THE PAST IN THE PRESENT

The Past
in the Present

History, Ecology, and
Cultural Variation
in Highland Madagascar

CONRAD PHILLIP KOTTAK

FOREWORD BY ROY A. RAPPAPORT

Ann Arbor   The University of Michigan Press

Library of Congress Cataloging in Publication Data

Kottak, Conrad Phillip.
  The past in the present.

  Bibliography: p.
  Includes index.
  1. Betsileos. 2. Madagascar—Social conditions.
3. Madagascar—History. I. Title.
DT469.M264K67 1980   969.1'00499   80–14575
ISBN 0–472–09323–1

To Betty Wagley Kottak

Foreword

This comparative study of three Betsileo communities constitutes an important addition to the ethnography of Madagascar, an insular world not well-known to most English or American anthropologists. But it is much more than that. To a degree that remains rare in the anthropological literature despite decades of admonition, Conrad Kottak locates these communities in time, in space, and in the larger political entities that have encompassed them: the early proto-Betsileo states, the Merina empire, the French colonial administration, and now, the Malagasy Republic. Through the careful use of oral and documentary historical materials, the consideration of regional environmental differences, and ethnographic observations supplemented by extraordinarily extensive survey data, Kottak has been able to construct a model of adaptive radiation that not only accounts for variations among the three communities in which he lived and worked, but also places the Betsileo as a whole in the pan-Malagasy context. This book is a significant contribution to the literature of adaptive radiation of sociocultural systems, a literature that remains small because of the complexities that confront those who would undertake it. In this instance the complexities are especially great. The evolutionary processes that underlie the sociocultural differences Kottak observes include not only the development of *variations* as responses of similar and related sociocultural systems to different material circumstances—a process analogous to speciation—but also the process of *general evolution*, the emergence of increasingly complex organization. This study is a contribution to our understanding of the development of stratification and of the origins of the state as well as a study of adaptive radiation and of Betsileo society and culture.

Readers will discover that Kottak has faced the complexity of the Betsileo material squarely, producing a remarkably lucid and balanced account that in nondoctrinaire fashion gives full due to ideological, social structural, environmental, and historical factors in the production of the outcomes observed by the ethnographer. At the same time, although implicitly rather than explicitly, he gives full due to each of the four Aristotelian forms of cause or determinant: material, formal, efficient, and telic (or final). In the matrix of adaptive radiation, environmental factors (broadly construed to include not only physical and biotic factors but external social and political agencies as well) can qualify as efficient causes not only of events in societies but also of changes in their contents and structures. Sociocultural systems respond to efficient causes, or perturbations, within the constraints of their previously existing orders; that is, their structured contents. Sociocultural contents may be regarded as material cause, the entailments of their organization or structure as formal cause. The relationship between the response of a system characterized by particular formal and material features and its own unbroken continuity is the domain of final, or telic, cause. This would all seem too obvious to bear discussion were it not for the confusion vexing anthropological accounts. To claim that the specific characteristics of environments or perturbations in them cannot account for the specific nature of the responses to them, a rather common complaint, is hardly to discredit efficient cause. It is simply to say that efficient cause is not material or formal cause. The related complaint, that functions do not specify how they are to be fulfilled, in like manner criticizes final cause for not being material or formal cause. Conversely, it is clear that structural descriptions, from which formal causes may be derived, cannot by themselves account for the conditions of their own transformations. It may be that various schools of anthropology do give privilege to one or another of the Aristotelian forms: the ecological schools emphasize efficient cause; symbolists and historical particularists, material cause; functionalists, final cause; and structuralists, formal cause. These simple tendencies are probably exaggerated by their antagonists, but be this as it may, each form must be given its proper place in any reasonably comprehensive account of any of the living entities in which anthropologists immerse themselves to produce ethnographies. Kottak has done so here, producing a volume that is at once devoid of polemic and full of theoretical interest.

That the varied responses of cultural evolution, in both its general and specific aspects, are oriented is implicit throughout this entire work. This is not to say that that sociocultural evolution is orthogenetic, for it can be assumed that the goal of such systems is so low in specificity as to seem a virtual nongoal. It is simply to persist. Persistence does not stand opposed to evolutionary change but, rather, guides evolutionary change. Such a view of evolution, which is espoused here, is in accord with what Hockett and Assher (1964) called "Romer's Rule" after the zoologist who enunciated it in a discussion of the emergence of the amphibia from the lobe-finned fish (1933). Romer's parable proposes that those fish did not take to dry land to exploit the opportunities it offered. Rather, relatively minor modification of their fins made it possible for them to migrate from one drying-up pond or stream to another still containing water during the intermittent droughts he assumed were frequent during the Devonian era. Structural changes thus made it possible for them to maintain their general aquatic organization during a period of frequent and serious environmental perturbation. This is to say that evolutionary changes in the components of systems are an aspect of the homeostatic processes of the more inclusive and enduring systems of which they are parts. To put it a little differently, evolutionary changes can be understood in terms of that which they maintain unchanged.

That which is maintained unchanged in the adaptive radiation of the Betsileo and, indeed, in the more inclusive adaptive radiation of the Malagasy generally, Kottak tells us, is "the essentials of an ancestral cultural plan—their *fombandrazana*. . . ." In this respect the Betsileo illuminate the condition of that large segment of humanity composed of "tribal populations [being] pushed rapidly from a world governed by kinship and reciprocity toward one of political regulation, inequality, and exploitation."

The maintainance of culturally specified values under changing circumstances can be self-destructive: witness the tenacity of our own commitments to consumption, corporate capitalism, and industrialism in the face of ecological degradation and decreasing social, political, and economic stability. But at the end Kottak suggests, contrary to much received opinion, that in the very rapidity of their modernization may lie the salvation of the Betsileo for, unlike those populations in which the long, slow growth of industrialism and capitalism originally unfolded, they proceed through the late twentieth century with communal forms and values, although altered, generally intact. As such they may be better able to respond humanely and effectively to the unforseeable stresses of the twenty-first century than are "more developed" societies.

To discuss the general orientation of this book does not do justice to the more particular arguments in which it abounds and the wealth of data that it presents. Kottak's discussion of *hasina*, for instance, along with Bloch's (1977) consideration of that concept, enlarges our understanding of both sacred kingship and the cybernetics of the holy (Rappaport 1971, 1979), and the mass of economic and agricultural data offered in both the text and the appendix will make this book invaluable to students of subsistence agriculture. But I have kept readers from the riches of the work itself long enough.

Roy A. Rappaport

A Note on Names

Most personal names, along with the names of the three main villages, their satellites, and two canton seats have been changed to preserve anonymity. In addition, I have translated many personal names into approximate English equivalents, and used French and English first names frequently encountered among the Betsileo. I did this because prepublication readers were unanimous in complaining that untranslated Betsileo names were difficult for nonspecialists to follow and remember. (Most begin with R, include assorted a's, i's, and o's, and have several syllables, e.g., Rainivelomaly, Rainijomalahy, Ramijalahy, Rainikalavaha, Randrianasoana.) Names of such historical figures as kings and queens are unaltered, except for a few prominent senior commoners whose names were changed to preserve their descendants' anonymity. My practice of name changing would no doubt be acceptable to the Betsileo themselves, since most change their names two or three times during their lives.

Preface

Madagascar, great island of unity and contrasts, has, until the last decade, been neglected by English-speaking scholars. This is particularly unfortunate since Malagasy cultures and history exemplify in microcosm, and suggest solutions to, so many of the problems that traditionally have engaged anthropologists, historians, and geographers. Among the problems considered here are: the nature of sociopolitical transformation and the origin of the state; relationships between prior structure, ideology, and material conditions; and the forms, functions, and context of customs and institutions focusing on death, corpses, ancestral spirits, kinship, marriage, fosterage, and economic activities. Along with other recent studies of Malagasy groups, this historical and ethnographic account of unity and diversity among the Betsileo of the southern highlands is an attempt to enlarge understanding of both the distinctiveness and the comparability of Malagasy beliefs and behavior. More generally it aims at clarifying how cultures are constituted, how they work, and how and why they change. It is based on six months study and preparation in Paris and fourteen months fieldwork among the Betsileo, as well as on background reading and archival research.

Several people and institutions offered gracious assistance prior to, during, and after the field research on which a large part of this study is based. I thank the Foreign Area Fellowship Program for a postdoctoral research grant, entitled "The Socioeconomic Effects of the Expansion of Wet-Rice Cultivation," which supported my fieldwork among the Betsileo and initial preparatory study in Paris. I also thank the Horace H. Rackham School of Graduate Studies of the University of Michigan for a Rackham Faculty Fellowship (summer, 1969) and grant that supported the analysis and write-up of data gathered in Madagascar. Georges Condominas, as a visiting professor at Columbia University, originally stimulated my interest in Madagascar and has offered me guidance during my graduate and postgraduate career. In Paris I benefited from the advice of Paul Ottino and several other French scholars.

I cannot forget the hospitality and kindness, the intellectual stimulation, and the sharing of knowledge about Madagascar that I received from my good friends Pierre and Juliette Vérin in Madagascar in 1966 and 1967. Of my many friends in Madagascar, I am especially indebted to Emilienne Randimbiarisoa, Léon Razanadimby, Etienne Razafimandimby, Jean-Noël Rakoto, François Rainijomalahy, Marcel Rajomalahy, Philippe Radilahy, Jean-Albert Rahaovalahy, Marcel Ramijalahy, Elois Rainibotovao, Basil Rambelson, Therese Razanakolona, Therese Ramoma, Laurent Raphael, Marie-Esther Razanamasy, Ramichel, Ravao-Michel, and Ravao-Koto.

The kindness and patience of several Betsileo villagers are deeply appreciated, but I am especially grateful for the hospitality, trust, and interest of the people of the village herein called Ivato.

I thank my field assistant Joseph Rabe for his help, for his knowledge, efforts, and good intentions, and for the meticulous field notes he gathered in Mahazony during my stay in the southern highlands. Jean Verger shared his knowledge of the southern Betsileo and helped tremendously in providing accommodation and contacts in a strange land.

My interest in materialist, evolutionary, and ecological interpretations reflects my association with Marvin Harris, Morton Fried, Roy Rappaport, Eric Wolf, Kent Flannery, Richard Ford, and several other colleagues. My graduate work with Robert Murphy and Elliott Skinner drew me to social and political organization. More recently, I have had the opportunity to share my interests in Madagascar here at Michigan with Henry Wright, Michael Lambek, and Susan Kus. All of us have learned from the others' fieldwork with the Malagasy.

I wish particularly to thank Maurice Bloch, Shepard Forman, Joseph Jorgensen, and Roy Rappaport for careful readings of a previous draft of this manuscript, and for their detailed and extensive suggestions for revision. Although I alone am responsible for still existing deficiencies, and although some areas of disagreement remain, all of them will recognize the impact of their guidance on the present work. Daniel Gross, Marvin Harris, Maxine Margolis, Charles Wagley, Henry Wright, and students too numerous to name have also read all or part of this study, and I am grateful for their comments, criticisms, and suggestions. I wish to thank Catherine Cross, Lynda Fuerstnau, Karen Shedlowe, and John Alden for their assistance in preparing the manuscript.

Since 1962, through every day of my work in anthropology, and especially during fieldwork in Madagascar, I have been accompanied and assisted by Betty Wagley Kottak. Her adaptability, sensitivity, anthropological expertise, and indefatigability in the field are responsible for much of the information collected for this study. I dedicate this book to her and thank her not only for working with me, but also for discussing with me before, during, and since our stay in Madagascar the nature of Betsileo life, for sharing her impressions and interpretations of what we were observing, and for understanding why the composition of this book took so much of my time.

Contents

I
INTRODUCTION

CHAPTER ONE

Studying the Betsileo

THE BETSILEO

In the highlands of central Madagascar live a proud though conquered people who call themselves Betsileo. Having possessed their own rulers and petty states during the eighteenth and early nineteenth centuries, the Betsileo were among the first objects of conquest of their northern neighbors, the Merina. Following their annexation of the Betsileo early in the nineteenth century, the Merina went on to subdue other groups and to extend their hegemony over two-thirds of Madagascar until their conquest by France in 1895. Although outside the island their work has been largely forgotten, the Merina were responsible for the creation of one of the largest and most cohesive indigenous empires of the tropics (cf. Bloch 1971; Condominas 1960; Delivré 1974).

This book, however, is a study of the Betsileo. As an analysis of variation in historical and contemporary aspects of economy, polity, religion, and social organization in general within an ethnic group that numbers some 800,000 people, it is also intended as a contribution to anthropological theory. The variation to be examined here exists in time and in space. Not only have major changes (most notably the emergence of state organization) taken place in the development of Betsileo society since the seventeenth century, there is also contemporary variation, both broad variation encountered over the approximately 40,000 square kilometers of the Betsileo homeland and microvariation between Betsileo villages located in a more restricted region. As we know from Charles Darwin, analysis of variation is vital, for variation is in one sense—as product—the result of, and in another sense—as raw material—the basis of, adaptation and evolution through natural selection. In contrast to other animals, however, much of the raw material on which natural selection operates among human populations is sociocultural (transmitted through learning) rather than genetic (transmitted through DNA). Such sociocultural variations will concern us here.

How have natural selective forces—material conditions—affected

Betsileo society and culture? In this book I attempt to identify and explicate ways in which variable material conditions have historically determined, and still affect, sociocultural variation among the Betsileo. Material conditions are those that govern a group's access to valued and strategic resources. As such, they include the physical environmental and biotic variables (rainfall, temperature, land forms, plants, and animals) that affect the formation of local ecosystems (see p. 47). They also include culturally available means of production and relations of production within such ecosystems and such regional forces as warfare, trade, and migration that join local systems into larger networks. However, most significant for understanding contemporary sociocultural variation among the Betsileo are the material conditions that create and are created by systems of socioeconomic stratification: artificial, human determinants of differential access, conditions not of nature but of a particular social form, the state.

Because of the book's broad comparative and historical aims, its agenda should be made obvious at once. The first chapter introduces the reader to Betsileo village life and to my fieldwork strategy and techniques. Thereafter, in successive chapters I focus my analysis on a gradually narrowing scale of sociocultural variation, starting with historical and contemporary diversity encountered within the total Malagasy population (chapters 2 through 4) and ending with contrasts between three villages in a restricted region, the southern part of the Betsileo heartland (chapters 4 through 8). As scale narrows, the types of material conditions responsible for the major sociocultural contrasts also change. Thus in chapters 2 and 3, in which the adaptive radiation and sociocultural evolution of the Malagasy population as a whole and of the Betsileo in particular are examined, I focus on variation linked to physical environment, local ecological and economic adaptation, and regional interaction. Chapters 3 and 4 trace the genesis and changing nature of socioeconomic stratification and state organization among the Betsileo. Chapters 5 through 8 focus on the effects of growing inequality and state intervention on rural life and on participation by Betsileo in national culture. Before considering Betsileo diversity, however, let us see what unites them.

Who Are the Betsileo?

The Betsileo are one of twenty contemporary *ethnies* or ethnic units into which the census of the Malagasy Republic divides its population. The Betsileo distinguish themselves from other Malagasy by calling themselves Betsileo, and thus contrasting themselves with their immediate neighbors, the Tanala to the east, the Bara to the south and southwest, the Sakalava to the west and northwest, and the Merina to the north. However, Betsileo have not always shared this consciousness of themselves as a distinct ethnic unit. Prior to their conquest by the Merina, there appear to have been no Betsileo.

Rather, there were several statelets and chiefdoms located in different parts of what is now the Betsileo homeland. Their conquerors, the Merina, produced unity where previously there had been competition. They created the Betsileo province of the Merina state, constructing a Betsileo capital at Fianarantsoa, now seat of the province and of the prefecture that includes the Betsileo homeland, and, in so doing, provided a basis for Betsileo ethnic consciousness to develop through the present.[1]

The Betsileo are agriculturalists who, for almost three centuries, have lived in state-organized societies, first under their own rulers, after 1830 under Merina administrators, and subsequently, following its annexation of Madagascar in 1896, under the rule of France. They are currently part of the population of the Malagasy Republic, which attained its independence in 1960. Thus, the Betsileo are peasants: agriculturalists in a state-organized society. They grow rice on permanent plots which are cultivated with a single annual crop from year to year, with few or no breaks, and which are passed on to their descendants. Those who are fortunate may transplant their rice seedlings in October, or even earlier, before the advent of November rains. Those whose fields lack sources of water for artificial irrigation must wait to plant and harvest later. The Betsileo do not form an egalitarian society. Access to water, land, labor, and other strategic resources is unequal. Some Betsileo are more fortunate than others in terms of wealth, prestige, ritual status, and power.

Their economic activities are not limited to the cultivation of rice, though rice is their preferred food and its cultivation is their primary concern. Cattle are essential to agriculture as most Betsileo practice it. Cattle dung is used to fertilize rice fields, as well as the nursery beds where, over a period that ranges from forty days to three months, rice seeds grow into transplantable seedlings. Before transplanting (an activity performed by women) takes place, fields are flooded. Young men drive cattle through the flooded fields and excite them to a frenzy which, as the cattle trample the field, produces a mud of even consistency in which the rice is transplanted. In addition to their traditional role in trampling, for the past fifty years Betsileo cattle have been attached to plows and harrows. They also take part in the harvest, as ox carts transport paddy (unhusked rice) from distant fields to village granaries.

The importance of cattle is not limited to their economic utility; they also enter social, ceremonial, and dietary contexts. When Betsileo marry, a steer is traditionally given by the family of the groom to the family of the bride. When large groups of people come together to take part in ceremonial, cattle are slaughtered and meat is distributed. Since beef is always distributed at funerals, which occur throughout the year, animal protein, in which the Betsileo diet would otherwise be deficient, is available on a fairly constant basis.

The relationship between people and their cattle varies over the Betsileo homeland, and it has also changed over time. Cattle are still bred and raised, rather than merely grazed, in some Betsileo villages, but stockbreeding is said to have been more widespread in the past. Today many adult Betsileo have never raised a calf and own no cows. Although their ancestors drank milk from their herds, as some Betsileo still do, most contemporary Betsileo are content to buy cattle from other Betsileo or from non-Betsileo cattle merchants. In either case, wealth may be stored in cattle and converted, through sale, exchange, or slaughter, to provide material, social, ceremonial, and nu tritional benefits.

Most Betsileo work is directed toward rice and cattle. However, Betsileo supplement a diet of rice and beef with other livestock and with a great variety of secondary crops. Manioc, sweet potatoes, Irish potatoes, taro, beans, maize, greens of various sorts, tomatoes, onions, and a variety of fruit trees adaptable to the tropical highlands complement the caloric staple. Chickens, ducks, geese, and turkeys are found and eaten in every village. Some women raise pigs. Formerly goats and sheep were kept. Some Betsileo raise tilipia fish, which were introduced by the French during the 1950s, in ponds. Others merely fish in rivers and streams, which abound in central Madagascar. Locusts are occasionally caught and cooked in oil.

The Betsileo economy demands long and hard work at certain seasons, and in no area of Betsileo economic life are labor requirements greater than in rice production. In the southern part of the Betsileo homeland, considering three villages where most of my ethnographic fieldwork was carried out, an average of approximately 1,700 hours of human labor are needed each year to farm one hectare of rice land and about 1,400 hours for the average household rice holding. This figure does not include, however, the daily chore of pounding unhusked paddy to produce edible white rice, one of many jobs that devolve on Betsileo women. When one considers, too, the hours invested in caring for cattle and in secondary crop production, it becomes apparent that productive work occupies much of the nonsleeping hours of adult men and women. Work is not spread evenly throughout the year. Variable labor requirements reflect stages of rice cultivation, beginning with preparation of the fields which, for some, starts as early as August, ending with the harvest which, for others, comes as late as May. June, July, and August, the austral winter, the season of cold and drizzle, is the agricultural off-season, a time rather of ceremonial activity.

The intensity of Betsileo work sometimes posed problems for me, the ethnographer, seeking people to talk to. I had previously done fieldwork in a community of oceangoing fishermen in northeastern Brazil. Sea fishing is basically an extractive activity and, given the limitations of the primitive sailboats and equipment of the Brazilian fishermen, the people I studied were often prevented from working by the vagaries of weather, as storms churned up the sea. Sedentary agriculture, on the other hand, especially involving artificial irrigation and drainage, is very different. Notable is the regularity of rice cultivation and the constancy of work in the working season. The water level must be regulated and labor conscripted for transplanting, one of the major collective tasks in the Betsileo economy. Not only must peasants be willing to work for others if they expect others to work for them, they must try not to deviate from their schedules of agricultural activity, since they draw on a common labor pool. I still recall a man and his sons tilling his field in the midst of a heavy thunderstorm because transplanting had been set for the following day. Having prior research experience only among fishermen, the scheduling and intensity of work were aspects of Betsileo life that I found particularly noteworthy.

A Betsileo Looks at Betsileo Culture

To give the reader a somewhat greater feel for Betsileo life before discussing my fieldwork strategy and research goals, I shall write briefly about the way in which one of my Betsileo friends and informants conceptualized his world and the cultural nature of Betsileo society.

As I was approaching the end of my stay among the Betsileo, I asked Jules, a young household head, a very general leading question designed to reveal something about his conception of his society. Having observed Betsileo rural life over more than a year, I wanted an insider's attempt to give a capsule impression of the significance of what I had seen and inferred. The question I asked Jules may be translated as "What is Betsileo culture?" The question was possible because Betsileo have a word which is very similar to some anthropologists' definitions of the term and the concept "culture." The Malagasy word *fomba* may be translated as "customs" or "traditional ways of doing things." Often it is used in an expanded form, *fombandrazana*. *Razana*, its modifier, is the word for ancestor(s). These terms refer to certain behavior patterns, things, events, values, beliefs, and rules of conduct that Betsileo regard as normal and appropriate. *Fombandrazana*, meaning the ways of the ancestors, underscores the fact that these customs are seen as sanctified by tradition and by repetition. The same term, with a similar meaning, occurs in all Malagasy ethnic groups (cf. Bloch 1971, pp. 35–39; Wilson 1971, p. 194), and throughout the island not only the ancestral ways, but the ancestors and their mortal remains themselves are sanctified, objects of rites and offerings. In subsequent chapters, it will be shown how relationships that Betsileo perceive between dead ancestors and living descendants act to sanctify and to reproduce aspects of their socioeconomic structure.

To an extent, all Betsileo recognize the same *fombandrazana*; that is, conceptions of the nature of traditional Betsileo life and appropriate behavior are shared. However, as Delivré (1974, p. 124) observed about Merina *fom-bandrazana*, any Betsileo's understanding of *fombandrazana* is certainly not to be regarded as an accurate reconstruction of things that went on in the actual Betsileo past. To a lesser extent than the Merina studied by Maurice Bloch (1971), contemporary Betsileo draw a contrast between Malagasy times and modern times. Bloch reports that Merina see themselves as participating in two distinct and incompatible social systems, that of today and that of the ancestors. Merina who have left their ancestral lands as emigrants to recently colonized areas or as bureaucrats, merchants, or other participants in the pan-Malagasy political economy reconcile the competing claims of their two social systems by maintaining a strong attachment to the ancestral tombs in which they will eventually be buried. These are located in, and help make concrete their attachment to, the village and homeland (*tanindrazana*) of their ancestors. For Betsileo the dichotomy is not so clear-cut for two main reasons. First, a far larger percentage of the Betsileo population continues a peasant existence in the homeland. Second, because of a succession of conquests and foreign rulers, Betsileo perceive a less sharp contrast than the Merina between precolonial and European times. Nevertheless, the notion of *fombandrazana* allows Betsileo, like the contemporary Merina (Bloch 1971, p. 37), to view certain customs and beliefs as expressing eternal moral values that remain constant, reproducing Betsileo ethnicity despite the flux of history.

Still, since there is variation in age, sex, locality, wealth, and socioeconomic stratum among contemporary Betsileo, it is not surprising that some of this variation shows up in ideology. Because there have been differences in ways of the ancestors of different Betsileo, not all Betsileo would agree that a given act accords with tradition. Betsileo who are descendants of slaves, for example, are forced by circumstances to have notions about behavior appropriate to Betsileo life that differ from those of descendants of the former nobility. *Fomba* Betsileo also vary with locality. Ways of doing things and ideology are not the same for the extreme northern and the extreme southern Betsileo. Therefore, the picture that Jules presents of Betsileo *fomba* should be taken for what it is—one composed by a particular thirty-year-old married household head and father. To some extent other residents of his village would agree, although there would be modification and perhaps disagreement.

Jules's response to the question "What is *fomba* Betsileo," "What is Betsileo culture," reveals that for him the need to work and the organization of economic activities are intrinsic to Betsileo life and to the traditional Betsileo way of doing things. I shall first give his responses in the order he gave them, then discuss the significance of some of his comments by relating them to my own knowledge and observation of Betsileo life. Jules divided *fomba*

Betsileo into six named categories and further distinguished specific traditional expectations, obligations, and activities within each category. The categories are numbered, and his specifications within each are then noted. They are as follows: (1) care of livestock, including care of the cattle corral, the supervision of grazing cattle, the use of cassava (sweet manioc) and the gathering of grasses to feed them; (2) plant cultivation after the manner of the ancestors, involving the cultivation of rice and of sweet manioc. Although he merely stated that manioc cultivation was traditionally Betsileo, Jules broke up rice cultivation into specific activities: seedlings are grown in a nursery bed for three months; cattle dung borne in water is used to fertilize the rice seedlings; the rice fields are tilled with a spade; rice field walls (bunds) are cleaned; rice fields are flooded; cattle trample the rice field; seedlings are transplanted; the growing crop is weeded; the paddy is harvested. (3) Jules's third category of Betsileo customs consists of events that bring people together: funerals, thanksgiving celebrations, cattle slaughter at funerals of "big people." (4) Next, he named the relationship between adult child and parents: concern over parents' health, the necessity to feed parents unable to feed themselves, to respect them, and to show them affection. Also associated with this relationship, according to Jules, is the custom that if a woman is dirty and unable to wash herself her daughter-in-law washes her. Finally Jules pointed to a man's obligation to work for his father or older brother. He then named (5) the relationship between parents and nonadult children: parents must spread a paste thought to be necessary to growth on an infant's head and work their rice fields to feed their children; parents expect boys to cut firewood and watch over grazing cattle; children are now encouraged to study. The final category was (6) marriage. Jules mentioned the gift of the groom and his group to the bride and her group; taking one's wife home to one's village; inscribing the marriage in the government registry.

Notable in Jules's response is the fact that he first mentioned economic domains. Furthermore, his specification of activities was more detailed in the domains of livestock care and rice cultivation than in other categories of Betsileo *fomba*. Included in his discussion of livestock practices was the cattle corral. I would hesitate to say that most other Betsileo would give cattle care priority over rice cultivation, but it is a fact that in the course of Betsileo history there has been a shift from a more pastoral economy to an agricultural economy based on wet-rice. Hamlets, the preferred Betsileo form of settlement, have often grown into villages, but in most Betsileo villages the ancestral cattle corral, constructed when the village was still a hamlet, remains an enclosure for cattle at night. The words for corral and hamlet (*vala*) are identical. Corrals are circular semisubterranean structures whose walls are built of layers of small flat stones laid out in bricklike fashion and held together by weight and mud. The ancestral corral is the scene of festive bullbaiting by young men and the place where cattle are slaughtered during ceremonial events. Because of the labor involved in their construction, since the abolition of internal slavery in Madagascar soon after French conquest, these corrals are no longer built. Instead, wooden fences surround new cattle pens.

In traditional Betsileo agriculture, zebu (*Bos indicus*) dung accumulates in the corral and, prior to transplanting, pond water is allowed to flood the corral. Mixed with the manure by the rice field owner, the water flows out of the corral in a ditch to his rice fields. For Jules, water transport of dung was an ancestral custom no longer practiced in his village, where dry manure is carried in baskets and dumped in fields. For other Betsileo, however, the ancestral way remains the usual means of manuring their nurseries and transplanted rice fields.

According to Jules, several areas of cattle care are also customary. The task of watching the cattle as they graze, unlike many in the Betsileo economy, is not very onerous, and boys and old men are the usual cattle guardians. The principal task of the guardian is to make sure that, while grazing on the uncultivated hillsides in summer and around the village and in the rice fields after harvest, cattle do not stray into someone's cultivated plot to destroy plants and to eat food intended for humans. For old men, it has an additional function, though not one they admit: it keeps them from being bothered. On many occasions I arrived in a village and found that an older man I had wanted to interview, having seen my car approach, had managed to take to the hills to relieve his grandson as cattle herder.

When, in evening, the zebu return to the village and are driven into the cattle corrals, they are given a meal consisting of various grasses that boys gather in the afternoon. As the grass cover begins to fail prior to November rains, manioc tubers are also fed to the cattle. Jules mentioned this evening cattle meal as intrinsic to Betsileo culture.

In his discussion of traditional cultivation practices, Jules mentioned the most typical Betsileo farm tool, the long-handled, iron-bladed spade used in various phases of rice field preparation, bund cleaning, and the maintenance and repair of irrigation ditches and drainage canals. The congeries of tasks surrounding transplanting is also validated by tradition: tillage, flooding the field, trampling by cattle, transplanting itself. He mentioned weeding, an arduous task associated with the Betsileo way of growing rice; a weeding may require work for a month for a family of four. According to my calculations, it is the most time consuming part of rice cultivation.

Jules went on to describe large assemblies of people, occasions generally of the winter, of July and August. Since ancestral times, funerals have occasioned large congregations from several hamlets and villages. Also bringing people together, but in a more festive context, are events known as *lanonana*. People are convoked by a host to a celebration of thanksgiving.

Hosts have vowed to sacrifice a zebu if some wish has been fulfilled—a child has returned from a stay outside the Betsileo homeland, the host or a close relative has recovered from an illness. It is also traditionally Betsileo for numerous cattle to be slaughtered when assemblies are hosted by or for some "big person." The greatest number of cattle are killed, and their meat distributed among all who attend, at the funeral of a person with a regional reputation.

Next came a discussion of the relationship between adults and their parents. Noticeable in it is a stress on respect and the subordination of adult child to parents, particularly to father and older brother which, as subsequent chapters will show, reflects values that pervade Betsileo social life. It is significant, and typically Betsileo, for the obligations due one's senior to be stressed rather than one's rights in him. Jules said that a child should be concerned about his parents' health, and, if adult, should care for them and see that their illnesses are treated. In the past, local curers were widely employed. Today children must accompany their parents to a nurse or doctor in an administrative town.

Finally, Jules mentioned a man's obligation to work for his father or older brother. His own father, Vernon, died when Jules was twelve. Administration of Vernon's estate passed to his oldest son residing in the village. Jules's older brother is, in fact, a half-brother, thirty-eight years his senior, son of his father by a previous marriage. According to custom, and this is one of the most often heard dicta of Betsileo culture, the oldest son replaces his father. Jules therefore treats his older half-brother very much as he would have treated his own father. He assists him in rice cultivation and in other activities. He calls his brother "father," and his brother's teknonymous name, assumed following Jules's birth, means "father of Jules." The culturally appropriate relationship between the two men is thus substantiated in their actual relationship.

Jules went on to say that parents must act so as to insure normal development of their children. One of the culturally appropriate ways of doing this is to spread a paste prepared from several ingredients on a baby's head in order to help the soft spot harden. If the preparation donated by the mother's family is found ineffective, the father's group will prepare a new mixture. It is significant that Jules did not mention discipline. In fact, I rarely observed disciplinary acts by father, mother, or other adults. When a baby is born, or when a child has been weaned, he or she is usually supervised, carried, and cared for during most of the day by an older sibling. Children wander in and out of the houses of their parents, grandparents, and other relatives. Enculturation is an informal process that goes on in the community rather than principally in the parental household. Jules mentioned the parents' obligation to feed their children, and he talked of work expected of Betsileo children by their parents. Nowadays, it has become customary for children to study. There is a Roman Catholic primary school in Jules's village, and most children begin to attend classes around age six. I was impressed with the extent to which Betsileo value education. They often invest considerable sums in their children's secondary education in a major administrative town because they correctly perceive education as a means to a prestigeful and lucrative position in the national political economy.

Jules completed his encapsulation of Betsileo culture with a discussion of marriage customs. He mentioned the custom whereby money and livestock pass from the groom's family to the wife's family. Under the French and in the modern Malagasy administration, marriage is registered with the government, so that it has civil status. However, Jules included the notification of the local representative of government as traditional in Betsileo culture. Indeed, it was an observance that their Merina conquerors also required of the Betsileo.

Jules's domains, including marriage, the recruitment of labor for economic activities, the importance of age and seniority, the relationship between parents and children, and ceremonial, all represent important constituents of Betsileo social life. The elucidation of these and other aspects of Betsileo culture is the object of this book. My brief description of the Betsileo economy and my discussion of the major domains of Betsileo culture as identified by Jules are intended to acquaint the reader with Betsileo rural life. A few other introductory comments will complete the general outline of Betsileo society and culture.

First some observations about villages and settlement pattern. There is no standard size for Betsileo villages. The three main villages examined in this book, Ambalabe, Ivato, and Tanambao, for example, have populations of 217, 175, and 82, respectively. The usual Betsileo settlement pattern is one of villages and hamlets located on higher ground and hills in valleys where rice is cultivated. Streams and rivers flow through these valleys, offering water and alluvial soils from rainy season flooding, and, once canals have been constructed, water for artificial irrigation of many of the rice fields. More rarely, villages are located high in the hills above or between elaborate spring-fed rice terraces. Even more mountainous sites atop massive granitic outcrops were occupied in the past for purposes of defense.

House construction materials are varied, and several house types are visible in any village, which the traveler normally sees from a distance, as he or she moves along a road above the valleys, rice fields, and settlements. Status differences show up in house type; older men, who control land, labor, and other strategic resources, have the most elaborate homes. The best houses are painted or whitewashed and have two or three stories, four to six rooms, tile roofs, and at least some brick or wood. The poorest houses have a single story with one or two rooms; their frames are wattle and daub and their roofs, long grass collected on hillsides near the village. There is often a striking visual contrast in the Betsileo settlement pattern, between the bareness of the village, whose mud-walled houses and red ground stand out in the absence of trees, and the vivid colors of the vegetation below—the rice in the valleys and terraces and the secondary crops growing between village and rice field.

Any traveler will also notice works in stone in and around Betsileo villages. These include monoliths raised to commemorate particular events, memorials of people who have died outside their homeland, and family tombs. The most commonly encountered tomb is a rectangular semisubterranean structure that rises a few feet above ground level; modern tombs are built of cement, more traditional sepulchers of small stones, like those used in the cattle corral. Inside the tomb on three walls are the beds (between six and nine) where the ancestors (*razana*) are deposited. Betsileo beliefs about the continuing role of the ancestors in their lives are examined fully in chapter 7. Here it will suffice to say that the Betsileo hold several kinds of ceremonies in order to appease, thank, please, or recall their ancestors. Most ceremonies are held during July and August, the rainy season. The ceremony of largest scale is the inauguration of a recently constructed tomb, in which corpses are transferred from one or more old sepulchers to the new one. In other rituals, corpses are rewrapped in new shrouds inside or outside the tomb. These are all joyous occasions, in contrast to the funeral, which can occur at any time of year, and which attracts hundreds of kin and neighbors.

Betsileo belong to descent groups of several sorts and sizes, and these are discussed fully, particularly in chapter 6. A capsule anthropological description of Betsileo social organization would call it ambilineal (or cognatic) with a strong patrilineal bias. Almost all marriages are virilocal; that is, the couple resides in the husband's village, which is usually his father's. Any Betsileo is simultaneously a member of several descent groups. One is the *local* descent group (i.e., its members reside together) where a man cultivates his main rice fields. Most men eventually inherit and cultivate their father's estate, but many Betsileo simultaneously cultivate fields inherited from father and mother. They usually reside near the larger inheritance, and this is generally the father's. Aside from one's primary membership in a mostly patrilineal local descent group, a Betsileo also belongs to several totally ambilineal *tomb-groups*. People have the right to be buried in any tomb where they have an ancestor, and this can (in theory, but rarely in practice) extend right back to eight great-grandparents. Betsileo maintain their membership in tomb-groups by taking part in their ceremonials and by contributing to the construction costs and upkeep of the ancestral tombs. However, the social organization of the dead people in the tombs turns out to be patrilineally skewed, since most people choose to be buried in the tomb of their local descent group.

The disposition of land and other strategic resources is subject to national law, but in practice estates are cultivated and passed on in accordance with generations-old customs of the countryside. Thus, an old man controls an estate that will eventually be split among his descendants. On his death, custom demands that the oldest son allocate the estate among himself and his brothers. Since women are expected to have the benefits of their husband's estate after marriage, they generally receive no rice fields at home. However, husbands and sons of such women are sometimes allowed to cultivate her ancestral estate if need is great, or if there are no other heirs. Furthermore, the inheritance rights transmitted through women are guaranteed in national law and can be enforced legally in those rare cases where close kin become enmeshed in a legal dispute.

Subsequent chapters will discuss at great length the manner of articulation of rural villages with national life and nation-state administration. Having briefly presented here the economic, ideological, and social materials for an outline of Betsileo society, I now consider why and how I did this study. Subsequent chapters will fill in the outline from both historical and contemporary perspectives.

FIELDWORK AMONG THE BETSILEO

I think that many readers are interested in, but are too seldom told, how anthropologists' interest in their subject arose, how they got a chance to study it, and what problems they faced in carrying out the study. Of interest to those evaluating and planning ethnographic fieldwork is a degree of knowledge about the practical as well as theoretical reasons for undertaking research, how universes for study were determined, how data were collected from members of each universe, how the observer and the observed interacted in the field to produce, finally, a report such as this. The aim of the rest of this chapter is to provide such information.

The Background

A course on peoples of Madagascar taught at Columbia University by Georges Condominas in 1963 first demonstrated to me that Madagascar was anthropologically fascinating. I was particularly struck by two aspects of Malagasy cultures: (1) tremendous diversity and (2) contrasts in scale and complexity, attributes of Madagascar that still strike me as important.

After finishing the course, I put aside the study of Madagascar, did fieldwork in northeastern Brazil, and wrote my dissertation about the egalitarian socioeconomic structure of a marine-fishing community. However, Condominas and others at Columbia had been encouraging me to do postdoctoral research in Madagascar. The idea was attractive for several reasons. Madagascar seemed an ideal laboratory to study some of my major interests: the evolution of political organization, socioeconomic stratification, and covariation of behavior, beliefs, and material conditions. On one island one could find groups that spanned in a rough way the general evolutionary gamut (cf. Sahlins and Service 1960), from isolated foragers (the Mikea of the southwestern interior, about whom very little is known) through tribal horticulturalists (the Tanala) and pastoralists, through agriculturalists combining features of both tribal and state organization (the Betsileo), to the Merina empire. I was amazed that, in view of this diversity, so little had been published about Madagascar in English. There were the ethnographically informative accounts of missionaries in the *Antananarivo Annual*, whose publication ended around 1900, soon after French rule was established. There was Ralph Linton's work, but his fieldwork had been superficial and had ended in 1927.[2] French works on Madagascar were numerous. There was even a 1,500-page monograph on the Betsileo by the Jesuit Father H. Dubois. In general, however, the concerns of the early French scholars were with the foreign origins of Malagasy cultures and culture traits, and information I regarded as basic was missing. Dubois includes, for example, virtually no information on the social organizational questions discussed in this book. I hoped to provide a study in English of Madagascar, and to orient it toward those interests in variation, comparison, adaptation, and change that I had developed as a graduate student and still maintain.

The Problem

My research proposal was to study the socioeconomic effects of the expansion of wet-rice cultivation in southcentral Madagascar. I proposed to study the relationships between Betsileo and their immediate southern neighbors, the Bara, that had developed following Betsileo migration to the northern part of Bara country. From the literature, I correctly perceived Betsileo migration into Bara country as part of a general ongoing expansion of wet-rice cultivators in Madagascar (cf. Deschamps 1959). Like Merina peasants and Taisaka from the southeast coast, Betsileo agriculturalists are colonizing the river valleys and other areas of irrigable land within the homelands of more pastorally oriented populations. This expansion has followed the cessation of internecine raiding and warfare in Madagascar. It began in the nineteenth century in the areas regulated by the Merina administration and was accelerated with French conquest and pacification. Peasants and pastoralists are now living together in the homelands of the latter (cf. Gardenier 1976, p. 27–31). The site where I proposed to do research was Ihosy, seat of the northernmost subprefecture of Bara country, where 18 percent of the population is now Betsileo.

In April 1966 I left the United States to go to Paris, where, under the research design I had written, I was to perfect my rudimentary French, begin to learn Malagasy, take some additional courses on Madagascar, and get to know people who had worked in Madagascar or who could provide me with contacts there. Most of what I had planned to do in Paris turned out to be impossible. There was no beginning Malagasy course available, nor were any other courses related to Madagascar being taught. However, I met several people who had been in Madagascar, and, as a result of conversations with some of them I began to revise the problem I had intended to investigate. I learned that the literature had been somewhat deceptive in leading me to believe that Betsileo settlements in northern Bara country were long-established. In fact, most of the Betsileo colonies around Ihosy had developed after the imposition of French rule. Furthermore, the problem I had chosen to investigate involved relationships of Bara and Betsileo in Bara country and the modifications in Betsileo social organization and economic roles near Ihosy. I had been aware when I originally wrote the proposal that there was a massive monograph on the Betsileo that Father Dubois, a long-time resident of the Fianarantsoa region, had published in 1938. An early and cursory look at this work had given me the impression that the Betsileo had already been well-studied. This, I assumed, had two implications. First, fieldwork in the Betsileo homeland would merely repeat a job already done rather than extending knowledge of Malagasy diversity. Secondly, I could use Dubois's material on Betsileo social organization and economy as a basis for understanding changes among Betsileo colonists in northern Bara country. As I read Dubois's book more carefully in Paris, trying to develop hypotheses to test in my fieldwork, I soon realized that it was most deficient in treatment of social organization and economic activities—exactly the areas I needed to know most about (cf. Southall 1971, p. 145).

Since my main interest had always been in the Betsileo, as wet-rice cultivators, rather than in the Bara, I was receptive to suggestions of some French scholars who had worked in Madagascar that I change the site of my fieldwork from Ihosy to Ambalavao, the southernmost town of the traditional Betsileo homeland. By starting my research in Ambalavao, I thought, I would become acquainted with traditional Betsileo economy and social organization and could later assess departures from the homeland pattern among Betsileo emigrants. Furthermore, Ambalavao was an appropriate place to begin a study of the interaction of Betsileo and Bara for several reasons. I surmised—correctly it turned out—that most Betsileo migrants to Ihosy, 150 kilometers south of Ambalavao, came from the subprefecture of Ambalavao. Furthermore, the southern and western areas of Ambalavao's circumscription traditionally had been transitional between Betsileo and Bara. Thus, through research in these transitional, ecoclinal regions I could learn about Betsileo-Bara interrelationships. Finally, I learned that Ambalavao was the site of one of Madagascar's major cattle markets. Stockbreeders from Bara country and further south bring their cattle to Ambalavao, where Betsileo peasants and Merina businesspeople buy them. They are then herded along the main highway to Fianarantsoa, and some as far as Tananarive. Basing myself in Ambalavao, then, would enable me to get to know the nature of traditional Betsileo economy and social organization, while also illustrating something of the interaction between Betsileo and Bara. I was later to learn that the national government had instituted agronomic and hydraulic programs in the rural zones of Ambalavao. Since new rice land was being put under cultivation, it also turned out to be very appropriate for studying the expansion of wet-rice cultivation—my original research aim.

My stay in Paris enabled me to learn French sufficiently well to do research in Madagascar, to revise my research site, and to do additional background reading on Madagascar. The research period in Madagascar, which began in October 1966, was fourteen months, with about thirteen spent among the Betsileo. Accompanied by Betty Kottak throughout the fieldwork, I spent my first two weeks in the capital, Tananarive; we made our existence known to the national bureaucracy, bought books, government records and publications, and established contacts and friendships with several people. Driving down the central highlands, we spent some days in Fianarantsoa, making our intentions known to government officials in the Betsileo province, obtaining authorizations, and buying supplies before making the move, fifty-four kilometers south, to Ambalavao.

Ambalavao

Ambalavao was typical of the subprefecture seats (formerly district seats under the French) of the Betsileo prefecture, and, since the national administration, using a modified French model, had a standardized roster of officials for all subprefectures, it was like all Malagasy subprefecture seats in its government personnel. Ambalavao was also one of the largest Betsileo towns; only Fianarantsoa was larger. There was a city hall, an office and residence of the subprefect, who was a career administrator (unlike the mayor, who was elected). A marketplace marked the center of town. Around it were stores: two large grocery and dry goods stores run by Chinese, some Indian-owned fabric shops, and, on the northeastern side of the square, a hotel run by a

Frenchman born in Madagascar. Each Wednesday—market day in Ambala-vao—the usually quiet marketplace became the scene of animated and col-orful activity as people from the rural areas came, in their best clothes, to buy, sell, gossip, listen to Malagasy music, see government officials, make sexual liaisons, and do the several things a Betsileo does at the market.

Originally established by the French, Ambalavao ("New Town") was an administrative and an economic center. Its economic attraction was not only its weekly market, nor even the weekly cattle market that was held on Wednesdays, too. The French hotel owner ran a rice mill that converted paddy, bought by his truck-borne collectors in the countryside, into white rice. He sold some of this milled rice in his store, which was adjacent to his hotel, and he exported the remainder to other parts of Madagascar. Ambala-vao was also a collection point for tobacco, which peasants, if they chose to grow it, were required to sell to the government. Another Frenchman ran the tobacco curing plant.

Ambalavao was an educational center, though not as important as Fian-arantsoa, the provincial capital, because it lacked a high school. Excellent primary schools were run by the government. They were staffed by skilled instructors who were generally as proficient in French as Malagasy. The skills and progress of instructors and students in Malagasy public schools were measured by the same examinations that were used in France.[3] When I was in Ambalavao, its junior high school was run by two young Frenchmen, fulfilling their military service as schoolteachers. Neither junior nor senior high schools in Madagascar demanded bilingualism, and neither of these men spoke Malagasy.

Our first few weeks in Ambalavao were spent renting and equipping a small house, finding a field assistant, experiencing the residue of French co-lonial rule—which was much more obvious in towns than in the country-side—getting to know people, and making contacts with Ambalavao resi-dents who knew or had ties with the rural zones. It turned out that it was the first two people we met in Ambalavao who became our best friends there and who were most responsible for our success in fieldwork. These were two teachers at the government primary school. A young man and a young woman, they were first cousins whose fathers (who were brothers) had been born in a rural Betsileo village, Ivato, in the southern part of the subprefec-ture of Fianarantsoa, but located as close to Ambalavao as to the town of Fianarantsoa. This village was to become the site of my most intensive field-work among the Betsileo.

Fieldwork Begins

Soon after our arrival in Ambalavao, the two school teachers invited us to visit their ancestral community, which they considered a truly traditional Betsileo village. We drove to Ivato for the day. Most of the household heads assembled in the largest house for our visit. I asked them about the history of the village and drew up a genealogy tracing the reported migrations of their remote ancestors from Merina country to the southeast coast, and, thereafter, into Betsileo country where they settled near the present village, seemingly during the eighteenth century. Interested in the household composition of the village, I made cards for each household and learned its membership, and incorporated the kin links among households within the master geneaology. I also inquired about rice fields and found that some fields were artificially irrigated, whereas other peasants had to await the rainy season to transplant. I was impressed by the ready rapport I encountered among these villagers and assumed that—as had been the case in Brazil—it was going to be easy to obtain ethnographic information. It was only later that I was to understand the importance of this village and to comprehend what turned out to be an unusual willingness to give me ethnographic information.

Survey Research

I had seen one rural Betsileo village, but before deciding on one or more villages to study intensively, I wanted to have some idea about the nature and extent of variation in rural social organization and economy, as well as reasons for this variation. Accordingly, I returned to Ambalavao planning to spend a month or more visiting several villages in the southern Betsileo region. To assist me in this survey, since my Malagasy was rudimentary at best, I sought a man who would teach me Betsileo pronunciation and vocabulary (I had grammar books for the closely related Merina dialect), who could serve as interpreter in the village survey, and who would become, after I spoke Malagasy myself, a general assistant in fieldwork. Through the French hotel owner, I found a remarkably active seventy-year-old man who had spent twenty-five years of his life in France. Joseph Rabe, who spoke beautiful French, was a Betsileo born in Tanambao,[4] a rural village of the subprefecture of Ambalavao. Having served as an accountant in Ambalavao's city hall for many years, he was fully literate. He also had an enviable ability to make quick mathematical calculations, which turned out to be useful when we were gathering quantitative data.

He worked with me on the Malagasy language in Ambalavao for a few days, and with him I got to know most of the local officials. Since I was still interested in the expansion of wet-rice cultivation, we visited the local headquarters of several agencies concerned with rural development. These included a program known as Rural Animation that was designed to select one or two peasants from each village, explain to them the government's plans for agricultural development, and inspire them with enthusiasm that they would in turn convey to others in their villages. Another government agency sold fertilizers and agricultural equipment. Near subprefecture seats, experimental farms were run to demonstrate to peasants the benefits in yields that came with such techniques as using chemical fertilizers and transplanting rice seedlings in rows rather than haphazardly, as was the Betsileo custom. Row transplanting reduced labor because it enabled peasants to use rotary weeders made in Japan. Weeding is the most time consuming and tiring aspect of traditional rice cultivation. The government's agricultural schemes were not confined to subprefecture seats. In many rural areas, young men were acting as agricultural advisers, showing Betsileo how to transplant in rows and to follow other parts of the government agronomic scheme, and spreading news of the success of the new techniques to traditionalists and doubters. During our survey, these men often introduced us to villagers and told us about their problems and progress.

Most of our daily forays into the countryside were not to visit agricultural advisers, however. Interested in economic variation, we visited seats of rural cantons, talked with canton chiefs, and copied government statistics on crop acreage and yields, livestock holdings and price in these rural zones. Over about two months we visited perhaps twenty-five villages and went to most of the cantons of Ambalavao. Visits to the canton seat were always combined with research in at least one village. In some cases villages were chosen because of contrasts in rice cultivation patterns. Thus, we traveled to villages located on hillsides above elaborate rice terraces, and we investigated villages whose rice fields covered large valley floors. We attempted to find villages where ancestral canal systems of Betsileo construction and maintenance irrigated or drained rice plots. We also visited villages whose peasants had to wait for November and December rains to transplant, and other villages representing a combination of the two water sources.

In most places, in addition to our questions about rice cultivation techniques and changes in them, we asked about the history of the village and of the surrounding region. We collected the oral traditions of particular local groups (cf. Delivré 1974, p. 35–36). Where had ancestors come from—from the forest to the east, from Betsileo areas to the north, or from the west? What petty state or states had ruled over village ancestors? What had become of noble families? Did they live in the same villages as commoners or in their own hamlets? We also collected genealogies, trying to ascertain how many unrelated ancestors had founded or subsequently settled the village, how many different "families" (*fianakaviana*, see chapter 6), now lived in the village. We inquired about household composition and links among households. During the survey we visited some nobles, many commoners, and undoubtedly some descendants of the slave stratum, though, because of the stigma attached to slave ancestry, we usually were unable to identify them. We also tried to get some notion about how Betsileo looked at and divided up the world, some statements from peasants giving their opinions about kinship, rice cultivation, and other aspects of Betsileo life. We asked them to describe differences between their village and those of their neighbors.

After about a month of surveying we made an important discovery: that the "families" whose genealogies I had been collecting belonged to larger named, supralocal (i.e., territorially spread out) groups. An informant in a village near Ambalavao described three different "families" as the founders of her village. She provided me with names which later research showed to be those of three populous and geographically extended Betsileo descent groups. Throughout the remainder of the survey and of my fieldwork among the Betsileo, I investigated the number, the origins, the geographical range, and the general significance of these named descent groups and of descent groups formed at different genealogical levels (see also chapters 3 and 6).[5]

After about two months of surveying, I had developed a provisional classification of Betsileo villages. In terms of sources of water for rice cultivation, most villages were heterogeneous, with some peasants irrigating and some relying on rainfall. There were, however, differences between villages in terms of average size of rice plot, and there were contrasts involving modern versus traditional technology and cultivation practices. A more clear-cut basis for a typology, however, lay in descent organization. Some villages included members of only one named descent group; others had two or more; and in still others, descent was unimportant or completely absent as an organizational principle. Later I was to discover how the relationship between village and descent group organization itself reflected demography, history of settlement, physical environment, and particularly socioeconomic stratification.

Choice of Villages for Intensive Study

I chose to study three Betsileo villages representing these three broad types of descent organization. Ivato, whose core population represented a single descent group, was to be one. To represent the third type, a village in which descent group organization was unimportant, I chose Tanambao, the village of origin of my field assistant. A third village, Ambalabe, located two kilometers from Tanambao and, like it, in the canton of Mahazony in the southeastern part of the subprefecture of Ambalavao, had multiple descent group organization. (I later learned that the three villages sampled two additional and more fundamental contrasts that have produced variation among Betsileo. Tanambao and Ambalabe, on the one hand, and Ivato, on the other, sampled the historical contrast between the more pastoral south and west and the more agricultural east. Further, the three communities sampled contrasts in socioeconomic stratification among the Betsileo, with Tanambao near the bottom of the hierarchy of wealth, prestige, and power, Ambalabe intermediate, and Ivato near the top. The contrasts in region and stratum, it turned out, underlay the descent group typology that initially led me to select these villages.)

Reasons for the differences among the three villages in descent group organization are considered in subsequent chapters. However, whatever the reasons for the kind of descent structure, or lack of it, characteristic of a particular village, the fact of variation in village descent group structure was related to a number of other things including, as will be seen in chapters 5 through 8, size of peasant holdings in that village, solutions to problems of labor mobilization, the allocation of scarce resources, and the manner in which the village related to twentieth-century Madagascar.

Having decided on three villages to study in depth, we made preparations for finding lodging in each one. Ambalabe was located on a dirt road and from the point of view of supplies would have been a good place to rent a house. Tanambao was two kilometers and three steep hills away from the road, and smaller. We looked for a house in Ambalabe, and, though there were several vacant ones in the community, no one would agree to let us rent. Thus, we began to set up a household in my assistant's village, Tanambao.

Suspicion

The reluctance to rent us a house that we encountered among the peasants of Ambalabe came as no surprise in view of some of our experiences with Betsileo during our survey. We had been impressed in Ivato, the first Betsileo rural community we had visited, with the willingness of villagers to answer our questions and with the fullness of their responses. We soon found that this attitude was not typical. During the survey we became accustomed, as our car drove into, or, in many cases, drove by a village, to see children run crying and often screaming to their mother, telling her that some white people (*Vazaha*) had come. To greet us, adults stopped what they were doing and retreated into their doorways. Usually one of the men would take a few steps toward us and cautiously greet us. During the survey, field assistant Rabe would explain, in speech full of Betsileo regionalisms to make his own identity known, that we were studying Betsileo life and culture. I would join in with my growing body of Malagasy words, phrases, and sometimes complete sentences, and our reception committee would grow. The explanation of our purpose would be reiterated. Often we were told that the village chief was away, but we had learned from experience in other villages that the village chief was more of an errand boy for the village elders than a local authority. Usually the reception committee included some members of the village power structure, and ultimately someone would usually agree that we could ask our questions.

No matter what subject we opened with, after about four or five questions, the respondents would again reveal their suspicions, and we would begin another series of explanations of our aims. Usually, further assurances would be necessary as we progressed. Sometimes our arguments were persuasive and people opened up. At other times it became obvious that we were getting lies. If so, I would ask about the inconsistencies. Sometimes, when people found that we were actually interested in the minutiae of their lives and those of their ancestors, they would enjoy communicating, or when they found that we knew more about Betsileo villages than other outsiders they had met, their answers became more plausible—or their lies more devious. Clearly, an approach to fieldwork that involves creating rapport with a different group each day limits the amount and the reliability of the information. This, however, is something I had realized when I began the survey. Developing the kind of relationships with informants that are necesary among even the least suspicious villagers takes time. The time had come for intensive study.

Toward the end of the survey in February and March, after we had decided where to settle, we concentrated on Rabe's village, Tanambao, and Ambalabe, its neighbor. Our study of these two communities continued over ten months of our stay. It took time to establish rapport in both villages, although, because of Rabe's presence, we had an easier time in Tanambao than in Ambalabe. We made some friends in both villages, and we observed all stages of the rice cycle, measured fields, weighed crops, collected genealogies, attended ceremonials, and observed everyday behavior.

The Primary Village

Our rapport with the people of Tanambao and Ambalabe would undoubtedly have continued to improve had we in fact moved into either village. We never did. Our schoolteacher friends in Ambalavao invited us to go back to Ivato in late March to see one of the earliest and largest of the rice harvests there. We went and stayed over a weekend. Again, we were impressed by the instant rapport that our two friends' sponsorship created for us. Again we asked and had detailed answers providing information that it would have taken a week to obtain, with less certain accuracy, in the other villages. From this weekend, we determined to move to Ivato at once to be on hand to observe the harvests, which were just beginning. Influencing our decision to move immediately to Ivato were delays in preparing accommodations in Tanambao. I was eager to begin intensive work with peasants. From the survey I had developed a detailed interview schedule on ownership, inheritance, and cultivation of rice fields, and I wanted to use it as a basis for formal interviews and to provide quantifiable data.

I was also convinced that if I was ever going to become fluent in Malagasy, I would have to leave my interpreter behind and work directly and continuously with Betsileo informants. Not to derogate Mr. Rabe's good will, I had also discovered that there were some kinds of questions—either particularly naive or particularly nosy—that I could not expect him to ask for me. Since he was a Betsileo, and presumably more attuned to their notions of propriety than I, neither could he expect to get answers to such questions if he asked them. Often I found that complete strangers, because they are expected to know less about customary cues, have greater latitude than a partial stranger, someone like Rabe who is simultaneously in and out of the system. When we moved into Ivato, Rabe's assignment was to stay in Ambalavao to copy government statistics. We thought we would move to Rabe's village for awhile after the harvest season in Ivato. Because we became interested in phases of data collection I shall describe below, we never did.

The contrasts in our relationships with people in different villages were not fortuitous; they must be explained. Consider Ivato. We came with two "children of the village." Their fathers, themselves brothers, had been born in Ivato. One of the brothers, a physician trained in France, was also a nationally important politician. Since his schoolteacher daughter and her schoolteacher cousin—his (classificatory) son in the Malagasy kinship system—had brought us there, the villagers knew that our stay and our investigation had his approval. Our rapport, however, was not merely a matter of having been introduced by someone with a kinship tie to the village. Since Ivato had a powerful patron and protector in our sponsor, the physician-politician, the villagers had nothing to fear. His approval, and the schoolteachers', enabled people to accept our professed aims, which were honestly stated to be an investigation of Betsileo *fomba* and all things encompassed by that term, as our actual aims. Their protector had never brought them anything bad, and had been responsible for much that was good.

In the case of Tanambao, on the other hand, my sponsor Rabe lacked ties to either the regional or the national power structure and had long ago removed himself from village life. His financial means had always been limited and had brought his covillagers very little. Who, even in Rabe's own village, but especially in Ambalabe, could be sure that there was no evil-intentioned complicity between us, that he was not, as one villager suggested to him, conspiring with us to rob the farmers of their land and sell it to the United States? A man who had spent twenty-five years of his life in France could not evoke trust and loyalty as could a proven benefactor.

In our case, the fears of the Betsileo were unfounded, but their fears, suspicions, and reluctance to talk to outsiders should be placed in historical context. Since the eighteenth century, Betsileo have seen few unmixed blessings come from the outside. Among the petty states of the eighteenth and early nineteenth centuries in the southern Betsileo homeland, war and raids were endemic. Betsileo captured in raids became slaves. Under King Radama (ca. 1809–27) the Merina brutally subdued the populations of those Betsileo polities that resisted their attempts at annexation. Burdens in taxes, labor, and other contributions to their conquerors were sometimes intolerable. Fear and suspicion of outsiders already established for good reasons, French rule brought reinforcements. One Betsileo told me that no Frenchman, other than some priests, ever entered a Betsileo village without demanding something that strained or hurt the villagers. Forced labor was the plight of many Betsileo and other Malagasy, especially during the 1930s. Of course the Betsileo were afraid of us. History has given them every reason to maintain fears that usually have been neither irrational nor unfounded.[6] Our fortune was that we were able to dispel some of them.

We moved into Ivato in late March. We saw most of the rice harvests, weighed many of the yields, saw who helped whom, and began conducting formal interviews about the socioeconomic context of rice. Soon we could not imagine moving to another village. We were doing what we had determined to do: interviewing, conversing, being taught Betsileo *fomba*, observing life on the local level, getting to know Betsileo as individuals, appreciating their ideas, values, and traditions, and becoming acquainted with surrounding villages and their relationships with Ivato. There were other practical reasons to stay. A good road ran to our front door; our sponsor, the physician, had loaned us his brick vacation house; through his efforts, Ivato had piped running water; there was a village outhouse.

The implications of our luck began to strike us as fieldwork in Ivato progressed. Rapport and conditions were so good there because of the physician's success. What in the social context of his village of origin had promoted this success? It turned out that he was merely the latest, and most successful, in a long line of regionally important individuals from Ivato. My subsequent ethnographic and oral historical research documented the long-term importance of Ivato in its region. The reasons for this importance will be discussed in chapter 4.

Intensive Fieldwork Begins

During my first visit to Ivato I had made separate notebook pages for all households there, inquiring about the age, sex, birthplace, and kinship connections of their members. I had met most of the adults. My first visit had been spent with the elders of the eastern side of the village. I had also met the village chief, a young married man, and another young household head, Jules, the physician's half-brother and one of my closest neighbors. Almost immediately, in addition to daytime interviews and observation, I established a pattern of evening fieldwork that continued throughout my stay in Ivato. Around five or six o'clock, when their work was done, villagers came to the living room of the physician's house for wine, conversation, and, especially as our stay was coming to a close, for dinner. From these evening gatherings I soon learned that one man of the village's senior generation, in his mid-fifties, stood out in knowledge, intelligence, and verbal skill among village grandfathers. This was Rakoto, and I was not the first to recognize him for these qualities.

Many Betsileo local groups have such an individual, someone especially interested in traditions, a man given to oratory, and the customary speaker for the group on ceremonial occasions. People like Rakoto occupy no formal office in Betsileo society. They are simply individuals who, because of their extraordinary interest, oratory skill, and intelligence, are encouraged to assume this role. Sometimes there are two spokesmen for the same group. Rakoto's oldest son shows some of the same interests and skills and will probably replace his father. Jules, Rakoto's cousin, is also a likely successor. Often there is no member of a local group who is especially adept. When this is the case, short[7] speeches are made at ceremonies, and for the ethnographer, fieldwork loses some of its richness.

Ivato has Rakoto, and he became my most valuable single informant, cataloging the rules of Betsileo culture, providing me with genealogical and oral historical information about Ivato and other villages with which he had ties of descent or marriage. Though, as the most observant older man in Ivato, his fund of general knowledge of his village and region was greatest, he also facilitated my research by readily admitting gaps in his knowledge and by directing me to appropriate sources. When I asked him about people buried in his family tomb, for example, he made me call his cousin, Tuesdaysfather,[8] a well-informed informant on the tomb because he had witnessed its construction and consecration and had interred the many victims of the influenza epidemic of 1919, two years after the tomb was completed.

Despite Rakoto's knowledge and willingness to cooperate, an anthropological field study cannot be based on work with only one informant. Furthermore, pleasant evenings with informants, although conducive to rapport, had to be combined with observation of daily life. April, the month when most rice fields were harvested, was a good time to arrive. I had a chance to weigh yields, to observe preparations for several harvests, the arrival of personnel, the tasks and the division of labor, the threshing of the paddy, its drying and winnowing, and its transport to household granaries. I met outsiders who had come to help. I charted the composition of various task groups. I ate meals served by rice field owners. I began to see the importance of age, seniority, kinship, descent, and stratum in the recruitment of groups for different tasks and in everyday encounters. I visited all households in Ivato. I timed people working at various activities and I began to fill out my interview schedules on rice fields and cultivation techniques. As the harvest closed, the ceremonial season began, and I traveled with Ivatans to ceremo-

nies, meeting their kin and neighbors, assimilating the cultural significance—
so strange to a late-twentieth-century American—of dead ancestors to ongoing social life.

Interview Schedules

Observations, conversations, and informal interviews were gradually creating
an impression of Betsileo rural life in Ivato. More detailed information was
being gathered in formal interviews centered on the rice schedule, which had
been mimeographed in Ambalavao. It was written in the Betsileo dialect of
Malagasy. It was four-pages long and included queries on location of rice
field, distance from house of respondent, informant's estimate of size (later
checked with other estimates), number of plots, type of land (Betsileo distinguish several categories, differentially evaluated in terms of ease of cultivation, environmental hazards, and productivity), manner of acquisition (generally inheritance), kinship or other relationship of successive cultivators,
and source of water. For cultivation techniques I asked about date, number
of workers, time expended, and cost in food and/or in cash to the owner for
each task in the annual cycle: seeding, tillage, transplanting, weeding, reaping, and threshing.

For several tasks, informants were able to list all personnel and their
kinship or other relationship to the field owner. For a subsample of the total
sample, all people who took part in all activities connected with rice cultivation for the field in question were ascertained, through my own observations, supplemented with informants' recollections. For the major cooperative tasks—transplanting and harvesting—I recorded complete personnel for
all cases I observed. In Ivato the rice schedule was completed for forty-four
fields. Rabe and I, later, did the same questionnaire in Tanambao (twenty-
five rice fields) and Ambalabe (thirty-three fields).

After doing about five formal interviews based on the rice schedule, I
found that my Malagasy had improved to a point where I could understand
answers to virtually any question I might ask concerning rice fields or their
cultivation. Most interviews lasted about an hour. Since a separate schedule
was completed for each rice field of a given peasant, I sometimes worked on
this for four hours with a single informant.

By June, since the rice schedule had yielded such complete and comparable data for an almost total sample of Ivato's rice fields and had done so
much to improve my Malagasy, I designed several additional interview
schedules on other domains of Betsileo life. One that is particularly significant to the analysis that follows (especially in chapter 6) involved questioning
informants about villages where they had relatives and the nature of these
relationships. These questions were designed to see how wide the kinship
networks of an individual were, whether father's or mother's side tended to

be favored, whether relatives by marriage, blood ceremonies, and adoption were included under the same label as kin, and if the nature and extent of kinship calculation varied with sex, age, stratum, and position in descent group. This interview schedule also included queries about fictive kinship (e.g., "blood siblinghood") and fosterage, and was completed for all male and female residents of Ivato over seventeen years old, and for smaller samples in Tanambao and Ambalabe.

A third interview schedule on migrations and displacements gathered histories of temporary and extended extravillage employment, marketing, ceremonial attendance, and visiting. A fourth schedule was concerned with the cultivation of secondary crops, trees, and livestock possession. Like the first three, this schedule was carried out for a less complete sample in Tanambao and Ambalabe than in Ivato. Finally, a very detailed schedule on income and budget was done for a small sample of Ivato's households, roughly stratified by sex of household head, residence on father's or mother's estate, and relative wealth. This last schedule often took about five hours to complete and allowed intensive study of a few contrasting cases selected on the basis of my knowledge during my last two months in the field. Questions included in the first four schedules provided a larger but less detailed sample of income and budgetary data for all Ivato households.

While interviewing with the schedules from April through December, we continued to observe activities and behavior of Ivatans, to learn informants' opinions, and to gather information about ancestral values. We saw people assemble to build a house, to repair a community building, to repair the village water supply line, to open the tomb, and to attend ceremonies elsewhere. Over more than a year spent among the Betsileo, we observed tasks associated with all phases of rice production, its preparation, and distribution. I did time and motion studies of most phases of rice agriculture. I weighed cooked food consumed in different households. I drew genealogies and learned household composition for all neighboring villages. In sum, I tried to learn as much about variation among Ivatans and between them and their neighbors as I could through formal and informal interviews, observations, measurement, conversation, and questioning.

By the end of the harvest season in Ivato, we wanted to return briefly to Ambalavao and to renew our study of the villages to the south in the canton of Mahazony. The ceremonial season in 1967 was much fuller in Mahazony than around Ivato (for reasons spelled out in chapter 7), and we attended a major ceremonial event, the consecration of a new tomb, there that July. Bodies from two ancient tombs were being transferred to the new one. Since an ancestor of a woman in Tanambao was to be moved, we had an obvious reason for our interest. The event, analyzed in chapter 7, lasted three days and nights and brought representatives from most villages in Mahazony and neighboring cantons. My interest in the Mahazony villages rekindled, but unwilling to abandon intimate fieldwork in Ivato, I asked Rabe if he would be willing to live in Tanambao, his natal village where he occasionally vacationed, and do some of the structured interviews that Betty Kottak and I had been doing in Ivato.

He agreed to live in Tanambao on and off from August through November. To show him what I wanted, I did some of the interviews around the rice schedule myself. As we subsequently returned to Ambalavao from our respective villages at one or two week intervals, I checked the questionnaires he had completed in Tanambao and Ambalabe and asked him to clarify incomplete or doubtful responses. I returned several times to Mahazony myself to seek further information and clarification and to find out to what extent informants' estimates to Rabe of the area they cultivated corresponded to actual measurement. The information included in the forms he had completed was also suggesting new questions about the southern villages which I had to pursue myself. Although my knowledge of them is, of course, much less complete than for Ivato, I was able to develop models of their economy and social organization based on observation, informal fieldwork, and a large sample of quantitative data.

Macroregional Inquiry

Descent group organization had been one of my main interests before I went to Madagascar, and differences in their descent organization initially led me to choose the three villages for intensive study. Excluding the descendants of slaves, the core of Ivato was a branch of a widespread descent group called Tranovondro. Ivatans claimed that their own descent group and another whose members lived in nearby villages had been influential throughout Betsileo history. I wanted to test their claim by determining for the entire Betsileo territory the importance of named descent groups, the approximate number of these groups, their population sizes, their geographical ranges, their origins and movements, and the extent to which descent group distribution reflected environmental and economic variation. To obtain such large-scale comparative and historical information, I devised, in August, another form, this time a true questionnaire rather than an interview schedule. Unlike the others, this form was distributed and completed more in the sociologist's than the anthropologist's tradition.

I could never have used this questionnaire without the hierarchical administrative structure which, in the central highlands, represents the result of over a century of Merina, French, and Malagasy rule. I also could not have distributed this questionnnaire without the cooperation of several Malagasy officials. The first assistant to the province chief approved my request to distribute my form through the government hierarchy. He directed us to the assistant to the prefect of the Betsileo prefecture, who wrote a letter to each of the seven subprefects within his circumscription. In September we traveled to all seven subprefecture seats and personally delivered the questionnaires, of which 5,000 forms had been printed. The forms were picked up later by the seventy-four canton chiefs on their monthly visits to their subprefect. Below this, there was considerable variation in how the information was gathered. In some cantons the forms were sent to each village, where they were completed by village elders. Results were best, however, when the canton chief called in elders from each village in his circumscription on market day to answer the questions in his presence as his secretary transcribed them. I doubt that there are many ethnographers who have inconvenienced and who are, therefore, indebted to such a large number of officials and informants.

I had intended the sample to be as total as possible. The sample that I eventually collected is therefore very large, but not random. Of 5,000 forms distributed, 1,500 were returned, representing as many villages. About 1,300 contained useful information on oral traditions and contemporary distribution of descent groups, indicating that my queries had been understood.

Sociocultural Variation and Traditional Ethnography

Having identified some of the techniques I used to obtain information about the Betsileo, some similarities and differences between my approach and other ethnographic fieldwork strategies should be emphasized. Like most other ethnographers I lived in and studied one community that was in some ways representative of "my people's" way of life. I think of this as the most important and most deeply informative part of my fieldwork. I temporarily became a part of life in a Betsileo village. I studied intensively and intimately a community and its web of interrelationships with its natural environment, its neighbors, and the outside world. I also learned about its history, which lives so vividly in everyday conversation. I got to know Betsileo not as fearful peasants, and not only as oral historians and well-informed informants, but as individuals—as humorists, orators, diligent workers. I learned to appreciate personality differences, and I made some good friends. I was fictively incorporated into the Tranovondro descent group localized in Ivato and even had the name of one of its ancestors conferred on me.

Although I employed many usual ethnographic strategies, perhaps the major difference between my own and more traditional ethnographic research was my focus on variation. I am unable to say how characteristic of contemporary anthropologists this interest is.[9] Most ethnographic descriptions I have read have not been concerned with a population and territory as large as that of the Betsileo. Despite this, it seems to me that many ethnographic reports attempt to develop models that are more concerned with establishing uniformity than demonstrating diversity. Communities have been treated as representative of some larger unit. The larger unit customarily of interest to the anthropologist has been the "culture" of the society being studied. Anthropologists' traditional aims have included documenting the range of human diversity by presenting each culture as in some ways unique. Following such an approach, I might have emphasized contrasts between Betsileo culture and Tanala, or Merina, or Bara, cultures. Some of the uniformities in Betsileo culture, embodied in their notion of *fombandrazana*, have already been mentioned. They certainly cannot be ignored in any ethnography of the Betsileo. However, variation, like that between the three Betsileo villages I studied, is an equally important attribute of a complex society, and as such merits anthropological attention.

Furthermore, a shortcoming of some ethnographic reports is their failure to specify the universe described, how it is like or unlike other universes that might have been studied, and how much it can tell us, therefore, about the larger unit being abstracted from observation of the smaller. Of course these are not blanket indictments of most ethnographic reports. In the band-organized and small-scale horticultural societies in which ethnography grew up, sociocultural heterogeneity exists, but is a less severe problem. However, as their familiarity with techniques for analysis of large quantities of data increases, sociocultural anthropologists are paying more attention both to complex societies and to variation.

Subsequent chapters show another reason for detailed studies of intracultural variation in space: evolutionary processes can be reconstructed not just through historical information, but can be inferred from variation in space at a single time. We will see, for example, that Betsileo who have settled in contrasting environments have been subjected to different selective forces and that the material conditions that promote sociocultural adaptation and differentiation have changed historically, as physical environments have themselves been processed differently by different sociocultural systems. Examining contemporary contrasting villages such as Ivato, Ambalabe, and Tanambao, one sees the end products of adaptive divergence, expressed sometimes in different sociocultural forms, but more often in the actual behavior underlying these forms and in the manner of their functioning, their effects, and their interarticulation with other forms.

Sociocultural variation at a given time, when viewed as reflecting diversification in response to variable material conditions, may offer clues about actual historical processes and temporal relationships among variables. Consider one example, the contrast between contemporary Betsileo stockbreeders and agriculturalists. Historically the Betsileo economy has shifted toward specialization in crops. Areas that over centuries have been converted into rice paddies were once idle marshland or were used for grazing zebu cattle. Contemporary regional variation among the Betsileo documents this shift and its many ramifications in progress.

Government Statistics

I had distributed my macroregional questionnaire to gather information on oral traditions and in order to test hypotheses involving covariation of social organizational, demographic, and economic data. For economic information, my limited means could not permit even an attempt to duplicate the labors of more than 200 Malagasy government officials, a few thousand village chiefs, and many more cooperating peasants. To test my hypotheses at all, I had to incorporate certain government data.

Since some of these government data enter my analysis, it is appropriate to say a bit about how they were collected. Accompanying long-established centralized rule in the highlands have been fairly reliable means of collection of data of interest to the government. Bloch (1968) has discussed the role of long-established literacy in facilitating administration within the nineteenth-century Merina empire. Taimoro scribes from Madagascar's southeast coast, who had been rendering Malagasy languages in Arabic orthography since at least the sixteenth century, taught writing—used for divination and administration—to court officials during the reign of Merina king Andrianampoini-merina (1783–1809), as dated by Delivré (1974, p. 221–27). In 1820 two London Missionary Society pastors and a Frenchman adapted Roman script for Malagasy, and by 1827 at least 4,000 citizens of Imerina were literate. Bloch attributes this quick spread of literacy, on which the detail of colonial and contemporary government record-keeping rests, to the Taimoros' prior role in familiarizing the Merina with writing. Bloch (1968, p. 287) notes that Imerina is probably the area of the Third World with the highest literacy rate (and probably the highest rate of Christianization as well). Betsileo, unlike Bara (cf. Huntington 1974, p. 53–54) also value Christianity and education. These facts make government records for highland Madagascar more useful than for other parts of the island. French colonial rule, which retained many Merina as bureaucrats, fostered and perpetuated the collection of statistics.

I was able to consult annually compiled government records on crop production, cultivated area, yields, livestock, market prices of certain goods, and demographic variables. Although the manner of collecting information on production and yields varied from one canton to another, most government estimates of crop yields agreed roughly with calculations based on my own measurements. Prices were ascertained by canton personnel in weekly markets. Malagasy were required to notify canton authorities of births and deaths. Each village chief, assisted by village elders, notified the government about local residence shifts and collected a head tax (subsequently abolished) on all adult males and livestock. Information derived in this way is more likely to be accurate for the Betsileo than for Malagasy groups that are less sedentary and whose experience with state authorities has been of shorter duration, for example, the Tsimihety described by Wilson (1971). To be sure, biases and inaccuracies turned up in the government statistics. However, most of the biases appeared to be constant. To evade taxation, few Betsileo declared the full number of their cattle, and young men frequently, and through various machinations, successfully lied about their ages. Peasants usually underestimated the size of their rice fields, to which a tax was attached, when they listed them with the government registry.

How does this affect data analysis? There is every reason to believe that the same biases toward underestimation held for all areas of the Betsileo homeland. Government statistics should therefore be regarded not as arithmetically precise (equal interval) variables but as somewhere between interval and ordinal accuracy. My analysis recognizes this and uses appropriate statistics. Even though the absolute figures cannot be trusted completely, government data for one Betsileo canton relative to others do have value since biases are constant.

Aims of Analysis

The present analysis strives to produce a structural model abstracted from information on several different levels, supported by statistical data and illustrated with cases of real people. Responses collected in the three villages, government data, and the comparative and historical macroregional descent group questionnaire have all been analyzed statistically, and some of the results are discussed in subsequent chapters. Also, in the pages that follow, I have tried to place Betsileo rural life and variations from one village or region to another in human terms. A statistical approach makes the discussion of cases of individual Betsileo more meaningful by firmly substantiating what is typical and what is deviant. Statistical correlations, too, become more meaningful when they are brought down to the level of an individual concerned with those problems of existence that a coefficient or ratio expresses abstractly. By presenting some historical and contemporary examples, in human terms, of the normal and degrees of variance, I hope to show factors that motivate individual Betsileo to different decisions, actions, and life patterns.

My picture of Betsileo society has a statistical foundation, supported by discussion of cases, but it is more than this. It is a composite picture based also on my observations of behavior, my discussions and conversations with Betsileo, conscious teaching of me by people like Rakoto, and my own impressions and informal manipulations of information I received in the field. Most of my empirical generalizations, confirmed by statistics, represent hypotheses originally formed as qualitative generalizations—relationships I had seen exist which must therefore, I thought, receive statistical validation. In reality, some did; some did not. Some of my generalizations keep only a qualitative base. Though I cannot validate them, so strong is my impression of their validity that I could not exclude them.

The analysis that follows also incorporates, but tries to keep separate, both emic and etic research strategies (Harris 1968, chapter 20). I also paid attention to Rappaport's (1968) similar distinction between an operational (Harris's "etic") model and a cognized (Harris's "emic") model of cultural behavior. The Betsileo cognized model, briefly, is the native interpretation of the world, the set of rules and expectations, orienting principles, concepts, meanings, and values that are significant to an individual Betsileo—why he or she does things. The operational model, in Harris's (1968) terms "etic," or "intersubjectively valid," is the ethnographer's abstraction from and analysis of what he or she studies—an outsider's account of behavior, its material determinants, context, and results, and specification of the limits that determine what individual actions may be tolerated without destroying the system that includes them. It is the trained outsider's interpretation of why people do certain things. Such distinctions, however, should not confine the ethnographer. The material world feeds back on the cognized model, which in turn affects individual actions that may maintain or modify the system. Informants' conceptions of their world do not just mirror, they may also mask from informants, aspects of their concrete situation. Yet they may also suggest to the ethnographer the possibility of things and events in the real world and prompt inquiries directed at developing and refining the operational model. Much of my reconstruction of Betsileo history, for example, involves trying to build an operational model out of a cognized model.

In the following chapters several sources of information will be the basis for a comparative and historical study of the Betsileo of southcentral Madagascar. These include intensive fieldwork in three Betsileo villages, a regional survey, written questionnaire responses, governmental data, ethnohistorical research, and previously published accounts of Malagasy history and ethnography. The analysis of the material context of sociocultural variation begins with a consideration of the Betsileo against a background of historical and contemporary variation encountered within the total Malagasy population (chapter 2). Sociocultural diversity is viewed through a model of adaptive radiation of populations bearing a similar cultural heritage into a variety of physical and biotic environments. Such regional factors as trade, warfare, and migration represent other material conditions that have influenced unity and diversity among Malagasy populations. In chapter 3, local and regional determinants of the emergence of state organization in the Betsileo homeland are examined. The scale of analysis is narrowed by focusing on divergent evolution—attributable to local ecological and economic differences—of the eastern Betsileo and the more pastorally oriented Betsileo of the south and west.

Chapters 3 and 4 document the emergence and increasing importance of socioeconomic stratification among the Betsileo, from its genesis in their native states to its sharpening and modification under Merina and French rule. Chapters 5 through 8 bring a still narrower focus to the analysis of variation of material conditions—those that promote differential access to valued and strategic resources—and other sociocultural phenomena. It will be seen that systems of socioeconomic stratification have become the major factors that produce and reproduce several types of sociocultural variation. In the final analysis, however, the contrasts in stratum exemplified by three contrasting villages reflect the historical contrasts in material conditions documented in previous chapters.

Tanambao, Ambalabe, and Ivato were originally chosen for study on the basis of contrasts in their descent group organization. They sample a typology of Betsileo villages structured respectively by no descent group organization, multiple descent group organization, and single descent group organization. Chapters 3 through 6 demonstrate, however, the historical, demographic, economic, and political basis for this typology. The three villages also exemplify the highly important regional contrast between the more arid, traditionally more pastoral Betsileo south and west, where Tanambao and Ambalabe are located, and the more densely populated, better watered, traditionally more agricultural east, where Ivato is. Lastly they sample the hierarchy of wealth and power that now includes all Betsileo, running from Tanambao near the bottom to Ivato near the top.

Fieldwork techniques used in these three villages included quantitative and qualitative data collection through interview schedules, measurement, observation, informal interviewing, conversation, participant observation, and my conscious instruction by well-informed informants. I learned that a certain unity in Betsileo culture is maintained by the native concept of *fombandrazana*, the notion that ancestral customs and beliefs provide eternal moral values still orienting Betsileo behavior despite the flux of history. History and the ancestors are very much on everyone's mind. My decision to begin with a detailed examination of Betsileo history in part reflects this convergence of my own interests with the Betsileo view of what is important in studying them. Yet, despite *fombandrazana*, sociocultural forms still vary and change, as do the behaviors underlying them, their functioning, and the interarticulation of these sociocultural forms with others. Subsequent chapters examine concrete variation in economic, social, and ceremonial organization. The major aim of this study is to uncover reasons for some of the diversity that exists in any complex society. Historical and ethnographic information both have a contribution to make, since reasons for contemporary variation are historical and since contemporary cultural variation sheds light on evolutionary processes.

II

VARIATION IN TIME

CHAPTER TWO

Themes, Instruments, Variations

In order to understand variation among Betsileo of the past and present, it is first necessary to place them within the more general context of natural and cultural diversity in Madagascar, and to identify the contemporary Betsileo as merely one variation on a theme that recurs, in a number of transformations, among the twenty or so contemporary ethnic groups descended from Madagascar's original settlers. The range of physical environmental contrasts encountered on the world's fourth largest island is broad. Madagascar is 1,580 kilometers long from north to south and 600 kilometers across at its widest point. The island's total area is 590,000 square kilometers or 228,000 square miles. It is located in the southwestern Indian Ocean, between the southern latitudes 12.5° and 25°. The shortest distance between the western Malagasy coast and Africa, from which it is separated by the Mozambique Channel, is less than 250 miles. Its nearest continental neighbors are Mozambique and Tanzania.

Madagascar's first settlers, the Proto-Malagasy, appear to have begun to colonize the island no longer than 2,000 years ago. A mixed population combining African and Indonesian ancestry, their descendants have proliferated and have occupied a variety of different habitats on the near continental island, including the rainy lowlands of the east coast, the tropical forest of the eastern escarpment, the valleys and plains of the central highlands, and a variety of more arid environments in the south and west. In the process of this population explosion and adaptive radiation, both the sociocultural legacy of the Proto-Malagasy and subsequently invented, borrowed, or diffused sociocultural contributions have been subjected to screening effects of a variety of Malagasy environments.

A great deal of additional archaeological work needs to be done in Madagascar in order to determine its manner of original settlement, and the times of and reasons for divergence of its populations. At present, many speculations about early Malagasy history and subsequent divergence are suggested by the study of Malagasy languages. Most scholars who are acquainted with Madagascar have been impressed by the uniformity of the speech patterns of its inhabitants. Malagasy speech communities are more closely interrelated than the Romance languages derived from Latin. All indigenous Malagasy languages share a unity of origin in Proto-Malagasy, a member of the western Indonesian subgroup of the Malayo-Polynesian language family. Although the problem of ascertaining the particular Indonesian languages most closely related to Malagasy languages has not been, and perhaps never can be, conclusively resolved, Dahl in 1951 first made a convincing case for a close relationship between Malagasy languages (Merina for the most part) and Maanyan, a language spoken in southeastern Borneo. Hudson's publication (1967) of word lists for several Barito speech communities of Borneo does much to confirm the close relationship between Malagasy languages and Maanyan and other related Barito speech communities of southeast Borneo. My own preliminary comparison of Malagasy dialects and languages with those in Hudson's East Barito subgroup suggests that the percentage of shared cognates in basic vocabulary between certain Malagasy languages, on the one hand, and certain East Barito languages (including Maanyan), on the other, may be as high as fifty percent. Since I was also able to find two Malagasy languages that shared only sixty-one percent of the same list of cognates, it is unlikely that any other Indonesian languages will turn out to be closer to Malagasy than those of the East Barito subgroup. Thus, the closest linguistic relatives of the Malagasy almost certainly live in southeast Borneo.

Although we can say where the nearest linguistic relatives of the Malagasy live today, this does not, of course, tell us where the common ancestors of the Malagasy and the East Barito lived, nor does it give us much information about Malagasy history. According to a joint glottochronological study of Malagasy speech communities, the Malagasy languages separated from their nearest Indonesian relatives most probably between 100 B.C. and A.D. 200, and, with considerably less probability, as early as the fourth century B.C. or as late as the fourth century A.D. (Vérin, Kottak, and Gorlin 1970, pp. 60–61). Because of several problems with the glottochronological formula used to calculate divergence times of related languages these dates are included as broadly suggestive only. It seems reasonable, however, to date the initial settlement of Madagascar to the first millenium A.D. Carbon 14 dates for an early ceramic assemblage—apparently a local development linked only to ceramics on Mayotte in the nearby Comoro Islands, excavated at sites at Irodo on Madagascar's northeast coast (Battistini and Vérin, 1966; Vérin 1975; Wright n.d.)—suggest occupation around A.D. 800–900.

THE SETTLEMENT OF MADAGASCAR

Speculations about how Madagascar was settled are too numerous, varied, and often farfetched to review here: Vérin (1979) provides a useful summary.

To me, the most probable theory is that of Deschamps (1965), who argues that the Proto-Malagasy were an oceangoing population of traders who participated in a vast Indian Ocean trade network that tied Indonesia to points east and west. To the west, the Proto-Malagasy traveled, never too distant from the coast, along the Indian, Arabian, and East African shorelines, eventually to reach Madagascar. A hybrid gene pool has been enriched over the centuries, since Malagasy populations, especially those of the coasts, have remained within an exchange system linking them to East Africa and even to Arabia (cf. Bloch 1968; Ferrand 1891; Kent 1970). This has led to the tremendous diversity in physical types observed among present-day Malagasy.

Diversity marks the phenotypes of Malagasy and suggests their hybrid ancestry; so, too, do their gene pools point both to Africa and to Indonesia. In a study of blood groups of contemporary Malagasy it has been demonstrated that, in terms of certain chromosomes determining Rh blood groups, contemporary Malagasy are about one-third Indonesian and two-thirds Bantu (Singer et al. 1957; pp. 119–21).

The Proto-Malagasy found their new island home to be devoid of prior human inhabitants. Having separated from the adjacent African coast several million years ago, Madagascar also lacked most of the mammalian fauna of Africa. There were no monkeys or apes, only the prosimian lemurs, which, in the absence of primate competitors underwent an evolutionary diversification and adaptive radiation that foreshadowed a similar radiation of the human population into contrasting Malagasy environments during the past 2,000 years. The large fauna of the island consisted of crocodiles, a lemur the size of a zebu steer, extinct since the seventeenth century, and a large flightless bird, the aepyornis, similar to the African ostrich and the moa of New Zealand, and, like the latter, soon rendered extinct by the hunting and egg-collecting habits of the early human population. A pygmy hippopotamus suffered a similar fate. Zebu cattle, now more numerous than Madagascar's human population, were brought in from East Africa, as were sheep, goats, and some crops, sometime during the first millenium. Rice, to become so important in the diet of most Malagasy, also came from outside, though we do not know where or when. Manioc, a New World crop which supplements grain diets throughout the island, was introduced by Europeans during the sixteenth or seventeenth century.

ADAPTIVE RADIATION

Madagascar is a particularly appropriate laboratory for studying comparative and historical problems of interest to anthropologists, because within a fairly clearly bounded area one encounters several related populations who are linguistically quite similar, but nevertheless diverse in terms of behavior patterns and institutions. In the terminology of Claude Lévi-Strauss (1967,

p. 22), the variant sociocultural manifestations associated with Malagasy populations can be viewed as a series of transformations on common structures or themes. What makes Madagascar particularly appropriate as a laboratory for studying and explaining sociocultural differences and similarities is the fact that sociocultural heritage can be held relatively constant. The problem of whether variation among populations is attributable to differences in cultural heritage or to material variation is therefore avoided, at least more so than in other parts of the world.

Adaptive radiation, of course, refers to the production of heterogeneity out of homogeneity, the development of an array of diverse types out of a relatively homogeneous ancestral population as a result of population increase, subdivision, and adaptation to a variety of circumstances, including, in the Malagasy case, occupation of contrasting environments, historic participation in a variety of local and regional ecosystems, and other factors that influence the nature and allocation of strategic resources. The model, when applied to contemporary and recent human populations, assumes that evolutionary divergence and adaptive radiation have been accomplished primarily through modifications in sociocultural means. Such divergence may involve the behavior underlying sociocultural forms, the forms themselves, the functional context and import of these forms, and their articulation with other forms. Sahlins's *Social Stratification in Polynesia* (1958) stands as an early application of the model, as do Gulliver's (1955, 1965) studies of the Jie and Turkana and the work of Steward (1956) and his students in Puerto Rico. A model of adaptive radiation is best applied to a group of human populations all of whom are descended from a common ancestral population with a common ancestral culture. Furthermore, for the model to work ideally, daughter populations or subgroups, once they have split off from the parental population to occupy new environments, should lose contact, i.e., become completely isolated from both the parental population and from other daughter populations.

If the above conditions are met, and if the range of environments occupied by the daughter populations is wide, theoretical questions vital to explaining the process of sociocultural diversification and reasons for parallelism (related populations' coping analogously with similar selective agents) can best be answered. Unfortunately for the anthropologist, there are few actual cases in which all these assumptions correspond to fact. Perhaps the closest correspondence of the expectations of the model and reality is among island populations, notably in Polynesia, where daughter populations have colonized an array of environmentally contrasting islands dotting a wide expanse of ocean. Contacts between populations of different islands, although sometimes happening, were far less frequent than for diverging continental populations. Introducing the most noise into the application of the model of adaptive radiation are cases like the Indo-Europeans. Collateral populations have diverged, converged, rediverged, and reconverged many times as trade routes, migrations, and other contacts have linked them. Indo-Europeans have been forged together, divorced, and reunited with other daughter populations by the erection, demise, and reconstruction of national boundaries.

The situation in Madagascar is intermediate, but still the model of adaptive radiation through sociocultural means is revealing. The traders who departed from Indonesia bore their own culture and social organization, no matter how partial a slice of what they left behind in Indonesia it may have been. Of those who were eventually to colonize Madagascar, some stopped here, some there along their continental coastal trade network. To Madagascar the Proto-Malagasy brought a heritage that would be common to their descendants, but this legacy was a mélange of genes and traditional ways of behaving, living, and organizing ultimately derived both from Indonesia and from East Africa.

The model of adaptive radiation set forth above demands a single, relatively homogeneous, shared protoculture as a base from which adaptive divergence has taken place. For several reasons it is impossible to know to what extent the Malagasy fulfill this assumption. Although there is a marked linguistic uniformity throughout all Malagasy speech communities—the result of the common protolanguage—there is no doubt that the hybrid Proto-Malagasy cultural heritage has been enriched over the centuries by contributions from several extra-Malagasy sources. Madagascar was founded by traders, and economic links with other world areas have been maintained throughout Malagasy history, although at times trade has been interrupted or scaled down in volume as new maritime powers have arisen in the western Indian Ocean (cf. Vérin 1975: Wright n.d.).

Furthermore, not only have Malagasy had dealings with outsiders, coastal Malagasy have not been isolated from interior ethnic units. Warfare, trade, marriage, migration, and other kinds of exchange systems have linked Malagasy populations of littoral and hinterland, so that eventually all Malagasy ethnic units have been exposed, either directly or indirectly, to cultural influences derived from East Africa and Arabia. Bloch (1968, p. 285), for example, comments on widespread travel throughout Madagascar by scribes from the southeast coast which, along with the northwest coast is one of the two main centers of Arabic and East African influence in Madagascar. Certain pan-Malagasy similarities in divination, astrology, medicine, and magical practices are traceable, not to the protoculture, but to this kind of diffusion. Wilson (1971, p. 194) also notes that "a striking feature of all Malagasy peoples is their penchant for perambulation all over the island."

Although, in the absence of the kind of detailed data needed to specify the characteristics, time, and duration of contacts, it is impossible to demonstrate the nature of either the protoculture or subsequent cultural diffusion, the model of adaptive radiation through sociocultural means is still appropriate. This is because both the protoculture and later accretions from non-Malagasy areas have been available to all Malagasy. Through time, both ancestral and borrowed sociocultural forms and the behavior undertaken with these forms in mind have been subjected to the screening effects of the diverse selective agents encountered by the expanding Malagasy population.

THE ORIGIN OF UNIFORMITIES

My own feeling is that the matter of geographical origins of particular sociocultural traits, patterns of behavior, and institutions must be approached very cautiously. This is because I think of creativity and flexibility as being intrinsic attributes of human populations, and, in fact, the major reason for the success, measured in terms of sheer numbers and range of environmental niches occupied, of *Homo sapiens.*

In economic, social, and political organization, of course, geographic origins are difficult to discern because certain customs, institutions, and beliefs are encountered all over the world and have independently arisen among the most remote human populations. Independent invention, common heritage, and borrowing are equally plausible explanations for the possession of similar sociocultural items among different populations.

Although I would therefore argue against trying to assign specific origins in either Indonesia, Africa, or Arabia to certain broad cultural similarities encountered generally among Malagasy populations, I do believe that such shared forms should be indicated, since they provide a framework of constant reference points for assessing and explaining adaptive radiation expressed in sociocultural transformations. Many are undoubtedly homologies derived from the Proto-Malagasy heritage; others represent contributions introduced early in Malagasy history that have spread among the island's populations. Although I am unable presently to identify specific homologies as aspects of Malagasy protoculture or as subsequently borrowed, some of these shared sociocultural forms may now be indicated. Descent groups that are biased patrilineally are apparently encountered among all Malagasy ethnic units except the contemporary Merina (Bloch 1971, pp. 44–50).[1] However, most Malagasy societies, although stating that an individual should join his father's descent group, also allow him the choice of affiliating with his mother's descent group. Almost universally, individuals on both maternal and paternal sides are considered to be kin. Huntington (1974, pp. 66–69) finds throughout Madagascar a widespread ideological connection between ideas of order, morality, father, patriline, tomb, and ancestor. However, among cousins the relationship between children of sisters is generally considered closest, and the taboo on cousin incest applies with greatest force here (Bloch 1971, p. 52; Huntington 1978, pp. 17–21; Southall 1971, p. 150). Despite this, Huntington (1978, p. 30) correctly notes a preference for some kind of endogamy throughout the island.

Most Malagasy say that a bride should go to live in her husband's village after their marriage, and most marriages follow this rule. Fictive kinship, usually based on rituals that turn nonkin into structural analogues of blood relatives, is another Malagasy universal. Most Malagasy use Hawaiian cousin terms, designating their first cousins with the terms they use for brother and sister. Except among southern-western tribes like Bara (Huntington 1974, p. 86) and Sakalava (Gardenier 1976, pp. 90–98) where cross-uncles and/or aunts are distinguished, reference terms for aunt and uncle are generally those used for mother and father, and children of sisters and brothers are designated by the terms for children. Malagasy generally distinguish between their siblings on the basis of their relative age with (at least) terms for older and younger sibling.

Most Malagasy pay special attention to their ancestors, and most perform rites venerating bones and relics of deceased persons. All use the same word, *mpanjaka* or a variant, to designate individuals who exercise authority over territorial units and over the people who live within them (cf. Rakotoarisoa 1979). All Malagasy believe in a spiritual being or beings called by some variant of Andriananahary, and in an efficacious, mana-like force called *hasina*. Most Malagasy circumcise their children, and in all Malagasy societies some form of divination and astrology is practiced. What is important is that although these general forms are shared, they and the behavior, functions, and contexts associated with them vary with specific material circumstances.

CULTURAL DIVERGENCE, ETHNICITY, AND ECOLOGY

Subgrouping on the basis of glottochronology (Vérin, Kottak, and Gorlin 1970) suggests a fairly early split between the languages of the west and south, and those of the east coast and central highlands. There was a later split between east and central (Merina, Betsileo, Sihanaka) linguistic groups (see Map 1). A few broad contrasts in economy are roughly correlated with the linguistic differentiation. Thus, whereas eastern and central populations rely on (usually wet-) rice cultivation, mixed economies involving cattle herding and horticulture (of rice and other crops) are basic to all members of the western-southern subgroup. And, associated with the later split, central populations have added irrigation (given much less rainfall in the interior) to the agricultural techniques (drainage, leveling, terracing) practiced by some groups on the east coast. Given this broad divergence, how are Madagascar's twenty contemporary *ethnies* or ethnic units, as recognized by French and

Map 1
ETHNIC GROUPS OF
MADAGASCAR

TANKARANA

SAKALAVA

TSIMIHETY

SAKALAVA

SIHANAKA

BEZANOZANO

BETSIMISARAKA

MERINA

BETSILEO

SAKALAVA

TANALA

TAMBAHOAKA

TAIMORO

ZAFISORO

TAIFASY

BARA

TAISAKA

MAHAFALY

TANOSY

TANDROY

o   km   200

Malagasy administrations, related to adaptive radiation, to ecological and cultural differentiation?

Unlike the Bushman band (Lee 1968), the local territorial group of 200 people known as the Tsembaga Maring (Rappaport 1968, 1971b), or the Betsileo communities—Ivato, Ambalabe, and Tanambao—examined in subsequent chapters, the Merina, Betsileo, and other Malagasy ethnic units are certainly not ecological populations if one defines an ecological population either as "an aggregate of organisms having in common a set of distinctive means by which they maintain a common set of material relations within the ecosystem in which they participate" (Rappaport 1971b, p. 238) or as "groups exploiting resources entirely, or almost entirely, within certain demarcated areas from which members of other human groups are excluded" (Rappaport 1971b, p. 250). Furthermore, it is often difficult to specify the ecosystems, defined as "the total of living organisms and non-living substances bound together in material exchanges within some demarcated portion of the biosphere" (Rappaport 1971b, p. 238), in which Malagasy participate. Indeed, anthropologists (Rappaport 1971b; Kottak 1972b) distinguish between local and regional ecological populations, and local and regional ecosystems. Rappaport notes that ecosystems are not sharply bounded and that their discrimination rests to a considerable extent on the aims of a particular analysis. It is probably even truer for the Betsileo and other Malagasy than for the Maring of highland New Guinea that "local ecological populations . . . participate in regional exchange systems composed of several or many local populations occupying wider geographical areas" (Rappaport 1971b, p. 251).

For a large-scale comparative and historical study such as this one, ecological adaptation can perhaps best be evaluated by focusing on the sociocultural contexts and associations of bundles of interrelated material variables rather than by trying to define and demarcate precise local ecosystems. Especially among territorially large or populous groups like Betsileo, Merina, and Sakalava, environment, modes of production, and other sociocultural means of adaptation display considerable variation. Similarly, the existence of ecoclines, regions of gradual rather than abrupt shifts from one local ecosystem to its neighbor, makes it difficult to demarcate even broad ecosystemic contrasts.

The Betsileo illustrate the noncorrespondence of ethnicity and ecology. Most Betsileo live in the highlands as peasant cultivators of wet-rice. As one moves south or west, however, temperature gradually rises, rainfall gradually declines, and sources of water become scarcer and scarcer. Cattle herding becomes more and more important, and rice is gradually replaced by maize, manioc, and other crops. As one travels through this ecocline, if he wishes to know where Betsileo ethnicity stops and Bara ethnicity begins, he will probably have to ask someone (cf. Shaw 1876, p. 103). Drawing an ecological boundary would be arbitrary, since similar ecoclinal shifts continue as one moves to the west and south in Madagascar generally. There is a gradual shift in historical and contemporary selective forces and, correspondingly, in sociocultural means employed by humans to adapt to such gradually changing circumstances.

There *are* sharp environmental boundaries and contrasts in adaptive means between some Malagasy populations. The highlands fall abruptly, more than 1,200 meters in 50 kilometers, to the narrow eastern littoral. On the eastern side of Betsileo country an abrupt shift in natural environment accompanies the sharp descent to the intervening forest homeland of the Tanala, whose adaptive means also contrast strongly with those of the Betsileo. No Tanala is a sedentary cultivator of wet-rice. No Betsileo is a swidden horticulturalist (yet there are many ecoclinal Betsileo communities that approximate the Bara in their penchant for cattle breeding). The name Tanala has ecological import; it means "people of the forest." In the past Betsileo who moved to the forest became Tanala, and Tanala who migrated to the highlands became Betsileo; there were no intermediate steps.[2] On the other hand, a long-established Betsileo population in Bara country are known as Barabory, something not quite Betsileo, but also not completely Bara.

If the ethnic units are not united by a single economic activity or characteristic type of local ecosystem, what did bring common ethnicity about? In many cases Malagasy ethnic units are creations of political confederations and states, which have forged unity on a large territorial scale in Madagascar since early in the eighteenth century. Many of the ethnic labels employed since French conquest in 1896, "Betsileo" among them, do not appear on a list of Malagasy societies published by Etienne de Flacourt in 1661, prior to the formation of the Sakalava confederation of the west coast and to the development and expansion of the Merina empire. Many of the ethnic units designated today must be recognized as products of Merina expansion. For example, no evidence I have examined convinces me that the Betsileo constituted an ethnically conscious or even environmentally circumscribed unit prior to their conquest by the Merina. Previously several polities, each with its own name, which also served as the ethnic designation of the population residing in its territory, had been autonomous entities. Nor, in the absence of the political cohesion provided by a single territorial administration, did the pre-Merina Betsileo have any kinship basis for unity. No common genealogy links all Betsileo or even the noble lines of the once independent political subdivisions.

States have solved, to an extent, the problem of establishing and maintaining ethnic diversity. For example, the Merina drew an administrative line between the Betsileo province, with its capital at Fianarantsoa (established in 1830) and the Bara province, with its northern capital at Ihosy (established in 1877). Merina rule over the Betsileo was firm, but their administration of the Bara was tenuous at best. Ten years elapsed after French annexation before Bara were effectively brought into a nation state (Huntington 1974, p. 17). Still, through state administrative boundaries the division between Betsileo and Bara eventually came to be regarded as an ethnic distinction. Today Betsileo who migrate to Bara country remain Betsileo. They do not, as informants say they did in pre-Merina days, become Bara (or even Barabory). Thus, many of the ethnic units enumerated in the Malagasy census originated as labels for provincial and territorial divisions of the Merina state. Employed and enforced by the French, they were reinforced and today ascribe ethnic status for life.

CULTURAL ADAPTIVE TYPES

Recognizing that many contemporary ethnic units were creations of the Merina state, one can still incorporate these units into a discussion of adaptive radiation of Malagasy populations leading to a variety of types of ecosystem. Adaptive problems to be solved through sociocultural means have been posed by local physical and biotic environments as well as by incorporation of local ecosystems and their populations into wider or regional networks involving material exchanges among Malagasy populations and between Malagasy and outsiders. Considering both immediate environment, economy, and regional exchange relationships, it is possible to group the twenty Malagasy ethnic units into a limited number of "cultural adaptive" types. The typology incorporates adaptive divergence and parallelism. The six types are divergent, representing the sociocultural and sociopolitical results of broadly different adaptive problems. The ethnic units within a given type, on the other hand, represent parallel development, where local and regional selective forces acting on a relatively uniform sociocultural heritage have been broadly similar.

The reader will see that because of the administrative rather than ecological basis of many of the ethnic units, in some cases part of the population of an ethnic unit is placed in one adaptive type whereas another part belongs to a different type. This is because some of the ethnic units span large territories over which there is adaptively significant variation. Even in those cases where I have placed an ethnic unit in only one type, a minority of its population may actually belong to another. A case of this is the Betsileo ethnic unit, placed in type VI, Irrigation Agriculturalists. Although this is the adaptive type of most contemporary Betsileo, pastorally oriented Betsileo would more accurately belong to type III. Variation of this sort among the Betsileo will be examined later.

Type I—*River valley agriculturalists and ritual specialists (southeast coast).* Five of the ethnic units listed in the census, all located on the southeast coast, are included in this cultural adaptive type. They are Taisaka (325,000),[3] Taimoro (211,000), Zafisoro (43,000), Taifasy (40,000), and Tambahoaka (22,000) (cf. Deschamps and Vianès 1959). Manioc, sweet potatoes, beans, taro, and other crops have been cultivated since precolonial days, but the staple is wet-rice. The southeast coast is an area of abundant rainfall and rich alluvial valleys, formed as short watercourses descend rapidly from the eastern escarpment. Artificial irrigation is unnecessary to the cultivation of wet-rice; drainage and flood control techniques are important, however, and transplanted rice fields in sometimes terraced alluvial soils are permanent plots cultivated from year to year. Population densities between 50 and 100 are found in a few cantons, and most cantons have between 20 and 50 inhabitants per square kilometer. The figure rises to over 200 in some of the areas of richest valley soils. Ethnic group consciousness is emphasized by geographical compartmentalization. Rivers mark the boundaries of the ethnic units. To the immediate west, on the escarpment that leads to the highlands, lies the tropical forest, home of the Tanala. Under French rule, the southeast coast became a region of cash cropping, principally of coffee, and of small plantations owned by French Creoles from Reunion Island.

For several centuries, the populations of the southeast coast have participated in regional ecosystems spanning large areas. As previously noted, there is considerable evidence of contact between southeast Madagascar and the African coast. Segments of these populations have recent coastal African ancestry (Kent 1970, chapter 3). Taimoro and Tambahoaka possessed knowledge of writing (Arabic script used to render Malagasy words) prior to the arrival of the London Missionary Society. Since at least the seventeenth century (Bloch 1968, p. 282) a group of specialists in ritual and esoteric knowledge has traveled widely throughout Madagascar. They served as diviners at the courts of Merina, Betsileo, and Sakalava rulers, and they brought home cattle and money which they had obtained through application of their ritual knowledge and for instruction in certain skills. Because of heavy population densities, southeast populations migrate easily to other parts of the island. About one-fourth of these groups are presently settled outside of their traditional homeland (Deschamps 1959, p. 39).

Type II—*Coastal trade states and political confederations.*   Included in this type are the Sakalava (360,000) of the west coast, the Betsimisaraka (915,000) of the east coast, and the Tanosy (149,000) of the extreme southeast. In these ethnic units the basis of political organization and the differential access of elites to wealth and power was control of resources strategic to regional systems that linked Malagasy ethnic units to a number of non-

Malagasy economies (cf. Sibree 1978, p. 55). City states thrived on the Malagasy coasts prior to the first arrival of western Europeans (the Portuguese) in Madagascar in 1500. The ruling groups of Malagasy port towns oversaw the provisioning and exchange of local products—principally rice, but also cattle, beeswax, and slaves—for East African and Arabian imports (Kent 1970, pp. 178–80). Still, the rule of such city states did not extend far beyond the port town and its immediate hinterland (Gardenier 1976, pp. 19–22). The arrival of Europeans on the Malagasy coasts did not create an immediate change in scale of coastal political organization. During the sixteenth and early seventeenth centuries, European ships collected subsistence provisions along the Malagasy coasts. In the latter half of the seventeenth century, however, Europeans began to exchange munitions for Malagasy cattle and slaves. It was the trade in muskets and slaves that transformed coastal Malagasy society, producing territorial integration of coastal populations beyond the city state.

The earliest, territorially most extensive, and most successful of the trade states, more aptly called political confederations, was that of the Sakalava.[4] A group of southern Sakalava, who were to become the ruling lineage of the Sakalava confederation, appear to have been among the first Malagasy to obtain European munitions in exchange for Malagasy products, principally cattle and slaves. European arms entered the exchange network in about 1660, and by about 1700 the southern Sakalava had extended a very loosely organized polity along much of the west coast, a length of approximately 1,100 kilometers (Kent 1970, pp. 198–202). The Sakalava confederation persisted through the early nineteenth century, when the major port cities of both northern and southern Sakalava territory were conquered and annexed by the Merina.

As has been generally the case with Malagasy coastal polities, the authority of the Sakalava rulers appears to have been absolute only in and immediately around the major port towns. Away from the coast the Sakalava practice cattle transhumance. Interior Sakalava were controlled, tenuously, by the threat and the fact of raiding parties organized by the nobility and their representatives. Sakalava raiders, seeking war prisoners for European slavers, also harassed the populations of the western central highlands until the expanding Merina state built stockades to protect the highlands from Sakalava marauders (Gardenier 1976, p. 21). As will be seen, the raiding pattern stimulated by the demand for slaves also affected the adaptations of pastorally oriented Malagasy south of the highlands.

The slave-firearms trade came later to the east coast than to the west. A trade state, that of the Betsimisaraka, developed a half-century later, with the introduction of European firearms on the Malagasy east coast (cf. Julien

1909, vol. 1: p. 38; Sibree 1897, 1898a). Its ruling lineage was also founded on control of the exchange of Malagasy war prisoners for European munitions. In addition to war prisoners, rice and other local products figured prominently in the trade with Europeans. As in the west, state control was most effective in the immediate vicinity of the ports. Interior groups of shifting horticulturalists were temporarily subdued, only to reassert their autonomy and be raided again during the century of Betsimisaraka existence as an independent polity, prior to its nineteenth century conquest by the Merina.

Finally, among the Tanosy of the extreme southeast, a city state and a ruling family appear to have come into existence prior to the arrival of Europeans, to oversee the exchange of Malagasy and East African products (cf. Kent 1970, p. 16, 96). European trade items subsequently enabled the Tanosy nobility to expand its subject population, but apparently there was never even the nominal large-scale territorial integration characteristic of the cases just examined.

Type III—*Mixed pastoralists (south and west)*.   Three of the twenty officially recognized Malagasy ethnic units—Bara (228,000), Mahafaly (91,000), and Tandroy (327,000)—may be placed in this cultural adaptive type along with the noncoastal Sakalava and Tanosy. Madagascar's lowest population densities (between one and ten per square kilometer) are encountered here. Most Malagasy pastoralists combine horticulture with transhumant herding of zebu. In areas of Bara country where water sources permit, wet-rice is cultivated in annually flooded river valleys (Huntington 1974, p. 13, 32–42). Among the Tandroy (cf. Decary 1930) there is groundwater cultivation of sorghum, maize, manioc, and other crops. Elsewhere the cultivation of these crops depends on rainfall.

During the eighteenth and nineteenth centuries, interior Malagasy of the south and west also became involved in the slave-munitions exchange networks that had produced the coastal trade states. However, the effects of a pattern of adaptation that came to be oriented as much toward raiding of neighbors as toward cattle herding was centrifugal, contributing to political fragmentation among these interior populations. Away from the ports, access to European arms was indirect, mediated through exchange with the coastal Malagasy, and no single interior group enjoyed a monopoly on European firearms. The inability of Sakalava and Tanosy rulers to maintain effective control on a permanent basis over interior populations has been noted above. The sparse population and relative mobility of the pastoral Malagasy were also responsible for failures of Merina military expeditions sent to subdue these areas (cf. Huntington 1974, p. 17; Gardenier 1976, p. 21–22). Difficulties in the administration of these nonsedentary cultural adaptations have continued to plague both French and modern Malagasy governments.

Type IV—*Swidden cultivators of the tropical forest (eastern escarpment).* The Malagasy whose economies are oriented less toward pastoral transhumance and more toward plant cultivation have higher population densities,
but here, too, there is a contrast involving the nature of the economy, to some
extent a reflection of physical environmental variables. Subsistence for the
Tanala (237,000) and, north of them, the Zafimaniry (Bloch 1975; Coulaud
1973; Southall 1979) and the interior Betsimisaraka, depends on swidden
cultivation of dry rice, maize, sweet potatoes, manioc, and many other crops.
These swidden cultivators have densities between ten and twenty per square
kilometer. The southern Tanala (Shaw 1875) were never conquered by any
other Malagasy population. During the eighteenth and early nineteenth centuries, in response to an increased demand for slaves on the east coast, the
southern Tanala carried out raids on the Betsileo and exchanged their prisoners of war on the east coast. They also preyed on caravans that crossed
their country conveying products to and from the east coast. Access to firearms and trade goods created temporary "kings" out of Tanala descent group
leaders. Normally dispersed in small villages throughout the forest, members
of several Tanala descent groups assembled on fortified hilltops when Betsileo and, later, Merina military expeditions invaded their country. They dispersed again when the military force withdrew. Tanala "kings" were simply
temporary military coordinators and heads of raiding parties whose positions
rested on possession of firearms (cf. Linton 1933, pp. 36–37).

Type V—*Mixed pastoralism and horticulture (northeast and north).* With
less ethnographic information available, this type and its separation from type
III is more tentative than the others. Included are four ethnic units: Tsimihety (428,000), Tankarana (42,000), Sihanaka (135,000), and Bezanozano
(44,000). The homelands of the Sihanaka (Sibree 1877) and the Bezanozano
(Peake 1878) were two of the first additions to the expanding Merina state,
and the services and local ecosystems of Sihanaka and Bezanozano eventually became specialized appendages of the Merina economy, supplying fish,
basketry products, pastureland, wood, charcoal, and labor to their overlords.
In the absence of archaeological investigation and written documents, their
pre-Merina adaptations are difficult to reconstruct, but did, like the Tsimihety
and Tankarana (Batchelor 1877) involve cattle herding as well as cultivation
of wet and dry varieties of rice and other crops. Tsimihety and Tankarana are
remote northern populations traditionally isolated from one another and other
Malagasy by natural environmental barriers. Peter Wilson's (1971, 1977) descriptions of the importance of cattle herding among the Tsimihety suggests
that they might just as well be placed in type III along with most populations
of the interior west and south. More ethnographic knowledge of the Tankarana is necessary before their placement in type V can be confirmed.

Type VI—*Irrigation agriculturalists (central highlands).*   A major topographic contrast is provided by the central highlands. With a median elevation of about 1,200 meters above sea level, and a maximum width of about 300 kilometers, the central highlands extend from north to south for approximately 1,200 kilometers. The highest area of the highlands, comprising the homelands of the Merina and the Betsileo, extends some 600 kilometers from north to south between latitudes 18° and 22.5°, and its maximum width is 200 kilometers.

Because of the productivity of their agricultural economies, Merina and Betsileo (the two Malagasy ethnic units who rely most intensely on wet-rice cultivation) are first and third respectively in population size among twenty Malagasy ethnic units. Comparison of population size data from 1900 and 1964 (table 1) may underestimate actual growth for both of these highland populations, since they could be more easily censused than other ethnic units in 1900, because of sedentary communities and an elaborate administrative hierarchy. The national rate of population increase apparently rose from 1.8 percent per year in 1947 (Bastian 1967, p. 48) to a 1963 figure of 3.4 percent,

TABLE 1

Population Growth of Malagasy Ethnic Units
Between 1900 and 1964

Ethnic Unit	1900 Population	1964 Population	Percentage Increase 1964 over 1900
Tsimihety	45,000	429,000	953
Tambahoaka	4,000	22,000	550
Taimoro	44,000	211,000	480
Sihanaka	37,000	135,000	365
Betsimisaraka	288,000	915,000	318
Tandroy	103,000	327,000	317
Taisaka	121,000	325,000	269
Mahafaly	34,000	91,000	268
Sakalava	155,000	360,000	232
Bezanozano	21,000	44,000	210
St. Mary Islanders	7,000	14,000	200
Makoa	33,000	65,000	197
Merina	847,000	1,570,000	185
Betsileo	408,000	736,000	180
Tankarana	25,000	42,000	168
Bara	140,000	228,000	163
Tanosy	96,000	149,000	155
Tanala	157,000	237,000	151
Taifasy	33,000	40,000	121
Zafisoro		44,000	
Total	2,602,240	5,999,331	231

Sources: 1900, Julien 1909; 1964, Malagasy government statistics.

with the most rapid rates of increase recorded for the Merina and the Betsileo, and the lowest for pastoral populations of the extreme south and west. One of the major reasons for population increase has been a decline in the death rate following the eradication of malaria, particularly in the central highlands, as a result of public health programs begun under the French and continued by the Malagasy government.

The Merina state,[5] its development eventually blocked by French conquest and control, represents a major culmination of one of the divergent routes followed by the Malagasy population in its adaptive radiation. One of the attributes of evolution—the production of diversity through adaptive differentiation—was essential to its origin, first because it was necessary for orientation toward hydraulic agriculture, manufacture, and long-distance trade to converge in a single population, and second, because the Merina eventually were able to incorporate a variety of ecotypes developed over centuries of divergence by other Malagasy. The Merina state represents yet another important attribute of evolution, progressive centralization. Progressive centralization is the incorporation and coordination of an array of regionally, ecologically, and functionally specialized populations, and the elaboration of special-purpose subsystems, (e.g. military, administrative, judicial, enforcement, and fiscal) that serve both to maintain and to expand the larger system—in this case, the Merina state—of which they are parts.

By at least the nineteenth century, the Merina economy was firmly founded on irrigated rice agriculture, long-distance trade, and manufacturing. Though there is a difference in scale, Betsileo (736,000) and Merina (1,570,000) are placed together in this cultural adaptive type because of similarities in their agricultural economies. Due to similar peasant economies and the dense, sedentary Betsileo population, Merina rule over the Betsileo was more effective than in other parts of Madagascar. The differences between Merina and Betsileo appear to be quantitative. Both manufactured certain goods for export to other Malagasy populations, but the Merina manufacturing and distribution system was much more developed. I shall argue in chapter 4 that the Merina conquest truncated what had been an essentially parallel independent development of this cultural adaptive type and political organization by the Betsileo.

Commonalities between contemporary Betsileo and Merina include agricultural techniques, principles of recruitment to social groups, patterns of socioeconomic stratification and political organization, cosmology, and the nature of ceremonial life. Analogous hydraulic economies provide some reasons for this, but there are several others. Physical and biotic environments of the highlands are common to both. Both Merina and Betsileo had begun to live in fortified settlements linked through territorial political organization by at least the eighteenth century. This was a response to raids by coastal states and to other outside pressures in the form of trading and exchange emanations from European states and their subsidiary trading partners. Merina and Betsileo also share recent common ancestry, at least in language. There is no Malagasy ethnic unit whose basic vocabulary is closer to the Betsileo's than the Merina.

Because Merina and Betsileo apparently represent recent descendants of a single ancestral population radiating in the highlands with similar sociocultural adaptive kits, there is, as is true of Betsileo and Bara, no abrupt transition between them. Traveling south from Tananarive, one officially leaves the southern Merina province and enters Betsileo country when he crosses the Mania River, located at 20° south latitude. However, there is no ecological contrast at all between northern Betsileo and southern Merina. The extreme south of Merina country is topographically more rugged than Merina areas to the north, and the southern Merina have constructed rice terraces on hillsides in the absence of the broad plains that rice farmers prefer to cultivate. South of the Mania River, the Betsileo also cultivate terraced rice fields. The linguistic change is as gradual as the ecological shift. In fact, the Betsileo of the northernmost Betsileo town of Ambositra share exactly the same percentage of cognates in basic vocabulary with the Merina of Tananarive as they do with the Betsileo of Fianarantsoa (cf. Vérin, Kottak, and Gorlin 1970).

As noted previously, distinctions between the ethnic units of the central highlands have been political. Merina conquests brought formerly independent polities, first those of what is now considered to be southern Imerina, later northern Betsileo, and finally southern Betsileo, under a single administration (cf. Delivré 1974, p. 226 et seq.). The Mania River became the administrative boundary between the southernmost province recognized as Imerina and the Betsileo country.

Thus, the two highland populations are similar because economically, ecologically, historically, and geographically, they are close to one another. Of course, the early conquest of the Betsileo by the Merina incorporated them as members of the Merina polity, and since 1830, when the Betsileo province was officially created as the sixth major subdivision of Imerina, the two ethnic units have once again had a common history. In chapter 4 the nature of Merina rule over the Betsileo and resulting modifications in Betsileo life are examined in detail.

Having now provided a framework for the historical, economic, ecological, and political events that created the contemporary ethnic unit known as Betsileo, I turn to the historical events and processes on which many dimensions of their current lives are founded.

Perhaps two millenia separate the culturally and biologically composite Proto-Malagasy settlers of Madagascar from their contemporary descendants.

Yet their language and their cultural legacy continue to provide a framework for unity among Malagasy populations. Although it is extremely difficult, and perhaps impossible, to identify specific geographic and temporal origins of certain institutions and orienting principles of behavior that are common now to all or most Malagasy, similarities—some shared not only by all Malagasy but generalized in Indonesia and throughout the Malayo-Polynesian world—constitute a set of sociocultural constants with reference to which variations in time, space, and scale can be seen as variants or transformations. In chapter 2, a model of cultural adaptive radiation has been applied to the biologically, linguistically, and culturally related ethnic units of contemporary Madagascar. Historical splits have been inferred from linguistic subgroupings and have been linked to broad economic and environmental contrasts. A more detailed classification of similarities and differences among Malagasy populations was suggested in a typology consisting of six cultural adaptive types, summing up both divergent and parallel evolution.

In subsequent chapters, the analysis changes scale. In this chapter, broad differences and similarities have been linked to broad characteristics of local and regional ecosystems. The role of the Merina state in exacerbating economic and ecological differences, while providing a common framework of territorial political organization to most Malagasy, has been mentioned. In chapter 3 sociopolitical variation in time, space, and scale is confronted through a speculative reconstruction of the process of state formation in the southern highlands of Madagascar, a process which, in the absence of archaeological confirmation, is inferred and suggested rather than proved, but still of interest to scholars concerned with explaining sociopolitical process and the development of civilization. Final comparison of major ecological contrasts, and their effects on sociopolitical development, between two areas of the southern highlands reduces the analytic scale still further and paves the way for the analysis of variation among successively smaller units in chapters 5 through 8.

CHAPTER THREE

The Process of State Formation

Most anthropologists agree that the state differs significantly from more "primitive" forms of sociopolitical organization. In a classic article, Fried (1960, p. 728) defines the state as a form of sociopolitical organization whose primary functions are to maintain general order and to support an order of socioeconomic stratification. All states develop specialized subsystems that fulfill a variety of what Fried calls secondary functions: population control, the disposal of trouble cases, the protection of sovereignty through military and/or police forces, and fiscal support. Carneiro (1970, p. 733) defines a state as "an autonomous political unit encompassing many communities within its territory, having a centralized government with the power to collect taxes, draft men for work or war, and decree and enforce laws." The attributes that define state organization vary quantitatively with the growth of centralized government: more and larger communities are included within the state's territory; the fiscal support of the state increases; labor and military conscription power also grow; and legal codes and associated personnel evolve. Characteristically, settlement size, hierarchy, and functional differentiation increase gradually as the state matures.

Flannery (1972) has suggested that anthropologists apply a cybernetic model to the evolution of state organization. Like many other scholars he rejects single cause, prime-mover approaches to the origin of the state. Flannery recognizes that several kinds of socioenvironmental stress may select for state organization, which he sees as incorporating the universal processes of segregation (increasing internal differentiation and specialization of subsystems) and centralization (tighter linkage between the various subsystems and the highest-order control systems in the society). In addition to variable conditions of socioenvironmental stress and universal processes of segregation and centralization, Flannery adds to his model two evolutionary mechanisms, promotion (ascent of an institution from its place in the control hierarchy to assume a higher level) and linearization (complete or permanent bypassing of lower order controls by higher-order controls, usually after the former have failed to maintain variables in range for a critical length of time).

58

Flannery's approach is a dynamic one in which state formation is treated as an aspect of the general evolution of systems. Complexity may be assessed in terms of increasing segregation and centralization, both of which may be compared and measured. Segregation, for example, involves an increasing amount of internal differentiation and specialization, and centralization involves tighter linkage within a control hierarchy with more, and more differentiated, levels. Quantitative aspects of these processes are the generation of increasing numbers of institutions that process, store, and analyze more and more information, and the general evolution of institutions that process more data and perform more regulation than institutions of less complex societies. For Flannery the distinction between states and chiefdoms is quantitative: in states, the managerial superstructure is more elaborate, multilevel, and more centralized. Presumably archaeological, historical, ethnohistorical, and ethnographic data should be gathered to assess these trends.

BETSILEO STATE FORMATION : PRESTATE PERIOD

Events in the southern highlands of Madagascar between 1650 and 1815, when the Betsileo were brought under Merina rule, illustrate these and other processes of state formation. Map 2 represents the Betsileo heartland between approximately 1650 and 1900. Bounded roughly on the north by the Ankona River and its confluence with the Matsiatra[1] and on the east by the escarpment and tropical forest homeland of the Tanala, the more arid western and southern parts of the heartland were less clearly circumscribed, eventually becoming Bara territory. The largest of the southern highlands polities were Lalangina in the east and Isandra in the west. South of these lay the six formerly independent polities that the Merina overlords eventually designated collectively as Arindrano: northern and southern Vohibato, Tsienimparihy, Manambolo, Lalanindro, and Homatrazo.

One may draw an opposition, realizing that in fact the contrast in ecotype is gradual, ecoclinal, and ongoing, between the agricultural east (similar to cultural adaptive type VI in chapter 2) consisting of Lalangina and northern Vohibato, and the arid and more pastorally-oriented west and south (similar to cultural adaptive type III in chapter 2) including, among others, Isandra and southern Vohibato (see fig. 1). The three villages studied and described sample this contrast. Ivato in northern Vohibato represents the agricultural east, and Ambalabe and Tanambao are in the canton of Mahazony, once a part of southern Vohibato, thus sampling the more pastoral south and west. Early agriculture in the east proceeded on the basis of higher annual rainfall and use of swampy valleys and floodwaters of several rivers and streams. Contemporary agriculture in much of the west and south, however, depends on artificial irrigation, which largely came to these areas under the Merina

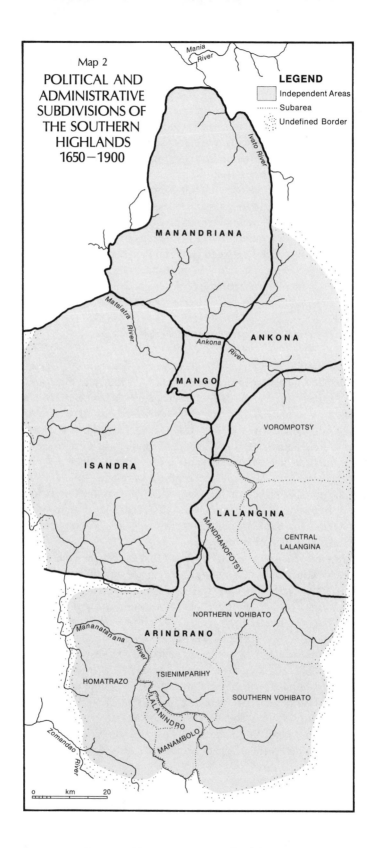

Map 2

POLITICAL AND
ADMINISTRATIVE
SUBDIVISIONS OF
THE SOUTHERN
HIGHLANDS
1650–1900

LEGEND

Independent Areas
Subarea
Undefined Border

Mania River

Ivato River

MANANDRIANA

Matsiatra River

Ankona River

ANKONA

MANGO

VOROMPOTSY

ISANDRA

LALANGINA

MANDRANOFOTSY

CENTRAL
LALANGINA

NORTHERN VOHIBATO

Mananatanana River

ARINDRANO

TSIENIMPARIHY

HOMATRAZO

SOUTHERN VOHIBATO

LALANINDRO

MANAMBOLO

Zomandao River

0   km   20

and French colonial administrations. Geographical areas are not, obviously, irrevocably bound by their physical environments to one or another ecotype, since physical environments are processed by changing cultural systems. In large measure the transition from tribal society to state organization among the Betsileo was accompanied by a shift from pastoral to agricultural orientation. Furthermore, this transition in ecotype is not yet complete, although Isandra, southern Vohibato, and other parts of the Betsileo west and south are more agricultural today than at the time of Merina conquest. Chapters 5 through 8 examine some of the sociocultural implications of this contrast by focusing on variation among contemporary Betsileo villages. Here we examine the implications over time of this broad contrast in ecotype for sociopolitical developments.

In the eighteenth century, the commitment to agriculture was greatest in Lalangina and northern Vohibato, although wet-rice cultivation was spreading south and west. As rainfall declined, moving west and away from the major river valleys where annual floodwaters could be used to nurture rice, the pastoral orientation of Isandra became more and more pronounced. In fact, a pastorally oriented economy predominated over most of Isandra's territory, west and south of the river that gave the kingdom its name. Southern Vohibato and other parts of Arindrano were environmentally and ecologically similar to Isandra and evolved along parallel lines during the eighteenth century.

Although the types of local ecosystem within their boundaries differed, Lalangina, Isandra, the Vohibatos, and the other political units of the Betsileo heartland were constituted during the late seventeenth and early eighteenth centuries as common responses to common exposure to socioenvironmental stress, in the form of a major modification in the regional ecosystems in which they participated. During the seventeenth century, southern highlanders had gradually been exposed to various effects of the presence of European trading interests on the coasts. The emergence of the coastal Sakalava as west coast trading subsidiaries of the Europeans initially affected interior Sakalava and Bara and other mixed pastoralists but eventually reached the highlands as Bara and Sakalava themselves sought booty for trade through raiding. Europeans appear to have begun to exchange firearms with coastal Malagasy around 1660–70 (cf. Kent 1970, pp. 27, 200–201), but several decades were to elapse before firearms, exchanged for slaves, reached the Betsileo heartland.

The contrast between mixed pastoralism and wet-rice cultivation may have existed in interior Madagascar prior to Portuguese discovery in 1506.[2] Not only do Betsileo oral historians throughout the heartland, whether in pastoral or agricultural areas, recall a pastoral orientation as antedating Lalangina, Isandra, and the other polities, written history also suggests that although the contrast between wet-rice cultivation and mixed pastoralism existed in the highlands in 1650, the pastoral area was far larger then than today, and may, in fact, have covered most of the Betsileo heartland, including what was to become the agricultural east.[3]

An early historical account of the southern highlands, written by Etienne de Flacourt (1661), governor of the short-lived French post at Fort Dauphin on the southeast coast, reported secondhand the observations of a trading party consisting of Frenchmen and coastal Malagasy who apparently reached the southern highlands in 1648. Flacourt's account names Vohitromby (a populous rice-cultivating region) and Arindrano (a land of fewer people and more cattle) as two interior areas. Scholars have argued about whether Vohitromby is Lalangina or Imerina, and whether Arindrano, therefore, refers to the southern and western Betsileo or to the entire Betsileo heartland. However, the cultural adaptation that Flacourt describes for Arindrano is pastorally oriented, representing cultural adaptive type III. Such an adaptation is fully consonant with Betsileo traditions of the early history of the southern highlands. The party left Fort Dauphin for the interior seeking zebu to bring back to the coast for eventual export. Although Europeans were not yet exchanging firearms with Malagasy for cattle or slaves, Flacourt's account does report that the French members of the trading party, themselves bearing firearms, helped Arindrano in a skirmish with Vohitromby.[4]

Oral Traditional Accounts: Origin Myths and Quasi-Historical Documents

If Flacourt's account is unsatisfactory, written documentation of events in the southern highlands during the next two centuries—precisely the period of state formation—is completely absent. Archaeological research may eventually help to confirm the following reconstruction based largely on oral historical materials.[5]

If ancestors of the Betsileo relied on (or were stimulated by) French riflemen in their seventeenth-century raiding, as Flacourt reports, by the eighteenth century they were able to bear their own munitions, for muskets, bullets, and gun powder were becoming the standard exchange items for cattle and slaves. All the evidence indicates that it was this new eighteenth-century exchange system that fully committed southern highlanders to state formation. The change of scale in Betsileo warfare is reflected in their oral traditions. The impact of Europeans' demand for slaves and of the Malagasy marauders who undertook to satisfy it must have triggered an ongoing migration from coasts to interior at least by the late seventeenth century. An influx of migrants, mostly from the east coast, is recalled in Betsileo oral history. The settlers of Ivato in the agricultural east, for example, are supposed to have arrived from the southeast coast in the eighth generation above Ivato's seniormost resident, who was born in 1902. Their migration may have corresponded with an intensification of the coastal slave trade early in the eighteenth century.

The Origin of Nobilities

How did Lalangina, Isandra, the Vohibatos, and other Betsileo polities originate and develop in the context of this regional change, and how did their nobilities come into being? Reflecting the fact that the first ethnic unity of the Betsileo was a product of Merina expansion, there is no single oral history of the southern highlands. Different polities, and even different areas and descent groups within these polities, give diffferent accounts of historical events and relationships among pre-Merina states and chiefdoms.[6] These accounts are, nevertheless, worth examining for their sociological as well as historical value.

A quasi-historical oral tradition of the agricultural east (Dubois 1938, p. 114) posits an idealized but still plausible origin for nobilities, and an initial kick toward state formation. Due to attacks by easterners seeking cattle and slaves, the oral tradition recounts, southern highlanders were forced to reside in and to fortify hilltop settlements. In each, heads of the most populous and influential descent groups provided defense chiefs and their advisers. Eventually, in ways that oral history neglects, some settlements prevailed over others, as organizations created for defense assumed offensive functions.

To help test this tradition's plausibility, I distributed about 5,000 printed questionnaires through the Malagasy government's administrative hierarchy. Initially presented to the seven subprefects[7] whose circumscriptions included substantial Betsileo populations, the questionnaires found their way to canton chiefs and thereafter to village elders. About 1,500 questionnaires, sampling about half the population of the current Betsileo territory, were returned. About 1,300 of these contained useful information concerning names of descent groups localized in each village, their region of origin according to their genealogical histories, and their immediate residence prior to settling in their present communities. About 1,000 different descent group names were mentioned in responses from these 1,300 villages. An estimate of total sampled size of each named group was obtained, and its geographical range was approximated from the number of villages in which it appeared. About half of the 998 descent groups named existed only as local descent groups, confined to a single village; another 154 spanned only 2 villages, while 244 spanned between 3 and 9 villages, and only 83 (less than 10 percent of the total) appeared as local descent groups in 10 or more villages. Only 16 named descent groups spanned 50 or more of the villages in the sample, with the largest and most geographically dispersed located in 183 villages.

I assumed that the contemporary ranges of named descent groups were at least roughly correlated with their differential population growth and dispersal, and my questionnaire data seem to support the oral tradition about the origin of Betsileo nobilities recounted above, since those contemporary named descent groups that are largest on the basis of estimates of population and of range are precisely those that supplied the nobles and influential (senior) commoners of pre-Merina polities in the southern highlands. Since, however, I suspected that people, for prestige, might be attempting to claim spurious affiliation with elite descent groups, I examined in greater detail a subsample of the responses in the region where most of my fieldwork was concentrated. By questioning genealogists representing senior branches of noble and senior commoner descent groups, I found that those more junior local descent groups that claimed affiliation were indeed recognized as genealogically related.

I thus grant a large measure of plausibility to the oral tradition for the origin of southern highlands nobilities cited above. Those groups, organized on the basis of descent, which had been previously important by virtue of their numbers and range at a time of tribal sociopolitical organization, were rearranged in a more formally hierarchical organization to confront threats from outside the heartland; they ultimately would provide the controlling descent groups of Betsileo polities during the eighteenth and nineteenth centuries. Adaptation to changed circumstances by human populations proceeds on the basis of, and often involves restructuring of, organizational material at hand when the change begins. In this case, basic structural units of a population organized by kinship, descent, and marriage were rearranged hierarchically in response to a perturbation introduced from outside the system, which provided an initial kick in the direction of state formation. My argument here is that the potentiality of ranking was inherent in the demographics of the prior structure. Given a need for defensive reorganization, the implicit ranking began to be formalized.

However, a contrasting oral traditional account of Betsileo noble origins, which both Dubois (1938, pp. 115–16) and I collected, seems more realistically interpreted as myth than as history or pseudohistory. It gives Betsileo nobles a single and external origin; it makes all Betsileo nobles descendants of a princess descended from Arabs who settled on the southeast coast, apparently around the fourteenth century. The migration of this princess and her entourage from coast to highlands is supposed to have taken place in the sixteenth or seventeenth century. Somehow she was accepted as a ruler by whatever population occupied the Betsileo heartland when she arrived, and she had seven children who became the apical ancestors of the noble descent groups of Lalangina, Isandra, Vohibato, Tsienimparihy, Homatrazo, Lalanindro, and of the Bara. This version is particularly popular in the Betsileo south (Arindrano), because it places the princess's first highlands residence there; it thus places the nobles of the minor polities of Arindrano (see fig. 1)

AGRICULTURE	MIXED PASTORALISM		
East	*West*		
Lalangina	Isandra		
northern Vohibato	southern Vohibato		
	Tsienimparihy		
	Homatrazo	}	Arindrano after
	Lalanindro	}	Merina conquest
	Manambolo		

Fig. 1 Summary of Pre-Merina Economic Orientation of
Southern Highlands (Proto-Betsileo) Political Units

in the same genealogy as those of the major states of Lalangina and Isandra,
in fact giving the southerners seniority. It proposes the seniority or greater
sanctity of some territorial groups over others by asserting that they are not
local in origin, and it argues that the source of whatever unity the pre-Merina
Betsileo had can be traced to Arindrano rather than to Lalangina or Isandra.

Several other accounts of noble origins can be interpreted similarly as
myths that argue for differentiation of the noble descent group by virtue of
external origin, usually in a commercially or politically prominent area.
Thus, Isandra's history brings its noble ancestor from Lalangina, the major
proto-Betsileo polity. In terms of relative development of state organization,
Isandra stood to Lalangina as Lalangina stood to Imerina, and, as one might
expect, an oral tradition of Lalangina brings its first noble from Imerina. His
departure, or in some versions his expulsion, took place during a prestate
period recalled in Betsileo traditions as the "epoch of many rulers", a time of
feuding between territorial descent groups each claiming the status of
"noble"—an epoch probably reflecting the early inability of any one descent
group to arrogate noble status to itself.[8] Lalangina's first "noble" moved south
into the Betsileo heartland where he met and married a mermaid.

Unless we are dealing with mermaids, it is difficult to separate history
from myth in traditional accounts of the origin of noble descent groups.
Nevertheless, the body of oral traditions is significant for several reasons.
First, there is no uniform belief in the unity of origin of the different descent
groups that provided rulers in each of the Betsileo petty states. The myth of
the Arab princess and her seven children, which is neither uniformly nor
generally accepted, stands as merely one among several accounts. For Imerina, which evolved into a single polity, there seems to be more agreement
about royal genealogy (cf. Delivré, 1974, pp. 58, 69–70), and the same
applies to Isandra, whose king in 1892—after the Merina had confirmed his

power—instructed local oral historians to provide his court historian with an official history of his realm (Dubois 1938, p. 112). By and large, oral traditions about noble origins seem to be *ex post facto* arguments developed or generally accepted only after state organization had matured.[9] They use history to sanctify present contrasts in status, wealth, and authority.

LOCAL ECOSYSTEMS AND EVOLUTIONARY DIVERGENCE

I focus now on oral accounts that are closer to history than myth in order to demonstrate the relationship between degree of political development and ecotype in two broadly contrasting regions of the southern highlands. Lalangina, representing the agricultural east, and Isandra, representing the more pastoral west and south, will be compared in order to suggest types of local ecosystemic changes that helped or hindered the process of state formation, given similar initial kicks through regional ecosystemic change. The sequences that I reconstruct (largely on the basis of oral historical accounts collected and published by Father H. Dubois in 1938)[10] have implications considerably beyond the Betsileo and beyond Madagascar.

In terms of chapter 2's cultural adaptive typology, Isandra, southern Vohibato, and other southern and western political units of the Betsileo heartland were at least as similar to type III populations (mixed pastoralists) as to the wet-rice cultivators (type VI) of Lalangina and northern Vohibato in the agricultural east. For the understanding of political developments and the process of state formation outside of Madagascar, the comparison of Lalangina and Isandra will illustrate some of the variables that link complex political developments and agricultural economies, and some of the impediments to state control over transhumant pastoralists. Furthermore, just as it was argued that a model of adaptive radiation can help explain sociocultural differences by holding prior cultural heritage constant, a similar but more specific analysis of variation—of adaptive radiation focusing on a smaller area and fewer contrasts—also aids explanation of sociopolitical differentiation. For, as will be seen, the sparser population of Isandra carried into the eighteenth century a tribal heritage and structural units shared with the population of Lalangina. Furthermore, Lalangina and Isandra were exposed equally both to "the idea of the state" and to an identical form of socioenvironmental stress with regional trade, raiding, warfare, and other aspects of penetration of Madagascar by European economic interests and their trading subsidiaries. However, because the local ecosystems of Lalangina emphasized sedentary wet-rice cultivation whereas those of Isandra did not, the process of state formation made considerable progress in the former but not in the latter. Consider now this variation in time and scale.

The adaptive radiation of the descendants of the Proto-Malagasy expressed itself, as in other cultural domains, in a wide and rich variety of precolonial sociopolitical systems. One commonality of all Malagasy socio-political variants, which may be part of the legacy of the protoculture, is the existence of a sociopolitical status called *mpanjaka*, which can be roughly translated as head of a territorial unit that may or may not include co-resident nonkin as well as kin (and affines). However, despite general recognition throughout Madagascar of the status of *mpanjaka*, there is substantial varia-tion in the determinants of *mpanjaka* status and its context and behavioral results in different parts of Madagascar, as the contrast of Lalangina and Isandra will demonstrate.

Lalangina

Little of significance is recalled about Lalangina's first *mpanjaka*. However, beginning with his successor,[11] whose administration Dubois has placed be-tween 1680 and 1700, oral history is more detailed, plausible, and uniformly recounted through Lalangina (at least in Dubois's monumental collection of ethnohistory).

Detailed consideration of the oral history of Lalangina (based largely on my analysis of traditions collected by Dubois 1938, pp. 174–200) beginning with its second *mpanjaka* illustrates problems in distinguishing between chiefdom and state organization in a specific sequence. It also reveals the gradual nature of—and structural impediments to—the process of state for-mation, and the difficulty of agreeing on a specific time at which a chiefdom becomes a state. Oral traditions do not specify the nature of Lalangina's economy under its second *mpanjaka*, although of probable importance were the stockbreeding and herding of zebu cattle and the cultivation of rice, in small valleys, relying mainly on rainfall. Oral history suggests a population organizing for defense in response to a growing coastal threat, but not yet involved in the slave-firearms trade. The reign of Lalangina's second *mpan-jaka* is remembered for its formulation of the first code of crimes and sanc-tions in the southern highlands (cf. Dubois 1938, pp. 174–75). The code's articles, however, suggest a weak *mpanjaka* compared to heads of the major commoner descent groups. Although some concern with safeguarding prop-erty is indicated, the code itself was primarily a formalization of principles intrinsic to sociopolitical organization founded on kinship, descent, and mar-riage. Many of the stipulations were general: children were enjoined to re-spect their parents, the living cautioned not to speak ill of the dead, especially of their own ancestors; a sacrifice of cattle was specified as the penalty. Filial disrespect brought public humiliation. The penalty for stealing moveable property was return to the owner of four times its value. An indemnity in kind was expected for damages to crops. A man whose wife was discov-ered in adultery was entitled to kill the adulterer and to claim his personal possessions. Suspected sorcerers were tried by ordeal. For none of these offenses is it specified how sanctions were to be accomplished and enforced. Only three of the articles related to emerging socioeconomic stratification and differences between the nobility and other Betsileo. Nobles were enjoined to marry other nobles. (Subsequent Lalanginan reigns demonstrate, however, that women of inferior stratum did become wives and mothers of prominent *mpanjaka*.) Offenses against members of the *mpanjaka*'s descent group were punished with stoning; the oral tradition reports, however, that the wealthy—and therefore influential (senior) commoners—could escape this penalty with strategic bribes.

Although oral tradition recalls that tribute was offered to the *mpanjaka* in first fruits and livestock, there is no indication of the volume of these prestations or of the extent of the probable redistribution. Also recalled as associated with this second reign are a corps of *mpanjaka*'s spearsmen, hunting and fishing parties, public reunions, songfests, and gift-giving ceremonials convoked by the *mpanjaka*. At the end of the seventeenth century the Lalanginan *mpanjaka* seems to have been a ritual figure associated with redistribution, who had limited authority and privileges. To this era of Lalanginan history, one might attribute at most a chiefdom level of sociopolitical organization.

Oral traditions recount under the third and fourth *mpanjaka*, a woman and her son, the institutionalization and growth in authority of a group of advisers known as *mahamasinandriana* (maha·masin·andriana), literally "those who make the leader or noble (*andriana*) sacred." The term *mahamasinandriana*, which designated the senior commoner descent group heads who began to serve formally as governmental agents under Lalangina's fourth *mpanjaka*, incorporates a concept—*hasina*—that Delivré (1974, pp. 140) has called the basis of Malagasy thought. *Masin(a)* is an adjective derived from the noun *hasina*, a complex notion whose religious, social, and political significance for the Merina has been analyzed by Delivré (1974, pp. 140–59) and Bloch (1977). Further discussion of the *hasina* concept, which is common to Merina and Betsileo, will reveal some of the cultural mechanics of state formation. In nineteenth-century Imerina, *hasina* had become a complex idea linked in several ways to the preservation and reproduction of the king's authority and the legitimacy of the Merina state. However, *hasina*'s several other meanings suggest that, like *mpanjaka*, it represents one of those important pan-Malagasy cultural forms whose meaning has changed in a process of sociopolitical transformation.

Delivré's (1974, p. 198) observation that the evolution of the Merina kingdom involved not a series of *ex nihilo* cultural innovations but a gradual buildup of power through minor religious, social, and economic acts also applies to state formation in Lalangina. Changes in the meaning of *hasina* were part and parcel of the gradual transformation of tribal society into state organization in the Malagasy highlands. Yet in describing the transformation of the *hasina* concept among Merina and Betsileo, it will be argued that the very maintenance of this ancestral concept helped mask from people taking part in the process of state formation the fact that their society was changing from a tribal form to one of inequality, stratification, and state organization. Over the generations the *hasina* concept itself differentiated in tandem with increasing sociopolitical complexity. And, although an increasing number of hierarchical levels of *hasina*-wielders came to separate common people from nature, preservation of the familiar idea helped make sociopolitical transformations appear less radical than they were in fact.

The Sacred in Lalanginan Evolution

In deciphering the evolution of the *hasina* concept, let us begin by considering its various meanings and their functions in the nineteenth-century Merina state. *Hasina* in its most general sense is a *mana*-like notion that Delivré (1974, pp. 140–42) describes as a life force possessed by any being, a supernatural essence that makes something good or efficacious. For example, the knowledge, words, techniques, paraphernalia, and persons of diviners, curers, and sorcerers rely on their possession of *hasina*. Because of the intervention of the sacred, of *hasina*, no outcome has a purely secular explanation; no event belongs solely to the profane order (Delivré 1974, p. 146).

Along with living people, dead ancestors and ghosts can manipulate *hasina* to work harm or good. Delivré (1974, p. 147) also reports that *hasina* has a malicious aspect, called *hery*, which can be used to attack the proper social order; witches are people who have been seduced by the dark side of the force. The dualism of the concept permits its use in explaining, for example, both illness and curing and both the quality that makes something taboo and the force that punishes taboo violations.

By the nineteenth century at least, among both Betsileo and Merina *hasina*'s meanings had ramified into the political order; the *hasina* concept had differentiated along with society and polity. Certain beings were endowed with superior *hasina* to others. Although the ruler of Imerina was the supreme possessor, a graded distribution of *hasina* was the basis of an intricately graduated hierarchy of ranking that, in the native view, organized Merina society. Bloch (1977, pp. 324, 315–16) reports that each deme (local kin group) of Merina society had a ritual status slightly different from every other deme, through their differential possession of *hasina*. Each deme retained its proper measure of *hasina* through endogamy. This ritually based hierarchy materialized in behavior through the presentation of gifts to superiors, the rendering of homage, special clothing, a few minor differences in legal rights, the use of certain titles and forms of address, and granting of precedence in seating and speaking on formal occasions (Bloch 1977, p. 322). Fathers' *hasina* surpassed sons', and that of deme ancestors stood above that of the living. Accordingly, fathers, elders, and ancestors were recipients of gifts and homage, as is still true among Merina and Betsileo.

Bloch (1977 pp. 315–17) correctly notes that Merina ideology misrepresented the distribution of power by seeing it as an orderly, harmonious, finely graded ranking system with no sharp breaks in privileges. But real power was held by a few (and not necessarily those with the highest ritual status). As among the Betsileo (see chapter 4) the ideology of a graded hierarchy, rather than a stratification system with sharp breaks, has impeded Merina class consciousness.

The continuity of the nineteenth-century Merina state was therefore facilitated by the cultural illusion that actual differential power was congruent with differential possession of *hasina*, whose multiple meanings included supernatural power, vigor, fertility, efficacy, and sanctity. Bloch's (1977) analysis also points up one of the main contradictions in the Merina meaning of *hasina*. What he calls *hasina* mark I is the more general meaning, the sacred force that has been discussed so far—the supernatural virtue that is differentially possessed by all beings and concentrated, among the living, in the Merina king. *Hasina* mark II, on the other hand, refers to an action by inferiors—rendering homage, *hasina*, to superiors. (Note the similarity of *hasina* here to "honor" in English; superiors possess honor but can be honored by inferiors.) Merina subjects regularly presented *hasina* mark II in the form of homage, titles, forms of address, deference, observation of a traditional order of speaking on formal occasions, and gift-giving, particularly of an uncut coin (the Maria-Theresa thaler, sometimes called dollar or piaster, widely circulated in Madagascar during the nineteenth century, usually cut in fractions). This coin was also called *hasina* and was given by subjects to the ruler on the occasion of major state rituals, of which four were particularly important. Three were occasional: a ruler's coronation or funeral, and mass circumcision, which took place at seven year intervals. One was annual: the New Year's ceremony climaxed by the ruler's ritual bath. (Detailed discussions of the New Year's ceremony, on which the following description is based, can be found in Bloch 1977, pp. 324–29; Delivré 1974, pp. 153–57; and Molet 1956.)

These state rituals shared certain features that demonstrate the king's role in transmitting the *hasina* of the royal ancestors and the royal talismans (pre-Christian idols maintained by guardians at certain centers and believed to benefit sovereign and kingdom in various ways) to the people. Holy water (*rano masina*) was manipulated by the sovereign to renew *hasina*; at the coronation ceremony the king incorporated the *hasina* of his predecessors by drinking water mixed with earth obtained from their tombs. When circumcision was held, or for the royal bath, the holy water was drawn from certain fixed places. The king, emerging from his bath, ritually stated "Let me be *masina*." His contact with holy water apparently renewed his own *hasina* and enabled him to transfer it to the people. These state rituals also renewed the link between current and past sovereigns. As noted, water mixed with earth from the tombs of the royal ancestors legitimized succession. Offerings and prayers at tombs were part of the circumcision ritual, again followed by the king's request "Let me be *masina*." Tombs were opened and tidied up prior to the annual bath ceremony.

All these state rituals—most regularly the royal bath—occasioned the presentation of *hasina* mark II not just by subjects to king, but by ritual inferiors to superiors throughout the entire ranking system, right down to a son's gift of *hasina* to his father. Through such rituals, says Bloch (1977, pp. 325–27), the entire Merina social structure was activated in a series of ritual acts whose purpose was to renew life. Each year the royal bath symbolized rebirth as the month of death yielded to the month of fertility. Merina state rituals were designed to reproduce the cosmos—the established social, political, and ritual order—through several acts that manipulated *hasina* (used in both senses) in order to renew and increase it. Bloch (1977, pp. 322) recognizes the similarity between the Merina sovereign and the role of the Inca ruler and his assistants (as analyzed by Godelier 1977) in mediating the sacred gift of fertility. In both systems regular gifts by inferiors were necessary to recreate the supernatural efficacy of superiors.

Bloch (1977) and Delivré (1974) seem to disagree about how permanent the possession of *hasina* is in Merina thought. Delivré (1974, p. 143) characterizes *hasina* as the possibility of having a sensible effect on other beings. Bloch (1977, p. 319) calls *hasina* an unchangeable essence that is given at birth and is inherent to certain people. The apparent disagreement can be resolved by recognizing that potential *hasina* is given at birth; this potential will be continually expressed as actual *hasina*, given the continuation of the established social and cosmic order. Ceremonies are therefore necessary to renew *hasina* and to reproduce the social and cosmic order on which it rests. Bloch (1977, p. 323) does recognize the ambiguity that although *hasina* is unchallenged, given, and religious, it also depends on the actions of others. According to Delivré (1974, pp. 140, 146), the possession of *hasina* is not immutable; customs like the royal bath were designed to renew and augment it, particularly in the king, who never permanently possessed it. Bloch (1977, pp. 322–24) notes that Merina participated in state rituals because they believed that everyone benefitted; preserving *hasina* in others—the king, for example—granted continued fertility of people and crops. By giving *hasina* mark II during state rituals, notes Delivré (1974, p. 159), all Merina could share, with the king as mediator, a much more fundamental *hasina*—that of the ancestors.

Speculating about the development of the ritual ranking system of nine-teenth-century Imerina, Bloch (1977, pp. 332–33) argues that the essentials of the hierarchy were produced through successive conquests, with new rul-ers requiring that members of the kin group of the old ruler grant them *ha-sina*. The *hasina* that had flowed through the previously established hierarchy to the old ruler could be maintained, but now was transmitted up one more level, from the kin group of the old ruler to the new sovereign. However, Bloch's reconstruction does not at all explain how *hasina* came to be associ-ated with hierarchy to begin with, a question now to be considered.

As noted previously, *hasina* appears to be one of those generalized Mal-agasy concepts, perhaps inherited from the protoculture, whose meaning has been transformed during the adaptive radiation and sociopolitical evolution of the Malagasy people. Although in other parts of the island *hasina* is also associated with the maintenance of cosmic orders, these orders are *not* the intricately graduated Merina ranking system. Just as there are contrasts be-tween the meanings and behavioral results of *mana* between Melanesia and Polynesia (Kottak 1978, pp. 366–68), the nature and effects of the *hasina* concept differ with degree of sociopolitical evolution. Delivré (1974, p. 154) asserts that a preoccupation with ensuring success permeates Malagasy cul-ture. In attempting to establish control over things and events—including those that are actually beyond realistic human control—all Malagasy groups use astrology. Successful transplanting, harvesting, trance, or ceremonial re-quires that an astrologer set a propitious date. Throughout the island, indi-vidual fortunes are told at birth as horoscopes are computed through an intri-cate system based on weekday, a lunar cycle, and twelve astrological directions (cf. Delivré 1974, pp. 148–49). Astrology links up with *hasina*: the *hasina* of each person is determined by his or her position in time, namely the destiny or *vintana* that is calculated at birth (Delivré 1974, p. 148). Here again, however, an element of potentiality seems to enter; ritual specialists can sometime avert the consequences of unhappy destinies.

With the growth of differential access to strategic resources in Betsileo and Merina society, the determinants of individual *hasina* became more com-plex. Birth horoscopes were still drawn up, but several other factors helped determine placement in the social order. Order of birth, for example, is im-portant among both Betsileo and Merina. Bloch (1977, p. 325) notes that in state rituals younger brothers offered *hasina* to their older brothers, just like sons and fathers. As Huntington (1974) observes about the Bara, one's place in an established, enduring, social order is determined at birth by horoscope, birth order, mother's status if offspring of a polygynous union, and the genealogical status of the individual's father, paternal grandfather, and other patrilineal ancestors following the same principles of ranking. Bloch (1977, pp. 320–21) notes that principles that structure ritual status and authority relations within households are writ large in state rituals. A son presents his father with an uncut coin (*hasina*), which the father anoints with water. The father blesses his son (augments *hasina* in his son through his own superior *hasina* and the *hasina* the son has presented) by blowing water in his direction. This custom may be the prototype of the Merina king's ritual use of holy water to ensure the kingdom's survival.

To return now to the Lalangina sequence, we can see that a *hasina* concept that had formerly operated in a society organized by kinship, descent, and marriage was incorporated into the process of state formation. The term *mahamasinandriana*, used to designate the heads of the major commoner descent groups (senior commoners) who were officially recognized as government agents, includes the prefix *maha-*, which means to make something the way it is, to constitute. Delivré (1974, p. 144) shows that the term *mahamasina* refers to the process whereby certain beings communicate their power (*hasina*) to others. Use of the term *mahamasinandriana* for the senior commoners who were beginning to serve formally as government agents, and whose basis of political legitimacy was therefore shifting from simple descent group role to position in a territorial administrative hierarchy, linked the tribal principles of the past to the state principles of the future in this sociopolitical structure in transformation.

The *mahamasinandriana* were rendering the leader (*andriana*) *masina* in three ways. First, they were communicating their power (*hasina*) based on their descent group positions and their links to local ancestors, and through them to nature, to the *mpanjaka*. The ruler of an emerging structure would rule by grace of the personnel that ran the established institutions and by virtue of the religious beliefs on which the social order was founded. Second, the senior commoners were elevating the *mpanjaka* to a sacred status. In their view they were not just legitimizing a particular leader, but actually creating sovereignty (and a nobility as its legitimate source, since the transmission of leadership was based on descent and ties through ancestors to land and nature). On the political level, leadership would unite diverse interest groups from the prior structure to meet external threats. On the ritual-cosmic level, central leadership, created and maintained through the support and prestations of lower level units, would ensure an uninterrupted flow of *hasina* through a changing social order.

Finally, the senior commoners and, in turn, the remaining Betsileo who paid homage to the senior commoners were actually rendering homage (and tribute) to the *mpanjaka*. Perhaps before, and certainly after their nineteenth-century conquest by the Merina, Betsileo, like Merina subjects, were expected to present uncut coins to the sovereign on certain formal and ritual occasions. Lalanginan oral traditions noted above suggest that early in the development of the Lalanginan state *hasina* was rendered in the form of first fruits, and that its return was material, through redistributory ceremonials sponsored by the *mpanjaka*, rather than illusory as among nineteenth-century Merina. Prior to state emergence, in other words, *hasina*'s link to production and reproduction—materialized in the actual presentation and distribution of food—was concrete and direct rather than mystical, symbolic, and illusory. Later, following revisions in ceremonial sponsorship discussed below and in chapter 7, *hasina*'s link to production and reproduction became indirect and symbolic, as among the Merina.

Structural recognition of the *mahamasinandriana* in Lalangina can therefore be interpreted as a formalization of the previously established privileged position of heads of major commoner descent groups within a sociopolitical organization undergoing segregation, differentiation, and centralization. Senior commoner descent groups provided advisers and judges at the *mpanjaka*'s court. Like the elevation of Betsileo nobilities from the fund of hierarchically undifferentiated descent groups, the formalization of senior commoner status as agents of state organization represents Flannery's (1972) "promotion," the ascent of an institution from its previous place in the control hierarchy. That is, decision-making and adjudicative functions formerly associated with autonomous descent groups were now seized by, and received their legitimation through, hierarchical administrative organization, but units previously important on the basis of population and range continued to provide regulatory personnel for the emerging organization. Furthermore, moral principles that had been part of a previous structure based on descent groups helped effect the sociopolitical transformation. Not just the *hasina* concept, but principles of seniority that had formerly operated within the individual descent group—generation and age—were now validating a model of ranking and relative seniority of *several* descent groups and their branches within the evolving structure.

Merina Idols and Betsileo Descent Groups

Promotion of basic units of the prior structure also played a part in the evolution of the Merina state, but differences between prestate structures of Imerina and the southern highlands meant that different kinds of units were promoted.

In discussing ways in which Merina sovereigns used previous cultural elements for political ends, Delivré (1974, p. 145, 191, et seq.) examines the critical role of certain royal talismans or idols (*sampy masina*). To understand the functional parallel that seems to have developed between Merina talismans and their guardians, on the one hand, and Betsileo senior commoners on the other, we need to look at another compound of *hasina—manamasina* (not to be confused with *mahamasina*). The subject of this verb is always ritually inferior to its object. Thus, *Ny ambanilanitra manasina ny Andriana* means that the people (*ambanilanitra*) must render homage to the sovereign (*Andriana*). Delivré (1974, p. 145) reports the recurrence in Merina historical texts of two expressions that expose the basis of the Merina sovereign's legitimacy: *Ny Andriana manasina ny razan'Andriana* ("the king must render homage to the royal ancestors") and *ny Andriana manasina ny sampy masina* ("the king must render homage to the sacred idols") (Delivré 1974, p. 145).

The Merina king therefore received his legitimacy from his royal predecessors and from certain sacred idols, of which four—each achieving prominence in different reigns—were paramount at the time of Radama I (1809–27). The *hasina* of the Merina sovereign, who occupied a ritual position between subjects, and royal ancestors and idols, rested on idols and ancestors, just as the *hasina* of the Betsileo ruler was founded on that of senior commoners and ancestors.

Despite the unification of the Merina talisman cult and its integration with the cult of the royal ancestors by King Andrianampoinimerina (1783–1809), most of the royal idols retained a local cult and guardian in a particular region of old Imerina. By correlating the sites of these local cults with the history of territorial accretions to the Merina state, Delivré (1974, pp. 192–98) has demonstrated a progressive confiscation of regional talismans by and on behalf of growing royal power. The principal talisman, Kelimalaza, whose local cult was observed in the southeast (an early addition to the Merina state), was the most functionally general of the royal idols—retaining, to paraphrase Delivré (1974, p. 194), all the characteristics of the *ody* (*hasina*-bearing charms) of the people, out of which the royal idols had evolved. Unlike the royal talismans that were incorporated later and that were concerned with such state ends as revealing disharmony and obstacles, or symbolizing the perfection and unity of government, Kelimalaza retained a class of functions associated with talismans of the people: preserving harvests and health, fending off hail and locusts, protecting against enemies, as well as creating the sovereign's reign. However, as the oldest of the royal idols and the closest to the people, Kelimalaza was still regarded as king of the royal talismans in nineteenth-century Imerina (Delivré 1974, p. 195).

We can now see that Merina and Betsileo states used the same evolutionary mechanism, promotion, to solve the problem of legitimizing growing royal power with reference to prior structural units and cultural beliefs. But the prior structural units differed. The Merina countryside was organized into localized kin groups enclosed by the custom of in-marriage. However, the prestate sociopolitical organization of the more sparsely populated Betsileo consisted not of enclosed local kin groups packed closely together in space, but of territorially dispersed descent groups linked by ties of kinship, marriage, and fictive kinship (see chapter 6). This prestate structure was controlled by the heads of the major descent groups, who were most closely linked through their own superior *hasina* as descent group elders to the even greater *hasina* of the ancestors. Kinship, marriage, and fictive kinship therefore linked Betsileo who belonged to different descent groups into a regional social system, as is still true. Because the Betsileo had these other alliance mechanisms, they had no need for (and lacked) regional cults based on sacred idols.

In contrast, the talismans described by Delivré (1974, 192–98) seem likely to have provided a unifying focus for members of different kin groups localized in particular areas of Imerina. Their promotion to serve as the source of royal *hasina* therefore had an effect that paralleled that of promotion of Betsileo senior commoners, i.e., incorporation within state structure of prior structural units larger than the local kin group, and use of these groups' most prominent members (guardians or descent group heads) to confer royal legitimacy by channeling already established *hasina*.

Furthermore, just as senior commoners were used as agents by, and to enhance the legitimacy of, the Lalanginan state, Merina sovereigns used the idol system to augment royal authority. Citizens' participation in the cults of the major regional idols was a form of support of local branches of what was becoming a state church. Further, the four paramount idols, called "mothers" among the royal talismans, acquired the ability to transmit their power to other regional and familial idols. In other words, a hierarchy of talismans with differential efficacy developed in tandem with the sociopolitical and ranking hierarchies, just as descent group ranking was developing among the Betsileo. Understanding now some of the basic beliefs, contexts, and sociopolitical units that were caught up in the process of state formation in the Malagasy highlands, we can return to the Lalanginan sequence.

The Emergence of the State in Lalangina

Several roles began to converge in senior commoner status under Lalangina's third and fourth *mpanjaka*. The *mahamasinandriana* served as administrative officers of territorial subdivisions, advisers to the *mpanjaka*, judicial officials, and generalized information processors, while simultaneously retaining functions associated with their ancestral territories, which now hierarchically incorporated junior descent branches, new immigrants, and a variety of clients seeking protection in a more and more dangerous environment. The rewards distributed by the *mpanjaka* continued to be confirmed by his senior commoner advisers. The elevation of new groups to senior commoner status was permitted in return for loyal services to the *mpanjaka*. While the fourth *mpanjaka* is recalled as an adulterer and debaucher who was killed in a battle with Isandra, his reign is remembered as associated with an administrative reorganization involving the establishment of four districts. By the fourth reign, hierarchical administrative organization was also beginning to intervene in hitherto private delicts. For example, no longer was a husband entitled to kill and seize the possessions of his adulterous wife's partner; adultery was punishable by a fine to the *fanjakana* ("government," same root as *mpanjaka*).

Oral traditions of this period make only passing reference to economy. To determine the amount of corvée labor due the *fanjakana*, it is said that rice fields were divided into units with standard productivity, suggesting that some form of rice cultivation had been important previously, along with cultivation of taro and other crops and stockbreeding. A degree of information processing and supervision of measurements, at least territorial allotments, is clearly present during this reign, along with other types of hierarchically organized regulation, management, and enforcement.

Following the death of Lalangina's fourth *mpanjaka* came an interregnum during which the *mahamasinandriana* officers are supposed to have governed until one of them hastened the succession, with himself as regent, of a young prince who was to become one of Lalangina's most illustrious political figures. During the reign of Lalangina's fifth *mpanjaka*, Raonimanalina I, between 1715 and 1740 (according to Dubois 1938, pp. 182–84), the process of sociopolitical transformation was hastened by Lalangina's definite incorporation within an interregional trade network. In contrast to preceding reigns, this one showed progressive growth in the power of the *mpanjaka* at the expense of senior commoners. The first muskets were imported to the Betsileo heartland. Oral traditions tell of the manner in which the firearms-slave exchange began. A Lalanginan trading party went to Sakalava country hoping to negotiate an exchange of cattle for firearms. The trading party returned, however, with the information that the Sakalava required slaves rather than cattle for firearms. Foreigners, either Europeans or Arabs, are recalled as returning with the trading party, residing for a time in Lalangina and serving as intermediaries in the trade with the Sakalava.

The demand for slaves led to increased administrative intervention in Lalanginan life. A military reorganization involved the formation of a standing army, adding riflemen to the spear corps, and land grants to the best soldiers. The growing authority of the *mpanjaka* was maintained by such devices as establishment of a group known as "the eyes of the king," roving agents who traveled throughout Lalangina overseeing senior commoner officers. Here one sees a notable increase in, and seizure by the *mpanjaka* of, information gathering, storage, and processing.[12] Modification in codes of crimes and sanctions included reduction to slave status for a variety of hitherto private crimes and the definition of new crimes and penalties that functioned to meet emerging governmental needs. Humans to serve as items in exchange with the Sakalava included prisoners of war as well as indigents and debtors reduced to slave status.

A far-reaching modification in ceremonial suggests that the fifth reign marks a transition between chiefdom and state. Formerly the "right" to slaughter cattle consecrated to the ancestors had been confined to nobles and senior commoners. During this reign the "privilege" of cattle sacrifice was extended down the hierarchy. Note that as long as ceremonial sponsorship had devolved on the wealthiest Betsileo, as among the contemporary Taimoro of the southeast coast (cf. Collins 1897), ceremonials functioned as leveling mechanisms, since the richest people footed the bill. As the "privilege" of such sponsorship was extended, however, it could be regulated and manipulated to increase, rather than to level, differential access to strategic resources, as it continues to do among contemporary Betsileo (see also chapter 7).

State formation, however, is not an inevitable onward and upward process, but is subject to setbacks, either occasional or of a more definitive nature. The process of sociopolitical transformation in Isandra, the polity to the west of Lalangina, illustrates some of the more permanent impediments, whereas the reign of Lalangina's sixth king illustrates temporary setbacks to progressive centralization in the form of royal authority. Lalangina's sixth king was ousted by the *mahamasinandriana* after proposing that no longer would their successors be appointed by the senior commoners themselves but by the *mpanjaka* from within the descent group of the previous official. This *mpanjaka*'s privilege, which was allowed to stand in subsequent reigns, allowed royal manipulation of the relative positions of descent group branches.

Between about 1745 and 1794 the seventh *mpanjaka* of Lalangina, Andrianonindranarivo, ruled a territory and headed a sociopolitical organization to which few would deny the status of state. Oral tradition (cf. Dubois 1938, pp. 188–95) associates with the reign of the seventh *mpanjaka* a major administrative reorganization, state intervention in the agricultural economy, and progressive growth in military apparatus. The capital now presided over three districts, each with four major towns. The districts and towns were headed by senior commoner governors. The governors' assistants, similar to contemporary village chiefs, were the state's representatives in villages. Oral tradition suggests, therefore, at most a five-, at least a three-, and, most probably, a four-level settlement hierarchy: capital, district town, possibly subdistrict town, village, and possibly hamlet.

Oral tradition associates with this reign an increase in population throughout Lalangina, expressed in the growth of new fortified hilltop towns. Administrative intervention in agriculture is recalled as augmenting rice production, by increasing the area cultivated in rice through a state-administered drainage program. Manuring and intensified cultivation of existing rice fields were also fostered by state officials. For the first time, the Lalanginan state was initiating a hydraulic program.[13]

A likely precondition for such an agricultural program is a military sufficiently effective to protect such investments from external marauders. Oral traditions recall expansion of the army and establishment of defensive posts on the southern and western boundaries of Lalangina. The eastern frontier was still plagued by Tanala raiders, who attacked and retreated into the forest with their captives. The fact that a military career could still be rewarded with elevation to senior commoner status and land grants by the *mpanjaka* suggests that population pressure was not critical. Lalangina's military subsystem was not only defending, but also attacking and conquering parts of Vohibato to the south, Isandra to the west, and areas to the northwest and northeast. As Bloch (1977, pp. 311–12) notes, Lalanginan military exploits also supplied slave labor to drain and work the large marshlands that supported king, court, and, in a positive-feedback relationship, the military.

Oral tradition also reports enlargement of the judicial role of administrators. In particular, a change in inheritance laws increased litigation.[14] The former custom of patrilineal inheritance of land was changed to legally enforced bilateral inheritance. Although increased litigation is recalled, it is likely that this more flexible inheritance rule enabled descent groups to redistribute, while retaining, their estates in the absence of patrilineal heirs. The change may be a response to population growth; it certainly indicates the state's concern with population distribution.

It is possible, too, that it was during this reign that a sociocultural mechanism that may have formerly served to limit population was converted into a mechanism promoting population redistribution and increase. The pastorally oriented Bara (Faublée 1954, pp. 46–50; Huntington 1974, pp. 153–56) and Sakalava (Gardenier 1976, pp. 40–46), like many contemporary Betsileo (and most Malagasy), routinely employ an astrologer to determine the destiny (*vintana*) of newborn children through calculations based on zodiac signs, a lunar cycle, and weekday of birth. Faublée reports that should the child's destiny be found dangerous to its parents, kin, or society in general, and should the astrologer be unable or unwilling (because of the horoscope's extreme danger) to remove the threat through various rituals, infanticide was a Bara custom. Gardenier (1976, pp. 40–46) and Deschamps and Vianès (1959, p. 59) have reported similar customs among Sakalava and Taimoro respectively. Among the Betsileo, however, diagnosis of incompatible destinies of child and parents often leads the diviner to search for a relative with a more compatible destiny; usually the relative who is selected to foster the child is someone with few or no real children. (The fosterage system is analyzed further in chapter 6.) This change in the behavior underlying a generalized custom could be related to population growth and redistribution during this reign. A progrowth cultural attitude would certainly be expectable in a state whose regional economy was based on supplying people for export. And, as Bloch (1977, pp. 311–12) has noted, labor of royal slaves also freed citizens to strengthen the military, thus increasing the supply of slaves and booty. In the positive-feedback process that developed, agricultural innovation was necessary to free the growing population, and the larger army offered more protection to fields and crops.

Increasing differentiation of stratified groups in Lalangina is also associated with this reign. The slave stratum included at least three groups: those to be exchanged for firearms with the Sakalava, slaves of the king, and a group of stigmatized former slaves whose relatives had been allowed to buy back their freedom. However, neither market sales of slaves nor widespread slave ownership by senior commoners were apparently characteristic of Lalangina prior to its conquest by the Merina.

Public addresses of Lalangina's seventh king are also recalled in oral tradition; they demonstrate attempts by an emerging sovereign to incorporate traditional cultural themes within a structure in transformation. The *mpanjaka* could assert both that the state had been confided to him by the ancestors, thus linking himself to the traditionally important descent groups, and, claiming divine right, that "the state is ours (we exclusive); we have received it from Andriamanitra ("the sweet lord") and not taken it by force" (Dubois 1938, pp. 193, 195).

Lalangina's eighth *mpanjaka* ruled only a year; his ouster through a senior commoner rebellion again illustrates a temporary setback in emerging centralization. He is remembered (Dubois 1938, pp. 196–98) as a sorcerer who ignored his advisers and was ultimately forsaken by his corps of riflemen who, with the assistance of a neighboring petty state, drove him from office.

The final *mpanjaka* of an independent unitary Lalangina, Raindratsara, ruled only a decade, between about 1795 and 1805. He is recalled (Dubois 1938, pp. 198–202) as having encouraged senior commoner officials to supervise the major tasks of rice cultivation in their circumscriptions, to oversee drainage work, tillage, trampling, and harvests (cf. Chapus and Ratsimba 1958, pp. 647–48). Lalangina's military received training in European battle techniques from a European merchant from Fort Dauphin, who came initially as a trader. Warfare between Lalangina and polities to the south is recalled. Prior to his death in battle, the ninth king divided Lalangina into three parts, to be governed respectively by the children of each of his three wives. An attempt by one to reunify the kingdom was only partially successful, but was ended by an invading Merina army around 1815.

The evolution of independent Lalangina therefore ends early in the nineteenth century. The process of state formation, of increasing segregation, differentiation, and centralization, in Lalangina illustrates not only the gradual nature of the transformation and its restructuring of prior units and cultural themes, but also temporary setbacks involved in such sociopolitical changes.

Isandra

More definite handicaps characterized a process that can more accurately be described as "attempted state-copying" in what is remembered as the other major polity of the southern highlands, Isandra, to the west. Contemporary descendants of Isandra's *mpanjaka* conjur up a glorious past and describe their ancestors as the seniormost Betsileo nobles. Their claim of seniority, however, reflects the decision by an Isandran *mpanjaka* of the late eighteenth or early nineteenth century to seek Merina assistance and support by declaring himself a vassal of the Merina king. In recognition of his early submission, the Merina king Radama, on occupying the southern highlands, made Isandra the seniormost of the three Betsileo provinces and granted to its royal heirs, who retained the title of *mpanjaka* while serving as agents of the Merina state, prerogatives that their ancestors had never enjoyed as rulers of an independent Isandra (cf. Shaw 1875, p. 64). The Merina also gave to their noble Isandran agents the means to rule: military fortresses protecting Isandra against external threat and internal dissension. Merina protection also permitted Isandra to develop a more productive economy supporting an increasingly sedentary population who began to irrigate in extending their rice fields. During the nineteenth century, one-half of the tribute and taxes collected from the Isandran population for the Merina state remained with the Isandran *mpanjaka* (Dubois 1938, p. 147).

During the 1700s, Isandra and Lalangina were equally exposed not only to the same regional ecosystemic changes but also to "the idea of the state," the ethnomodel of state organization which, by diffusion, migration, trade, warfare, and other contacts ultimately linking all Malagasy populations, had been available as a model of sociopolitical organization since perhaps the late seventeenth century. However, mere exposure to "the idea of the state" or to regional ecosystemic change does not guarantee that the process of state formation will or can take place. Local ecosystemic variables play a key role in the actual process of state formation. The gradual evolution of sociopolitical organization in Lalangina took place in the agricultural east, an area of greater rainfall where rice cultivation could proceed without artificial irrigation. Isandra, on the other hand, was a more pastorally oriented region, one in which hydraulic rice cultivation—through irrigation and a state military force to protect it—has become important only during the past 150 years. Prior to Merina occupation, the economy of most of Isandra was essentially one of mixed pastoralism (type III) involving stockbreeding and herding of zebu cattle, goats, and sheep, and cultivation of rainfall-dependent and flood-plain rice, manioc, maize, millet, taro, and other horticultural crops. Greater annual precipitation in the east permitted earlier transplanting and harvesting than in the west and south. Vulnerability to attacks, not just by Sakalava and Bara, but by earlier-harvesting Lalanginans also may help explain why Isandra's agricultural economy did not flourish until the nineteenth century. As noted previously, such southern Betsileo polities as southern Vohibato and Arindrano-Tsienimparihy shared Isandra's physical environment, cultural adaptation, and political organization (cf. Chapus and Ratsimba 1958, p. 662 et seq.). A sparser, more mobile seventeenth- and eighteenth-century population in Isandra can be still inferred from contemporary population densities. Whereas a single capital served as administrative center of Lalangina throughout its history, the Isandran capital shifted several times, as many as four times under a given *mpanjaka*.

The figure whom oral history remembers as the most illustrious *mpanjaka* of an independent Isandra is its third *mpanjaka*, Andriamanalimbetany, who ruled jointly with his full brother between about 1750 and 1790 (Dubois 1938, p. 229). The oral historical description of Andriamanalimbetany suggests that he was little more than a highly successful brigand chief similar to *mpanjaka* described among the Bara in the late nineteenth century (Nielsen-Lund 1888). Although he is recalled as having conquered areas to the south, north, and west, what does conquest mean in an area of sparse population and mobile cultural adaptation when no perpetual occupying force holds the conquered? Although Isandra's territory is generally stated to have been larger than Lalangina's, the actual geographic extent of its political effectiveness is difficult to assess. Isandra fortified and guarded neither its southern nor its western frontiers, and so continually faced not only desertion by its subjects but also attacks by Bara and Sakalava.

Firearms were introduced to Isandra under Andriamanalimbetany, some fifty years later than in Lalangina. As in Lalangina, a few foreigners are recalled as having resided in Isandra, acting as intermediaries in the slave-firearms trade. In contrast to Lalangina, however, Isandra's slaves were exclusively prisoners of war; no legal code supplied slaves. The Isandran *mpanjaka* administered the distribution of slaves, cattle, and other booty, and headed a supply node of a distribution network that also provided cloth woven from Isandran silk, cotton, and banana fiber. Rice was only cultivated in the river valleys of eastern Isandra, principally as an export crop. Staples of the Isandran diet are reported to have been manioc, sweet potatoes, and taro. The consumption of rice and beef at the same meal was specifically prohibited (Dubois 1938, p. 126).

A group consisting of heads of the major commoner descent groups arose as the structural equivalent of Lalangina's *mahamasinandriana*, and, as the latter did early in the eighteenth century, they checked the prerogatives and power of the *mpanjaka*. For example, the senior commoners are recalled as having forced the foreigners to leave Isandra on learning that the *mpanjaka* wished them to instruct Isandrans in the use of firearms. Perhaps they recognized in the *mpanjaka*'s control over riflemen a threat to their own position (cf. Dubois 1938, pp. 123–31).

Isandra's most illustrious *mpanjaka*, therefore, presided over a poorly demarcated and defended territory, a sparse, mobile population, and a regional exchange network involving local manufactures, prisoners of war, cattle, and rice. Though well-exposed both to European economic penetration and to "the idea of the state"—to the ethnomodel of state organization— Isandra maintained for some years the illusion of state organization while teetering on the edge of anarchy.

VARIABLES IN THE PROCESS OF STATE FORMATION

Comparison of the agricultural east with the more pastoral west and south demonstrates the gradual process of sociopolitical transformation, some of the local ecosystemic requirements of state organization, and some of the factors involved in progressive segregation, differentiation, and centralization. Of the factors that anthropologists and historians have suggested as variables in the origin of the state in other world areas, can we identify any as important in the development of state organization in Lalangina? The need for defense and its fulfillment through reorganization of units in the previous sociopolitical organization has been posited as an initial kick in the process of sociopolitical change.[15] Other variables known from other world areas to be important in state formation also appear in the Lalanginan sequence, but none can be identified as a unitary cause in the process. Regulation by state officials of a hydraulic network, which Karl Wittfogel (1957) viewed as a major selecting variable in the origin of the state, does not characterize Lalangina until the reign of its seventh king. This hydraulic intervention is associated, according to oral tradition, both with increasing population and with the development of a military apparatus capable of defending hydraulic works against outsiders.

There is no evidence that regulation of ecological diversity, which Sanders and Price (1968) and others have associated with the genesis of the state, was an important function of hierarchical administrative organization in Lalangina. On the other hand, interregional trade—participation in the widespread slave-firearms exchange network—provided a major administrative function and stimulus to centralization under Lalangina's fifth *mpanjaka*, some half century before state intervention in hydraulic agriculture. However, as Isandra teaches us, such regional ecosystemic participation was only a necessary, but not a sufficient, condition for the evolution of state organization.

One of the most intriguing and most generally valid approaches to the origin of the state has been proposed by Robert Carneiro (1970), who suggests that state organization eventually emerges in the context of population increase, warfare, and environmental circumscription. Environments may be circumscribed either physically or socially. Physical circumscription is exemplified by small islands and river valleys in arid areas, such as the Peruvian coast and the alluvial plain of the Tigris-Euphrates. Social circumscription involves the inability to expand because of boundary pressure by neighboring groups. One manifestation of physical circumscription is resource concentration, which Carneiro uses to explain a concentration of chiefdoms in the fertile *varzéa* area on the fringes and islands of the Amazon River.

Environmental circumscription of increasing population may have played a role in Lalangina's development. Sometime during the seventeenth century southern highlanders were forced to deal with an environmental perturbation reflecting events on the Malagasy coasts, and, if oral traditions and descent group genealogies are to be believed, had to absorb an influx of immigrants. In an atmosphere of increasing internecine warfare, migratory possibilities were eventually limited; however, archaeological investigation is needed to confirm and approximate population increase in the southern highlands around 1700. It is also possible that, because of external threats, early Lalanginans may have been forced to concentrate their attention on a smaller variety of resources, and that concentration of resource use in combination with the necessity of a defensive pose may have been early inputs in the process of sociopolitical transformation. Oral history does not focus on population growth other than through immigration until the reign of Lalangina's seventh king, some 100 years after the process of transformation had begun. Increasing population could have accompanied a change in the functioning of a system of population regulation based on astrological divination, an expression perhaps of a progrowth cultural policy related to the need to capture slaves for export, to increase military personnel, and to intensify production of rice to support the military, royal slaves, and temporary war prisoners.

Immigration, the need for defense, interregional trade, militarism to supply slaves for export, and eventually population increase, sedentarization, and hydraulic agriculture all contributed to the process of sociopolitical transformation in Lalangina between the seventeenth and nineteenth centuries. Once they developed, these variables interacted synergistically. Instances of state formation involving the systemic interaction over time of such variables may profitably be compared for different world areas. Different initial kicks may trigger analogous positive-feedback relationships. For other world areas anthropologists may also examine processes of sociopolitical transformation that can be speculated about on the basis of ethnohistorical data, documented or confirmed through archaeological and historical records, or assessed in space, through synchronic comparison of sociopolitical variance (cf. Kottak 1972, 1977).

If we are to study concrete processes of state formation, we will be faced in all cases with identifying specific initial kicks and specific interacting variables necessary to produce the reality as well as the illusion of state organization. Although neither Lalangina nor Isandra was a pristine state—one that developed in isolation from other states (Fried 1960, pp. 729–30)—the process of state formation, given similar conditions of socioenvironmental stress, took place in Lalangina but not in Isandra. The sparser and smaller Isandran population carried into the eighteenth century the same tribal heritage and similar structural units, was exposed equally to "the idea of the state," was affected by similar regional threats, and was eventually incorporated into the same interregional exchange network as Lalangina; yet, because of local ecosystemic impediments, Isandra never underwent the process of state formation. A revision in relationships of Malagasy with outsiders, which occurred first on the coasts and subsequently as interior populations joined the trade network, served as an important early stimulus to state formation in the southern highlands. If similar perturbations can be demonstrated to have occurred in other sequences, then they are likely to be significant variables in the process of sociopolitical transformation.

But analysis of the process of state formation requires much more. It is relatively meaningless in an evolutionary context merely to present evidence purporting to link through diffusion the growth of the state in one area to the prior growth of the state in another if the specific conditions whereby contact might have provided an initial kick or a sustained impetus favoring directional change are not specified. Arguing the opposing view, Betty Meggers (1975) has pointed to certain similarities in notation, settlement orientation, and art motifs to suggest that Shang dynasty China may have been responsible in some way for the appearance of Olmec "civilization" in Mesoamerica. If indeed Mesoamerica had somehow been incorporated within a transoceanic trade network with Shang dynasty China, this could have been a significant factor in Mesoamerican state formation. However, even if trans-Pacific contact were confirmed, and even accepted as a stimulus to the growth of state organization in Mesoamerica (which most anthropologists find unlikely), the process of state formation in Mesoamerica would not have been explained. Rather, the situation would be comparable to that of the several Malagasy populations who had to contend with major externally introduced perturbations beginning in the seventeenth century. The prospects for and directions of sociopolitical transformation would depend in large measure on local ecosystemic options.

Nor can conquest alone, any more than diffusion alone, explain sociopolitical transformation. Conquerors must enforce their claims and organizational schemes. If anthropologists and historians are unable to demonstrate the concrete means whereby conquerors have created and maintained state organization, they have provided little information about process.

Although the origins of the first civilizations lie in the remote past and may be susceptible only to archaeological investigation, processes of sociopolitical transformation go on today throughout the world. The Betsileo are similar to many other tribal societies who have undergone, as a result of factors beyond their control, a rapid transformation of sociopolitical organization based on kinship and descent into one of territorial, formally hierarchical, centralized administration. The study of such transformation is available through ethnographic, historical, archaeological, and ethnohistorical techniques. Only a processual approach to state formation can combat assumptions of limited inventiveness and intrinsic backwardness (unless stimulated by outsiders) that are currently attributed by a variety of scholars and the public to the populations that anthropologists have traditionally studied.

Chapter 3 has continued the examination of cultural variation, adaptive radiation, and other evolutionary processes in Madagascar, through comparative and historical consideration of sociopolitical organization. A diachronic perspective demonstrates the processual nature of the origin of the state and the role of environment, mediated through economy and other sociocultural means of adaptation, in favoring or hindering the emergence of complex society. Physical environments, since they are perceived and used differently at different times, through different techniques, and in the context of regional changes, do not pose static problems for cultural adaptation. In the case of the Betsileo there has been a historical shift, still in progress, away from pastoral transhumance, with its relative mobility and sparse populations, toward wet-rice cultivation, with its larger, denser, and more permanent communities. On the basis of written and oral historical accounts, this shift appears to have been underway in the eastern part of the southern highlands, at least in Lalangina, by the latter half of the seventeenth century. In the absence of irrigation and in the presence of sparse population and more direct exposure to raids of Bara and Sakalava, which impeded development and protection of hydraulic systems, the more arid western and southern parts of the Betsileo heartland constituted an inhospitable habitat for the process of state formation.

The contrast of Lalangina and Isandra applies the model of variation and adaptive radiation to a smaller area than in chapter 2, where diversity among all Malagasy populations was seen in this framework. Comparison of variation in scale of sociopolitical organization in Lalangina and Isandra is also of general interest to the comparative study of political organization and state formation since it illustrates several generalized phenomena: the synergistic interaction of several variables; the gradual nature of sociopolitical transformation; the restructuring and recontextualization of prior units and cultural themes during evolutionary processes; impediments, temporary or more permanent, to the origin of the state; and the relationship between material variables and different degrees of sociopolitical development. Furthermore, the application of an adaptive radiation framework to Isandra and Lalangina illustrates that given original sociocultural and structural homogeneity, given equal exposure to the ethnomodel of state organization and to diffusionist processes, and given identical modifications in regional ecosystems, local material variables can still dictate generally the direction and progress of change.

Chapter 4 will examine modifications in Betsileo society under their Merina and French overlords. In the presence of a stronger, better-defended Merina state organization, and with incorporation within a regional political economy of far larger scale and complexity, the economy of Isandra changed as people began to irrigate their rice fields and to devote more time to agriculture. Chapter 4 examines the ways in which structural units and cultural behavior of the Betsileo prior to Merina conquest were preserved, restructured, or otherwise modified by their overlords from the north. It also examines a major change in scale of the Betsileo stratification system, as domestic slavery became important for the first time throughout the Betsileo heartland.

The genesis and development of a stratification system of different scale is vital to understanding the ethnographic data discussed in chapters 5 through 8, for variation among contemporary Betsileo is linked more closely to their relative position in the stratification system than to physical environmental variables. In preceding chapters, emphasis has been on differential access to strategic resources that is largely attributable to broad differences in sociocultural adaptation to regional economic and physical environmental features. In subsequent chapters, however, cultural variation is examined in terms of differential access to strategic resources attributable to politico-economic factors. In other words, variation in previous chapters has been viewed mainly in terms of adaptation to different natural biases; hereafter such variation is seen as primarily a function of the stratification system.

CHAPTER FOUR

The Impact of Conquest

The first formal declaration of the Merina as administrators of the southern highlands was a speech that Merina king Radama made in Isandra in 1815 (cf. Dubois 1938, p. 144). The sixth *mpanjaka* of Isandra would retain his title and would represent Radama in Isandra. Northern Lalangina and Vohibato, polities that had resisted Merina annexation, were placed under the administration of leaders who had voluntarily accepted Merina rule. In what became the (Betsileo) province south of the Matsiatra River, three territorial subdivisions were recognized: Isandra, Lalangina, and Arindrano. Isandra attained its first effective and operational unity under the Merina. Arindrano, the southernmost province, formerly consisting of a half-dozen independent polities, became a single political entity governed by the *mpanjaka* of Arindrano-Tsienimparihy. Radama fortified administrative centers, usually traditional capitals, for each subprovince. To these centers would later be added other fortified administrative towns, including Fianarantsoa, which became a military garrison and provincial capital in 1830 (Dubois 1938, p. 152).

Several factors explain Merina success in governing the Betsileo when compared to other parts of their empire. An increasingly sedentary population and agricultural economy facilitated Merina rule. Also important were the skills of Radama and some of his successors in maintaining the illusion that Betsileo ancestral customs were being preserved. The official Merina policy was that the administration would allow traditional practices that did not conflict with Merina law (cf. Chapus and Ratsimba 1958, p. 649–51). In fact, the southern highlands came increasingly under Merina law, as codes of crimes and punishments were proclaimed by successive Merina rulers, culminating in a code of 118 articles designed specifically for the Betsileo and proclaimed in Fianarantsoa by the Merina queen Ranavalona II in 1873 (cf. Dubois 1938, p. 885).

What the Merina brought to the Betsileo heartland, especially to those areas that had not resisted annexation, was a system of indirect rule. Those who had traditionally held authority—ruling nobles and senior commoner governors—retained their functions, but as Merina representatives (cf. Shaw 1877, p. 84–85). In areas that had resisted—northern Lalangina and northern Vohibato in the east, southern Vohibato in the south—formerly ruling nobles suffered more than senior commoners, some of whom became Merina agents. The presence of a Merina administrative bureaucracy also offered possibilities of advancement to certain commoners whose previous influence had been slight. In the Merina state a judicial apparatus had differentiated out of the administrative structure, and Betsileo judges, whom senior commoner governors chose among themselves, heard cases in the major settlements (Shaw 1877, p. 85). And, especially in the less agricultural areas of the Betsileo west and south, Merina rule sharpened contrasts in wealth, prestige, and power. The Merina did not, however, leave the administration of the southern highlands entirely to the Betsileo. Merina governors, lieutenants, and soldiers occupied the major towns throughout the Betsileo province. As the Betsileo population increased during the nineteenth century, so, too, did the number of Merina overseers.

THE NEW ELITE

Nobles

Accompanying growth and differentiation of the administrative structure were more complicated and less fluid criteria of social ranking. The population of the southern highlands became ethnically heterogeneous, including Merina soldiers, officers, administrators, and merchants who brought a market economy to rural rice growers and stockbreeders. Although the ruling[1] Betsileo nobles and noble "fief holders" (see p. 91) were, along with the Merina, members of the new elite of the southern highlands, their status was placed below that of prominent nobles of Imerina itself. Formerly, as in Imerina, the Betsileo noble group had been known as *andriana*. After Merina annexation, however, Betsileo *andriana* were gradually demoted to the status of *hova*, the term used in Imerina for its commoner stratum. Verbally, and in the eyes of the Merina *andriana*, the Betsileo rulers eventually became their social inferiors, though equal in rank to the Merina merchants and administrators who were *hova* (cf. Dubois 1938, p. 210). In Lalangina, the senior commoner descent groups became *mahamasinkova* rather than *mahamasinandriana*; the literal translation of the new term is "those who make the *hova* sacred" or, as was discussed in chapter 3, "those who render tribute (*hasina*) to the *hova*." The term *andevo-hova*, literally "servants of the *hova*," became widespread to designate the Betsileo senior commoner descent group heads who were the lower level agents (but with variable power, reflecting the size of their circumscription) in an administration in which Merina ruled and certain Betsileo nobles, now sharing the *hova* status of Merina commoners, were intermediaries. The mass of Betsileo commoners became *olompotsy*, "clean people" or "just plain folks" (see table 2.).

Merina sovereigns concerned themselves directly in maintaining social distinctions among the Betsileo, as in Imerina itself. The change in status of Betsileo *andriana* to *hova* appears to have been gradual. Callet's collection of the oral traditions of Imerina (Callet 1908; French translation, Chapus and Ratsimba 1953–58) describes negotiations between emissaries of the Merina king[2] and Betsileo leaders. Throughout these negotiations, Betsileo nobles were spoken of as *andriana*, thus approximate social equals, though political inferiors, of the Merina king. However, although recognizing them as *andriana*, the Merina king also stipulated that Betsileo *andriana* should henceforth consist only of rulers and their children (Chapus and Ratsimba 1958, p. 652). This limited the proliferation of Betsileo nobilities by hiving off and demoting to *hova* status those children of *andriana* who never ruled.[3]

Consistently in Callet's collection, the Betsileo rulers posed to the Merina emissaries the problem that in their kingdoms there were many *andriana* (Chapus and Ratsimba, 1958, pp. 649, 661). Merina king Radama eventually solved the problem by recognizing only the kings of Isandra and Arindrano-Tsienimparihy and the queen of central Lalangina as *andriana* and as his representatives. The Merina king additionally stipulated that not all children of a Betsileo ruler were equally entitled to rule. Although not prohibiting intermarriage between *andriana* and commoners, only children of full *andriana* parentage would have the right to represent the Merina king (Chapus and Ratsimba 1958, p. 652, 662). Formerly, succession to office among the Betsileo had tended towards strict patriliny and, in Lalangina at least, children of senior commoner mothers and *andriana* fathers had become *mpanjaka*. For the purpose of inheriting political office, though not wealth, the Merina introduced a rule of hypodescent: the offspring of an interstratum marriage would share the affiliation of the lower-ranking parent.

Under the new administration, those Betsileo nobles who were recog-

TABLE 2

Stratification in the Southern Highlands under Merina Rule

Emic Category	Etic Constituents
andriana	Merina nobility
hova	Merina commoners, Betsileo nobles
olompotsy, including *andevohova* (no native term)	{ Betsileo commoners, including Betsileo senior commoner governors (and derivatively their local descent branches) Betsileo junior commoners
andevo	Merina and Betsileo slaves

nized as *mpanjaka* and allowed to rule as Merina representatives, along with certain other important Betsileo nobles, became—like top-ranking Merina nobility—*tompomenakely*, small estate lords or fiefholders, heads of areas that they administered and from which they received a share of taxes and labor. Major representatives—the three *mpanjaka* of Isandra, Lalangina, and Arindrano—apparently kept half of the taxes collected whereas small-scale fiefholders kept only a third, transmitting the rest to the Merina sovereign (cf. Dubois 1938, pp. 167–68, 214). The Betsileo *hova* stratum continued to grow during the nineteenth century as a customarily endogamous group incorporating children of *andriana* who never ruled, other members of the noble descent groups of each of the pre-Merina polities, and the composite and geographically dispersed descent group known as Andrianaby who claimed descent from the earliest Betsileo nobles and who served as sources of holy water used in the circumcision ritual.

Sometime during the nineteenth century, Betsileo began to reserve the term *andriana* for the nobles of Imerina. Today most Betsileo classify descendants of the traditional Betsileo rulers as *hova*. Because of this, lines between the strata of Betsileo society are not as sharp as in Imerina, where a noble's marriage to a commoner may entail psychologically severe sanctions, including expulsion from the ancestral tomb (cf. Condominas 1960, pp. 127–28). Among the Betsileo only unions between descendants of slaves and those of free people entail this sanction. Endogamy is preferred but not prescribed for nobles. The fact that Betsileo and Merina perceive gradations of rank within strata also dulls the distinctions between the strata. For example, members of the royal descent group of Lalangina prefer to marry members of their own or another royal descent group, but frequently marry Andrianaby, the largest and lowest status noble group. Andrianaby prefer to marry other Andrianaby or members of royal descent groups, but often marry senior commoners. Although senior commoners prefer to choose their spouses from either their own descent group, another senior commoner descent group, or, with more reluctance,[4] one of the noble descent groups, practice is now departing from preference as unions between senior and junior commoners increase.

While there was a reduction in the relative prestige of the Betsileo nobles in a society dominated by Merina, the material rewards of political office were considerably expanded. In Isandra especially, a state organization for the first time exercised effective control over its subject population. The gap widened between rulers and commoners, with marked differences in their life styles, wealth, and power. Merina rule also helped promote Isandra's internal pacification and reduced the threat of outside attack. Transhumant pastoralism and rice cultivation replaced raiding as the dominant concern of Isandra's cultural adaptation. Protected by the Merina state's military apparatus, sedentary agriculture spread through investment of human labor in irrigation systems. With more numerous and more stable subject populations, the authority of rulers in the pastoral south and west grew.

Incorporated within the Merina empire and with new means of support available to its administrators, the political organization of nineteenth-century Isandra began to parallel that established in Lalangina a century earlier. The privileges of kingship under Merina rule are recorded in Isandra's official history. The Merina empire imposed several new taxes on the people of Isandra. Its *mpanjaka*, who was responsible for collecting these levies, was allowed to keep half. In addition, the Merina overlords allowed him to expropriate one steer from each household and to convoke work parties to build a new palace (Dubois 1938, pp. 147, 151, 167). Other burdens placed on Isandrans as tribute for subsequent rulers are discussed below.

In Arindrano, similar support for the noble line of one of its formerly autonomous polities, Tsienimparihy, was guaranteed by Merina rule. The rewards associated with the status of *mpanjaka* in the Merina empire were great. Moreover, the changes effected under Merina rule have left their imprint on Betsileo oral history. No evidence that I could gather supports claims (Dubois 1938, p. 17; Shaw 1877, p. 74) of preeminence of Isandra or its leaders prior to incorporation within the Merina empire. Oral historical accounts containing such claims reflect post-Merina history, a period in which Isandra, because of its early submission, was treated as most senior of the Betsileo areas, and in which its nobles did finally rule, but as Merina agents (cf. Shaw 1875, p. 64).[5]

In the traditionally agricultural east, the nobles of Vohibato and northern Lalangina appear to have suffered, at least in the early years of Merina rule. Their leaders had refused to submit to the Merina. Northern Lalangina's *mpanjaka* was put to death by the Merina army. According to oral traditions, apprised of the approach of Radama's army, some of the nobles and most of the population of northern Vohibato took refuge among the Tanala, whose chief was the blood brother of their king. Southern Vohibato also resisted, and many perished at the hands of the invaders. After the Merina had subdued the countryside, they let it be known that no further reprisals would be taken against either nobles or commoners of recalcitrant areas, and refugees returned home. Under the Merina administration Vohibato was split, parts of the north (including the village of Ivato) placed under central Lalangina, whose ruler was also awarded the administration of northern Lalangina. Most of Vohibato was, however, included in Arindrano and placed under the administration of the *mpanjaka* of Arindrano-Tsienimparihy. (see table 3.)

Though demoted from *andriana* to *hova* status and deprived of their right to rule, Vohibato's nobility was allowed to retain some of the privileges of their position. In contrast to Isandra and Arindrano-Tsienimparihy, where

Merina support greatly increased differential access to wealth and power between nobles and commoners, in Vohibato Merina rule seems merely to have maintained the prestige, ritual status, and some of the privileges of the nobles at the pre-Merina level. It is significant that the Merina did not attempt to destroy the native nobility in Vohibato. This is probably because the distinction between noble and commoner—based, as noted in chapter 3, on the distribution of illusory *hasina*—had become so basic to Merina society that Merina rulers were unable to conceive of a social unit lacking such a distinction in any part of their empire (cf. Condominas 1960, p. 54). Accordingly, some of the Vohibato nobles who would have ruled had not the Merina intervened became holders of fiefs, and were entitled to certain goods and services from the people living within their domains (cf. Dubois 1938, p. 214). However, my own observations of descendants of nobles led me to believe that differences in wealth and influence between nobles and senior commoners in Vohibato were insignificant. Today, members of Vohibato's noble descent group, the Zanakatara, living near Ivato control less productive land, have smaller estates, and live in less impressive houses than Ivato's senior commoners. The nobles I visited in the former capital of southern Vohibato also stood out from their commoner covillagers neither in wealth nor life-style.

However, the present day situation of the descendants of Betsileo nobles who submitted voluntarily to the Merina is much more favorable. In a hamlet in Arindrano-Tsienimparihy I visited an impressive compound housing two noble brothers and their descendants, spouses, and other dependents. Nearby were the tombs of their great-grandfather (MFF), a *mpanjaka* who had represented the Merina in Arindrano, and of his first cousin (MZS). The latter was the Arindrano-Tsienimparihy ruler who had offered voluntary submission to the Merina king and who had become his first representative in Arindrano. Together these brothers owned a large agricultural estate, twelve hectares of rice land which produced twenty metric tons annually, supporting their household and their hired agricultural workers. These men were enjoying the residue of a post-Merina *mpanjaka*'s estate that included between

TABLE 3

Incorporation of Formerly Autonomous Betsileo Polities into
Merina Administrative Units

Merina Administrative Division	*Betsileo Polities Incorporated Therein*
Isandra	Isandra[a]
Lalangina	central Lalangina[a], Mandranofotsy, northern Lalangina, northern Vohibato
Arindrano	Tsienimparihy[a], southern Vohibato, Homatrazo, Lalanindro, Manambolo

a. Ruling territorial division

3,000 and 5,000 slaves in around 1875 (Shaw 1877, p. 80). Thus, for certain Betsileo nobles voluntary submission to the Merina brought advantages that have been transmitted to their twentieth-century descendants.

Commoners

We have seen that in formerly nonagricultural areas especially, the Merina administration offered vertical mobility to the indigenous noble stratum. In the agricultural east, however, those who profited most were not nobles, but senior commoners, who were governors representing important commoner descent groups. The *mahamasinandriana* of Lalangina retained their administrative and judicial functions as governors under Merina rule, as did the heads of populous commoner descent groups of Isandra and Arindrano-Tsienimparihy. However, appointment as governor was also opened to other commoners. King Radama began a policy pursued by subsequent Merina sovereigns of encouraging groups of loyal supporters to settle in once rebellious areas.[6] From loyal Isandra and central Lalangina to resistant Vohibato came members of descent groups that had shown their loyalty to the Merina empire, for example, through military service. Not only did the Merina require the native population of Vohibato to find land for these colonists, they also appointed some of them governors.

In most cases, however, the senior commoner governors were drawn from descent groups long-established in an area that included several villages or hamlets. Members of a given descent group elected one of their own as governor. Despite the convention of election, the governor seems usually to have been the oldest living male of the senior generation of a senior descent branch. Branches of descent groups are still roughly ranked according to descent from oldest (particularly important), older, or younger brothers of the sibling group that first settled in the region. Some Betsileo commoner descent groups were sufficiently populous and dispersed to provide the governor in several areas. For example, different branches of the widespread Taray descent group provided many governors both in Lalangina and Vohibato. Under the governor's jurisdiction were other members of his own descent branch, junior branches, immigrants who had come as individuals rather than as colonists sent by the Merina, members of less populous descent groups whose ancestors had settled in the area at various times, and slaves, usually owned by the governor and other members of his senior descent branch. Disputes involving any of these people were submitted to the governor, though as a last resort they could be taken before a judge in an administrative center. Governors also administered tax collection, labor mobilization, and military conscription, and disseminated proclamations, edicts, and information about policy of the Merina state.

The economy of the southern highlands became more uniform under the

Merina, primarily because greater security allowed more attention to increasing rice production. Functions of senior commoner governors in different parts of the southern highlands had differed significantly prior to Merina rule. In Lalangina, for example, many of the governor's duties had been related to rice cultivation. In negotiating the conditions of her submission to the Merina king, the queen of central Lalangina informed him of several traditional rights of senior-commoner descent-group leaders in her polity: to receive first fruits of all harvests; to use, inherit, and distribute land; to divide estates; and to grant land to immigrants or other people in need of it. Furthermore, one of the most important functions of the senior-commoner leaders of Lalangina was to oversee the distribution of water for rice cultivation and to make sure that riverbanks were maintained against flood damage. Lalangina's governors also watched over a relatively sedentary population. Customarily when someone died, his relatives presented a basket to his governor; this was regarded by the Lalangina queen as a means of tallying deaths (Chapus and Ratsimba 1958, p. 647–48).

The privileged position of the nobles and senior commoner chiefs of preagricultural Arindrano-Tsienimparihy, on the other hand, rested on their participation in regional trade networks involving cattle, cocoons, raw silk goods, and slaves. The major product was silk cloth, woven into *lamba*, colorful mantles for the living and shrouds for the dead. Accounts of late nineteenth-century European missionaries describe the husbandry of silk worms in Tsienimparihy (Shaw 1876, p. 103). One of the functions of the senior commoner governors of Tsienimparihy, as reported by its *mpanjaka* in his submission to the Merina, was to collect silk from the people of his circumscription (Chapus and Ratsimba, 1958, p. 665 et seq.)

Thus, senior commoner chiefs, who had traditionally played major roles in the administration and economy of the southern highlands, were allowed to continue as important lower-level officials under the Merina. Although occasionally their ranks were infiltrated by colonies of Merina loyalists, Imerina allowed Betsileo senior commoners to retain many of their traditional privileges. Each year the people presented their senior commoner governor with first fruits of their harvests of corn, beans, and rice. Governors were honored at their funerals. In the south their subjects presented cattle, and a man's prestige was reflected in the number of cattle tails left on his tomb. In Lalangina stones were raised to mark the burial places of senior commoner governors.

The Rise of the Senior Commoners: A Case Analysis

Ambitious senior commoner governors could also profit from the plethora of opportunities available in the expanding economy and bureaucracy of their new rulers. In Vohibato, to whose noble descent group resistance to the northerners had brought relative disfavor, there are several examples of governors who increased their wealth and influence over other commoners, often rivaling and even surpassing descendants of native *mpanjaka*. Consider the Tranovondro descent group of the village of Ivato in agricultural northern Vohibato. Ivantans contend that their remote ancestors were Merina nobles who lived near Tananarive, and they tell of how their more recent ancestors used their claim of common descent with the Merina nobility to gain favors from the northerners.

According to their oral traditions, the Tranovondro settled in in the Ivato region in the eighth generation (P8) above Tuesdaysfather, the current head of the senior descent branch localized in Ivato. The P8 generation ancestor[7] is remembered as having fought against the Vazimba; who were quasi-mythical early highlands inhabitants. His son and grandson are supposed to have been governors in Vohibato and to have resided along with the *mpanjaka* of northern Vohibato atop the mountain that rises above Ivato's rice plain. By matching the events associated with their lives in oral tradition with Dubois's (1938) chronology, and by calculating an average of twenty-five years per generation, it seems likely that these three ancestors lived during the eighteenth century. The P6 generation ancestor, Hundredmaster, is also remembered as representing the Tranovondro when the Merina conquered Vohibato. The Tranovondro took refuge from Radama's army among the Tanala. Once it became apparent, after his conquest, that Radama planned no further reprisals against Vohibato's senior commoners, Hundredmaster declared his allegiance to Imerina and returned home. Radama appointed him as one of the governors of northern Vohibato.

In the time of Hundredmaster's father, when Vohibato was still independent, its *mpanjaka* had lived near Ivato. Later he had changed his capital to another fortified mountain to the east. Radama and subsequent Merina sovereigns recognized the region around the new capital as the fief of the Vohibato noble line. In Ivato and elsewhere in northern Vohibato, however, senior commoner governors were allowed to represent the Merina. Ivato's P6 generation ancestor, Hundredmaster, the oldest son of an oldest son, had two daughters but no sons. Customarily Betsileo marry people from villages other than their own, and women move to their husband's village. On the other hand, examination of genealogies shows that high status Betsileo have often been able to prevent the loss of their daughters and their grandchildren in two ways. Hundredmaster persuaded the husband of one of his daughters to accept a land grant near Ivato and the couple resided there. This woman is remembered as the founding ancestress of a small village about one-and-a-half kilometers west of Ivato. Furthermore, when Hundredmaster's oldest daughter married, he stipulated to her husband that her first son should return to Ivato to be raised by Hundredmaster as his heir and successor. It was this daughter's son, Peter, who was to sire Karl Fridaysfather, the most illustrious senior commoner governor of Ivato (see figure 2).

As governor during the last quarter of the nineteenth century, Karl Fridaysfather was the administrative subordinate of the Merina governor at Fianarantsoa. Karl used his position as a Merina official to enhance his own wealth and that of his relatives. By the end of his life he had accumulated a valuable estate in cattle and rice fields, which has maintained the wealth, reputation, and influence of his descendants and enabled one of them to become, during the 1960s, a high official of the Malagasy Republic. No doubt Karl was an intelligent and ambitious man, but his success must be understood in the context of local and regional changes, particularly a major modification in the regional economy supervised by the Merina empire—the abolition of export slavery.

By the 1820s the Merina state was enforcing an agreement with the English governor of Mauritius Island to stop the export of slaves from Madagascar. English support of the Merina army was given in return. Since the

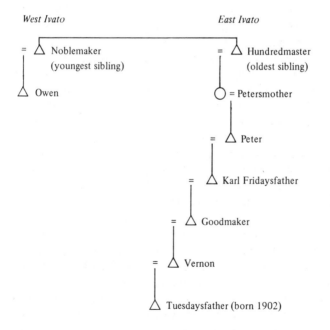

Fig. 2 Genealogy of Ivato's Senior Commoners

sources that had pumped slaves into the Merina exchange network—warfare, debt slavery, reduction to slavery for many crimes, and natural increase of the slave population—remained open, the Merina had to devise new uses for human chattels. Two of these were most significant to the Betsileo: the Merina established slave markets in the southern highlands, and slaves became agricultural laborers for wealthy commoners. Associated with the growth of a stratum of slave laborers during the nineteenth century was an increase in productivity of wet-rice agriculture in the southern highlands.

It was in this context that Karl's intelligence, ambition, and skill in manipulating Betsileo and Merina customs and institutions were rewarded. Karl was not the first, however, of the Tranovondro of Ivato to profit from an official position within the Merina administration and from a more productive agricultural economy based on widespread use of slave labor. Another Ivatan, Owen, had been senior commoner governor before him.

Contemporary Ivato is divided by a road and by separate tombs into two socially significant groups, an eastern and a western descent branch descended respectively from the oldest and the youngest of seven siblings on the sixth generation above Tuesdaysfather, the contemporary village leader (see figure 2). The oldest brother, Hundredmaster, ancestor of the eastern village, had no sons. It was he who stipulated that a grandson, Peter, should be his successor and eventual heir. The youngest brother, Noblemaker, the founder of the western village, however, did have sons. It was one of them, Owen, who in the next generation actually succeeded his uncle Hundredmaster as governor. Since he was the son of a youngest brother, Owen, although one generation above Peter, was actually his age peer.

The fact that Owen and Peter were age peers raised problems about seniority and about who should be governor. Owen's western branch ranked below eastern Ivato on the basis of seniority of descent, since Owen was the son of a youngest brother. On the other hand, he was one generation above Peter. Furthermore, Peter, though a member of the senior branch, was a nonagnate, a daughter's son. Patrilineal succession and generation prevailed over seniority of descent, and Owen became the first of the Tranovondro governors to derive substantial benefits from a position in the Merina administration. His life also partially overlapped with that of Peter's son, Karl Fridaysfather.

Again, conflicting principles of succession enabled the position of governor to revert to the eastern and senior branch under Karl. Owen's father had been polygynous, and Owen was the only son of his principal wife. Furthermore, although Owen adopted several of his half siblings and their children, he had no children of his own. The easterners could therefore argue for Karl as next head of the Tranovondro, since he represented the senior branch, was residing in his father's village as a member of his father's descent group, and since none of his female ancestors had been other than senior wives.

Because contemporary Ivatans recall more about Karl than Owen, he will be used to illustrate advantages associated with the status of senior commoner governor. As a fiscal agent of the Merina empire, the governor received a fraction of the taxes he collected; by Karl's time, taxes were paid in money. There were still other sources of wealth. When any Betsileo died, the administration claimed cattle from his estates; the governor had the right to a steer. The governor also judged disputes involving people in his circumscription, and litigants were expected to compensate him for his services. Indirect access to wealth, however, was perhaps as significant as these direct rewards. As one of a limited number of Merina representatives in the Betsileo countryside, the senior commoner governor had personal contact with higher officials whom he was in a position to influence. Various advantages therefore brought revenues to the senior commoner governor and gave Karl his start as an influential man. It was in the Merina economy, however, with its abundant investment possibilities, that Karl made most of his fortune. Cattle and money could be converted into slaves, and Karl's papers show that he owned at one time about 100 slaves, whom he set to work at rice cultivation. They dug drainage canals that converted marshes into productive rice fields. They built dams across rivers and streams and from them dug canals to irrigate rice fields. Areas once used as cattle pasture began to grow rice. As rice production increased, it fed the governor, his slaves, and other dependents, and left a surplus that Karl converted into more slaves or stored on the hoof in cattle.

Karl's increasing force of chattel laborers augmented rice production not only through the creation and maintenance of new fields, but also through intensification, the land was cultivated more carefully. Today, most Betsileo weed their growing crop twice; with slave labor there were three weedings. In addition to agriculture, Karl found other productive use for his slaves. They were guardians of his growing herd of cattle. Since an agricultural economy was encroaching on the local pasture land, Karl sent most of his cattle and their slave guardians to areas where it was warmer and grazing land was more plentiful, usually to the south. Some of his twentieth-century descendants still employ guardians, including descendants of Karl's slaves, to herd their cattle in pastures seventy-five kilometers south of Ivato.

So grew Karl's wealth and with it his regional reputation among Betsileo and among his Merina superiors. His growing prestige and his administrative position opened a new source of wealth: people began to adopt him. Anticipating his (or his descendants') inheritance of land, Karl acted as son and protector, arranging their funerals and handling their relations with their neighbors and with the Merina administration. Karl's descendants now farm several rice fields acquired through his adoption.

Like other senior commoner governors, Karl and Owen were agents of change in the local and regional ecosystems that included the population of the southern highlands. A tenfold increase in the area around Ivato devoted to rice cultivation occurred during the lifetimes of Owen and Karl. Moreover, their slaves created rice fields not only for Ivato, but also for several neighboring villages and hamlets. Some of these fields are now cultivated by the descendants of their slaves, while others are farmed by Owen's heirs and Karl's descendants.

The estate of Owen, who had no children, was distributed among his half siblings and their descendants. There has been less fragmentation of Karl's estate. His only son, Goodmaker, who died in 1928, succeeded his father as a figure of regional prominence, serving as a canton chief under the French. His descendants remember Karl as an astute man, but they also acknowledge that he profited from the advice of a French priest who lived as a Catholic missionary in Ivato in the last years of Karl's life. The priest warned Karl and his son Goodmaker that the French would soon defeat the Merina and incorporate Madagascar into their empire. They would, said the priest, abolish slavery in Madagascar. Heeding the priest's prognostications, Karl and Goodmaker sold many of their slaves during the 1890s. They reinvested in more rice fields and cattle. Karl also became a usurer. His account book shows that forty-one people, representing several villages and hamlets, owed him money in 1898, two years after French rule began. Ivato's western villagers—Owen's heirs—on the other hand, lost their slaves when the French abolished slavery in 1896.

The case of Karl's ascent is not isolated. Many senior commoner governors used their administrative positions to tap the riches of the Merina economy and to enhance their descent groups, especially their senior branches. When I first talked with people of Ivato, they told me that they were "sort of noble."[8] Though not members of Vohibato's noble descent group, they stipulate remote descent from the Merina nobility. More important, however, they were talking about their historic influence in their region. This influence grew inordinately under the Merina. It is no wonder that my principal informant Rakoto recalled the years under the Merina administrator at Fianarantsoa as a golden age when there was peace, cattle roamed pastures with little danger of robbery, and extensive rice fields supported the social and ceremonial life of Ivato as a regional center. It is also in this context that one should consider assertions of the contemporary Tranovondro about the nobles who ruled in Vohibato before the Merina conquest. Their remembrance of the *mpanjaka*s of Vohibato is neither fond nor respectful. Vohibato's nobles came there to rule, several Ivatans told me, because the P7 generation ancestor of the eastern village (Hundredmaster's father), combined with other senior commoners to depose the former *mpanjaka* and sought a new ruler.

The ideas of Ivatans about the relationship between nobles and senior commoners no doubt reflect a mixture of historical truth and modification following the rise of Vohibato's senior commoners under the Merina. The oral history of agricultural Lalangina, with its numerous commoner rebellions, ousters, and installations of new *mpanjaka*, certainly testifies to the importance of senior commoners in Vohibato's closest neighbor. Without exception, oral traditions, even those of nobles and their descendants, stress the authority of the senior commoners in pre-Merina political organization. Ivatans say that the *mpanjaka* ruled the people, while the senior commoner descent-group leaders ruled the land, and use of the *mahamasinadriana* of Lalangina to connect ruler to ancestors and the land has been discussed in chapter 3. A statement similar to the Ivatans' was made by the queen of Lalangina to the king of Imerina at the time of her submission and is inscribed in Merina oral tradition (Chapus and Ratsimba 1958, p. 647–48). Certainly in the contemporary economic status and life-styles of Vohibato nobles, there is no indication that they were superior in landed wealth to senior commoners. Although royal authority did grow in Lalangina during the eighteenth century, senior commoner chiefs never relinquished their decision-making, judicial, and managerial roles.

The accounts of Ivatans suggest an even more limited role for the *mpanjaka* in Vohibato. My informant Rakoto's analysis of politics before the Merina came may be astute. He claims that Vohibato's senior commoners installed and maintained a noble *mpanjaka* more or less as a figurehead. In fact, he said, it would have been as appropriate for his ancestors to kill a ruler who displeased them as to oust him, which they did more than once. Perhaps, in contrast to Lalangina, kingship in smaller Vohibato is best explained not by virtue of its regulatory or administrative functions but in terms of its symbolization of political organization beyond the level of the single descent group and its creation of a rallying point for offensive and defensive organization.

Thus, having created Betsileo ethnicity, the Merina also bounded and stabilized major horizontal divisions among them, the socioeconomic strata that possess a continued relevance to Betsileo life.

It is as true for the Betsileo as for the Merina described by Bloch (1977, p. 315) that the native (emic) representation of sociopolitical hierarchy does not correspond to an objective analysis of the actual distribution of wealth and power. Thus, as among the Merina, the Betsileo category of *andriana* encompasses a graded hierarchy similar to what we would expect to find in a chiefdom (Service 1971), in which the ritual status of *andriana* increases in minute increments. However, the persistence of a chiefdom ideology in a state-organized society certainly demands an explanation. As Bloch (1977) suggests in different terms for the Merina, and as is spelled out below, maintenance of a chiefdom ideology helps mask the reality of stratification and limits resistance to state rule. Just as few Merina *andriana*, or Betsileo nobles prior to conquest, ever ruled, only a few Betsileo *hova* ever served as Merina agents or were awarded fiefs by the Merina administration. Only in defining the terms of Betsileo annexation did the Merina king bring ritual and political status of Betsileo nobles together by reserving the term *andriana* for his Betsileo representatives and their children of full *andriana* parentage. However, even this distinction failed to survive the nineteenth century, as all Betsileo *andriana* were eventually termed *hova*.

An equally important contrast between the native representation of the status hierarchy and etic analysis is the lumping of all commoners under a single term, *olompotsy*. This masks, for the Betsileo as well as for the ethnographer who is not careful, the effective locus of wealth and power in the hands of senior commoners. It also obscures the kinds of distinctions among commoners that explain so much of the variation examined in subsequent chapters. Maintaining the terminological opposition of undifferentiated nobles (*andriana* or *hova*) to undifferentiated commoners (*olompotsy*) is one of many kinds of cultural manipulations that Betsileo senior commoners have been able to use to their own advantage.

The native view thus masks the facts that (1) senior commoners often have more wealth and power than all but a few nobles, and (2) the major contrasts in differential access to strategic resources lie within the commoner stratum and below, among slave descendants. The eventual demotion of Betsileo *andriana* to *hova* status should not be seen as just a Merina plot or simply as part of the conquerors' arrogance, since its effect was to place two social layers (Merina *andriana* and Betsileo and Merina *hova*), above the commoner group in the emic hierarchy. Betsileo could now view both Merina *andriana* and *hova* and Betsileo *hova* as their oppressors or as most privileged when, in reality (despite the overarching fact of Merina domination) most of their local-level agents and most of the Betsileo who profited from Merina rule were senior commoners. The emic hierarchy thus partially shielded these senior commoners from the envy and resentment of the less fortunate because they were culturally identified as *olompotsy*—outside and below the ritually privileged group—and because they belonged to descent groups that also included junior commoners. The fact of internal descent group ranking was also emically ignored. Subsequent chapters show many other ways in which senior commoners have used established cultural themes to reproduce their favored position.

Distinctions between strata were maintained by a preference for stratum endogamy and by rules that defined the prerogatives of offspring of mixed marriages and assigned them to the lower stratum. Descendants of an *andriana* and a *hova*, for example, belonged to the *hova* stratum; they could claim neither the title nor the prestige of an *andriana*; they could hold no fiefs, nor could they exhibit any of the traditional signs of *andriana* status, e.g., a beaded headdress, long waiting period prior to burial of a corpse, distinctive funerary mantles; they had no rights to political succession. They could, however, share equally in the inheritance of their *andriana* parent's material estate. The other major distinction, that between free person and slave, was also maintained, but much more vigorously. Merina law interdicted their intermarriage, and even today such unions are very rare. I observed only one among the rural Betsileo, involving a slave descendant who had been an officer in the French army. Ivatans say that his commoner wife married him because of his pension.

THE STIGMA OF SLAVERY

Although distinctions between descendants of slave and free have been discouraged officially by the French and the Malagasy government, powerful social sanctions still operate against intermarriage. The commoner who marries a slave loses the right to be buried in his family tomb, as do his descendants. His relations with his kin also suffer. Furthermore, although his descendants may inherit his moveable property, they may be barred from the estate, including the rice fields, of his descent group. They may not hold positions of authority within his descent group. Oral traditions mention slaves of the kings of Isandra, Lalangina, and Vohibato during the eighteenth century. Ownership of slaves appears, however, to have been limited to the *mpanjaka* and, conceivably, to the most influential of his senior commoner advisers. Only for Lalangina does oral history recall royal use of slave labor in hydraulic works connected with agriculture. Throughout the pre-Merina southern highlands kings and courts collected and disposed of prisoners of war, most of whom were destined to be exchanged for firearms and other European imports. In the nineteenth century, however, with the abolition of export slavery, senior commoners acquired large numbers of slaves, and, as was seen in Karl's case, used their labor to effect major economic changes.

Contemporary Betsileo notions about relations between free people and slaves reflect the experience of their nineteenth-century ancestors. Under Pax Merina, Betsileo no longer acquired most of their slaves through raiding. Karl and other Betsileo bought their slaves in the slave market at Fianarantsoa or, once domestic slavery was widespread, from other slave owners. Throughout the Merina empire the slave population grew through natural increase and through Merina imperial expansion. Slaves were allowed to marry, but spouses could be sold independently, and sale could separate mother and children. When married slaves belonged to people residing in different villages, children became property of the mother's owner.

Slaves worked in rice fields and on hydraulic works, tended livestock, farmed secondary crops, fetched firewood and fodder for cattle, cleaned house, and did work now done by all rural Betsileo. Slaves were assigned small plots to grow their rice and other subsistence crops. They could sell surpluses, buy cattle and other moveable property, and had the right to repurchase their freedom. Descendants of senior commoner governors say that their ancestors treated their slaves like their own children, and, indeed, there probably was a similarity to contemporary paternalism.[9] Rural Betsileo fathers command their adult sons and allocate their labor. Sons tolerate the relationship because it is customary, and since only on their father's death will they receive his most productive rice fields.

The bonds of dependence and the warmth of feeling between masters and slaves were tested when the French proclaimed the end of slavery in Madagascar. I have heard some senior commoners complain that the slaves of their ancestors packed their few possessions and left the day they heard about emancipation. Many slaves, attempting to escape from the stigma and the dependence associated with their former condition, did leave their masters, some moving to other parts of the Betsileo homeland, others migrating out of the highlands altogether, contributing substantially to Betsileo colonies established among the Bara and on the west coast. Many slaves, however, remained on or near the estates of their former masters, where they continued to farm the plots assigned to them as slaves. Though free, the former slaves remained poor; abolition meant no immediate access to greater wealth. Freed slaves stayed on in Ivato and in satellite hamlets, but the position of their descendants remains subordinate. Slaves and their descendants have been granted a legal right, which may be transmitted to their descendants, to use their estates. However, although they cannot be dispossessed, their land is legally part of the estate of the descendants of their former masters. Lacking heirs, a slave's plot reverts to the use of the commoners.

The stigma of slave origin continues to limit those who form the *andevo* ("slave") stratum of highlands society. Their access to the means of production is impeded: on the average, *andevo* cultivate rice fields only one-third the size of those of descendants of senior commoner governors. Their lifestyles and their access to education—today the best route to vertical mobility—suffer accordingly. In a thousand encounters in everyday life, they are reminded of their origin. They are expected to assist their superordinates in agricultural work, and although agricultural help is supposed to be mutual, slave descendants do not usually enjoy an equivalent return. At ceremonies, they still receive the legs of slaughtered cattle, traditionally the portion for slaves and jural minors. When free Ivatans dance, they never choose an *andevo* as partner. Betsileo observe a seating order reflecting relative seniority when they assemble in any room, with the seniormost male seated nearest the ancestral (northeastern) corner, progressively less senior men along the eastern wall, and junior males and slave descendants along the south wall. If there is no place left in the room, slave descendants may stand outside; they are generally on the fringes of any group. Women and children occupy the west wall, with seniority increasing from south to north. Houses are traditionally oriented north-south, with the door always to the southeast. As among Bara (Huntington 1974, p. 147–53) and Merina (Bloch 1971, p. 184) hierarchical distinctions are made obvious by seating ritual.

I observed a group of *andevo* and free Ivatans assembled to build Jules's house. Preparing for the lunch break, one of the slave descendants washed the leg of one of the free men, his age peer. Although the *andevo* was equally dirty, there was no reciprocity. In the work party itself, a free man interrupted a slave descendant to send him on an errand. A younger free man was equally near and could have been designated. In the communal meal in Jules's kitchen, two *andevo* shared a common plate while each free man had a plate of his own. "It is easy to identify an *andevo*," free Ivatans told me; "they lack a certain finesse; they don't know how to behave properly. Besides, they have ugly feet."

In 1967 Tuesdaysfather, senior man of Ivato, maintained an *andevo* couple as his dependents. He fed and clothed them and paid the man's taxes. The woman helped Tuesdaysfather's wife around the house, and the man did agricultural work under the supervision of Tuesdaysfather's son and grandson. Four households in Ivato are headed by *andevo*, but most descendants of its slaves live in satellite villages and hamlets. Many of them hire themselves out as agricultural workers for Ivatans, especially in rice field weeding.

Merina and Betsileo share a heritage of domestic slavery. The slave stratum of Imerina, however, formed a much larger percentage of the total population. Estimates of the contemporary percentage of *andevo* in the Merina population run as high as fifty percent (Bloch 1971, p. 35). I would estimate that about fifteen percent of the contemporary rural population of traditionally agricultural northern Vohibato is *andevo*. In less agricultural areas, the percentage is smaller, perhaps five percent for southern Vohibato and the rest of Arindrano.[10] Only one of several villages and hamlets around the two communities I studied in southern Vohibato was mentioned as having some *andevo* families. On the other hand, twenty-three of thirty-one settlements for which information was available in the canton that includes Ivato had slave descendants. Most *andevo* live among free Betsileo. Only one of these villages was inhabited exclusively by slave descendants.

THE COSTS AND BENEFITS OF MERINA RULE

A final evaluation of the costs and benefits of Merina rule depends on the Betsileo area and stratum being considered. The initial popular response to

Merina annexation in Arindrano, which had been the most politically fragmented area of the southern highlands, appears to have been favorable.
Callet's collection (Chapus and Ratsimba 1953–58) of Merina oral historical
documents reports that prior to Merina rule, the "kings" who headed the petty
states of Arindrano, in the more pastoral south, resembled brigand chiefs in
their relationships with their subject populations. Merina emissaries reported
that the traditional rulers of Arindrano could seize at will cattle from their
subjects' herds. Furthermore, it was customary for the ruler to lay first claim
to the moveable property of his subjects on their deaths (Chapus and Ratsimba 1958, pp. 661–63).[11] Merina rule brought a single set of laws to the
southern highlands and extended uniform administrative and enforcement
structure throughout the Betsileo province. There can be no doubt that the
major benefit of Merina rule was Pax Merina, the internal pacification of the
southern highlands. The presence of the Merina army also reduced the number of external attacks until, as the Merina state began to break down while
fighting provincial insurrections and the French toward the end of the nineteenth century, Bara raids again became a problem to the Betsileo.

In a less dangerous social environment, Betsileo could increase their
efforts in rice production, and their livestock as well as their persons were
safer. From the point of view of the slaves sold throughout the highlands,
their lot may have been somewhat better under Malagasy owners than on
European slave ships and plantations.

Merina rule incorporated the southern highlands within a massive regional exchange network, thus opening to the Betsileo the resources of ecologically diverse areas, and conveying their own produce and manufactures
to other parts of the empire. Markets, whose trade was regulated by an officially established system of standard weights and measures and a means of
currency (European coins cut into separate fractions and weighed to determine their value), sprang up throughout the southern highlands (cf. Chapus
and Ratsimba 1958, pp. 665–66). Merina merchants peddled the wares of
Imerina. Betsileo and Tanala exchanged goods in the marketplace; Betsileo
silk cloth reached other areas of Madagascar with a demand for silk but no
local supply, and rice and cattle moved where need or avarice dictated within
the Merina empire. Peace, of course, was necessary for trade to flourish, and
Merina markets were usually protected by military forces. Taxes on trade
items were collected by market officials.

The Merina state accorded to the Betsileo nobility a new and permanent
prestige as a regional entity. Those nobles who represented the Merina, like
senior commoner governors in resistant areas, profited in wealth and power.
For slaves, the Merina government offered little more than the right to own
moveable property and the possibility of buying back their freedom. For jun-

ior commoners, who formed the mass of the Betsileo population, came greater demands of a more elaborate state machinery and those who ran it.

All free Betsileo had to support the Merina army. Each of the three Betsileo districts was expected to provide an identical number of men (initially 1,000, later 1,500 in each category) as soldiers and as porters for the army's equipment and food supply. In the circumscription of each senior commoner governor, three men were requisitioned as permanent soldiers, until their retirement from the Merina army. To get these soldiers, Ivato's Tranovondro offered them ownership of some of the best rice land.

More onerous and pervasive, especially after 1850, were demands for fiscal support and government service, a problem exacerbated by the fact that military and bureaucratic officials of the Merina state were unpaid and thus more likely to resort to such nefarious schemes for raising money as accepting bribes and delaying permissions for funerals and ceremonies, granting them only for exhorbitant fees (cf. Shaw 1877, pp. 80, 81, 85; Besson n.d. p. 541). Although a tax on each slave burdened only the elite, a graduated household tax siphoned wealth from all strata of Betsileo society, including slaves. At the time of accession of the throne of the ninth *mpanjaka* of Isandra, a transvestite woman, each cultivator was required annually to deliver three measures of rice, each weighing approximately twenty-five kilograms, to the Isandra ruler. Half would move up the hierarchy; half would support the palace life-style and agents of the Isandra *mpanjaka*. For her superiors, the queen collected the produce of estates of people who died without heirs, and fees to consecrate adoptions and rejections of children. Small sums were ritually collected as *hasina* mark II for the Merina sovereign whenever official pronouncements were made to the people of Isandra and at determined times during the year. Circumcision fees and portions of benefits acquired in litigation were also passed into Merina coffers. Senior commoner governors aided in collecting and shared in these fiscal receipts (Dubois 1938, pp. 166–68). Not just in Isandra, but throughout the highlands, peasants bore burdens that became especially severe in the declining years of the Merina empire. Uncompensated government service also included labor in palace and tomb construction, and in agriculture for ruling nobles and fiefholders.

To the regular schedule of fiscal and labor demands were added special requisitions of money and men to finance and staff military suppression of rebellions in several areas of the empire in the last quarter of the nineteenth century. The Betsileo had to endure other forms of cruel and unusual punishment devised by their overloads. Consider, for example, the demands placed on the Betsileo peasantry during the funerary ceremonies for the eighth king of Isandra, who reigned between 1861 and his death on April 3, 1892 (based on a native observer's account translated by Sibree, 1898). Betsileo custom dictated that he be honored with a lavish funeral, but the Merina state had long since been involved in regulating Betsileo burial customs. It was necessary for Isandra to officially notify the queen of Imerina, who would designate his successor and specify the conduct of the funerary ceremonies. It took four months for the queen to acknowledge the Isandrans' message. The official mourning ceremonies began after the Merina governor at Fianarantsoa had received her letter on July 30, 1892. The ceremonies lasted four months. Thus, a total of eight-and-a-half months elapsed between the death of the king of Isandra and his interment on December 17, 1892.

Demands were made on the people of Isandra throughout this period, but they were less severe in the four months preceding the queen's letter. In the absence of official recognition, the king of Isandra could not be declared dead, nor could public mourning begin. Instead, while his court made public that the king was "chilly" and "nursing himself," the assembly at his capital, which included his administrative subordinates and representatives from all the villages of Isandra, took part in festivities characteristic of a Betsileo ceremony of thanksgiving or rejoicing. The burden of feeding this congregation fell on the near relatives of the deceased, who served cooked rice and beef from cattle slaughtered every few days. To be sure, those who came brought presents of money, white rice, and poultry to the royal widow. So large was the assembly that a daily market was held. One of the principal items sold was rum, remembered as having been imbibed in quantities (Sibree 1898, pp. 195–201).

The burden of support shifted from Isandra's nobles to its subjects upon receipt of the letter from the Merina queen. The royal message ordered that, appropriate to a Merina official of the king's status, cannons and muskets were to be fired. Prescriptions and taboos were proclaimed to apply throughout Isandra until the noble's burial; the people were required to dress as mourners and were forbidden from manufacturing cloth or pottery.

More onerous than honors and an enforced code of behavior were fiscal demands. Isandrans were to deliver 100 oxen for ceremonial slaughter; they were also to give 400 dollars or piasters (equivalent in value to 400 cattle). In addition to these contributions, which were designed to finance the funerary ceremonies, the Merina queen used the occasion to collect a piaster from each Isandran male aged ten or older. Isandrans experienced difficulty in meeting these demands (Sibree 1898, pp. 201–5). The price of their products fell as peasants sold rice, poultry, cattle, and smaller livestock to meet the queen's levy. Some people who were forced to borrow and pay interest—with their livestock and sometimes their rice fields at stake—suffered long-term impoverishment, as they lost access to their means of livelihood.

The funeral, which began at the Isandran capital, continued as the royal corpse was transported to three regional capitals before arriving at its burial place. In each town the ceremonies were repeated on a slightly smaller scale; at one, "the people there were called up to pay their share, whether of oxen or money, and there was no end of beating and tying up before all was collected" (Sibree 1898, p. 205). The people of Isandra were clearly not totally mystified by the *hasina* of the Merina queen or her defunct representative.

Impositions did not end when the corpse reached Isandra's royal cemetery, a cave high on a sheer cliff. Isandrans gave their labor for two-and-a-half months to construct a ladder out of rope and wood necessary to reach and deposit the body in the place of interment. Even as they engaged in this work, the collection of money and cattle continued at the large village nearby. A final ceremonial slaughter of cattle following burial ended the funeral (Sibree 1898, pp. 206–8).

FRENCH COLONIAL RULE

Trends seen in the evolution of political organization in Lalangina during the eighteenth century therefore continued, became more pronounced, and became generally characteristic of the southern highlands under Merina rule. Merina control left an obvious imprint on contemporary Betsileo social organization. It was during the nineteenth century that the socioeconomic strata important in contemporary Betsileo behavior and ideology were formed. It was in the nineteenth century that Betsileo became conscious of themselves as an ethnic entity. It was under the administration of the northerners that many towns and regional centers developed. It was under the Merina that a sedentary cultural adaptation based on wet-rice cultivation began to spread rapidly outside the agricultural east.

The government officials of independent Lalangina had begun to intervene in what hitherto had been affairs regulated by principles of kinship and descent. The Merina generalized state intervention to all of the southern highlands. Adoption, inheritance, disinheritance, circumcision, and ceremonials became matters of concern to the state. The administration that succeeded the Merina in Madagascar, that of the French, was even stronger, and continued the pattern of governmental intervention in peasant life, often with a similar lack of concern about real benefits of national and international needs and decisions to peasants. Yet, the French also relied on the administrative structure of their Merina predecessors. Ethnic units such as the Betsileo that had been created by the Merina were frozen into the ethnic groups of French colonial Madagascar. Better armed and trained than the Merina, and able, by virtue of a fleet, to conquer from outside as well as from within, the French eventually subdued those areas of Madagascar that had successfully resisted the Merina.

Many trends that originated in the pre-Merina polities of the southern highlands and that were accelerated under Merina rule continued to develop under the French. A series of disputes between French and Merina, mostly between 1883 and 1885, culminated in partial Merina submission and a French resident general and military escort in Tananarive in 1885. Following the Merina government's rejection in 1894 of an ultimatum to surrender to France as a protectorate, an imperial French force of 4,000—its numbers reduced by disease and malnutrition—eventually reached and quickly captured Tananarive in 1895. The Merina queen's surrender ended the independence of a government that had been internationally recognized for more than half a century. During the first year of French rule Madagascar was a protectorate; French administration was indirect and depended on maintaining government structures created by the Merina. However, responding to pressure by business interests, prospective settlers, and French Catholics, all of whom wanted Madagascar's treaties with other nations abrogated, and following a series of antiforeign rebellions, France took possession of Madagascar as a colony in 1896 (Thompson and Adloff 1965, pp. 10–11). General Gallieni, later to become the first of a series of governors-general of Madagascar, was appointed the island's civil and military commander, a job he held for nine years.

Thompson and Adloff (1965, pp. 19–20) discuss the main tactics employed by Gallieni in bringing the first total national unity to Madagascar. His task was made somewhat easier by the common cultural and linguistic framework based on the Proto-Malagasy heritage, island-wide diffusion, and the Merina empire's previous unifying accomplishments. The ethnic diversity on which tribalism rested in many other French colonies was much less developed in Madagascar. Gallieni's official policy for dealing with Malagasy ethnic diversity was to employ a *politique des races*, using the native leaders of each ethnic group to bring that group within the French administration. He sought an end to Merina control over the island's political economy. He wanted to eradicate what he saw as feudal remnants of the Merina state, along with slavery, royalty, and the intricate status distinctions that characterized Merina society. When I asked Betsileo to assess the nature of French rule, several of them singled out "liberty, equality, and fraternity." On the basis of my observations in the late 1960s I would suspect that the French often treated Malagasy as inferiors. However, informants in Ivato were particularly disturbed not by the irony of the way Malagasy were treated by French, but by the abolition of slavery and the French demand, instituted under Gallieni, that the Malagasy forget about distinctions of stratum and status among themselves. As subsequent chapters demonstrate, however, distinctions related to historic ranking remain obvious features of contemporary Betsileo life, particularly in Ivato.

Despite Gallieni's professed *politique des races*, and the early assault on

the privileged position of the Merina, the general borrowed Merina structures—an established territorial administrative hierarchy and the *fokonolona*
or village councils that functioned as local governing bodies in central Imerina—in creating the French colonial government. Since elective politics
were virtually absent from Madagascar until the end of World War II, for
most of the twentieth century, in the minds of Betsileo and other rural Malagasy, government has meant appointed administrative officials. Governmental decisions and requirements have been communicated from the central authority in Tananarive through a hierarchical structure employed originally in
Betsileo and Merina state organization and modified by successive French
governors-general, and later by the independent Malagasy government. Hierarchical levels and their labels have changed, with provinces replacing regions, districts yielding to subprefectures, and the number of specific units at
each level contracting and expanding.

Modifications in local government have affected some parts of the island
more than others. General Gallieni was impressed with the village councils
of the Merina countryside. These *fokonolona* (cf. Condominas 1960) have
changed through Merina history and are not indigenous pan-Malagasy institutions. Betsileo, for example, consider the *fokonolona* a Merina-French import. In old Imerina (Bloch 1971, p. 5) residents of the same village and
hence participants in village councils were members of a localized kin group
interlinked by descent, marriage, agricultural cooperation, and burial rights
in a common tomb. However, today's Betsileo *fokonolona* lacks the historic
depth of the Merina institution. Over the past two centuries the Betsileo
settlement pattern has alternated between agglomeration and dispersal. With
Pax Merina Betsileo gradually abandoned fortified hilltop settlements for
hamlets in valleys near their rice fields. French colonial rule then forced
people back together; an edict of 1913 forced hamlet residents together in
central villages to facilitate administration. Thus, as will be seen in chapter
5, the typical Betsileo heartland village, unlike its Merina counterpart, includes members of multiple kin groups, and its village council or *fokonolona*
must mediate the interests of unrelated people.

In Gallieni's scheme, and even in the 1960s, village councils worked in
association with village chiefs, chosen by the notables (*rayamandreny*, literally "fathers and mothers") who composed the village council. The village
chief was to communicate information and requisitions—e.g., for forced labor and, in wartime, military service and compulsory sale of certain agricultural products—to the village council for discussion and action. However,
one of the main jobs of the village chief was to collect taxes, from which he
received a percentage. One hierarchical level intervened between village and
canton chiefs, the quarter chief, who was appointed after nomination by several village councils in a region. Among the Betsileo the quarter chief seems

to have been little more than a tax collector, entitled to a share of his receipts, and unpopular except among his own covillagers. Canton chiefs, to whom village and quarter chiefs reported, were Malagasy civil servants. Among the Betsileo, descendants of *mahamasinandriana* and senior commoner governors were often appointed as canton chiefs by early French administrators. Traditionally, however, canton chiefs were shifted from station to station. By the end of the colonial period, despite attempts by Gallieni and a few of his successors to equalize access to education and resources, Merina predominated among canton chiefs as in the civil service generally.

French colonial rule brought a variety of experiences to Malagasy in different parts of the island. The east coast, for example, witnessed an influx of settlers, particularly French colonials from Reunion Island. These predominantly lower-class, poorly educated colonists gained access to native lands and cheap labor and incurred the hostility of coastal populations, who, along with dissident Merina, played a prominent role in the large-scale anticolonial rebellion of 1947. Particularly in the highlands and on the east coast, Malagasy suffered through the revolt's bloody repression. The events of 1947 were responsible, directly or indirectly, for the deaths of between 11,000 and 90,000 people (Thompson and Adloff 1965, p. 56).

The psychological effects of French conquest on the Merina were pronounced, much more so than for the Betsileo, who merely saw one set of foreign rulers replaced by another. The Merina elite—*andriana* and *hova*—never adjusted to the quick fall of an empire that for more than half a century had been recognized internationally as the government of Madagascar. Yet the legacy of the past ensured continued Merina prominence under French rule, despite several attempts to quell Merina influence and to improve the relative positions of other ethnic groups vis-à-vis the Merina.

Contemporary Malagasy still talk in terms of a contrast between highlanders and coastal populations, essentially a contrast between Merina and all other Malagasy. More than any other group the Betsileo mediate the highlands-coast opposition. Cultural, linguistic, and economic similarities previously noted between Betsileo and Merina, their geographic proximity, early incorporation of the Betsileo within the Merina empire, and Betsileo participation in the Merina administration are some of the reasons why Merina and French alike have granted to the Betsileo a prestige second only to the Merina among Malagasy ethnic groups. The de facto second-most-favored status of the Betsileo is also revealed in their educational and professional advancement, particularly within the civil service.

Although always viewed as the most "evolved" of the Malagasy, the Merina experienced a series of ups and downs in their fortunes under French colonial rule. In the decade after annexation General Gallieni, following instructions from France and his own inclinations, took several steps toward equalizing the relative positions of Merina and coastal populations. The abolition of slavery, pacification of the entire island, inauguration of a road system, and the establishment of schools in coastal towns were some of Gallieni's measures designed to balance Tananarive's inordinate influence as political, educational, and cultural center. With the end of his stewardship in 1905, however, and continuing through the repression of the rebellion of 1947, Merina fortunes were on the rise. Economy measures by Gallieni's successors led to the closing of coastal schools and reinforced Tananarive's role as the colonial capital (Thompson and Adloff 1965, 20–21). Only in Tananarive, or outside Madagascar, could Malagasy receive training in teaching, medicine, and other civil service occupations. More than coastal populations, who were now effectively deprived of ready access to educational and professional opportunities, Betsileo shared in the advantages that accrued to highlanders. Our sponsor in Ivato, for example, whose own father had served as canton chief under the French, received medical training first in Tananarive, later in France. Highlanders, particularly Merina, enjoyed favored access to minor administrative and civil service positions in the French colonial government. French pacification promoted migration and allowed Merina business people to renew and extend commercial activity throughout the island, though they had to compete with a few large French companies, colonial entrepreneurs, and merchants from India and China.

The combination of favored educational, professional, and commercial opportunities, however, did not end the resentment of the descendants of Merina free men and women against their European rulers. Merina intellectuals, young dissidents, and other nationalists were implicated in several uprisings following French conquest, most significantly in the major rebellion of 1947. Two out of the three earliest Malagasy representatives elected to the French National Assembly were Merina. All three, and the Mouvement Dèmocratique de la Rènovation Malgache (MDRM) political party that they headed, were proponents of Malagasy independence at a much earlier date than their West African counterparts. These deputies and other members of the MDRM eventually were tried for organizing and inciting the 1947 revolt. Although the native reaction to foreign influence was most violent in eastern Madagascar, particularly against Reunionese settlers on the coast, the rebellion had considerable Merina guidance and support (cf. Thompson and Adloff 1965, pp. 43–69).

French suppression of the 1947 rebellion, which Bloch (1971, p. 29) sees as possibly "the world's most bloody colonial repression," was followed by another period of decline in Merina influence, one that continued through the early years of independence, into my fieldwork period, and that has only recently ended. In 1956, following the French parliament's passage of a liberal *loi cadre* which was designed to prepare French colonies for eventual

independence and which was to orient French colonial policy both in Madagascar and West Africa, the colonial government of Madagascar was reorga-
nized. Decentralization was one of the law's provisions. Provincial powers
initially established following a Free French conference at Brazzaville in
1946 were strengthened at the expense of Tananarive, again undercutting the
favored position of the Merina (Thompson and Adloff 1965, pp. 82–83).
This provincial structure had been essentially retained in the government
headed by representatives of "coastal" populations that ruled the Malagasy
Republic during my fieldwork there in 1966–67. However, a resurgence of
Merina influence followed the government overthrow of 1972.

Bloch (1971) has documented many changes experienced by the Merina
during the past century, particularly the complexity of the Merina reaction to
European cultural influences and French colonial rule. Since some of his
observations may be modified to apply to the Betsileo, they may be summarized. To a much greater degree than the Betsileo, the Merina accurately view
themselves as a people experiencing rapid social and cultural change. According to Bloch (1971, pp. 8–9) the Merina see themselves as having to
choose in their every action between two totally different sets of cultural
guidelines, the Malagasy way (*fomba gasy*) and the European way (*fomba
vazaha*). Some of the main oppositions that differentiate these contrasting
cultural principles are listed in figure 3. Generally the terms in the left-hand
column are positively valued; those in the right-hand column are aspects of
the change caused by European influence that the Merina see as having se-

Positively Valued	Negatively Valued
traditional-ancestral	modern-foreign
highlands	coasts
conquerors	conquered
free	slave
Protestant (London Missionary Society)	Catholic (Jesuits)
Christian	*barbare*
British	French
A.K.F.M.	Partie Sociale Democratique
tanindrazana (ancestral homeland)	*voanjo* (emigrant colonists)

Fig. 3 Prominent Contemporary Oppositions in Merina Thought
(based on Bloch 1971, pp. 14-36)

duced them away from the good life of the ancestors (Bloch 1971, p. 33). These oppositions have developed historically in the context of the rise and fall of the Merina empire.

Particularly important is the inclusion of Protestantism—an import—in the traditionalist left-hand column. Representatives of the London Missionary Society (LMS) arrived in Imerina in 1820, were welcomed at the court of King Radama, and helped introduce the roman alphabet, used to inscribe and transmit Merina law codes. Protestantism, which the Merina came to associate with the British, rapidly spread among the free Merina population, arrested only by a thirty-two-year period of reaction against foreign influence and the persecution of foreign and native Christians under Queen Ranavalona I (1827–61). During the 1860s the new Merina queen became a Protestant and Protestantism became the official Merina religion. The martyrdom of Malagasy Christians under Ranavalona I, the preponderance of Merina among Protestant pastors (compared to a largely European Roman Catholic clergy), and the association of Protestantism with the Merina empire are some of the main reasons why contemporary Merina link this variant of a foreign religion with their own traditional past.

Several other dimensions of the traditional-modern contrast are associated with the historic role of Protestantism. Merina in particular, Betsileo to a lesser extent, and Bara (cf. Huntington 1974, p. 53) apparently not at all, draw the contrast between Christian and *barbare* ("pagan," "wild," "uncivilized"). For the Merina, the term *barbare* conjurs up an older set of religious beliefs and practices than the Protestantism of the British or the Catholicism of the French. It brings to mind the pre-Christian days of the early Merina state, when the national religion focused on efficacious idols and on the sacred forces of nature and the established social order. Despite the association of Protestantism with the Merina state, most of the rebellions against Christian influence or colonial rule have employed the Christian-*barbare* opposition, using pre-LMS sacred symbols in reacting to the pervasive effects of the foreigners' religion. Charms and wizardry, for example, provided ideological support for many of the Malagasy who took part in the 1947 rebellion.

Except for the extreme circumstance of outright rebellion, in which the opposition of British Protestantism to French Catholicism has been converted into that of Malagasy ancestral religion versus foreign Christianity, the Merina have been able to use religion to express their hostility toward French conquest and rule with reference to the historic association of Protestantism with Britain and with Merina imperial expansion. Many of the other oppositions listed in figure 3 are linked to the Protestant-Catholic contrast. Thus because of Protestantism's early acceptance by Merina *andriana* and *hova*, Catholicism found a readier audience among the descendants of the slaves of Imerina and among coastal populations, particularly after conquest and abolition. Here again, the Betsileo are intermediate. The association of Catholicism and slave ancestry is much weaker among Betsileo than Merina, and both religions enjoy considerable support among descendants of free Betsileo. Ivato's residents, for example, are Catholic, while the two Mahazony (southern Vohibato) villages I studied include both Protestants and Catholics. Lacking the long head start that British Protestantism enjoyed in Imerina, the several Protestant denominations now represented among the Betsileo have competed for adherents jointly with Catholicism. Furthermore, like others who had been conquered or annexed by the Merina, those Betsileo who became Roman Catholics were in one sense choosing Christianity and modernity and in another rejecting the Protestantism of their Merina overlords.

Following Malagasy independence, the Protestant-Catholic opposition ramified into the politics of the Malagasy Republic. Outside the highlands, particularly outside of Imerina, the Partie Sociale Democratique (PSD) enjoyed widespread support and controlled the government until 1972. However, Merina support went to the Ankotonny Kongreiny Fahaleovantenan Madagasikara (AKFM). With many Protestant ministers among its leaders, this opposition party stood ideologically to the left of the PSD in international politics. Again Betsileo mediated this dichotomy. They were much less hostile to the government party than the Merina and less hostile to the opposition party than the populations of the coasts, south, and southwest.

For several reasons, these and other dimensions of the traditional-modern contrast are not drawn as sharply among the Betsileo as among the Merina. For the Betsileo, French conquest did not mean the end of independence and political power as it did for many *andriana* and *hova* of Imerina; Betsileo had been conquered long before. Although the French were more culturally different than the Merina from the Betsileo, they allowed some Betsileo to occupy lower-level administrative positions just as the Merina had done. By 1904 the French had pacified the entire island much more effectively than their predecessors. The end of internal warfare and slave raiding, along with the construction of a road network, hitherto neglected by a Merina state fearing attack from the coasts, promoted travel and migration on a large scale. Another of the oppositions mentioned by Bloch for the Merina and listed in figure 3 can be traced to pacification by the French. Through twentieth-century emigration many contemporary Merina live as colonists (*voanjo*) away from their ancestral homeland (*tanindrazana*). Bloch's study focuses on the Merina conceptualization of an ancestral homeland and community organized through kinship and marriage—and particularly on the expectation that one will be buried in a tomb located in the homeland—in providing enduring social identity through connection with ancestral times and customs for modern day Merina whose everyday lives are spent among non-kin in newly settled areas.

For the Betsileo the effects of pacification on emigration were similar but not identical. The shift from pastoralism and demographic mobility toward agriculture and sedentism, which Pax Merina previously had favored, accelerated under French rule. Now secure against attacks, irrigation networks increasingly supported permanent populations of rice cultivators in the Betsileo south and west. Colonies of former slaves and junior commoners left the status discrimination and more crowded estates of the agricultural east to found new settlements in Isandra and Arindrano, and Betsileo migrants also transplanted their techniques of rice cultivation to broad alluvial valleys of the west coast. Though mindful of their heartland origins, Betsileo emigrants, unlike most of the Merina that Bloch (1971) describes, relinquished their burial rights in the land of the ancestors for new tombs in the western and southern settlements they colonized. Their social ties with home and with other migrants were remembered not through common burial rights as in Imerina but through recollection of village of origin and common membership in the *foko*, or geographically dispersed named descent groups (to be discussed more fully in chapters 5 and 6.) However, like Merina emigrants, unrelated families who had settled the same areas were brought together after 1913 in administrative villages.

Economic changes also followed the abolition of domestic slavery, especially in the agricultural east. Although many of the freed slaves stayed on, farming small plots from the estates of their former masters, many others left. The wealthiest Ivatans, like other Betsileo whose ancestors owned slaves, continue to rely on the labor—now compensated in cash—of slave descendants. However, the freeing of the slaves shrank the labor pool available for village agriculture, and former slave owners and their descendants were forced to work harder in their own rice fields. If commoners now work harder than previously, this may help explain Haile's (1899) curious comments about the customarily low labor input of Betsileo women in agriculture, an assertion that contrasts sharply with my own observation that Betsileo women contribute at least one-third of agricultural labor prior to food processing (see chapter 5). The overall effects of abolition on labor requirements of Betsileo agriculture remain in doubt, however, because French rule also finally ended such former time- and labor-consuming demands as residence in hilltop settlements above rice fields and the need to defend fields, crops, and hydraulic networks against marauders. Causes and effects of contemporary labor shortages among the Betsileo are examined more fully in chapter 8.

As noted previously, geographic proximity, sedentism, familiarity with state organization, and cultural similarities permitted Betsileo, more than most Malagasy, to share with the Merina many of the more beneficial concomitants of French colonialism. In contrast to the east coast, little of the Betsileo heartland was appropriated for cash-cropping or for other commercial use by the foreigners. French colonialism simply allowed Betsileo to move further along a continuum they had been traversing for two centuries previously toward their contemporary life as small-scale rural peasants.

Even as peasants, however, the Betsileo have come to value education, and their access to schools staffed by mission and government personnel has been second only to the Merina. Even in the most remote villages at least a few people have a rudimentary knowledge of French, and literacy (in Malagasy) is higher than among the peasantry of an economically booming Brazil, perhaps even higher than among elementary school children in contemporary American urban ghettoes. Betsileo have followed the Merina into such professions as teaching, government service, and medicine, and are heavily represented in the Malagasy civil service. Other benefits of French rule included ready access to physicians, nurses, midwives, hospitals, and European medicines. The eradication of malaria and other endemic diseases under the French is one of the main reasons why population growth rates of Betsileo and Merina are the highest in Madagascar. When Madagascar received its independence in 1960, even remote Betsileo villages were linked to market towns and administrative centers through a well-maintained road system and the availability of relatively inexpensive transportation by *taxis-brousse* ("bush taxis"), passenger vans that link town and country. In virtually every village at least one person has made the trip via *taxi-brousse* to Tananarive, traveling a paved highway that extends to the southern boundary of the Betsileo homeland.

When enumerating the benefits of foreign contact and French rule, Betsileo mention roads, transportation, and medicine. They also single out plants, animals, and technology. The tropical highland climate permits cultivation of peaches, plums, avocados, and coffee along with tropical fruits. Several European vegetables now add variety to the ancestral diet of rice, taro, occasional beef and fowl, and native greens and legumes. European fowls and domesticated animals are found in every village along with older varieties. A program of reforestation, mainly with eucalyptus trees, has eased erosion in the highlands.

The French presence affected the technology of cultivation. Pacification, as noted, protected fields and irrigation systems, and concrete and cement were used in the dams and canals—many built with subsidies granted by the colonial administration or through forced labor—that made an agricultural economy increasingly characteristic of the Betsileo south and west. Plows, harrows, and ox carts supplemented human agricultural labor. Their diffusion to the Betsileo peasantry has been gradual; they have filtered down the previously established hierarchy of wealth and power and have spread from administrative and market centers. The road system helped peasants take their produce to market. The contemporary government of the Malagasy

Republic continues this technological change, making more recent agricultural tools, chemical fertilizers, and new varieties of rice and other crops available. Most of these changes have proceeded farther in Imerina than among the Betsileo, and, as subsequent chapters show, their spread among the Betsileo has been gradual and is related to historic patterns of differential access to strategic resources.

Like Merina rule, the slightly shorter period of French colonialism brought both advantages and disadvantages to the Betsileo. Again, pacification—relative freedom from the fear of attack—was the major advantage, with ramifications for migration, settlement pattern, social organization, and economy. Materially and psychologically, Betsileo seem to have suffered less under the French than either the Merina, who lost control of an empire and suffered ups and downs in their access to positions of power and influence, or the coastal populations who faced indignities and deprivations as French-speaking settlers gained access to ancestral lands and control over cheap native labor. Betsileo country lacks the rainy tropical climate that has favored cash-cropping of robusta coffee, sugar, vanilla, pepper, and perfume essences on either or both northwest and east coasts (cf. Hance 1957). Nor did Betsileo country include any major mining center. An assessment of the impact of European contact and colonialism on any of these other areas would inevitably pay more attention to detrimental effects, in reality and in native perception, than has this analysis of the Betsileo. Conversations with informants convinced me that Betsileo saw French annexation in terms of one set of conquerors replacing another rather than as an unprecedented event or radical change.

This can be confirmed by considering how Betsileo interpret some of the cultural oppositions listed in figure 3. For the Betsileo many of the negatively-valued poles of these contrasts are associated as strongly with the Merina as with the French. Betsileo, for example, view the Merina as arbiters of modern-foreign influences in opposition to the traditional practices of their own ancestors. As noted, despite ups and downs under colonialism, Merina participation in commerce, politics, administration, education, and professions has been disproportionate among Malagasy ethnic groups, and the majority of Betsileo are accustomed to dealing as subordinates with Merina. As Bloch (1971, p. 33) notes, westernized Malagasy and Europeans alike are feared by Merina peasants as vampires and heart-thieves. Betsileo generalize this fantasy, used to explain differential access to wealth, power, and the status symbols of a modern life-style, to those successful mobile Merina they most typically encounter, and from them to the entire Merina population.

However, Betsileo actually see themselves as mediating many of the oppositions between Merina and other Malagasy. They recognize their similarities to both groups due to geographic, economic, linguistic, and cultural proximity. But they also see themselves linked through physical characteristics (more African and fewer Asiatic phenotypes), language, and certain customs to populations of the east coast, such as the Taimoro, and of the west and south, principally the Bara. The religious oppositions so important in Merina culture are also much less sharply drawn for the Betsileo, who include Protestants, Catholics, and "pagans." As will be seen in chapter 7, even professed Christian Betsileo see no inconsistency in blending Christian and ancestral beliefs and practices. The southern Betsileo I studied, who seem similar in certain ways to the Merina described by Bloch and in others to the northern Bara described by Huntington (1974), provide evidence for their view of themselves as intermediate.

Contemporary Betsileo peasants interpret their history as a struggle to maintain their social, economic, and ceremonial life and ancestral customs in the face of warfare, conquest, pacification, and government demands. War, shifting political boundaries, and submission to new authority figures have characterized Betsileo life for at least three centuries. Merina and French alike are remembered as conquerors, and their rules are seen as offering both benefits and burdens. For some Betsileo—Ivatans, for example—foreign rule meant increased access to wealth and power. For others, burdens overshadowed advantages. Taxation, forced labor, military conscription, all familiar to the Betsileo at the time of French conquest, continued under the French. Under General Gallieni able-bodied Malagasy men between the ages of sixteen and sixty were required to give between thirty and fifty days free labor. This program served to spread roads and to build a railroad between Tananarive and Tamatave, Madagascar's major port, located in what came to be the main export region under the French, the east coast. Increased cash cropping and the possibility of wage work, such as on the transportation network after the forced labor requirement had been met, moved the Malagasy further toward a cash economy and provided the wherewithal for their taxation. A French law of 1900 demanded that colonies be generally self-supporting (cf. Thompson and Adloff 1965, pp. 15–20). Another, apparently less popular, forced labor program was used in constructing Madagascar's second railroad between Fianarantsoa and Manakara on the southeast coast in the 1920s and 1930s. One Ivatan recalled with distaste his military-camp-like life-style on the coast as a participant in this program (cf. Thompson and Adloff 1965, pp. 25–26).

Burdens intensified in wartime. During both World Wars Madagascar provided troops, laborers, money, foodstuffs, and minerals for the French war effort. About 46,000 Malagasy served in Europe during World War I, 41,000 of them as combat troops. Highlanders seem to have predominated among the soldiers (Thompson and Adloff 1965, p. 21). Prior to France's fall in World War II, 15,000 Malagasy troops embarked for Europe, including my field assistant and many other Betsileo. Another 28,000 were requisitioned once the Free French gained control of Madagascar in 1943. The Vichy administration of Madagascar was brief, ended by a British blockade and invasion by British and Zulu troops. During the Vichy period and British blockade, Madagascar had reverted to a subsistence economy and rationed goods had been reserved for Europeans.

Malagasy appear to have suffered most, however, under the Free French. Forced labor was used to repair the means of transportation and communication; Malagasy were pressured to increase export crop and mineral production and to contribute 150 million francs to the war effort (Thompson and Adloff 1965, pp. 34–41). Fostering most resentment was the creation of an Office du Riz, which forced peasants to sell their entire rice crop at a low price, then to repurchase their subsistence needs at a much more costly figure. Thompson and Adloff see resentment toward the Office du Riz, and the dietary deprivation for Malagasy, coupled with the black-market profiteering by some Europeans that it led to, as one of the main causes of the rebellion of 1947.

Their participation on behalf of the Free French in World War II therefore created the most distress for most Malagasy, including the Betsileo, whose sedentary, relatively dense, and relatively accessible population meant vulnerability to government demands. However, the Betsileo, particularly in the south, were able to escape most of the ravages of the 1947 rebellion and its repression, including a series of reprisals—executions, imprisonment, and more forced labor—that ensued. Some Betsileo went on to fight in other French colonial wars, and all Betsileo families continued to pay a variety of taxes to the colonial government and thereafter to the Malagasy Republic. As in Merina times, demands for taxes entered several areas of traditional social, economic, and ceremonial life. Taxes were levied according to units of rice land, by head of cattle, and per capita for every adult able-bodied male. In 1967 the government was still receiving a tax on each steer slaughtered for a funeral or ceremonial, and fees were required to gain governmental authorization to hold certain festivities. Many of the ways in which government demands continue to impinge on the rural Betsileo will be discussed in subsequent chapters. They are part of a three-century legacy of state organization and of differential access to wealth, power, and other strategic resources that continues to shape Betsileo life.

Certain trends that can be traced to the independent southern highland polities of the eighteenth century were intensified by Merina and by French rule. State demands and governmental intervention in social, economic, and ceremonial life of Betsileo peasants increased under the Merina and the French, as Betsileo were conscripted for military service and forced labor, and were required to pay diverse taxes and fees in order to observe their traditional customs. A system of ranking and socioeconomic stratification that continues to influence differential access to strategic resources was fully elaborated under Merina rule. Although some Betsileo nobles, particularly in the south and west, enjoyed enhanced wealth and power as Merina agents, the ritual status of the Betsileo nobility was gradually degraded to the level of Merina commoners. This helped mask actual socioeconomic contrasts within the commoner stratum of the emic hierarchy. As had been the case in pre-Merina polities, senior commoners continued to play important roles in lower-level administrative activities under the Merina and French.

Following the abolition of external slave-trading by the Merina, the domestic slave population grew among the Betsileo, though to a lesser degree than in Imerina. Concentrated under the ownership of the nobles and senior commoners who served as Merina agents, slave labor transformed Betsileo agriculture through drainage of marshy areas, irrigation works, and a greater labor input in ordinary cultivation. Pacification by the Merina, but even more notably by the French, also promoted the spread and augmented productivity of an agricultural economy.

A series of developments that had begun with the growth of Betsileo state organization therefore continued under Merina and French. More productive agriculture supported denser and increasingly sedentary populations; inversely, the pastoral component of the economy diminished in importance. More powerful state rule meant that some Betsileo tremendously increased their favored access to strategic resources, whereas others, particularly slaves and junior commoners, suffered through a series of burdens imposed by government.

The abolition of slavery at the beginning of the French colonial period, coupled with pacification and improvement in transportation under the French, had several results. The pace of migration increased. Dispossessed slaves and labor-poor commoners unable to cultivate their own estates, or lacking sufficient land to sustain their families, took up cash-cropping in some parts of the island. Through French pacification, access to markets improved, and irrigation networks spread. The population of the Betsileo south and west increased through colonization and irrigation.

In the face of conquest and of increasing governmental intervention in peasant life, the distinctions of the past that are linked ultimately to material factors discussed in previous chapters continue to produce social and cultural variation among today's Malagasy. The legacy of the Merina empire is clear in disproportionate twentieth-century Merina success in government, professions, education, power, wealth, and access to European goods. Those Betsileo who found favor from Merina and French still occupy positions of advantage in contemporary Malagasy society. In large part these people are descendants of those whose differential demographic growth gave them influence in the prestate highland society of the seventeenth century and before. Certain cultural forms and socioeconomic patterns of the past continue to influence contemporary Betsileo life, just as they have governed Betsileo adaptation to change over the past three centuries. It is to these contemporary Betsileo that we now turn, specifically to variation in economy, kinship, descent, marriage, ceremonial, and other cultural domains and principles that have remained significant in the context of historical change in the southern highlands and the adaptation of its population to it. In the following chapters we see that sociocultural variation among today's Betsileo is clearly related to historical material conditions created by state organization and socioeconomic stratification.

III

VARIATION IN SPACE

CHAPTER FIVE

The Contemporary Betsileo

Reflecting almost three centuries of life under state organization, contemporary Betsileo peasants inhabit a complex social world, living multiple identities, participating in activities of several groups and in relationships created by an array of social organizational principles. Part of contemporary peasants' social identity, their rights in and obligations to other members of the society that environs them, derives from their placement in a partially bureaucratized administrative and settlement hierarchy. At the lowest level each rural Betsileo is a member of an official village. In 1967 an official village typically included an aggregated population, that of Ivato, for example, along with surrounding hamlets. Today, throughout the southern highlands, the village is an important social unit. Betsileo normally see covillagers each day; they certainly know intimate details of each others' lives; household heads meet as a *fokonolona* or village council when emergencies arise or governmental demands arrive. The village is normally the most important unit of recruitment of mutual labor for trampling, transplanting, harvesting, and threshing, the customarily cooperative tasks in rice cultivation. If a special occasion, such as a funeral or other ceremonial event, brings large numbers of outsiders to a village, all its households normally offer lodging and rice for the guests.

Betsileo life is conceived by them as the life of a rural peasant. Although many Betsileo would prefer to live in hamlets near their fields so that cattle manure is readily available for rice cultivation, most contemporary Betsileo live in villages. As previously noted, the French colonial government, in 1913, ordered all Betsileo to move from hamlet to village. To a limited extent only, since there are still hamlets, the Malagasy government continues to reinforce the village pattern. Even longer ago, during the eighteenth and nineteenth centuries when warfare was rampant, the characteristic Betsileo settlement was a fortified settlement located on a steep hill, usually a massive granitic outcrop. The hamlet, the fortified hilltop settlement, and the village just above the rice plain are all familiar to the Betsileo. Not so familiar as these settlements, but traditional now, too, are towns. The towns that

Betsileo know are administrative and market centers.[1] Closest to most peasants and most frequently visited are canton seats. Ivato's canton seat is Sabotsy; the two villages I studied in southern Vohibato, Ambalabe and Tanambao, are in the canton of Mahazony. Cantons are units of subprefectures, the latter called districts under the French. Each canton seat has a market place where a market is held once a week on a given day. Often the town's name is that of the market day. Sabotsy, Ivato's canton seat, for example, means "Saturday". Ivatans, like most Betsileo peasants, live in walking distance of at least two market towns. Since markets in nearby towns are always held on different days, people can, if they wish, attend two or more markets in any week. Not all market towns are canton seats, though all canton seats have markets. Betsileo go to market with a frequency that depends on such things as age, sex, and need. Enterprising married and widowed women go often to sell mats, baskets, and other things they have made. The market is a place to form relationships, particularly for young people, to exchange gossip, to see kin, friends, and neighbors, as well as a place to buy and sell. When the market town is also an administrative center, a trip to market may also be a trip to pay one's taxes, to settle some dispute, or to see the canton chief.

The Malagasy government divides the island into six provinces, each of which is divided into prefectures. Most Betsileo live in the prefecture of Fianarantsoa, one of three into which the province of Fianarantsoa is subdivided. At a lower level, there are seven subprefectures in the prefecture of Fianarantsoa. Four of them, from south to north, Ambalavao, Fianarantsoa, Ambohimahasoa, and Ambositra (table 4), include most of the traditional Betsileo heartland. The Betsileo subprefecture seats and other urban centers in Madagascar are located on map 3. In table 4 the area, size, density of population of each, and population of their seats are indicated. As is the case when canton data are considered, there are strong contrasts in population densities among the subprefectures. These contrasts reflect physical environment, history of settlement, and economic orientation. Ambalavao, where two of the villages (Ambalabe and Tanambao) included in this study are located, encompasses most of what was Arindrano in Merina times. It is the

TABLE 4
Demographic Characteristics of Betsileo Subprefectures

	Area (km.²)	Total Population (1966)	Population Density (1966) (per km.²)	Population of Subprefecture Seat	Percentage of Betsileo	Actual Betsileo Population
Ambalavao	9,233	75,231	8.15	15,730	88	66,203
Fianarantsoa	9,266	237,489	25.63	43,907	87	206,615
Ambohimahasoa	1,824	79,958	43.84	4,600	92	73,561
Ambositra	4,157	147,082	35.38	14,800	81	119,136

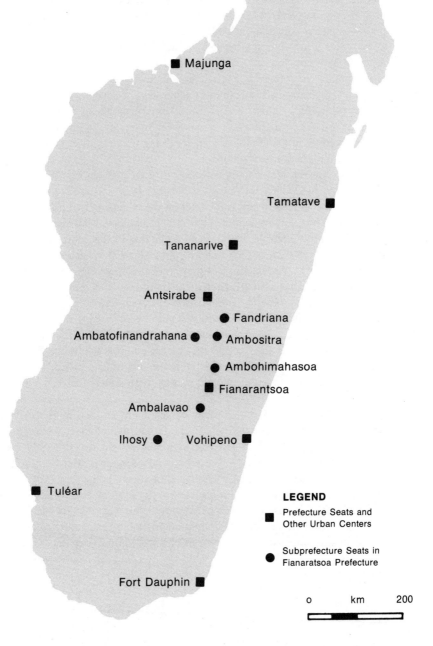

Diego Suarez

Majunga

Tamatave

Tananarive

Antsirabe

Fandriana

Ambatofinandrahana ● ● Ambositra

Ambohimahasoa

Fianarantsoa

Ambalavao

Ihosy ● Vohipeno

Tuléar

LEGEND

■ Prefecture Seats and
Other Urban Centers

● Subprefecture Seats in
Fianaratsoa Prefecture

o   km   200

Fort Dauphin

most arid subprefecture and stockbreeding remains more important than in Fianarantsoa, Ambohimahasoa, and Ambositra.

Among the Betsileo, and in general throughout Madagascar, subprefecture seats are also the largest population centers in their subprefectures. There is, as is demonstrated in table 4, considerable variation in the size of subprefecture seats. Fianarantsoa, Ivato's subprefecture seat, with a 1973 population of approximately 48,000, remains the largest city of the prefecture and province and is Madagascar's fifth largest city. Betsileo go to Fianarantsoa, as province seat, to argue disputes before a provincial court. There are government and parochial secondary schools in Fianarantsoa, as in other provincial capitals, and there are government and church-affiliated junior high schools and primary schools in most subprefecture seats. While there are also primary schools in most canton seats, some peasants in almost every Betsileo village have children who are studying in one of the subprefecture seats, either boarding in the church schools or living with relatives in the seat while attending the government schools.

Seats are the major market centers of their circumscriptions. As noted, markets are held on a set day of the week. It is on this day that peasants usually come in to buy and sell. Itinerant merchants arrive in large numbers on market day, traveling in their small trucks and vans from one major market to another throughout the week. Peasants normally feel more comfortable in their canton seat than in their subprefecture seat. They attend markets more often at lower-level centers, and they know more of the people there than they do in the urban setting. They try to transact as much as possible of their government business with canton officials, rather than calling on the subprefecture personnel, who are more distant, sociologically and usually geographically as well. Maternity wards are maintained in the canton seats, staffed by midwives and occasionally by male nurses whom the Betsileo call doctors. Better health care is available in the subprefecture seat, but is sought only if there is no "doctor" in one's canton, or in emergencies, such as difficult births.

In Fianarantsoa, a major urban center, there are two market days each week, and business goes on daily in the larger marketplace, where there are permanent stalls. Any Betsileo who visits the capital will probably visit the market. It is also normally in the provincial capital that Betsileo seek wage work. Young men and women who decide to leave home temporarily or permanently to work in cities must deal with subprefecture and even with national officials, as they fill out various forms required by the Malagasy government for wage work. Despite participation by a segment of their population in the professions discussed in chapter 4, most Betsileo remain rural peasants.

REGIONAL VARIATION, VILLAGES, AND DESCENT GROUPS

The population of any Betsileo village is subdivided into groups with different social identities expressed in different kinds of behavior. With the exception of descendants of slaves, most contemporary Betsileo claim membership in named descent groups (*foko* or *karazana*) whose branches reside as local descent groups in different villages and, in the case of the largest descent groups, in different regions. When buttressed by residence in the same village, membership in the same descent group provides an additional basis for cooperation and common social identity. A Betsileo descent group consists of people who maintain that they share common ancestry. Members of the same descent group typically share a descent group name, which they believe to have been taken by or bestowed upon early members; for example Tranovondro, Taray, Maromena. Often descent group members, most typically elders, claim to remember the name and some of the events associated with the life of the descent group founder—the ancestor, usually plausibly real, sometimes obviously fictional—who stands at the apex of their common genealogy.

On the basis of the macroregional sample discussed in chapters 1 and 3, the typical Betsileo descent group (52 percent of 998 named descent groups sampled) occurs only as a local descent group; that is, it is confined to a single village. Even so, it is usually only one among several descent groups in that village. Three-fourths (75.2 percent) of all Betsileo villages include 2 or more local descent groups, with a maximum of 32, a mean of 3.4, and a median of 3 local descent groups per village.

Computing village descent group organization in terms of Merina administrative subdivisions, the mean number of descent groups per village was 2.8 in Lalangina, 3.8 in Isandra, and 3.3 in Arindrano. There are fewer descent groups per village in the more agricultural areas. Arindrano's northeastern part was northern Vohibato, which was more agricultural and less pastorally oriented than the other statelets assigned by the Merina to Arindrano. Thus, in the number of descent groups per village, as well as in village population size and size of local descent groups, Arindrano stands between Lalangina, where reliance on agriculture was greatest, and Isandra (table 5).

These figures reflect patterns of migration discussed in chapter 4. The proto-Betsileo appear to have settled first and to have grown most quickly in the agricultural east within the boundaries of Lalangina and northern Vohibato. As noted in chapter 3, economic changes and a degree of pacification under the Lalanginan state favored differential growth of Lalanginan population, until Merina and French rule brought pacification to Isandra and Arindrano as well. Thereafter, with the economic and demographic trends

TABLE 5

Variation in Population and Local Descent Group Composition
of Villages of the Southern Highlands

Merina Administrative Unit	Mean Village Population	Mean No. Local Descent Groups per Village	Mean Size Local Descent Group
Lalangina ($n = 126$)	261	2.8	147
Arindrano ($n = 473$)	143	3.3	54
Isandra ($n = 107$)	99	3.8	30
Total sample ($n = 706$)	157	3.3	66

described in chapter 4, population appears to have grown rapidly throughout the heartland. As it grew, emigrants from the most densely populated area, the agricultural east (where Ivato is located), moved south, west, and north, where they petitioned land grants. The two villages I studied in the canton of Mahazony were settled as part of this diaspora. For these reasons present-day villages in the east tend to be inhabited by a few descent groups whose ancestral claims are deep, whereas in more recently settled areas the number of descent groups per village is typically higher. This is one of the major contrasts between Ivato and the two Mahazony villages. Its implications are examined throughout the remainder of this book.

If, as seems probable, in the prestate, proto-Betsileo past, the major descent groups had been associated with more discrete and exclusive territories, multiple descent groups came together for mutual defense in fortified hilltop settlements as states formed and evolved during the eighteenth and nineteenth centuries. The gradual pacification that accompanied Merina and French rule promoted a new settlement pattern as people abandoned the hilltops to settle in hamlets near their rice fields. Early in the twentieth century, as noted previously, descent groups were aggregated once again. In areas like northern Vohibato and Lalangina, because of early settlement by descent group ancestors, control of larger estates, and a longer period for demographic growth, those who were brought together in the same village were often members of different branches of one or two of the named descent groups long established in that region. As noted, the three villages where I did most of my fieldwork exemplify several contrasts between the agricultural east (Ivato in northern Vohibato) and the more recently settled, more sparsely populated, more pastorally oriented south (Ambalabe and Tanambao in the canton of Mahazony in southern Vohibato) and, by extension, west. The historical economic and ecological differences between east and south (and west) that have been discussed in chapters 3 and 4 are underlying material conditions that explain differential access to strategic resources in these three villages today. Ivato, Ambalabe, and Tanambao sample the major contrasts in actual wealth and power encountered in Betsileo society, from the favored senior commoners in Ivato through the impoverished junior commoners of Tanambao. We move now from the study of broad sociocultural variation across the centuries and from region to region to more detailed comparison of contrasting villages in the heartland subprefectures of Fianarantsoa and Ambalavao.

SOCIOECONOMIC VARIATION IN THE BETSILEO HEARTLAND

Ivato

As near to Ambalavao as to Fianarantsoa, which is its subprefecture seat, is Ivato, where I did most of my fieldwork. Like most Betsileo villages, Ivato is situated above the rice plain that it shares with neighboring villages and hamlets. Automobiles reach Ivato by traveling through Alarobia ("Wednesday"), the seat of the canton immediately to the north of Sabotsy ("Saturday"), the canton that includes Ivato. Nearing Ivato, one sees to the west the Outcrop, atop which the ancestors of Ivato and several other villages in the cantons of Alarobia and Sabotsy once lived. The Sabotsy River meanders through the plain between the Outcrop and Ivato. West of the river, nestled in talus slopes of the Outcrop, are two settlements, both inhabited like Ivato by members of the Tranovondro descent group, and founded after Ivato had been settled. East of the river, between it and the road, there are hamlets on many of the small hills that interrupt the rice plain. On a prominence a kilometer north of Ivato is Little Ivato, which like most of the other villages and hamlets, was also originally settled by the Tranovondro in their radiation within this rice plain. Descendants of the slaves of their ancestors now live in Little Ivato along with Tranovondro.

Because it is the largest settlement around the plain, Ivato immediately attracts attention. It is insulated by groves of trees, which are rare in the Betsileo countryside, except around abandoned hilltop settlements. The eucalyptus trees planted around 1900 actually form a backdrop for the village and break only to the north in the direction of the rice plain. Most Betsileo villages are open and sunbaked. One notes another contrast in the large number of buildings with tin and tile roofs and brick walls. Houses appear richer (and many of their residents are richer) than in other villages. It is not only its houses that distinguish Ivato, but also its Roman Catholic elementary school buildings and chapel. Ivato has become, as a result of its political importance (discussed in chapter 4), an educational and religious center.

To reach Ivato one turns west off the country road, which goes on through other rural areas and eventually reaches Sabotsy. The descent to Ivato is a rocky road, passable throughout the year. The road passes the village reservoir, a modern cement structure on the right. Pipes bring water from a hillside spring; others carry it from reservoir to village, about a kilometer away. Trees and other vegetation stand on both sides of the road, which has become level. To the east, the land descends to an eastern extension of the rice plain. Just above the rice fields, but obscured by vegetation, begin the areas where villagers grow their secondary crops. As the road enters a clearing fringed by eucalyptus trees, one sees the chapel and school buildings, forming Ivato's southern boundary. A Red Cross station, a wattle and daub hut where antimalarial drugs are dispensed, stands at the turnoff to another dirt road leading southwest to other villages.

Entering Ivato from the clearing, one passes between the chapel on the left and a school building on the right. The area to the right is occupied by a complex of school buildings built around a square that is the school playground. The peasant village lies behind, below, and west of these. Turning left, or west, one passes the chapel and stops the car in front of a church bell tower and small mud wall. Immediately beyond, a road descends north to the Sabotsy river and the rice fields bordering it. This road is passable for ox carts and is the path along which some Ivatans direct their zebu for daily grazing. More important, this road materially symbolizes the sociopolitical separation of western (junior) and eastern (senior) branches of the local Tranovondro. Just west of the road is the traditional Betsileo sepulcher, which to Ivatans more emphatically symbolizes the bifurcation, projecting it into an indefinite future. The easterners' burial place, a newer tomb, commissioned in 1917 by Goodmaker for his father Karl Fridaysfather, is located on the outskirts of the village. Tombs of slave-descended families and of clients are less imposing and are scattered just outside the village.

Ivato, whose population includes a single local descent group, a senior branch of the Tranovondro—a widespread named descent group that spanned thirty-nine villages in the macroregional sample—typifies the previously indicated trend toward fewer local descent groups, with larger memberships, in villages of the agricultural east. Cantons here have means of between 1.5 and 2.5 descent groups per village. As in Ivato itself, the social cores of most neighboring villages are represented by a single local descent group, often a branch of one of the major named descent groups whose ancestors are said to have entered Betsileo country prior to or during the early evolution of state organization. Internal contrasts based on socioeconomic stratum rather than multiple descent group affiliation are, however, much more typical of the agricultural east than of the south and west. Because nineteenth-century easterners owned more slaves, descendants of slaves now comprise a larger percentage of the rural population of northern Vohibato and Lalangina than of southern Vohibato and other parts of Arindrano. One hundred and forty-one or 81 percent of the one hundred and seventy-five residents of Ivato live in twenty-four households headed by Tranovondro, whereas twenty-three people, 13 percent of its population, live in five households headed by slave descendants. Eleven people, representing 6 percent of Ivato's population, live in two households whose heads are clients; they are non-Tranovondro, commoners rather than slave descendants, who farm land on the basis of use rights granted to their ancestors by ancestral Tranovondro.

Socioeconomic stratification remains obvious in Ivato today (table 6). Of the thirty-four hectares of rice land now cultivated by Ivatans, 89 percent is farmed by twenty-five Tranovondro owners. Merely 5 percent—1.8 hectares—is allocated to the four cultivators descended from slaves, to sustain twenty-three people, 13 percent of the village population. The mean rice holding of a Tranovondro in Ivato is 1.2 hectares, about three times the average of .45 hectare of a slave descendant. The two clients who reside as household heads in Ivato fare better; their holdings average a bit over a hectare each. However, neither clients nor slave descendants enjoy disposal rights over their rice fields, which are recorded in the government registry as property of elder Tranovondro. Slave descendants and clients are allowed to pass their use rights onto their descendants, but, should they leave no offspring, their fields would revert to the Tranovondro.

Automobiles cannot descend beyond Ivato's upper level, where the chapel-school complex is located. Cement staircases lead down about twelve feet to the level of the ground floors of the eastern houses and top of the eastern cattle corral, which is ten feet deep. Two stone-walled cattle corrals mark the historical centers of eastern and western villages. Houses constructed by influential Ivatans of the past and present surround the eastern corral (map 4). Towering over the southern side of the corral is our sponsor's three-story brick house. To the east, joined to it by a common porch, but not as tall, is the house of Tuesdaysfather, Ivato's most prestigious peasant. Tuesdaysfather is the second son—our sponsor the first—of three generations of eldest sons. While our sponsor served as regional and national representative of Ivato's senior line, in his absence Tuesdaysfather had become its local representative.

On the western side of the corral is their father's house, now inhabited by his youngest child, Jules, the only son of their father's second marriage.

TABLE 6
Aspects of Socioeconomic Stratification in Ivato

	Number	Percentage in Village Population	Number of Households	Percentage of Rice Land Farmed	Mean Holding (ha.)
Tranovondro	141	81	24	89	1.2
Clients	11	6	2	6	1.0
Slave Descendants	23	13	5	5	0.45

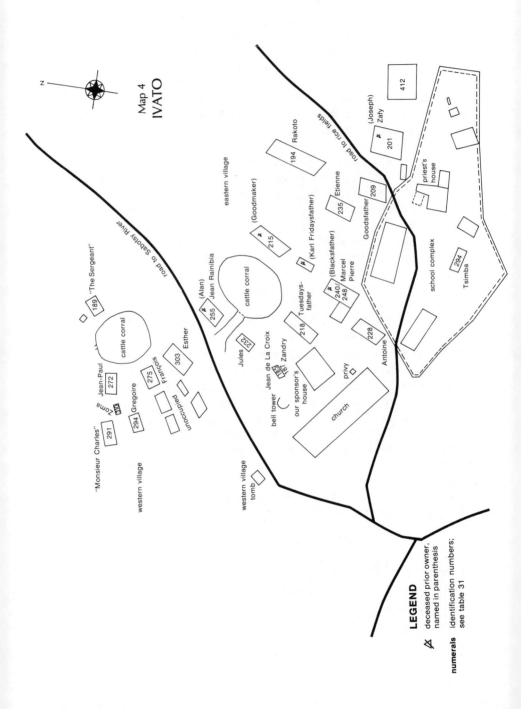

Map 4
IVATO

N

road to Sabotsy River

"The Sergeant" 189

"Monsieur Charles"
291
294 Gregoire
Zoma
Jean-Paul
272
cattle corral
275 Francois
303 Esther
unoccupied

western village

western village tomb

eastern village

255 Jean Rainibia (Alan)

cattle corral

Jules 232
Jean de La Croix
181 Zandry
bell tower

our sponsor's house

church

privy

218 Tuesdaysfather

228

Antoine

(Goodmaker)
215

(Karl Fridaysfather)

240 (Blacksfather)
248 Marcel Pierre

194 Rakoto

235 Etienne

209 Goodsfather

(Joseph) Zafy
201

priest's house

school complex

294 Tsimba

412

road to rice fields

LEGEND

⚔ deceased prior owner, named in parenthesis

numerals identification numbers; see table 31

Directly across stands the two-story, balconied house built by their grand-father, Goodmaker. Until our sponsor and Tuesdaysfather built their houses, Goodmaker's house, which occupies a ritually favored position northeast of all other houses in Ivato, had been Ivato's most imposing dwelling. Follow-ing the custom of transmitting houses in the junior line, its current inhabitant is the younger son (of two) of the builder's youngest son (of three). The house of Goodmaker's father, Karl Fridaysfather, stands closest of all to the corral, east of it, but south of Goodmaker's. Now dwarfed by the larger brick and two- and three-story houses of his descendants, this is an abandoned wooden house, which our sponsor planned to restore. Among Betsileo and Merina elites of the eighteenth and nineteenth centuries, the preferred house was constructed of wood. In the denuded central highlands, it was necessary to import timber from the eastern forest. Karl's slaves transported wood for his house from Tanala country. Rare in the Betsileo countryside, a wooden house testifies to a village's historical importance as a regional political and economic center. There was another wooden house in western Ivato, built by its last influential ancestor, Owen. Lacking a native son with our sponsor's wealth, western villagers had no means of restoring the ancestral cabin, and had recently torn it down. There were no wooden houses in any neighboring village.

In each generation, therefore, Ivatans have used their homes to validate their senior status and their local and regional importance. Although the con-struction media in vogue at different times have varied, the message has remained the same. In each generation oldest sons have constructed houses, whereas their younger brothers have remained in their father's home—when they are youngest sons, usually to inherit it. The prerogative of building new houses is not limited to senior sons. However, because they are usually wealthier, they are often the only ones who can afford this undertaking. The placement of houses in eastern Ivato only roughly corresponds to a ritual order of spacing that helps govern seating within a house on public occasions (see chapter 4) and house construction sites in villages. (For the system as it operates in the Bara hut and hamlet, see Huntington [1974, pp. 147–53]). Although men customarily build houses south or west (or both) of their sen-iors (fathers, uncles, older brothers), Goodmaker's house stands northeast of that of his father, Karl Fridaysfather, and the home of our sponsor—an elder brother—is west of his younger brother's. A magnificent third-story view explains our sponsor's choice of location. Goodmaker's probably reflects his desire to demonstrate for any visitor his headship of Ivato and prominence as canton chief under the French. As Huntington notes, several practical consid-erations, such as crowding or laziness, cause fact to depart from the theory of seniority's spatial expression. An Ivatan hut inhabited by two families of slave descent in the ritually least favored position—southwest of the corral—

does confirm partial translation of the cognitive map of Betsileo social ordering into actual residence choices.

The houses of less senior Ivatans are generally farther from the corral (see map 4 and the genealogy in figure 4). Behind Karl's wooden house, to the south, is the house constructed by his younger brother, Blacksfather. Their youngest brother Alan built his residence northwest of the corral. Farther south of the cattle coral is the brick house of Antoine, only son of Tuesdaysfather. Situated farther southeast of the corral is the house of Etienne, inherited from his mother Marie Claire, Karl Fridaysfather's daughter by the second wife in a polygynous union. Southeast of this is the house built and inhabited by Goodsfather, an oldest son.

Another oldest son, Rakoto, built his house immediately north of Goodsfather and due east of the corral. Moving further southeast, another road, passable by ox carts, leads down to the main rice plain, called Amparihibe. Just east of the road is another imposing house built by Rakoto's father, Joseph. In a lean-to next to his father's house, Rakoto kept the ox cart that he and his younger brother Zafy jointly owned. Zafy taught in a Roman Catholic elementary school in a village north of Fianarantsoa. Because salaries (and standards) for teachers in religious schools were far below those paid to schoolteachers employed by the government, Zafy maintained an interest in Ivato. Employing hired hands and relying on the help of Rakoto and his household, Zafy cultivated two rice fields in Ivato and had recently constructed a third, with terraces, in the eastern rice plain. Since as younger son (of two), Zafy was heir to his father's house, he and his wife stayed there on their weekend and vacation trips to Ivato. Zafy's widowed mother and sister and his daughter by a previous marriage also lived in his father's house. The last house to the east belonged to one of our sponsor's younger brothers, principal of a government school near Ambalavao, who planned eventually to retire to Ivato; he, his wife, and their children occasionally spent weekends and school vacations there.

The western branch of the Tranovondro of Ivato was established in the third ascending generation, reckoning from the oldest contemporary westerner (see figures 2 and 4). Since the founding ancestor, Noblemaker, was the youngest of seven siblings, whereas the eastern village founder, Hundredmaster, was the oldest, the western branch's third ascending generation now coincides with the eastern branch's sixth. Because of the generational difference, easterners sometimes joke that the westerners are their great grandparents—an irony since throughout Ivato's recent history the easterners have been senior. Socioeconomic implications of the resolution of an argument, in favor of the east, concerning relative seniority, which was analyzed in chapter 4, are evident today. The dispute involved Karl Fridaysfather and Owen, the western village elder. Karl's descent from an eldest son, as compared to

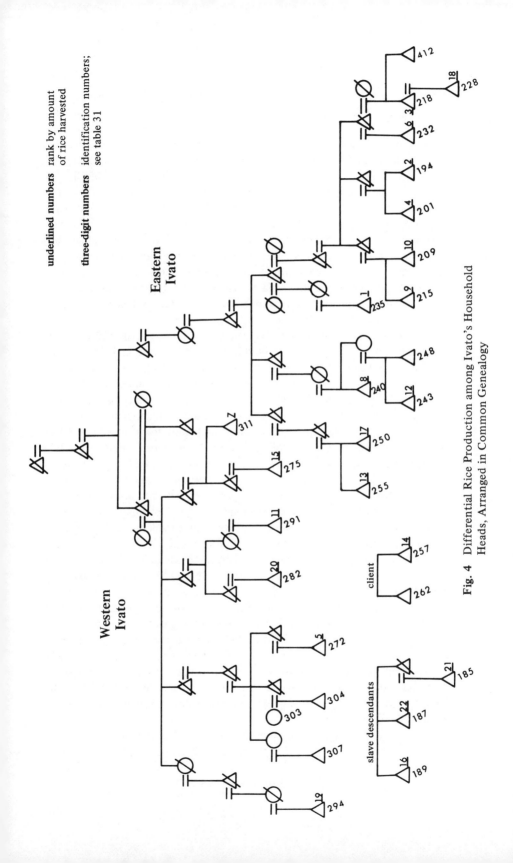

Fig. 4 Differential Rice Production among Ivato's Household Heads, Arranged in Common Genealogy

Owen's descent from a youngest son, was contrasted against Owen's generation and pure agnatic line. Owen's death without offspring left Karl and the eastern village with indisputable seniority. Heirs to Owen's sizeable estate included only children of his half brothers. Since Owen had himself been the oldest child of his father's senior wife (of three) his heirs, as descendants of junior wives, and in view of Karl's success as a Merina agent, could hardly challenge eastern seniority. In fact, most of them left Ivato altogether, to farm and to transmit to their descendants estates that Owen had assembled through purchase and by constructing new rice fields outside of Ivato. Karl was blessed with a son, Goodmaker, as able and as ambitious as the father. Together they used slave labor to transform marshland into productive rice fields, and to tap the Sabotsy River for irrigation, thus increasing the estate they would pass onto their descendants. The activities of these men who lived during the nineteenth and early twentieth centuries have influenced indelibly the distribution of wealth in Ivato today.

In 1967 no house in western Ivato was as imposing as most of those on the eastern side of the road. Household heads were younger, and most people recognized as head of the western village a retired teacher who had taught for many years in Ivato's Catholic elementary school. "Monsieur" Charles, called by the French title like all schoolteachers, was an incomplete leader, however, because Ivato was his mother's village. Although three western village household heads were full agnates, they were too young to be reckoned leaders. Not all western villagers were Tranovondro. Gregoire, a Taimoro from the southeast coast, was an agricultural advisor whom the government had assigned to Ivato at the request of our sponsor. Because our sponsor had promoted his acceptance, Gregoire encountered little difficulty in persuading Ivatans to adopt new cultivation techniques: planting rice in rows, Japanese rotary weeders, chemical fertilizers, and modern nursery care. In the western village as in the east were two households whose heads were descendants of slaves. One of them was Zoma, an odd man in his forties who did not plant rice, but was a manioc farmer. He sold his manioc to buy rice, which he cooked for himself in the small house where he lived alone, never having married. The other was the Sergeant, a slave descendant who had raised his status by joining the French army, serving as far away as Djibouti in French Somaliland. He received a handsome pension, for a peasant, from the French government. He and his wife represent the only known case I encountered among the rural Betsileo of a marriage between a slave descendant and a commoner. His rice fields were small and his rice bill was the largest in Ivato. He was attempting to remedy this, however, having hired workers to construct a new rice field.

Of contemporary Ivatans, 86 or 49 percent reside in the eastern village, and 46 or 26 percent live west of the road. Another 43 people, representing

25 percent of the official inhabitants of Ivato, reside in hamlets near the village proper. Socioeconomic contrasts are visible to the naked eye, in the more lavish houses and agricultural equipment of eastern villagers, but they reflect an underlying difference in the distribution of rice land, the most fundamental means of production (see table 31). Fourteen easterners own and farm a total of 18.1 hectares, with a mean rice holding measuring 1.3 hectares, while 8 westerners farm only 7.9 hectares, with an average holding of 1.0 hectare per cultivator. When one also includes hamlet residents who are genealogically affiliated with eastern and western villages respectively, 21 members of the eastern branch hold a total of 25 hectares, or 73 percent of the total. They are responsible for 118 Ivatans or 67 percent of the village, while 10 westerners, whose fields must sustain 57 people, or 33 percent of the inhabitants of Ivato, have access to only 9 hectares, the remaining 27 percent of the total.

Although these figures do demonstrate the privileged access to strategic resources on the part of eastern villagers, they actually underestimate the importance of seniority of descent ranking (as eldest son of eldest son, or where ancestors were polygynous, as descendants of the senior wife) because they include holdings of slave descendants and clients. The rice field owners descended from Karl Fridaysfather (the oldest son of a principal union) cultivate an average rice holding of 1.7 hectares, while the descendants of Karl's younger brother, Blacksfather, fare almost equally well, with an average rice holding of 1.4 hectares. Yet, measured by total area, Karl's descendants farm a total of 18.1 hectares while the three households whose heads descend from Blacksfather cultivate only 4.1 hectares. Three contemporary households are headed by descendants of Karl's youngest brother, Alan. The total legacy in rice land that Alan left to his heirs is 3.7 hectares. However, 1.8 of these are currently being used by slave descendants, leaving only 1.9 hectares for Alan's actual descendants, giving an average rice field size of only .6 hectare for each cultivator. Such is the plight of junior descendants whose shares, following Betsileo convention, have been assigned in previous generations by older brothers, like Karl and Blacksfather.

Village Economic Life

As typical of a Betsileo village as its houses and corrals are its granaries and kitchen gardens. Granaries differ in shape and construction materials. The Tanala-type granary is a wooden hut whose floor is raised about five feet off the ground atop thick, smooth poles. Between poles and floor are wide concave wooden plates, which, with the smooth poles, are intended to keep rodents out. An adaptation to the forest that requires bamboo and other woods, the Tanala-type granary is rare in the highlands, where most granaries are wattle and daub structures. Sometimes they are round and have conical roofs made of locally available long grass. However, in Ivato, most granaries are modeled after the most common Betsileo house type, rectangular structures with slanted roofs of long grass or tin. Many have wooden windows; all have wooden doors. Betsileo who cultivate more than one rice field usually grow at least two varieties of rice, which are stored in different granaries. One is used to feed hired hands and people who assist in transplanting and threshing. The other variety, considered tastier, is reserved for the family's daily meals. Some peasants in southern Vohibato have their granaries on the ground floors of their houses. In Ivato, all granaries are outdoors, but close to the owner's house.

Many Betsileo women keep kitchen gardens. Just outside their house, Jules's wife and mother have a fenced garden where they grow tomatoes, several varieties of greens, onions, garlic, squashes, beans and, other vegetables. The vegetable gardens of most women, however, lie outside the village proper on the slope towards the rice fields, near the areas where their husbands and sons grow secondary crops. Women also collect greens that grow wild in these gardens.

Whereas cattle are the charges of men, Betsileo women care for pigs and fowl: chickens, turkeys, geese, turkey fowl, and ducks. Before the French conquest, as numerous Europeans who traveled in the highlands described ethnocentrically, sheep, goats, and fowl slept in Merina and Betsileo houses. Older Ivatans recall when sheep and goats were kept in the village, but none are today. Nowadays, Betsileo put their fowl to sleep in coops, some made of stone, but usually of wattle and daub, and located near their houses. Pigs are kept in wooden pigpens. Tranovondro in other villages, like members of many other Betsileo descent groups, respect a taboo on raising and eating pigs. Ivatans, however, have raised pigs since the late nineteenth century. Eight women owned pigs in Ivato in 1967, though several died that year following an epidemic of a paralytic disease.

As one leaves the village proper and walks west, north, or east, he will pass, as he approaches the rice fields, areas where secondary crops are grown. An example will illustrate the pattern of land use. Between his house and the rice plain lie lands where Rakoto, his twenty-five-year old son Luther, his married stepson Claude, and other members of his household grow secondary crops. Immediately north of his house is one of three areas where he and the two young men planted tobacco, the principal cash crop in Ivato, the cultivation of which used about six hectares of land in and around Ivato. Below and north of Rakoto's tobacco plot is an area where sweet potatoes were grown, followed immediately by another tobacco field, a peanut field, a fallow area, and a plot cultivated in manioc and sweet potatoes. As mentioned, a road (cf. map 4) separates Rakoto's house from his father's, of which his brother Zafy is now head. Rakoto and Zafy share the land north of their father's house, including a grove of 120 coffee trees that their father

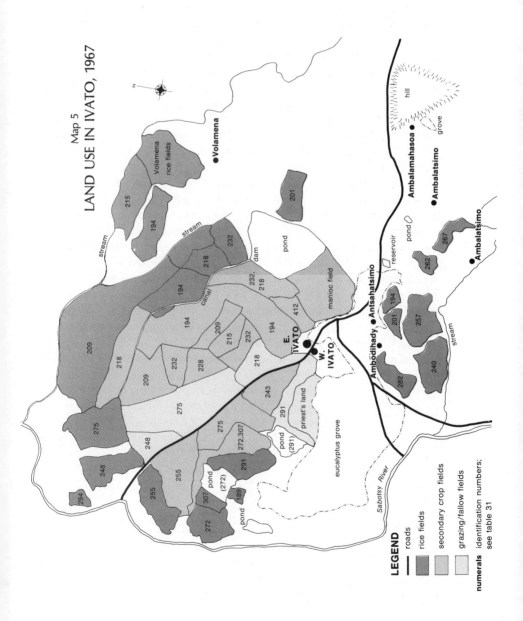

Map 5
LAND USE IN IVATO, 1967

LEGEND
—— roads
█ rice fields
▓ secondary crop fields
░ grazing/fallow fields
numerals identification numbers;
see table 31

planted. Twenty-six Ivatans owned a total of about 1,200 coffee trees, whose beans, harvested in September and October, were used locally and sold. Tuesdaysfather made 10,500 CFA[2] ($42.00 U.S.) in 1967 from the sale of surplus beans from Ivato's largest coffee grove, 450 trees inherited from his father.

North of Rakoto's coffee grove are located successively a third tobacco field; a peanut patch; a sweet potato field; a fallow area where his wife's pigpen is located; one of his threshing floors, with peanut fields on either side of it; a cornfield; another threshing floor; a plot where peanuts and tobacco are intercropped; a banana grove; another fallow area; and, just above his rice field, a grove of orange trees. There is a drop of eight feet to the drainage canal that runs alongside Rakoto's rice field. Like Rakoto, most villagers cultivate their secondary crops on land between Ivato and their rice fields in the plain of Amparihibe. The pattern is far from perfect because some Ivatans cultivate rice fields in other valleys but still are entitled to secondary crop land near home.

Areas farmed by Ivatans in secondary food crops in 1967 are indicated in tables 7 and 8.[3] Note that manioc is the major secondary crop, followed by sweet potatoes; together they account for more than half of the total area of secondary food crop cultivation. A total of about 45 hectares were used for secondary food crop cultivation in Ivato during 1967, representing a per capita area of .26 hectare for 175 Ivatans. With 34 hectares of rice land, which represents .2 hectare per person, Ivatans cultivate a total of 79 hectares, or .46 ha. per capita. With only 43 percent of their cultivated area planted in rice, Ivato's agricultural economy is more diversified than those of the subprefectures of Fianarantsoa and Ambalavao generally, where 53 percent and 67 percent respectively of all food crop land is rice field (see table 32).[4] Ivato's per capita rice holding is close to the Fianarantsoa and Amba-

TABLE 7

Secondary Food Crops in Ivato, 1967

	Number of Cultivators	Mean Plot Size (ha.)	Total Hectares Planted	Percent of Total Secondary Crops
Manioc	30	0.4	12.8	28.4
Sweet potatoes	32	0.35	11.1	24.6
Beans	25	0.2	4.9	10.7
Cape peas	21	0.2	4.2	9.3
Irish potatoes	18	0.2	3.8	8.3
Peanuts	19	0.2	3.5	7.7
Maize	18	0.2	2.9	6.4
Taro (*Colocasia*)	21	0.1	2.0	4.4
Total	—	—	45.1	100.0

Mean no. cultivators of a given crop = 23
Mean total secondary crop area per cultivator = 2.0 hectares

TABLE 8
Trees and Livestock in Ivato, 1967

	Ivato Total	No. Owners	Mean Holding	Maximum Holding
Trees				
Coffee	1170	26	45	450
Peach	440	31	14	80
Banana	320	28	11	45
Mango	240	24	10	30
Livestock				
Cattle	38	12	3	8
Chickens	212	32	7	24
Ducks	14	4	4	4

lavao averages of .22 ha. and .23 ha. per person, but Ivato's per hectare paddy yields are slightly higher, 2,250 kilograms compared to 2,200 for Ambalavao and 1,950 for Fianarantsoa. However, considering that at least 10 hectares of Ivato's rice fields now being cultivated by slave descendants in nearby hamlets are excluded from the preceding calculations, the relative prosperity of Ivato's senior commoners may be confirmed.

Division of Labor

The cycle of rice cultivation determines the most obvious seasonal changes in rural activities. The Betsileo have established a daily and seasonal division of labor on the basis of age and sex. Ivatans awaken between five and six in the morning. Women rise, wash, and prepare rice gruel, served between six and seven, often (in households that can afford it) mixed with canned milk. In the past, when there were cows in Ivato, fresh milk was used. Around seven a woman feeds her poultry in the court in front of her house or near the coops. Some women are removing paddy from granaries and placing it on straw mats to dry in the sun before pounding. By eight o'clock some women are pounding rice with wooden pestles in wooden mortars.[5] Others are working in their vegetable gardens. Between nine and eleven, women prepare the midday meal, cooking rice and the vegetables, the *laoka* as Betsileo say— usually beans or cape peas and seasonally harvested and collected varieties of greens—that accompany rice. Cooking done and awaiting their husbands' arrival from the fields, women converse with neighbors. Women with suckling infants commonly carry them on their backs, secured by flannel or cotton cloth wrapped around their waists, up around the baby. If there is no older sibling available to care for them, toddlers accompany their mothers, often grasping the hems of their cotton dresses.

Betsileo eat their major meal around noon. Neither men nor women commonly return to work before two. After eating, people visit or converse in front of their houses. In the early afternoon some women weave mats and baskets, occasionally to sell in the market, generally for use in their own homes. Other women sew on machines. Later on, women congregate in separate groups in front of a few houses and pound rice. Around half-past four or later, after rice for the following day's meal has been husked, women begin to round up their fowl. By five most women are cooking dinner. As their husbands and other members of their households return from the fields around six, families converse in the kitchen, generally a room on the second floor of the house. Most Ivatans eat dinner around half-past six. After dinner, in the absence of anthropologists, they retire to their rooms, and by eight most are in bed. Although women contribute about 35 percent of the labor used in rice cultivation (see tables 33 and 34), the demand for female labor in the rice fields is seasonal. Women's labor is extremely important during transplanting, weeding, harvesting, drying, winnowing, and transport to the granary. Their husbands, in contrast, attend to the fields on a more regular, almost daily, basis. The individual field owner must supply about 25 percent of the labor involved in rice cultivation and in rice field preparation and maintenance.

Men rise between five and six, wash themselves, go to the fields, come home after an hour of light work, eat the morning meal and return to the fields between seven and eight. The duration of morning work depends on the season. As they plow, hand till, or do other jobs preparatory to rice transplanting, in the transplanting season itself, and at harvest and threshing time, they often work until noon. In slack seasons they return to the village by half-past ten. Afternoon work in the fields begins around two and lasts until about half-past four. It takes those who own cattle from thirty minutes to an hour to prepare fodder: grasses cut in certain areas around the village and in the fields, for example, along the banks of the Sabotsy River. Beginning in February Ivatans also feed their cattle manioc tubers, stems, leaves, and peelings. Even if he shares a cattle corral with close kin, each man places the fodder for his own cattle in a determined area each evening, a shelf set in the corral wall. After he has fed his cattle a man visits or returns home, eats, and retires.

Cattle care is one of certain daily and seasonal tasks that males virtually always perform. The cowherd's work is not too strenuous. Older men and adolescent boys often do it. Etienne is a sixty-one-year-old man who cultivates two large rice fields in association with his twenty-six-year-old married son. They live in separate houses, but Etienne looks after their cattle while his son does most of the harder work, like tilling and plowing the fields. Another example: Rakoto hired a fourteen-year-old boy to watch his cattle. Occasionally Rakoto acts as cowherd himself, but rarely does he assign this job to his twenty-five-year-old son or twenty-year-old stepson, who also live with him. They are expected to do the harder work involved in preparing and maintaining his rice fields. Among young household heads who have no sons, fathers, or hired hands to guard their cattle, groups of two or three owners herd their zebu jointly, rotating as herdsmen on successive days. Men also fetch firewood from the eucalyptus grove south and west of Ivato. Male labor is important in the cultivation of secondary crops. With their spades, and sometime in manioc fields with plows, men prepare the land for planting. Women help harvest manioc and tobacco, which men plant and weed. With taro and Irish potatoes, men do all the work from preparing the soil to harvesting.

Women's work includes the daily household chores described above. Women spend about a half-hour each day removing paddy from the granary and sun drying it. The amount of time they spend pounding rice reflects their household's daily consumption and increases at certain times of the year when communal meals are prepared during the transplanting, harvest, and ceremonial seasons. Help from adolescent daughters frees an older woman from daily pounding and other chores. Given an average household consumption figure of 1,200 kilograms of husked paddy per year, the average adult woman must spend about 325 hours pounding annually. Women traditionally clean the interior of the house, cook, wash clothes, and fetch water, often traveling long distances to springs in villages that are not as fortunate as Ivato with its reservoir and faucets. The men of Ivato joke that women in other villages have become especially eager to marry men from Ivato because of the village water supply and consequent lightened work load. Before considering more fully the seasonal division of labor, I shall discuss the two villages in the canton of Mahazony where, with the aid of my field assistant Joseph Rabe, I also carried out field research. Following this, I shall indicate differences in patterns of cultivation between these two villages and Ivato.

Ambalabe

Some thirty-five kilometers SSW of Ivato, in another subprefecture (Ambalavao) and canton (Mahazony), lie the villages of Ambalabe and Tanambao (fictitious names, like Ivato), the latter located a kilometer or two east of the former. Both lie within the boundaries of southern Vohibato, which is more arid, more pastorally oriented, less densely populated, less stratified than Ivato and other parts of the agricultural east. Mahazony's population density of 9.2 people per km.[2] and a cattle to human ratio of .5 offer sharp contrasts to the comparable figures of 23.6 and .3 respectively for the Ivato region. In reality the contrast in the cattle/human ratio is even greater, since it is easier to hide cattle from government statisticians in sparsely populated areas than in the agricultural east. However, illustrating the historical trends discussed in chapter 4, Mahazony's economy, although still more pastoral than Ivato's, has grown more agricultural than it was in pre-Merina days, due to irrigation.

Because of greater aridity, proportionately fewer Mahazony rice fields rely on rainfall than in Ivato. More are tied into a stream-fed irrigation system. Ambalabe, with a population of 217 in 1966, is larger than Ivato, and is, in fact, one of the largest villages in the canton of Mahazony. Tanambao, the natal village of my field assistant Rabe, on the other hand, had only 82 inhabitants in 1966. A dirt road, passable by car throughout most of the year, leads from the canton seat to Ambalabe, cutting it into northern and southern halves. As in Ivato, this division has social implications. Reflecting immigration during the past century, the average village in Mahazony includes localized branches of about four named descent groups. Both Ambalabe and Tanambao exemplify this pattern. Branches of five named descent groups are localized in Ambalabe. Members of two of them (the northern groups) have built their houses on the northern side of the road and farm rice fields in the valley below them to the north. Branches of the other three (the southern groups) live south of the road. There is a steeper fall to the southern plain, where most of their secondary crop lands and rice fields are located.

The contemporary bifurcation of Ambalabe reflects a settlement pattern of the past. Following the French edict of 1913, the inhabitants of several hamlets were agglomerated to form the village of Ambalabe. The two descent groups that now reside in northern Ambalabe previously lived in hamlets to the north, whereas the three southern groups came from hamlets to the south and west (see table 9). Even earlier, the southern groups, along with still others, had inhabited the abandoned hilltop village of Mahazony, which has given its name to the present-day canton seat, located just below it.

Like the Tranovondro of Ivato, Ambalabe's three southern descent groups are senior commoners: local branches of named descent groups with relatively[6] deep genealogical ties and a history of political importance in their region. They composed, along with other senior commoner descent groups, a named phratry that, along with two other phratries, organized the council of elders of one of the administrative subdivisions of southern Vohibato prior

TABLE 9

Descent Groups of Ambalabe by Household and Population

Descent Group Name	Households		Household Population	
	No.	%	No.	%
Southern, no. 1	10	24.4	41	18.9
Southern, no. 2	7	17.1	57	26.3
Southern, no. 3	10	24.4	51	23.5
Northern, no. 1	5	12.2	20	9.2
Northern, no. 2	9	22.0	48	22.1
Total	41	100.0	217	100.0

to, or soon after, Merina conquest. Ambalabe's northern groups, on the other hand, are junior commoners whose genealogies bring their ancestors to Mahazony in the second and third ascending generations respectively, that is, well after the Merina conquest.

Although, as far as I could determine, no slave descendants live either in Ambalabe or Tanambao, clients have attached themselves to two of Ambalabe's senior commoner descent groups. In contrast to the two client households in Ivato, whose heads are distant genealogical kin of the Tranovondro, Ambalabe's clients have been fictively incorporated within their patrons' local descent groups after receiving land grants—at Merina administration direction—from them. Of the residents of Ambalabe who claim to be members of southern descent group number 2, just one-third are genuine, genealogically affiliated senior commoners. However, in contrast to Ivato, where Tranovondro officially own client lands, the government registry lists the land of Ambalabe's client cultivators in their own names. This reflects the Merina colonial land grant policy described in chapter 4.

The fact that the local founder of southern descent group number 1 left fewer descendants (only seven villagers descend from him) than other apical ancestors had implications both in and beyond the village. The ancestor of the clients who are now attached to this group arrived three generations later, but *his* descendants—who today stipulate affiliation with the admitting descent group—outnumber the former's nineteen to seven. The settlement of nearby Tanambao also reflects the paucity of this senior commoner's descendants relative to the size of the ancestral estate, which was originally approximately equivalent to that of Ambalabe's other two senior commoner groups. Most of the meager estate that the people of Tanambao now use once belonged to Ambalabe's southern descent group number 1. Local tradition reports that Merina agents in Mahazony "persuaded" ancestral members of this group—because there were so few of them—to grant land to northerners migrating south in the nineteenth century, including the early settlers of the hamlets that were eventually aggregated to form the village of Tanambao.

The houses of Ambalabe extend along a ridge running east-west, with the densest concentration of houses at the southeast end, closest to the main rice plain, where the southern groups originally settled. On both sides of the road, villagers have built new houses toward the western end, so that no longer are there precise clusters of households headed by members of the same descent group.

Tanambao

Ambalabe's large population justifies the dirt road that links it to Mahazony, making it a center for surrounding hamlets and villages like Tanambao. Tanambao's residents carried their paddy to Ambalabe to sell either to the governmental rice-buying cooperative located there and locally managed, or to private collectors from the subprefecture seat whose trucks came during the harvest season. For several other reasons Tanambao may be considered a satellite of Ambalabe. The people of Ambalabe have deeper historical ties to this region, the first of their ancestors having moved to the canton of Mahazony in the sixth ascending generation (above contemporary elders), whereas Tanambao's most remote ancestor arrived in the second. Like the land-poor junior commoners in Ambalabe, Tanambao's residents—because their ancestors arrived late rather than growing in situ—cannot, like senior commoners, count among their allies members of different branches of their own named descent group localized in nearby villages.

Located on the northern end of a ridge that runs north-south, Tanambao, like Ambalabe, was formed following the French colonial edict of 1913 as an agglomeration of several hamlets, some of which have subsequently been abandoned. The official village now incorporates two nearby hamlets. In contrast to Ivato and Ambalabe, no road divides Tanambao into historically related groups. In fact, social groups beyond the household are, when compared to the other villages, singularly insignificant. The people of Tanambao, if pressed, claim membership in five named descent groups. Yet demarcation of descent group boundaries is not clear, nor are the branches localized in Tanambao generationally deep. Rules of descent, as will be seen in chapter 6, help regulate access to estates, and where estates are meager or absent, as in the case of Tanambao and Ivato's slave descendants respectively, descent structure is also underdeveloped. A genealogy of all descent groups localized in Tanambao from apical ancestors to present-day residents shows marital links between them, but most of the descent groups lack even a skeleton of agnation. Reasons for this are spelled out in chapter 6.

Although it lacks the senior or core status of the Tranovondro in Ivato or any one of the three senior commoner descent groups in Ambalabe, more of the population of Tanambao belongs to the Maromena descent group than to any other. Forty-two or 51 percent of the people in Tanambao live in households whose heads claim to be Maromena. Beyond Tanambao, the Maromena are a populous, important, and widespread Betsileo descent group, represented in fifty-five villages and, with an estimated population of 10,500, ranking tenth on the basis of numbers and range in the macroregional sample. Their larger importance is obscured today in Tanambao by the fact that these forty-two people rely on about 4.5 hectares of rice land to sustain themselves. Yet their regional importance may have been a factor in their original settlement of Tanambao. Their local apical ancestor, a man whose ninety-five-year-old daughter was living in Tanambao in 1967, purchased his land from southern descent group number 1 in Ambalabe following French conquest of Madagascar. The Maromena of Tanambao descend from four of his five children, sons and daughters. All Maromena are buried in a single tomb, near Tanambao proper. One of the sons of the Maromena ancestor married a member of Tanambao's Maromaintso descent group, whose apical ancestor had arrived two generations earlier.

The Maromaintso ancestor, accompanied by his two daughters and their husbands, had received a land grant of approximately three hectares from southern descent group number 1 of Ambalabe. All the Maromaintso in Tanambao descend from the two daughters and have retained their Maromaintso affiliation even though established through females. In contrast to the single Maromena tomb, there are three for the Maromaintso. Two of the tomb groups reside in a hamlet, whereas members of the third live in Tanambao proper. Like the Maromena, the Maromaintso represent a populous and wide-ranging descent group, twelfth in the macroregional sample on the basis of range (fifty-two villages) and thirteenth on the basis of numbers (8,900). Maromaintso now head six of Tanambao's twenty households and account for 23 percent of its population, nineteen people.

Residing in a large house in another hamlet are brothers who claim to be Namodila-Maromaintso. Hyphenated descent group names are rare among the Betsileo, but they occur occasionally in Mahazony and adjacent cantons in the extreme south. The brothers are simultaneously claiming rights in the tomb built by their great-uncle (FFB), a Namodila who left no lineal descendants, and in the agricultural estate inherited from their father's maternal grandmother, a Maromaintso and granddaughter (DD) of the local Maromaintso apical ancestor. The household head, the oldest brother, is the most enterprising man in Tanambao, with experience in the French army. He has used his own labor and that of his wife and two brothers to increase his own rice holdings through purchase and now, with one hectare, exceeds any co-villager in rice land. Aspiring perhaps to be remembered as a prominent ancestor, he has added his father's regionally prestigious, but locally landless, descent group affiliation, Namodila, fourth on the list in the macroregional sample (ninety-two villages), to his mother's, from whose estate comes one of his two rice fields. Twelve people live in his house and eat at his hearth. Tanambao's two final local descent groups are represented in just three households.

Tanambao is poorer than either Ivato or Ambalabe. Its eighty-two residents obtain their livelihood from a mere ten hectares of rice land: .12 hectare per person compared to .2 in both Ivato and Ambalabe. The mean household rice holding of a slave descendant in Ivato matches that of the average junior commoner in Tanambao, .45 hectare. Compare this to mean holdings of .75 hectare and 1.1 hectares in Ambalabe and Ivato respectively, and a gap in access to strategic resources among Betsileo commoners is evident.

Socioeconomic differentiation is much more pronounced in Ivato than in Tanambao, with Ambalabe intermediate. In Ivato men of the same age, but different by virtue of the servitude, or lack of it, of their ancestors, farm estates whose size varies by a factor of eight. In Ambalabe the average junior commoner farms less than half the rice area of the average senior commoner. Alongside these contrasts, the people of Tanambao display a stark sameness of poverty. Reflecting limited access to land, they produce less rice per person (table 10), but they appear to work more intensively (2,610 hours per hectare

TABLE 10
Rice Production and Consumption

	Village		
Variable	Ivato	Ambalabe	Tanambao
Approximate total area cultivated in rice (ha.)	34.2	43	10
Total sampled rice area (ha.)	28.8	16.5	9.2
No. rice fields sampled	45	33	25
No. owners sampled	28	30	23
Mean area per sampled rice field (ha.)	0.64	0.5	0.37
Mean paddy yield per field, 1967 (kg.)	1450	1000	850
Mean paddy yield per ha., 1967 (kg.)	2150	2050	2225
Mean paddy yield per ha., average of 1966, 1967 harvests (kg.)	2250	2100	2350
Total paddy production of sampled rice fields, 1967 (metric tons)	62.3	33.9	20.6
Estimated total village paddy crop, 1967 (total ha. cultivated × mean per ha. yield)	73.9	88.4	22.2
Estimated total no. metric tons of white rice (after pounding) produced 1967 (61% of paddy crop)[a]	45.1	53.9	13.5
Total village population	175	217	82
Annual white rice production per capita (kg.)	260	250	165
Daily local white rice production per capita (kg.)	0.7	0.7	0.45
No. households	31	41	20
No. persons per household	5.6	5.3	4.1
Daily ideal white rice consumption per household (kg.)	3.3	3.9	3.9
Ideal daily white rice consumption per capita (kg.)	0.6	0.75	0.95
Annual ideal total village white rice consumption (metric tons)	37.9	58.3	28.6
Village white rice surplus or deficit (metric tons)	7.2	−4.4	−15.1
Total person-hours invested for average field (selected tasks)[b]	540	1020	970
Person-hours invested per ha. (selected tasks)[b]	840	2040	2610
Person-hours invested to produce 1 metric ton of paddy (selected tasks)[b]	373	1013	1153

a. Based on weights of rice before and after pounding in Ivato.
b. Those listed in table 11.

versus 2,040 in Ambalabe) and the land seems to respond, outyielding nearby Ambalabe 2,350 to 2,100 kilograms of paddy per hectare.[7] Because, as previously noted, aridity makes secondary crop cultivation more difficult in Mahazony than in the agricultural east, the people of Tanambao make up only part of their rice deficit with secondary crops, which, however, are considered inferior dietary staples. Nor do Tanambao's junior commoners own more cattle than their richer neighbors in Ambalabe.

Housing conditions also reflect differential access to strategic resources. Although few of the buildings in Ambalabe are as impressive or as substantial as those in Ivato, Ambalabe's houses are, as a rule, better than those of Tanambao. Some of the houses in Ambalabe are constructed at least partially of brick, and a few have tin or tile roofs. On the other hand, all the houses in Tanambao are wattle and daub, and all have roofs of long grass gathered on the hillsides. Houses in Ambalabe are also less crowded than in Tanambao. An Ambalabe population of 217 lives in thirty-nine houses, whereas there are only eleven houses for the eighty-two people in Tanambao, producing a mean of 5.6 people per house in Ambalabe and 7.4 in Tanambao. In each village, as is true also of Ivato and typical of Betsileo settlements, most houses have two stories. There are contrasts, however, in the social structures of these houses. So scarce is housing in Tanambao that twenty households live in eleven houses; the typical house includes two families, one above, one below. There are always ties of kinship or marriage between the families who share a house, but each is an independent hearth; they neither cook together nor rely on the same rice fields or secondary crop land, nor store their paddy in the same granary. In Ambalabe, in contrast, thirty-nine houses are almost adequate for forty-one households, and, as in Ivato, house-sharing is rare.

Relative to Ivato and Ambalabe, Tanambao is impoverished both in land and labor. Betsileo villagers generally cooperate to build houses. There is little cooperation, however, among the people of Tanambao. There are demographic reasons for this: Tanambao has a small population biased toward old people, and especially old women. Although information on age was not systematically collected in Ambalabe, such information gathered in Ivato and Tanambao shows an average age of twenty-two for the former and twenty-five for the latter. While only 48 percent of Ivato's population was fifteen years or older, the figure was 54 percent in Tanambao. Adult females accounted for only 25 percent of Ivato's population, but for 28 percent of the residents of Tanambao (see table 35).There are also sociopolitical impediments to cooperation in Tanambao: there is no basis, either in descent or in a tradition of historic coresidence, for community solidarity. Contrasts in labor recruitment and relations of production between the three villages are fully examined in chapter 8.

The extreme Betsileo south, including the canton of Mahazony, lacks

the historical political importance of the region around Ivato. Neither Tanambao nor Ambalabe has produced a native son with anything approaching
the regional reputation of our sponsor in Ivato. Nor can the estates of any of
the descent groups in Tanambao or Ambalabe rival that of Ivato's Tranovondro. In the absence of big men with regional reputations and connections
capable of materially improving the lot of villagers, Ambalabe and Tanambao
are in appearance more traditionally Betsileo and, in fact, more typical of
commoner villages in the subprefectures of Ambalavao and Fianarantsoa than
Ivato.

Neither, of course, has running water, and women perform the daily
chore of bringing spring water to their households. There is no school in
either, although there is a Roman Catholic chapel in Ambalabe. No priest
ever graces this chapel, but a villager leads weekly prayer sessions. The absence of ancestral cattle corrals for most of the descent groups in both villages
testifies both to recent settlement and to the inability of these village populations to mobilize the labor force, slave or free, necessary to build them. And
finally, the eucalyptus grove, a monument to the ecological foresight of one
of the ancestors of Ivato and the resident Roman Catholic priest who inspired
him, is missing. Ambalabe is especially bare of trees, and villagers cut firewood in a wooded area below, near the rice plain. There is more shade and a
better supply of firewood near Tanambao.

Contrasts between the Mahazony villages and Ivato also characterize the
technology and techniques of rice cultivation. This emerges clearly in a consideration of the seasonal tasks involved in rice cultivation.

VARIATION IN THE RICE ECONOMY

Division of Labor within the Rice Cycle

For the Betsileo, rice field care is virtually a year-round concern. Maintenance work begins soon after the harvest. In Ivato, 55 percent of the harvests
are in April, and all are completed by May (table 11). In May and June, adult
men, working individually, or, when the owner of the field has adult sons or
other male dependents, in small teams of two or three men, repair the bunds
(*manahalaka*, see tables 33 and 34).[8] Bunds are the earth walls that break up
most rice fields into plots and also bound fields of different owners. With
long-handled spades the men pile onto the top of the bunds earth that has
eroded below during the year. This is also the time of year when the same
workers drain the rice fields, transferring eroded soil and vegetation from the
drainage ditches that run along the sides of fields to the rice fields themselves.
If water remains in the plots, often because there are small springs below the
surface, the men expose these springs, digging furrows to conduct the water
into the drainage canal. It is almost always the owner or his dependents,
usually residents of his household, who do this work. Following foundation

TABLE 11

Calendar of Major Tasks in Rice Cultivation in Ivato, 1966–67

Task	*No. of Fields Worked (by month)* 6	7	8	9	10	11	12	1	2	3	4	5	*Number of Sampled Rice Fields*
Seed nursery	0	4	3	19[a]	10	6	0	0	0	0	0	0	42
Plow	3	1	9	15	5	1	0	0	0	0	0	0	34
Hand till	0	0	2	2	0	2	1	0	0	0	0	0	7
Fertilize	0	0	0	4	8	12	4	0	0	0	0	0	29
Transplant	0	0	0	0	10	18	13	0	0	0	0	0	41
1st weeding	0	0	0	0	2	12	16	7	2	0	0	0	39
2nd weeding	0	0	0	0	0	2	11	10	5	0	0	0	28
Harvest	0	0	0	0	0	0	0	0	1	11	22	6	40
Thresh	0	0	0	0	0	0	0	0	1	8	21	10	40
Store in granary	3	2	0	0	0	0	0	0	0	5	12	15	37
Number of fields worked in given month	6	7	14	40	35	53	45	17	9	24	55	32	

a. Modal month underlined

and drainage work are two or three months during which rural Betsileo enjoy comparative leisure from work in their rice fields (cf. table 11).[9]

Preparation and seeding of nursery beds initiate the new rice cycle. Most Ivatans seed in September, anticipating October or November transplanting. Ivatans can seed late because, following the advice of Gregoire, the local agricultural adviser, they use fewer seed in faster growing nurseries than other Betsileo and than their own ancestors. In Mahazony, where, because of greater reliance on irrigation, transplanting takes place a month or two ahead of Ivato, most seeding is done in May and June, three to four months earlier (table 12). Following traditional Betsileo practice, Mahazony peasants triple the seed and allow it to grow in the nursery for three months. Nursery preparation and seeding are also tasks devolving on the field owner and/or

TABLE 12

Calendar of Major Tasks in Rice Cultivation in Ivato, Ambalabe, and Tanambao (modal month for each village)

Task	*Ivato*	*Ambalabe*	*Tanambao*
Seed nursery	9	5,6	5,6
Plow	9	8,11	9
Hand till	8,9,11	10	9
Fertilize	11	9	11
Transplant	11	10	9
1st weeding	12	11	11
2nd weeding	12,1	12	12
Harvest	4	3	3
Thresh	4	3	3
Store in granary	5	3	3

his male dependents. Nursery preparation rarely involves more than a day's work of an adult male, and the actual seeding is usually a matter of minutes. For a day or two following seeding, the owner watches the nursery in the morning and in the evening when there is danger that birds might eat the seed.

Preparatory to transplanting, traditional Betsileo till with long-handled spades. More and more, however, are using plows, especially in Ivato. Eighty-one percent of the rice fields in Ivato, as compared to only 25 percent in Ambalabe and Tanambao combined, were plowed in 1966. Most Ivatans plowed in August and September, preparatory to transplanting in October, November, and December. The drainage and repair work described above must be done before plowing since, to be plowed, fields must be fairly dry. Those who plow may do it twice. After plowing they hand-till corners and other areas of the rice field where plowing was impossible and make sure that drainage furrows are closed. Standing water imposes fewer limitations on hand tillage. Thus, in Mahazony, where most tillage is still by hand, individual whim appears to determine month of tillage. Feeder canals for irrigated fields are also cleaned and repaired prior to transplanting.

Some of the tasks in rice production are dispensable, and for several reasons some fields receive more attention than others. Peasants who own more than one field invest less labor in traditionally less productive fields, paying more attention to their primary fields, which are usually located closer to their residences. Soil types influence cultivation techniques. About 40 percent of the rice fields in Ivato (versus only 11 percent of the fields in the Mahazony villages) had a soil type known as *baibo*, a term used for sandy (alluvial) soils located near river banks.[10] The permeability of these soils makes harvesting easier and drainage work unnecessary. To accomplish the major tasks in rice cultivation listed in tables 11 and 12, Ivatans invested an average of 670 person-hours per hectare for their seventeen sandy fields as compared to 820 person-hours for the seventeen fields whose soil type was the preferred, higher ground, muddier, more clayey *fotaka*. Since drainage work and other labor requirements of rice field preparation that are not included in tables 11 and 12 are also less onerous for sandy soils, the labor differential between the two soil types is even greater. Yields, too, vary, with clay outyielding sand 2,430 to 2,050 kilograms of paddy per hectare (see table 36). However, an hour's work in sandy soil produces the same payoff (3 kg.) as an hour's work in clay.

Work intensity also depends on plot size. In terraced fields, consisting of several small plots, plowing and harrowing are impossible, and, with more bund area, bunds are cleaned and reinforced as the same time. Bund repair, moreover, may even be neglected some years (see table 34). In valley fields, bunds are rebuilt after harvest, cleared of weed growth, and may be repaired again prior to transplanting.

Plate 1. Extended family of Rakoto (*right* of woman holding baby) of the village of Ivato.

Plate 2. Left of center, village of Ivato. Some of the rice fields have been flooded prior to transplanting, and others have recently been transplanted. Note, *bottom left*, the satellite hamlet and, in the *upper right*, the Outcrop, where Ivatans' ancestors once dwelled.

Plate 3. The *famadihana* (ceremonial tomb inauguration) held in July, 1967 near the village of Little Ambalavao, canton of Mahazony as described in chapter 7. *Lower right,* a party of men carries remains (the white bundle) from an ancient donor tomb to be placed in the new structure, *center of photo.* Note the terraced rice fields in this sparsely populated area, the Betsileo south.

Plate 4. A representative Betsileo village. One house has brick pillars; the others are wattle and daub, all with long-grass roofs. Note, *upper center*, the village tomb and, *upper and lower right*, rice threshing floors. Secondary crops are planted between the village proper and the rice fields (with growing rice) *below*.

Plate 5. Center of photo, the ancient wooden house of Karl Fridaysfather stands alongside the eastern village cattle corral in Ivato. *Far right*, the partially brick house originally constructed by Karl's younger brother, Blacksfather. Its current inhabitants include Marcel, Blacksfather's daughter's son, and Marcel's son, Pierre, the village chief. *Far left*, a small part of Goodmaker's house.

Plate 6. Betsileo settlement pattern and rice terracing.

Labor requirements and yields also vary with type of rice cultivated, which is only partially a function of soil type (see tables 37 and 38). The peasants of Ambalabe continue to concentrate on the ancestrally and gustatorially favored, tried and true, *vary lahy*, while more progressive Ivatans balance yield, flavor, and labor by favoring three varieties. The people of Tanambao, finally, faced with land and labor shortages, experimented with nine different rice varieties in 1966–67, in attempting to put their severely limited resources to maximum productive use. Ivatans plant higher-yielding varieties in small fields and farm these most intensively (see table 39). Of the three varieties that accounted for 90 percent of the rice in Ivato, the traditional *lahy*, whose taste is preferred, was planted in a fourth of the fields, averaging .5 ha. each. In contrast to *lahy*, *angika* was planted in larger (generally sandy) fields, yielded considerably less per hectare, and demanded considerably less work. Long-grained *lava*, grown in only four of the fifty-five fields sampled in the two Mahazony villages, had become Ivatans' most common rice variety, and stood between *lahy* and *angika* in field size, yield, and labor expended.

Irrigated fields are flooded before they are transplanted. His plowing completed, Rakoto let water into his primary rice field in the Ivato plain (see table 33) two weeks before he planned to transplant. Many Betsileo fertilize their flooded fields just prior to transplanting. Most Ivatans now employ a mixture of dry cattle dung and chemical fertilizer. If a peasant uses a harrow in his flooded field, he may choose to fertilize either before, along with, or following this operation. Like the plow, the harrow marks a departure from Betsileo tradition, and is more common in Ivato than Mahazony. In the past, trampling of the flooded field with cattle driven by young men accomplished exclusively what harrowing now assists in Ivato. Although Ivatans owned eleven harrows in the 1966–67 season, as compared to only one in the two Mahazony villages, so strong was the tradition of communal trampling prior to transplanting that trampling was totally abandoned in only three of Ivato's fields, even though most were also harrowed.

Male labor accomplishes field repair, maintenance, and preparation among the Betsileo. Women and children enter the rice cycle as transplanting time draws near, and female labor remains important throughout the remaining stages of cultivation. Women contribute about one-third of the person-hours expended in rice cultivation up to and including storage in granary (see tables 33 and 34). However, when daily drying and pounding of rice is added to productive labor, the female contribution exceeds 50 percent. In some cases in Ivato, the entire household participates in fertilizing the field, carrying baskets of cattle dung from corral to rice plot. Rakoto is the only Ivatan who takes zebu dung to his rice field in an ox cart. In 1967 Rakoto's son, stepson, and two hired hands dumped ten cartloads of dung, each weighing about 500 kilograms, on a hill near his rice field. They then carried baskets from the pile and scattered them in three of the plots in Rakoto's field. In this manner Rakoto fertilizes three of his seven plots each year. Like most Ivatans, Rakoto also bought some chemical fertilizer for his rice fields.

As in their use of plow, harrow, and modern nursery care, Ivatans also depart from Betsileo tradition in fertilizing, employing chemical fertilizers and transporting dung dry from cattle corral to rice field. In the two Mahazony villages, on the other hand, many of the peasants continued to employ the ancestral manuring technique in which water carries dung from cattle corral to flooded field. The peasant digs a canal between his corral and a water source, usually a pond or other reservoir located above it. Another canal leads down from the corral to the rice field, where it branches into several plots. The peasant stands in the corral using a spade to stir the water, mixes it with the cattle dung that has accumulated during the year, and sends it to the fields below.

Transplanting and harvesting are the main events of the rice cycle. They are cooperative occasions, involving several activities, associated with a traditional division of labor on the basis of age and sex. Trampling is the domain of males from their teens through their thirties. Done in each plot, this operation thoroughly mixes water, fertilizer, and tilled soil. As the tramplers leave one plot to go on to another, older men, in their forties, fifties, and sixties, enter the plot and use their spades to break up clumps of earth that the cattle have missed. Before his field is trampled, either the owner, his wife, or a close adult relative goes to his nursery to uproot the seedlings. Male and female adults, often household members, carry the seedlings from nursery to field. Following Betsileo custom, only women transplant. Transplanters range in age from late teens to middle forties, rarely grandmothers. They are usually women who live in the owner's village. In Ivato, the owner may choose to have his field transplanted according to the traditional Betsileo technique of haphazard placement of seedlings or according to the modern method of transplanting in rows. In row transplanting, two young men mark the rows by holding opposite ends of a string along whose length women stick seedlings into the soil.

Agricultural advisers often reported to me that Betsileo women are reluctant to learn the new technique. Even women in Ivato, who can now transplant as quickly using the modern as the traditional technique, contend that they prefer the old way of transplanting in which they made no attempt to line up the seedlings. The major advantage of transplanting in line is that weeding is much simpler and quicker. Weeds are easier to see, and, if the peasant has a Japanese rotary weeder at his disposal, he may weed faster and more often: perhaps four times rather than the traditional two. The four rotary weeders in Ivato belonged to Tuesdaysfather and Rakoto but were available for loan by any covillager. Neither row transplanting nor use of rotary weed-

The Contemporary Betsileo   159

ers had been adopted in Ambalabe or Tanambao. Despite women's expressed preference for traditional transplanting, most Ivatans had adopted row transplanting by 1966, reducing both absolute hours invested in weeding and the percentage of total rice field labor consumed by weeding; 28 percent of Ivatans' rice cultivating labor went to weeding, compared to about 50 percent in Mahazony. Variation in soil type (Ivato's larger area of sandy soil), less weeding time, larger fields, and a smaller percentage of artificially irrigated (versus rainfall dependent) fields are the main reasons why per hectare labor intensity is so much greater in Tanambao (2,610 hrs. per ha.) and Ambalabe (2,040 hrs. per ha.) than in Ivato (840 hrs. per ha.) (see table 40).

Not just technique differentiates transplanting in Ivato from Ambalabe and Tanambao. Ivato again departs from Betsileo tradition in that women who transplant in rows are paid cash for their labor. In Mahazony—and in Ivato when the traditional technique is used—the owner customarily prepares a good meal of rice, meat (usually poultry), and vegetables for the women who have transplanted his seedlings. Whether compensated in food or in cash, however, the transplanters are expected to return to assist in the rice harvest, at which time they receive a share in paddy of the rice they transplanted, averaging about twelve kilograms. Ivatans recall scenes centered around trampling and transplanting in the past, when more people came and when a basic economic activity was a large-scale festive occasion as well. Fields were, of course, bigger in the past. Inheritance has fragmented most of them. Owners of large fields—men like Karl Fridaysfather and Goodmaker—could afford to feast their workers, offering rice and rum, sometimes slaughtering a steer. There are important differences between Ivato and the two Mahazony villages in personnel and labor expenditures associated with the main phases of rice production, including transplanting and other activities: pulling up and transporting of seedlings from nursery to rice field, trampling, and transplanting (see tables 40, 41, and 42). For each activity, people in the Mahazony villages invest more time and assemble more people than in Ivato.

Weeding is the next task in the rice cycle; here, too, as noted, there are major differences between Ivato and Mahazony. Betsileo begin the first of two weedings of their rice fields approximately a month after transplanting. Each weeding takes from twenty days to a month, the first slightly longer than the second, which begins almost as soon as the first has been completed. Traditionally a task involving all members of the owner's household, some of the wealthier Ivatans now hire, for money and/or rice, people from surrounding villages and hamlets, generally descendants of slaves, to do one or both of their weedings. Fifty-six percent of the fields in Ivato used wage labor for one or both weedings, while fewer than one-third of the rice fields in the combined sample of Ambalabe and Tanambao were weeded by wage laborers. Weeding completed, there is little to do in the rice field until harvest time. When the rice grains first appear, owners must guard their fields against birds in the morning and early evening.

March is the modal harvest month (75 percent of all fields) for both villages in Mahazony. Harvest time comes later in Ivato; April is the modal month, with 55 percent of the harvests. In a sample of forty fields in Ivato, thirty-nine were harvested in March, April, or May. As noted, earlier transplanting and harvesting in the two Mahazony villages partially reflects differences in access to water. Owners of 40 percent of Ivato's fields, but only 28 percent of those in the two Mahazony villages, have to await November rains before transplanting. The peasants of Tanambao were especially lucky in this respect; only 16 percent of their fields (many of them purchased, remember, with reliable water in mind) lacked perpetual water sources. A reliable water source in years of normal rainfall does not, however, produce yields higher than those in fields whose owners rely on rainfall or the rejuvenation of springs in the rainy season. For Ivato and Ambalabe, fields with interrupted water sources actually outproduce, slightly and insignificantly, those with perpetual water (see table 43). In years of low or late rainfall, however, those with perpetual water sources have an advantage.

Anticipating this, virtually every Ivatan farms both irrigated and rainfall-dependent fields. In normal years the rain-watered field supplies a surplus that underwrites Ivato's prominence as a regional center and the market participation of its relatively progressive senior commoners. In Ivato irrigation is a hedge against drought. As noted in chapter 4 the recent spread of irrigation south and west has made rice cultivation prominent in the economy of Mahazony and similar areas. Whereas the land-poor junior commoners of Mahazony look to their irrigated fields to eke out a precarious survival, year in and year out, Ivato's senior commoners control varied productive means that almost always guarantee a generous surplus. Only four out of twenty-two Ivatan field owners lack at least one irrigated field. Expectably, only one of them descends from Karl Fridaysfather; the others are western villagers and slave descendants. For many senior commoners, therefore, an irrigated field means insurance; for many juniors it means life itself.

Like transplanting, the Betsileo harvest is a cooperative job with a traditional division of labor on the basis of age and sex. Reaping, done in the past with knives, nowadays with iron sickles, devolves on men, generally in their teens, twenties, and thirties. Females carry the harvested paddy on the stalk from the field to the threshing floor. Most of them are in their teens and twenties; some of the conveyors, however, are women in their thirties, and there is even an occasional subteen. Remaining at the threshing floor are women in their forties and fifties. As their younger covillagers dump the paddy on the threshing floor, the older women pick up the stalks and arrange them in a long bale-like pile. Elderly men and women stand atop the accumulating pile of stalks, compacting it by stomping. As in transplanting, the female's contribution to the harvest overshadows the male's. Men who are neither reaping nor stomping amble around, converse, and watch the harvest scene.

Threshing, to remove paddy from the stalks, is a male activity. In wetter Ivato, with a later harvest that is closer to winter and its morning drizzle, people like to thresh three days after the harvest. In Mahazony two weeks sometime separate harvesting and threshing. Young men and boys thresh by striking the stalks against large rocks that they bring to the threshing floor. Men in their forties and older then beat the stalks with sticks to make sure that all paddy has been removed.

In winnowing, the task that follows threshing, the labor contributed by adolescent and older male and female members of the owner's household is approximately equal. Winnowing is one of the postharvest tasks that depend on the weather. There must be at least a slight wind if one is to winnow, and the speed of winnowing increases up to a point with wind velocity. Drying the paddy also depends on the weather. As soon as the paddy has been threshed, and until it is transported to the granary, the woman of the household, or more rarely her husband, spreads it out each day on a straw mat to dry in the sun. Rainy weather can mean that a process which normally takes two weeks can stretch on for two months. The Betsileo dry their paddy both before and after winnowing.

Finally, all members of the owner's household, except for toddlers and infants, carry baskets of paddy from the threshing floor to the granary. The annual cycle of rice cultivation has been completed. Throughout the remainder of the year women will remove, dry, and pound paddy from the granary virtually every day in order to provide white rice for their household meals.

Constants and Variables in Rice Production

Emphasis in the preceding sections of this chapter, as throughout this book, has been on variation, here specifically involving three rural Betsileo villages with different histories and physical environments, differential sociopolitical significance and access to strategic resources, and variant patterns of rice cultivation, descent group structure, and socioeconomic stratification. The fact of variation, however, should not obscure certain constants. Any Betsileo would admit, for example, that certain tasks are more vital to and invariant in rice cultivation than others. Regardless of soil type, rice variety, and whether grown in terraces or plain, any rice crop demands nursery preparation and seeding, tillage, transplanting, weeding, harvesting, threshing, winnowing, drying, and transport to the owner's granary. Any Betsileo could also recite the age ranges and genders of the personnel who customarily perform specific agricultural tasks. Other constants, however, are not so readily enunciated by peasants, but still show up statistically. In all three villages, for example, the average peasant was around thirty years old when he started cultivating his rice field as its owner. This probably reflects the fact that most fields are inherited, often as a result of death of a parent or grandparent. When a grandfather dies his sons may take over his fields, relinquishing their former plots to their own sons. The average distance between owner's home and rice field was also constant in all three villages, slightly less than one kilometer.[11]

Most of my other statistical analyses of data on rice fields, however, revealed not uniformity, but variation, much of which can be attributed to historical and sociopolitical differences already discussed. Variation between the three villages in the nature, use, and distribution of productive resources also leads to differences in contemporary behavior examined more fully in subsequent chapters. For example, reflecting senior commoners' longer presence in each area, rice fields were older in Ivato and Ambalabe than in Tanambao. In Ivato the average field had been farmed by 4.3 previous owners, comparable to Ambalabe's 4.1, but in contrast to 3.2 in more recently settled Tanambao. Reflecting a combination of factors—including hillier terrain and smaller original descent group estates in Mahazony—Tanambao and Ivato stand at opposite ends of a continuum, with Ambalabe intermediate, in terms of average rice field size and individual plot size within a given field. For Ivato, Ambalabe, and Tanambao respectively, the average number of plots per rice field was seven, ten, and twelve, and the average size of a given plot was .1 ha., .05 ha., and .03 ha. In view of greater labor demands associated with *fotaka* ("muddy") soils and smaller plots, and because of differences in cultivating techniques discussed previously, one can easily understand why labor intensity per unit of land progressively increases from Ivato to Ambalabe to Tanambao (cf. tables 10 and 40).

The figures in table 10 summarize the major differences in rice production and consumption between the three villages. Peasants in Mahazony work between two and three times as hard as Ivatans to produce a given quantity or rice, and the land-poor junior commoners of Tanambao work harder for their rice than their neighbors in Ambalabe. Marginally, their work pays off, since their mean yield per hectare exceeded that of either Ivato or Ambalabe at harvest time both in 1966 and 1967.[12]

Yet hard work is not enough to overcome the rice field shortage in Tanambao. Women in each village were asked how much white (husked) rice they normally prepared each day for their household's consumption. Women measure their daily meals with empty Nestle milk cans of uncooked rice; three of these equal about one kilogram. As reported by informants, the amount of rice prepared each day, translated into kilograms in table 10, was greatest in Tanambao and smallest in Ivato. This partially reflects greater caloric demands resulting from harder work and the larger percentage of adults in Tanambao. It should be pointed out, however, that women were actually responding to my query by reporting how much rice they prepared when they ate rice. They were giving me their household's *subsistence ideal*. When their own granary supply runs out, Betsileo must either buy rice or consume secondary crops, which, when eaten without rice, are deemed to constitute an inadequate meal.[13] Only Ivatans produce a rice surplus (of approximately 7,000 kilograms for the village as a whole) over their subsistence ideal. The deficit in Tanambao (about 15,000 kilograms) is four times that of Ambalabe (4,400 kilograms). Any rice sold by all but a few of the peasants of Tanambao reflected their need to pay taxes. Privileged access to strategic resources on the part of senior commoners in Ambalabe and Ivato, of course, means that some peasants in these villages not only have adequate rice diets, but cash on hand, whereas covillagers who are junior commoners, clients, or slave descendants must look to secondary crops, tobacco cultivation, local employment for wages or rice, and doles from more prosperous villagers to sustain themselves and their families.

To perceive the magnitude of socioeconomic contrasts within a village, the reader may consider data on Ivato summarized in table 31. Although Ivato as a whole produces surplus rice, only ten of its twenty-two household heads for whom complete information is available produce more rice than they ideally consume. Eight of them are eastern villagers; all but one of the eight are descendants of Karl Fridaysfather. With two exceptions the ages of the ten are forty-nine years or older. Whereas Tuesdaysfather, seniormost easterner, heads the list—producing more than five times his household's annual rice consumption—none of the three slave descendant households produces as much as half of its own annual consumption. The readiness of Ivato's slave descendants to continue to serve senior commoners for wages in cash or rice, in order to sustain themselves, is apparent. A similar plight faces junior commoners in Mahazony.

In this chapter (and in various appendixes) a basis for a contemporary socioeconomic ranking of the three villages has been provided. Ivato, Ambalabe, and Ivato sample several historic and contemporary contrasts encountered in the Betsileo heartland. Ivato represents the agricultural east; the two Mahazony villages sample the more pastoral, drier south (and west). Reflecting historical economic and demographic shifts that accompanied Merina and French conquest and pacification, Ambalabe and Tanambao rely more on irrigation for rice cultivation, still have larger cattle holdings, and typically have multiple descent groups residing in the same village, descendants of late nineteenth-century and twentieth-century colonists. Ivatans, as descendants of senior commoner governors and as members of one of the major regional descent groups of the agricultural east, retain their historically favored access to strategic resources. They live in an area where socioeconomic stratification is more pronounced, reflecting an earlier process of state formation. All these contrasts ramify throughout local economy and influence relationships of these villagers to the contemporary world that surrounds and intrudes on them.

Of the three villages, Ivato's historical political importance has been greatest; today its senior commoner core, retaining differential and privileged access to rice land and other strategic resources, is more fortunate than most other Betsileo. The people of Tanambao, most recently settled and poorest of the three, represent the opposite end of the socioeconomic continuum among Betsileo villages. They suffer a land and labor shortage and must struggle to feed and house themselves. Now, as in the past, economically, politically, and in most cases socially as well, Ambalabe is intermediate. As the remaining chapters demonstrate, many aspects of contemporary life in the three villages reflect the historical, social structural, and economic differences already discussed. Throughout the Betsileo heartland, such varied histories, structures, and resources continue to determine reaction to and manner of participation both in local and in regional events. The past, in other words, provides information, opportunities, and impediments that pattern contemporary behavior. However, contemporary strictures always interact with and sometimes block historically appropriate behavior, and thus form part of the selective context that is creating variations of the future.

CHAPTER SIX

The Social Organization of Village Life

Detailed comparison of the principles that govern personal encounters and create social relationships among Betsileo reveals considerable variation following from historic and contemporary differences in access to strategic resources. Social interactions, identities, and distinctions are based on residence in the same or different households, settlements, neighborhoods, and regions. Betsileo social identity also reflects people's regular or occasional participation in the affairs of descent groups of various sorts, sizes, ranges, and genealogical depths. In addition to social ties created at birth through descent and residence, Betsileo routinely—but variably—use other social organizational principles to enlarge and extend their social networks. These include marital alliances, bilateral kinship calculation, fosterage, formal adoption, and ritual or fictive kinship.

Expectably, any Betsileo's access at birth to social relationships—which must be seen as among those strategic resources that are unequally distributed in Betsileo society—varies in accordance with those historically determined contrasts laid out in previous chapters. Focusing mainly on principles that structure everyday behavior, chapter 6 documents some of the significant social organizational contrasts between Ivato, Ambalabe, and Tanambao and relates this variation to differential access to strategic resources. Here again I will be attempt to show how Betsileo use and modify traditional cultural principles to deal with the exigencies of daily living. Chapter 7 will extend the analysis of Betsileo social organization to relationships and interactions, particularly those that are mobilized by ceremonial life, in a larger, neighborhood and regional, arena. But in both chapters the focus will be on functions and interarticulations of ancestral cultural forms within the context of varying material circumstances that influence their behavioral manifestations.

DESCENT AND DESCENT GROUPS

Among the contemporary Betsileo, descent and rules of affiliation with descent groups still play a major role in regulating—that is, assigning and limiting access to—resources strategic to life. These include resources essential to subsistence, such as land, water, and cooperative labor, and resources considered necessary to traditional Betsileo social life, such as a place to live and to be buried. Aspects of descent and affiliation, including seniority and agnation (the ability to trace descent through males) also have constituted avenues to power and prestige in a stratified society with a differentiated administrative subsystem.

Many French scholars have employed the term "clan" to characterize descent groups among the Betsileo and elsewhere in Madagascar. However, use of the terms "clan" and "lineage," which are appropriately applied to unilineal descent groups, is misleading in discussing Betsileo descent groups, since they are more accurately classified as ambilineal, only tending toward patriliny. I also prefer to avoid the terminology that has been developed to describe ambilineal descent groups, terms like ramage, sept, nonunilinear descent group, cognatic descent group, since their meanings and usage are by no means uniform (cf. Davenport 1959; Firth 1968; Goodenough 1968; Murdock 1949, 1968). Furthermore, the use of traditional labels developed for cross-cultural analysis, when applied to a single society, can mask a tremendous range of variation in patterns of affiliation with descent groups (cf. Huntington 1974, p. 92).[1] This variation, of course, is a major interest here.

To avoid both "clan" and "lineage," which should be reserved for unilineal descent groups, and such neologisms as those proposed by Murdock (1968, p. 249) I shall employ the terms "stipulated descent group" and "demonstrated descent group" to deal with analogous groups, with membership based on putative common ancestry among the Betsileo. The importance of stipulated and demonstrated descent varies regionally and with social rank. Betsileo nobles, for example, belong mainly to demonstrated descent groups, those that supplied rulers in the pre-Merina polities, whereas commoners are often members of both stipulated and demonstrated descent groups. Although today the named, maximal descent groups of Betsileo nobles are geographically widespread, most members of the same noble descent group demonstrate descent from their common apical ancestor. The fact that the names of noble descent groups are themselves compounds of the words "children of," "grandchildren of," or "descendants of," plus the apical ancestor's name reinforces demonstration. Thus, on hearing the name of the geographically dispersed Zanakatara descent group, one can immediately identify the ancestor as Rantara; the relatively unrestricted (cf. Goodenough 1968, p. 211) descent group comprises her "children" (*zanaka*) or descendants through males and females.

Although no nobles (except a few in-marrying wives) reside in any of the three villages I studied, senior commoners live in two of them. Senior commoners seem to lie midway between junior commoners and nobles in terms of the importance of stipulated and demonstrated descent. One might clarify the distinction by asserting that the maximal descent groups of junior commoners are always stipulated; nobles usually demonstrate their descent from the founder of their maximal descent group, and senior commoners strive for demonstration. Some achieve it; others do not.

I obtained genealogies for all descent groups, both junior and senior commoners, in Ivato, Ambalabe, and Tanambao, as well as elsewhere in the subprefectures of Fianarantsoa and Ambalavao. The descent group genealogy of the Tranovondro of Ivato can illustrate some of the problems involved in assessing the significance of stipulated and demonstrated descent groups. Starting with Tuesdaysfather, the (then) sixty-five-year-old elder, the Tranovondro of eastern Ivato trace their genealogy to the tenth ascending generation with no break and through only one female link (Petersmother, see figures 2 and 4) in the P5 generation.[2] According to tradition, a Tranovondro from the southeast coast settled near Ivato in the eighth ascending generation. Above the P10 generation a genealogical gap obscures an unknown number of generations of reputed Tranovondro residence on the southeast coast. Deeper in the past the genealogy begins again, this time extending back three generations through one male and two female links. Tranovondro maintain that their ultimate apical ancestress was the sister of a king of early Imerina. According to tradition, the Tranovondro assumed their descent group name during the second of these remote generations, when a colony of proto-Tranovondro settled in a mountainous region in southern Imerina. Some members of this colony thereafter migrated to the southeast coast where they resided until some of their descendants moved to Betsileo country. None of my informants could locate exactly the northern colony. Nor did Betsileo Tranovondro know if fellow Tranovondro continue to reside there or on the coast.

There are no social relations based on common descent, and there are no known contacts whatsoever, between Betsileo Tranovondro and collaterals stemming from the ninth ascending generation and above. For Ivato's Tranovondro, the eighth ascending generation establishes the effective maximal descent group. Tranovondro can locate, by region at least, all collateral groups that have diverged from the senior descent branch in or subsequent to this generation. When an Ivatan meets a Tranovondro from one of these branches, shared membership in the same named descent group can provide an idiom for social relations. Thus, when one considers socially significant, rather than theoretically possible, descent groups, the maximal demonstrated descent group coincides with the stipulated descent group.

In general, feelings of descent group solidarity and frequency of social interaction increase as genealogical depth, level of branching, and territorial distance decrease. On the P7 generation only the oldest of seven sons remained in Ivato to inherit his father's estate, thus establishing the senior branch status of his descendants. Two of his brothers settled in Tanala country and presumably became apical ancestors of Tanala descent groups. Another brother moved about sixty kilometers south; his descendants populate several villages in two cantons, including Mahazony. Tranovondro who have remained at or near the original settlement site do not associate at all with these distant collateral lines.

The senior Tranovondro, however, have maintained ties with geographically nearer collaterals. Of the seven brothers in the P7 generation, two settled between fifteen and thirty kilometers south of Ivato, and the youngest founded a village twelve kilometers to the east. Marriages have strengthened ties between Ivatans and these other Tranovondro. In the past senior commoners seem to have preferred to marry other members of their own named descent group. This practice reflected a more general preference that Tranovondro marry only those of their own stratum or higher. The village, on the other hand, if it contained a single descent group, was exogamous. Tranovondro men appropriately sought wives in other Tranovondro villages or in villages of other senior commoner descent groups. Thus, contemporary Tranovondro participate in social relations reflecting both common descent and affinal alliance with members of geographically near collateral descent branches.

Descent group endogamy among Betsileo senior commoners can be seen as one variation on a general Malagasy theme, preferred endogamy, which is, however, much more characteristic of the Betsileo's northern and southern neighbors, Merina and Bara, than of the Betsileo themselves. Prescriptive endogamy is associated with higher rank in many Malagasy societies. Betsileo nobles and senior commoners are similar to the higher ranking Merina demes (Bloch 1971, pp. 65, 175) in prescribing, or strongly encouraging, kin group endogamy. However, in traditional Imerina all free men and women belonged to demes: local, endogamous, cognatic (in theory and often in practice) kin groups. Demes were subdivided into smaller cognatic kin groups called *fianakaviana*, also normally endogamous, with the favored marriage between second cousins (grandchildren of a brother and sister) [Bloch 1971, pp. 50–54]. The tendency toward *local* endogamy therefore contrasted with Betsileo village exogamy, and Merina marriage ties (in native terms) not only kept marriages "pure" but kept ancestral land from passing to nonrelatives (Bloch 1971, pp. 54, 175). On the other hand, the Betsileo upper-rank custom of combining descent group endogamy with village exogamy cemented *regional* alliances already based on common descent.

The Tranovondro of Ivato represent one case of a senior commoner descent group in which there is no operational distinction between the stipulated descent group and the effective maximal demonstrated descent group. In theory, the stipulated descent group includes people who do not belong to the demonstrated descent group, but in fact it never does. The situation is different, however, for junior commoners whose occupation of an area has been recent and whose claims there are not well established, such as the junior commoner descent groups of Ambalabe and Tanambao. Shallow genealogies, never exceeding six generations, typify these local descent groups. Such newcomers originally received land from estates of senior commoners already settled in the region.

For these junior groups, stipulated descent has more significance than for senior commoners. For example, the Namodila descent group was widespread and important in Lalangina. However, because of Lalangina's dense population, junior members of many of its largest descent groups have migrated to the less populated south. People who call themselves Namodila in Tanambao and other villages in Mahazony normally trace their genealogies no farther than the ancestor who first arrived in that region. Although they may remember his village of origin, they cannot name his ancestors, nor can they link themselves genealogically with Namodila collaterals who remained in Lalangina or who emigrated to other Betsileo areas. When, therefore, migration involves long distances, and when demonstrated genealogical links are allowed to lapse and to be forgotten, the stipulated descent group becomes significant. Stipulation of membership in the Namodila descent group, rather than demonstration of descent from the apical ancestor of the Namodila as a whole, was employed when Namodila engaged in trade to the north, or today when they meet their senior collaterals in the original Namodila homeland.[3]

Despite the variation in the significance of stipulated descent, never do geographically dispersed maximal descent groups represent behavioral collectivities. Participation in common ceremonial activities depends on geographical distance. Neither all members of these large-scale descent groups, nor representatives of all their branches, ever come together. They can never mass as an entity against other such groups, since they are widely scattered in space, spanning modern administrative subdivisions and old political boundaries. Obviously such large-scale descent groups are not corporate in the sense of controlling access to any joint estate.[4] Stipulation of membership in the same named descent group, like the ritual kinship system described below, appears to have functioned principally in granting hospitality to travelers and traders. In the context of the modern Malagasy Republic, another function emerged. Politicians stipulated descent group membership to curry votes.

Corporate descent groups among contemporary Betsileo focus on estates consisting of tombs, houses, rice fields, water rights, and lands used to graze cattle and cultivate secondary crops. Ivato can again be used to illustrate relationships between more closely related descent branches. Ivato's senior status in its multivillage rice plain rests on demonstration of descent from oldest sons of the P8, P7, and P6 generations. The large rice plain, several smaller valleys, grazing land, woods, secondary crop lands, and a stretch of the Sabotsy River compose the estate originated by the P8 generation settler of Ivato and his extended family. The ancestral estate began to fragment in the P6 generation as brothers founded new settlements on the western and northern sides of the rice plain. The oldest and youngest brothers, Hundred-master and Noblemaker, remained in Ivato on the plain's southern boundary. Subsequent generations saw the growth of new settlements and further descent group branching. Today about a dozen villages and hamlets share access to the original territory. Five villages and large hamlets with a total population of approximately 800 surround the large rice plain. Smaller settlements have grown up in adjacent valleys.

As descendants of the first settlers, all Tranovondro claim superior status (as *tompotany*, owners or caretakers of the land) to more recent immigrants, who have obtained their estates through purchase, grants, and Merina policy. Yet only the senior Tranovondro of Ivato—the ceremonial, judicial, political, and economic center of a major rice plain region—invoke this claim. Residents of satellite and junior villages and hamlets traditionally brought unresolved disputes to the elders of Ivato for arbitration. Ultimate and binding arbitration of unresolved trouble cases has been a function of the state, rather than of the descent group, among the Betsileo for over two hundred years. Yet, because senior commoners, including men of Ivato, were themselves representatives of the state, junior commoners' recourse to administrative authority often involved the senior branch of their own descent group. In the past Ivato's elders also organized construction, maintenance, and repair operations, recruiting Ivatans and satellite villagers to work on the irrigation and drainage system shared by the villages of the rice plain. After sixty-five years of colonial rule, and in the context of the Malagasy Republic, each cultivator and his immediate family now maintain the water system, and peasants take disputes to a more impersonal tribunal in Fianarantsoa. Yet satellite villagers still defer to the elders of Ivato in speech and bearing. I observed no cases of agricultural labor exchange between these neighboring villages. Cooperative labor in rice cultivation normally involves people of the same village and, less regularly, affinals of the rice field owner. In the past, however, the agricultural work had a broader base.[5]

The division of Ivato into eastern and western branches has been discussed above. Concentrating on the eastern village, one observes further branching reflecting allocation of land. A section of the tomb of the eastern village is reserved for each of the three brothers in the P3 generation—Karl Fridaysfather, Blacksfather, and Alan. Social divisions stemming from these brothers are also recognized in everyday village life. Eastern villagers are said to belong to three different "families" (*fianakaviana*).[6] Ivatans identify these minor descent groups as "grandchildren of" or "descendants of" Karl, Blacksfather, or Alan. These groups now control their members' access to land. Unless all members of one of the three died or moved elsewhere, land currently controlled by one could not be reallocated to members of one of the others.

These groups are similar to the agnatically organized local corporate descent groups (*tariky*) of the Bara (Huntington 1974) and the patrilocally based Sakalava lineage segments described by Gardenier (1976, pp. 83–84). Sakalava lineage segments are joined together into "lineages" that share a common cemetery (Gardenier 1976, pp. 84 et seq.), and these are grouped into "clans" (*karaza, fahitsy*) that share certain cattle earmarks and taboos. Unlike both Sakalava lineage segments and Betsileo minor descent groups, Bara *tariky* do not belong to larger descent groups organized by similar genealogical principles.

However, as in the Bara *tariky*, each Betsileo minor descent group has a moral-political leader, normally the oldest living member of the group's senior surviving generation. The Bara leader must be agnatically affiliated with his *tariky*, and he (rarely she) alone may conduct essential curing and passage rituals. Confirming the slighter emphasis on jural agnation in Betsileo local descent group organization, one of eastern Ivato's three minor descent groups is headed by a nonagnate.[7] And reflecting greater missionary success among the Betsileo, one of the leaders—a staunch Roman Catholic— has relinquished his role in ancestral rituals to a more traditional junior member. As among the Bara, on the leader's death, succession passes to his brother or closest collateral, and this process continues until the generation is exhausted, when it passes to the oldest, or usually oldest surviving, son of the senior member of the previous generation. Since eldest sons allocate land, their own estates and those of their descendants profit at the expense of their younger brothers. Karl Fridaysfather's son Goodmaker, for example, granted rights to use the estate of his father's youngest brother, Alan, to slave descendants. Alan's descendants suffer today with mean holdings hardly more sizable than those of slave descendants, who use half of their land.

Descent group branching and its relationship to social ranking among the Betsileo may be summarized as follows: the maximal, stipulated descent group is functionally important for junior commoners. Maximal noble descent groups are usually demonstrated. (Slave descendants, with no estates to manage, belong to no descent groups at all.) The branching of a senior commoner descent group usually involves (1) a geographically dispersed and, in practice, nonfunctional named stipulated descent group (this name also describes all lower level divisions), (2) a geographically dispersed maximal demonstrated descent group, (3) a major descent group spread out around a single broad estate, (4) a descent segment localized in a village, (5) a descent segment with rights to burial in a single tomb, and (6) a minor descent or land control group. Levels 1 through 3 and their branches are ranked with reference to other named descent groups on the basis of priority of settlement in a region, numerical strength, and political role in the past. Levels 4 through 6 are ranked by degree of agnation and relative seniority—descent through oldest sons of oldest sons.

Descent Groups: Recruitment and Affiliation

Betsileo rules of descent and affiliation may be viewed as involving two principles. On the one hand, patterns of affiliation with local descent groups are in theory, as stated by Betsileo informants, and in fact, as measured by the ethnographer, patrilineally biased. On the other hand, Betsileo ideology allows individuals to affiliate with descent groups other than their father's and in addition to their father's.[8] Although such optative-nonexclusive affiliation may be manifest in land use, it is most commonly expressed in participation in tomb ceremonials, examined in chapter 7. The composition of Betsileo descent groups, as a result of this granting of alternatives, reflects the statistical outcome of multiple individual choices made across the generations.

To illustrate variation in residence and relationships between stratification and patterns of affiliation, the three villages where I carried out intensive field work may be compared. Recall that senior commoners form the core of Ivato's population, Ambalabe includes both senior and junior commoners, and all residents of Tanambao are junior commoners. The percentage of adult Betsileo (excluding in-marrying spouses) residing in their father's village never fell below 71 percent (table 13), confirming a patrilineal, patrilocal bias in group affiliation. This figure may seem low since, with the exception of slave descendants, postmarital residence is almost universally virilocal. However, most choices about residence are not, for males, made at marriage. Although virilocality is a definite preference, so that a woman almost always moves to her husband's village, he may have shifted his residence once or

TABLE 13
Village Rank versus Residence according to Village of Parent

| | Residence | | | | | |
| | Father's Village | | Mother's Village | | Total | |
Village	No.	%	No.	%	No.	%
Ivato	22	71	9	29	31	100
Ambalabe	49	83	10	17	59	100
Tanambao	19	86	3	14	22	100
Total	90	80.4	22	19.6	112	100

Note: Freeman's *theta* (θ) = .19. Rank associated with residence in mother's village.

more prior to their marriage, or he may do so, accompanied by his wife and children, later.

From birth, a Betsileo is endowed with several alternatives in terms of local descent group affiliation and residence. The father's group is usually chosen, but a man also inherits rights to live in his mother's natal village and to cultivate her ancestral estate. Marriage does not demand that a Betsileo woman sever ties with her original descent group. She, her husband, and their children take part regularly in economic, social, and ceremonial activities of her own descent group. An individual's range of affiliation rights encompasses still other groups. Every Betsileo of free ancestry has several options about descent group affiliation. Affiliation is optative and non-exclusive (Murdock 1968). One's descent group affiliation may be, relatively speaking, momentary and depends on where he or she is. In one's father's village, he identifies with his father's descent group. If he resides in his mother's village, a man regards himself, and others regard him, as a member of her descent group. But people change descent group identities even as they travel from village to village. When people take part in a ceremony held in their mother's mother's village, for example, they are regarded as members of her descent group. Individual Betsileo, then, have as many descent group affiliations as there are groups in whose social and ceremonial activities they ever participate as a descendant of a member of that group. In villages with which they have no ancestral connection, however, they are regarded as a member of the group whose estate they reside on and cultivate. A Betsileo thus has several occasional group memberships, and one that is more permanent, though it too may change.[9]

This does not preclude the possibility, moreover, that enterprising individuals can simultaneously reap benefits derived from rights in multiple groups. If one lives near his mother's community, or his mother's mother's, or his father's mother's, he may actually be able to remain in his father's village, farming his patrimony as his primary field, while simultaneously cultivating rice fields that are part of another ancestral estate. In a sample of ninety-eight cultivators representing all three villages, seventy-nine or 75 percent confined their cultivation to the estate where they resided. The remaining fourth also had rice fields elsewhere. Although a maximum of 29 percent of all Betsileo commoners in table 13's sample reside in their mother's village, a maximum of 40 percent of all rice fields cultivated (table 14) derive from the maternal side. The percentage of rice fields derived from the mother is higher in each village than the percentage of individuals residing in their mother's village. In these cases, the individual is obliged to lend agricultural assistance to both groups whose estates he cultivates, but his obligations are strongest in the community where he lives. Size of inheritance appears to be one determinant of residence choice and therefore primary

TABLE 14

Village Rank versus Inheritance of Rice Fields according to Parent

	Rice Fields Inherited Through					
	Father		*Mother*		*Total*	
Village	*No.*	*%*	*No.*	*%*	*No.*	*%*
Ivato	29	60	19	40	48	100
Ambalabe	56	78	16	22	72	100
Tanambao	19	76	6	24	25	100
Total	104	71.7	41	28.3	145	100

Note: Freeman's θ = .18. As rank increases, there is greater likelihood that an individual will cultivate rice fields derived through his mother.

descent group affiliation. The mean size of rice fields included within the estate of one's residence was .85 hectare (n = 79), whereas fields cultivated through rights derived from secondary descent group memberships averaged only .67 hectare (n = 19); (η^2 = .04).

With reference to descent group affiliation, then, Betsileo never face the problem of permanently relinquishing one affiliation for another. Through social visits and participation in ceremonials in multiple ancestral and affinal villages, they maintain multiple links that either they or their children might eventually need to exploit more actively. A man's primary descent group is that established by his residence; a woman's principal affiliation remains with the descent group that raised her. However, people's descent group identity changes whenever they go to the village of one of their other ancestors, either for a visit, as a temporary resident, or as a permanent occupant. Residence may and does change, but descent group affiliation remains multiple.

Contradiction and Flexibility in Betsileo Descent Structure

The system described above could not operate without certain ideological and behavioral supports, but there is a contradiction in Betsileo social structure between one's status as an *individual* parent and potential ancestor, and one's status as a member of a descent *group*. Betsileo assert that they like to have as many descendants as possible to comfort them in old age, to attend their funerals, and to conduct ancestral rites. For the Betsileo, who are fond of children, it makes no difference if these descendants come through male or female links. Lacking sons, a Betsileo commonly claims as heir his daughter's first son, and if she has no son, her first daughter.[10] So compelling is the desire to retain as many descendants as possible—personnel to cultivate the ancestral fields, to live in the ancestral village, to defend the group's interests, to be buried in the ancestral tomb, to perform the ancestral rites—that even daughters who have married out are never completely severed from their natal group. If they have borne children for their husband's group, they have the right to stay on as widows, supported by their sons, in their husband's village, and to be buried with the women in their husband's and sons' tomb. On the other hand, when such a woman dies, a delegation representing her own village customarily comes to her husband's village to ask to take her body home. The same request is made when one of her children dies. Neither is usually granted.[11]

On the one hand, the ancestors reach out and extend their estate, their village, and their tomb to all their descendants. On the other, those who are alive and who depend on the ancestral estate to support themselves and their immediate families seek to exclude nonagnates from the estate. Men do not want their patrilateral cross-cousins and their sister's sons competing with them and their children for the same resources. Thus, patrifiliation is stressed as the norm, and Betsileo contend that in their kinship system the father's side counts more than the mother's. Data described below, however, show that this commonplace ideal statement about what kinship calculation should be like does not accord with most Betsileo's actual descriptions of their own kinship relationships. One might speculate that agnates cultivate a patrilineal dogma in order to make nonagnate covillagers as uncomfortable as possible. Thus, although they have the right as descent group members, most Betsileo males do not choose to reside in their mother's village and to partake of her ancestral estate. They know that they will face problems if they do.

Within a primarily agnatic village there is a socially recognized difference between the children of sons and those of daughters. Agnates express their hostility to nonagnates, most commonly by leveling accusations of witchcraft against them. Most Betsileo are aware of the status of nonagnates in their own village. Extremely compelling reasons are needed before a Betsileo will reside in his mother's rather than in his father's village. Once the choice has been made, however, agnates can make no concrete move toward exclusion. The ancestors are believed to oversee village life, protecting all their descendants and guaranteeing a place for daughter's children, who are also protected legally as heirs. Informal ostracism, expressed in numerous everyday encounters, is the only form of exclusion that agnates can employ.[12]

Thus Betsileo descent must be understood in the context of two competing principles. On the one hand, the desire for children—for descendants—and the wish to retain the affiliation of one's descendants with one's own group work for ambilineality and allow people a multitude of affiliation choices. On the other, land pressure and the resulting desire of agnates to control exclusively access to the estate they cultivate tends to favor limiting rights to members of the patriline. On the one hand, stressing of patrilineal descent permits some degree of exclusion when population pressure on land increases. On the other, the possibility of multiple affiliation can also serve as a population adjustment mechanism. In times of special need the individual may face the choice of maximizing social harmony by remaining in an overcrowded father's village, or of insuring subsistence for himself and his family by residing in his mother's. The ideal solution, of course, is to live in one's father's village while cultivating one's mother's rice fields, too. If this cannot be done, and if the individual does not want to leave Betsileo country, then, as the 20 percent of Betsileo (on the average) who reside in their mother's village document, subsistence rather than social harmony is likely to be maximized.

The Relationship between Ranking and Affiliation Choices

Tables 13 and 15[13] reveal relationships between socioeconomic variation and affiliation and residence choices. Table 13 suggests an *inverse* relationship between rank and patrifiliation. Senior commoners are less likely to be living in their father's village than junior commoners.

Table 15, on the other hand, shows that when one considers antecedent generations, a *positive* relationship between rank and agnation emerges. This probably reflects political variables rather than land use. It has been pointed out that seniority depends not only on occupation of a long-settled ancestral site, but also on descent through eldest sons of eldest sons. Ivato includes a core—about two-thirds of the native population—that traces agnatic descent back (at least) three generations. The percentage of villagers of lower stratum who can do this is considerably less. As table 15 documents, only 15 percent of the junior commoners of Tanambao and less than half of the people of Ambalabe demonstrate pure agnatic descent from the P3 generation.

To summarize the association between stratum and patrifiliation: a seemingly inverse relationship between seniority and patrifiliation inferred from P1 generation figures is transformed into a strong positive relationship by the third ascending generation. Ivato enjoys a larger estate, a wider reputation, and traditionally a more important political role than the two villages in Ma-

TABLE 15

Village Rank versus Residence according to Village of Great-Grandparent:
FFF versus All Others

	Residence					
	FFF		All Others		Total	
Village	*No.*	*%*	*No.*	*%*	*No.*	*%*
Ivato	20	71.4	8	28.6	28	100.0
Ambalabe	23	44.2	29	55.8	52	100.0
Tanambao	3	15.0	17	85.0	20	100.0
Total	46	46.0	54	54.0	100	100.0

Note: Freeman's θ = .41. Rank associated with residence in FFF village.

hazony. Neither Ambalabe nor Tanambao has been settled as long, nor has either served as a political center. In neither, therefore, has long-term agnation been used to bolster political claims.

BETSILEO DESCENT GROUPS IN COMPARATIVE PERSPECTIVE

We may recognize parallels between Betsileo descent groups and those of other Malayo-Polynesian cultures. For example, resemblances to the Maori, Tongan, and Samoan ramages that Firth (1968, pp. 215–20) describes are extensive. Goodenough's (1968) detailed analysis of nonunilinear descent groups of the Gilbert Islands, however, offers perhaps the clearest comparative framework for analyzing the kinds of kin groups that structure Betsileo society. In attempting to reconstruct forms of Proto-Malayo-Polynesian social organization, Goodenough identifies four types of Gilbertese descent groups that have collateral forms in other parts of Oceania and Indonesia. All four show up, in outline at least, among the Betsileo.

The first of these is the Gilbertese *mweenga*. As among the Betsileo, where the term *fianakaviana* may be used either for extended family or for minor descent group as described above (e.g., all the descendants of Karl Fridaysfather), the Gilbertese term *mweenga* is now restricted to household, but formerly referred to a "predominantly patrilocal" extended family (Goodenough 1968, 198).

A second Gilbertese kin group, the *kainga* was a nonunilinear descent group based on parental residence. As among the Betsileo, Gilbertese postmarital residence was usually virilocal, in which case children inherited their father's *kainga* membership. Sometimes, however, residence was uxorilocal, and children then belonged to their mother's *kainga*. As in the Gilberts, a Betsileo's primary *local descent group* affiliation at birth is also determined by parental residence, and adult women keep this local descent group affiliation despite marriage. However, in apparent contrast to the Gilbertese, Betsileo enjoy the option of changing their primary local descent group affiliation prior to marriage by moving to another ancestral village, for example, from father's to maternal grandfather's or grandmother's, or paternal grandmother's ancestral village. In any case, however, primary local descent group membership for adult males is based on residence on and use of an estate originally settled or created by an ancestor. Furthermore, as among both Betsileo and Bara (cf. Huntington, 1974, pp. 73, 140), succession to local descent group leadership in the Gilberts was patrilineal. As in Ivato, with greater political prominence than the two Mahazony villages, eligible successors resided patrilocally in the Gilberts.

A third Gilbertese kinship group, the *ooi*, seems comparable to the Betsileo *common descent group*, which emerges in the context of tomb-centered

ceremonials, examined further in chapter 7. Like the people who constitute
the Betsileo common descent group, members of Gilbertese *ooi* are geographically dispersed, residing on the estates of their local descent groups, or
their spouse's. Members of an *ooi* trace common descent to an apical ancestor, the original holder of a tract of land. As among the Betsileo, inheritance
of land proceeds through sons and daughters, with the former receiving larger
shares. Brotherless sibships, however, insure that some substantial land rights
are always transmitted through women. By continuing to claim descent
through males and females from the *ooi* founder, its members, even if they
do not actually cultivate his estate, maintain potential land rights. Land may
revert to them when a cultivator dies childless.

Members of the Betsileo common descent group trace descent from an
ancestor associated with land (a village or hamlet and its territory) but, more
importantly, with the ancestral tomb and mortal remains located there.[14]
Common descent group membership is demonstrated by participating in
ceremonials centered on these tombs, and Betsileo may in this way reaffirm
their membership in up to eight common descent groups (those of all eight
great-grandparents).[15] Such ceremonial participation, especially when grandparents' remains are involved, helps preserve potential land rights and regional alliances.[16] On the other hand, most of the actual cultivators are those
members of the common descent group who, in each generation, have also
made this their primary descent group affiliation through residence.

A fourth Gilbertese kin group, the *bwoti*, also has a partial Betsileo
parallel. Like the Gilbertese *ooi* and *kainga*, members of the same *bwoti*
share a common ancestor who originally settled the tract of land that is their
focus. The restrictive principle that governs the composition of this type of
descent group is actual land use. *Bwoti* membership is demonstrated through
participation in public meetings held at a meeting house where each *bwoti*
member is formally seated in specific named places. According to Goodenough, anyone who cultivates even a miniscule share of the ancestral estate
may take a seat in the meeting house. Those who, as members of the
founder's *ooi*, have only potential rights, however, are excluded from *bwoti*
meetings. Nor do *bwoti* and *kainga* membership correspond, since one retains
the latter even when not using ancestral land (e.g., when residing in a
spouse's village), and since *bwoti* members need not reside in the same locality. Using the ancestral estate is the sole determinant of *bwoti* membership.

The Betsileo parallel is the *fokonolona*. This term, as noted in chapter
4, was probably borrowed from the Merina, and the composition and functions of the group to which it was applied were altered under Merina and
French colonialism. Like the Gilbertese *bwoti*, participation in a *fokonolona*
is based on cultivation of an ancestral estate. However, the distinction between the *fokonolona* and the Betsileo local descent group is not totally iso-

morphic with that between the Gilbertese *bwoti* and *kainga*. The *fokonolona* is primarily a local-level organization that regulates village affairs. Anyone who cultivates part of an ancestral estate may participate in *fokonolona* meetings in the village where the estate is located, even if he or she resides elsewhere. However, in practice, few nonvillagers attend *fokonolona* meetings.

A cultivation-based descent group more similar to the Gilbertese *bwoti* may have been more important in pre-Merina social organization in the southern highlands, but patterns of migration and settlement aggregation described in previous chapters have made the contemporary Betsileo *fokonolona* primarily a village-based, and only incidentally a descent-based, institution.[17] Thus in Mahazony *fokonolona* meetings bring together members of multiple local descent groups, and in Ivato descendants of free people, clients, and slaves attend (though the last have little input since they have no ancestral estate rights of their own).

The similarity with the Gilbertese *bwoti* lies in actual use of land as a criterion of *fokonolona* membership. Anyone who cultivates a rice field in a village has the right to attend its *fokonolona* meetings. Most participants are male household heads, but the following also take part: (1) separated, divorced, or widowed women who have returned home and control a rice field; (2) unmarried men who have inherited or been assigned a rice field while still residing in the household of a parent or other older relative; and (3) widows who manage their deceased husband's field in the name of their not-yet-adult children.

Note, too, the similarity between the formal seating arrangement of the *bwoti* meeting house and the astrologically-based ritual order that determines seating and placement of Betsileo at *fokonolona* meetings and on other formal occasions. Betsileo make seating dependent on age, seniority, and stratum, whereas *bwoti* members are assigned named seats. Nevertheless, the nature and organization of the *bwoti* and *fokonolona* suggest that they are variants on a single theme, perhaps cognate forms of social organization.

SUPRALOCAL DESCENT GROUPS AND MALAGASY SOCIAL ORGANIZATION

Despite these similarities, some aspects of the Betsileo descent system lack Gilbertese parallels. All the Gilbertese groups described by Goodenough are centered on particular tracts of land. In many cases, however, Betsileo ancestral estates are embedded in larger, supralocal, descent group structures, probably reflecting the contrast between small atolls and thousand of square kilometers of Betsileo heartland on a near continental island. As noted previously, many Betsileo local descent groups demonstrate or stipulate affiliation with geographically dispersed named descent groups that may span entire regions of Madagascar. Note that the tomb-centered common descent groups whose similarities to the Gilbertese *ooi* have been noted above are also grafted onto this supralocal descent structure since their ancestral tombs and estates are *simultaneously* foci of a local descent group and of a dispersed common descent group. Because of this linkup, and because it is possible to convert common descent group rights into local descent group membership by a residence shift, Betsileo do not terminologically distinguish supralocal descent groups in which membership is based on residence from those in which affiliation is demonstrated through ceremonial participation. The terms *foko* and (less regularly) *karazana* are used for named descent group in any context, local or regional, and regardless of whether membership is primary or subsidiary.

The structure of the Betsileo supralocal descent group thus is formed by two principles that govern affiliation at lower levels: (1) the everyday, restrictive principle, often agnatically based, that determines local descent group composition; and (2) the nonexclusive principle—totally ambilineal—that operates in a ceremonial context, keeps alliances between local descent groups alive, and creates the common descent group. Here again we see that use of labels like "patrilineal" or "ambilineal" to characterize Betsileo descent would mask the dynamics of a cultural system where both operate simultaneously, but variably, at different levels and in different contexts (cf. Huntington 1974, p. 69).

The structure of the Betsileo supralocal descent group also offers contrasts with other Malagasy peoples. For example, Huntington's research among the Bara has uncovered no such supralocal descent groups among the immediate southern neighbors of the Betsileo. Localized Bara patrilineages (*tariky*), in contrast to Betsileo estate-centered groups, appear never to be constituent segments of supralocal descent groups. Huntington (1974, pp. 186 et seq.) does describe a cognate, but structurally different, unit of Bara social organization, the *raza* (Betsileo *karazana*). The *raza* is a large, named, endogamous, cognatic kin group with a descent ideology. It may include 1,000 people or more, and its members share its name, a cattle ear mark (transmitted matrilineally from cow to female and castrated offspring), and certain traditions. Endogamy is much more characteristic of Bara than Betsileo. Huntington (1974, p. 191) reports that 75 percent of all residents of the village he studied had at one time been married to a first or second cousin. As among the Merina (Bloch 1971), where local and kin group (deme or *karazana*) endogamy has also been practiced, the resultant merging of kin and affinal ties obliterates distinctions between agnatic and uterine ancestors, creates multiple relationships with descendants, and erodes any semblance of a unilineal skeleton.

Betsileo trace descent farther back than their northern and southern neighbors, and they remember remote kinship ties between founders of different estates. Although they lack the precise segmentary structure of classic African descent systems, Betsileo descent groups, particularly those of nobles and senior commoners, do follow a clearer genealogical branching model than those of Merina and Bara. None of the more pastorally oriented populations of Madagascar, such as the Bara of Huntington (1974), Sakalava of Gardenier (1976), Tsimihety of Wilson (1967, 1971), or even the cultivating Masikoro-Sakalava of Lavondès (1967), trace genealogies (at least of commoners) more than three generations into the past. (Wilson's report [1971] does suggest, however, that Tsimihety belong to geographically dispersed stipulated descent groups organized through an agnatic skeleton.)

The Betsileo I studied thus present a sharp contrast to other Malagasy groups in the deeper demonstrated genealogies of even their junior commoners. Decades of permanent cultivation, but more significantly, for nobles and senior commoners, the desire to link current groups with historic agents of state organization, are probable reasons for this contrast. Contemporary Merina emigrants (a large proportion of the population) use different means to incorporate themselves in a segmentary structure; they link themselves to buildings rather than to specific ancestors. Through membership in a tomb-group in the "land of the ancestors," according to Bloch (1971, pp. 46, 111), contemporary Merina attach themselves to a complex segmentary system of (formerly) territorial and kinship based units: smaller demes, larger demes, villages, and districts.

There are several possible reasons why Merina demes, which in the traditional society had even deeper historical ties to their agricultural estates than Betsileo local descent groups, have shallower genealogies. First, demonstrated deme genealogies may have been deeper and more ancestrally focused in old Imerina than at present. Because deme members are now dispersed, their contacts are occasional and brief, focus on emotionally charged rituals, and do not permit the frequent retelling of ancestral stories that goes on in a Betsileo village. As Bloch (1971) demonstrates so well, contemporary deme membership is focused on collateral kinship, and the connection to the society of the ancestors is established through the tomb and the recently dead rather than through reckoning of lineal genealogy. Furthermore, unlike Merina free men and women, Betsileo cannot establish full social identity just by mentioning village or region of origin. They also need to demonstrate genealogy, since, in contrast to Imerina, the slave-free contrast was never phenotypically obvious among the Betsileo. Total relevant social identification therefore requires reference both to a place and to a genealogical connection. Despite these contrasts, use of demonstrated genealogy to establish links with politically prominent ancestors does characterize both Betsileo and Merina. The highest ranking Merina demes, particularly the descendants of rulers, do remember genealogical links for several generations.

Recent studies of Merina (Bloch 1971), Bara (Huntington 1974), Sakalava (Gardenier 1976), and Tsimihety (Wilson 1971) suggest that these populations use terms for basic units in their social organization more precisely than the Betsileo. My Betsileo informants, for instance, usually employed *foko* (like the Tsimihety, according to Wilson [1971, p. 192]) for named descent group, but accepted *karazana* (cognate terms are used by Merina, Bara, and Sakalava) as a synonym. However, as noted, Betsileo have no term that distinguishes between primary and subsidiary supralocal descent group memberships. Nor did Betsileo have separate terms for groups intermediate in size and genealogical inclusiveness between the minor descent group (*fianakaviana*) and the maximal descent group (*foko* or *karazana*). In the agricultural east, where many villages include a local branch of just one named descent group, village and descent group names can be used simultaneously for social identification, e.g., Tranovondro of Ivato. In Betsileo parlance the stressed units are household, minor descent group, village, and named descent group, regardless of range and mode of affiliation. The other units identified in the preceding analysis are the ethnographer's, not natives', categories.

VARIATION IN KINSHIP CALCULATION AND THE KINDRED

We have seen that no rigidly enforced descent rule governs composition of local descent groups among the Betsileo. Rather, people choose—from several potential descent group affiliations—one which, once confirmed by residence, will be primary. Groups have individual members, and individuals reckon connections with several groups and individuals. Like people everywhere, each Betsileo may be regarded as the center of a personal network, a set of people with whom he or she interacts regularly or occasionally. Unlike people everywhere, however, Betsileo have personal networks that are composed largely of members of their kindred, people whom they classify as relatives (*havana*): usually people who share a common ancestry, but sometimes also—in the Betsileo scheme of calculation—stipulated, ritual, or fictive kin, and even relatives by marriage.

The Betsileo dialect shares with the standard Merina (cf. Bloch 1971, pp. 58–60) form of Malagasy a word, *havana*, which one may translate as "relative."[18] To determine the meaning of this term to Betsileo, and to ascertain the nature and extent of kindreds, I asked several Betsileo to name all the villages in which they had *havana*. After completing the list, I asked additional questions—the names of ego's ancestors, if any, from each village, the names of ego's *havana* there, their descent group affiliation, and their specific relationship to ego.

Forty-eight adults responded to these questions in Ivato, compared to fourteen in Ambalabe and ten in Tanambao, where my field assistant did most of the interviewing. Because of the small size of the Mahazony samples for this interview schedule, Ivato provides the most revealing data for analysis of Betsileo kindreds. However, even the meager Mahazony data do bring out some contrasts between the three villages.

The responses confirmed my impression, based on several other lines of evidence, that Ivatans calculate extra-village kinship far more actively and enthusiastically than villagers in Mahazony. Significantly, however, the people of Tanambao responded with slightly more villages (3.4) and kin (3.4) on the average than informants in Ambalabe (2.5 and 2.7, respectively). (In some cases, respondents mentioned more than one relative in a given village). But neither Mahazony village rivaled Ivato, where the average respondent named 7.0 villages and 8.8 kin relationships.

When taken in conjunction with other evidence, especially that on fictive kinship presented below, the results of this interview schedule suggest that people of Ambalabe mentioned fewer extra-village kin than those of Tanambao because they have less need to extend kinship ties than the latter. Most residents of Ambalabe belong to larger local descent groups than the people of Tanambao. Furthermore, allies in cooperative labor in Ambalabe are provided not only by members of the same local descent group, but also through the historic association and coresidence of its three senior commoner descent groups as members of the same administrative phratry. Actual labor recruitment problems in Tanambao are contrasted with the more favorable social organizational basis for cooperative labor in Ambalabe in chapter 8.

The fact that Ivatans calculate extra-village kinship far more extensively than the people of either Ambalabe or Tanambao demonstrates, however, that no simple linear relationship exists between rank and extent of kindred. Ivatans can trace connections to a variety of villages of historical significance in their region. Furthermore, because Ivato has historically been a regional center, its residents have inherited a wide and ready-made network of relations with the outside world. Ivatans remembered links to other regional centers. Furthermore, in contrast to the villagers in Mahazony, they more often mentioned upwardly mobile, nonpeasant relatives residing in towns and cities like Ambalavao, Fianarantsoa, and Tananarive. And compared to Mahazony villagers, Ivatans—again for historical reasons—have more such kin to mention. These relatives are vital to the upward aspirations that many of Ivato's peasants hold for their children.

Dimensions of Variation

The nature and extent of the Betsileo kindred varies not only with village, rank, and stratum, but also according to sex. Generally men calculate kinship more extensively and more distantly than women. Female kindreds were narrower; the average alter was only 1.9 genealogical links away, compared to 2.6 links for relatives mentioned by men. Considering the total sample of 72 respondents provided by the three villages, the average male mentioned 7 kin relationships as compared to 6 for females. In Ivato, the ratio (11:7) was even larger. Lateral skewing—relative emphasis on mother's or father's side—also varies with sex and village. As previously noted, in characterizing ideal relationships with their *havana*, Betsileo often assert that although both mother's and father's sides are important, the father's is more important.[19] This ideal statement of patrilateral skewing is undoubtedly related to the previously described importance of agnation in local descent group organization.[20] Most men bring their wives to and raise their children in their father's village. Most Betsileo women grow up in their paternal villages and move to their husband's village when they marry. However, in a variety of ways, particularly through the system of fosterage to be discussed below, Betsileo also maintain close ties with their maternal villages.

Analysis of my interviews demonstrates, however, that despite the ideal statement favoring patrilateral kin, Betsileo actually mentioned maternal relatives slightly more often (219 references, as compared to 180).[21] Table 16 demonstrates that whereas males mentioned patrilateral about as often as matrilateral relatives, 62 percent of the women's responses involved the mother's side. As will be shown in the discussion of fosterage below, women are far more likely than men to be raised by their own parents, whereas men are more often fostered by other relatives for several of their childhood years. Yet most men eventually return to their father's village, where, as its political representatives, they must master its social links to other villages. Growing up in closer association to her mother than her father, the typical Betsileo woman learns more about her mother's than her father's favorite relatives. And she is rarely expected to equal the male's mastery of kinship and descent links needed in intervillage politics.

The customarily special bond of intimacy between sisters, also reported for other Malagasy groups (Huntington 1974, pp. 79, 87; Southall 1971), is another reason for matrilateral skewing in the kindreds of Betsileo women.

TABLE 16

Lateral Skewing by Sex of Respondent in Combined Three Village Sample

Respondent's Sex	Father's Side		Mother's Side		Total	
	No.	%	No.	%	No.	%
Male	123	49.4	126	50.6	249	100
Female	57	38.0	93	62.0	150	100
Total	180	45.1	219	54.9	399	100

Among the southern Betsileo I studied, as among the northern Betsileo described by Southall (1971) and the northern Bara studied by Huntington, the
sister-sister relationship is the closest bond in collateral kinship. Sisters, after
all, are more likely to grow up together than with their brothers, who often
are fostered out. The affective link between sisters is maintained through
frequent visiting, even if they marry, as they usually do, into different villages. Of first cousins, the incest taboo is strongest for the offspring of sisters. Related to these observations, the corresponding special closeness of the
mother-daughter tie shows up in women's naming of mother's own village
more often than men (22 percent of the women's responses, compared to 13
percent of the men's).

Variation also shows up in types of relationships mentioned. After ascertaining the specific genealogical or other connections between each informant and each of the relatives he or she named, I grouped responses into
six categories (see table 44). Arranged in descending order of frequency of
appearance, they were the following: relationship calculated to a parent or
other lineal (179), relationship calculated to a collateral residing in his or her
native village (163), relationship calculated to a kinswoman who married into
the village mentioned (115). These three categories accounted for 92.5 percent of all relationships mentioned. Other categories were far less significant:
relationship calculated to a relative of ego's spouse or a spouse of one of
ego's relatives (23 cases), fictive kin (9 cases), and adoptive relationships (3
cases).

Table 44 documents a few more contrasts between the kindreds of men
and women. Reflecting the intimacy of sister-sister and mother-daughter
bonds, female informants mentioned villages of their married kinswomen 28
percent of the time, whereas males did so only 20 percent of the time. And
reflecting the contrast in adult residence patterns and political roles of women
and men, all but 2 percent of the women's responses involved genealogical
relationships, whereas 11 percent of the men's responses involved affinal,
fictive, or adoptive relationships. The Betsileo term *havana* then seems to
apply principally, and for women almost universally, to "real" kin, ancestors
or people who share one or more ancestors with ego.[22] If women mentioned
their husband's village at all, they usually referred not to their relationship by
marriage, but to a previous genealogical link. Males, because of greater obligations, expressed in labor exchange and, as chapter 7 documents, in ceremonial, towards affinal villages, remembered their in-laws more often, but
still far less often than consanguineals.

Some additional contrasts between Ivato and the two Mahazony villages
also emerge in type of kin relationship mentioned. Whereas the modal kin
relationship (42 percent) in Ivato involves specification of an ancestral village, identification of collaterals provides the mode both in Ambalabe (55

percent) and Tanambao (65 percent) (see table 45). Although small samples
in the two Mahazony villages demand a cautious interpretation, an emphasis
on collaterality over ancestry is compatible with the greater importance of
stipulated descent among junior commoners. Not only do senior commoners,
and particularly Ivatans, trace their own primary descent group genealogies
further into the past than junior commoners, their historically more-favored
status means that Ivatans remember ancestral links to regionally important
villages inhabited by their own or other senior commoner descent groups.
Junior commoners, like Bloch's (1971, p. 50) Merina emigrants, on the other
hand, conceive of kinship as involving their contemporary collaterals rather
than their (not so illustrious) ancestors.

Familiarity with descent group affiliation of relatives also reflects rank.
Informants were asked to identify descent group affiliation of each of the
havana they mentioned. Ivatans failed to name a descent group in only 13
percent of their responses; comparable figures for Ambalabe and Tanambao
were 22 percent and 24 percent respectively. Ivatans mentioned members of
regionally important descent groups far more often than members of historically less significant descent groups. Reflecting descent group endogamy, 32
percent of the alters they mentioned were Tranovondro. Two other senior
commoner descent groups accounted for 37 percent of their responses; no
other descent group affiliation accounted for more than 5 percent. Neither in
Ambalabe nor in Tanambao was there such a clustering of descent group
identification of alters, reflecting the larger number of (shallower and less
populous) named descent groups in Mahazony, relaxation of the preference
for descent group endogamy, and therefore a greater choice in spouses among
junior commoners.

FICTIVE KINSHIP

In addition to its emphasis on bilateral kinship calculation and multiple descent group affiliation, southern highlands social organization incorporates
other means of extending and reinforcing personal networks. These include
fosterage and formal adoption and a relationship that, following the convention developed in the analysis of ritual godparenthood and coparenthood,
principally in the New World, may be called fictive or ritual kinship. All of
these relationships, although available to all Betsileo as part of their cultural
traditions, vary in the context of region, history, and stratification, and none
can be understood apart from the descent and kinship systems. As in the case
of the kindred, an examination of fictive kinship places major emphasis on
the individual. However, in contrast to the preceding analysis, in which
kindreds and kinship calculation were discussed as categories for analytic

purposes, fictive kin relationships among the Betsileo *are* primarily individual relationships. Egocentric kindreds reflect alliances between groups, both villages and descent groups, established in the past. Individuals recall these alliances, usually reflecting marriages, in their recognition of kinship relationships today. Fictive kinship, on the other hand, provides one of the few means available in Betsileo social organization of *creating* and sanctifying close personal relationships between individuals, without implying that their establishment entails major sharing of rights and obligations on the part of the groups of which the contracting individuals are members.

Unrelated invididuals can be converted ritually into kin, *vaki-ra*, the Betsileo term, or *fatidra*, the more generally used Malagasy term that Betsileo occasionally employ to describe the relationship. The expression *vaki-ra* refers to spilling of blood; in the ritual that establishes kinship between two hitherto unrelated people, each makes a small incision in his or her chest. Each partner then drinks the blood, mixed with water and other ingredients, of the other. Thereafter, they are *vaki-ra*—friends, allies, and kin. The ritual usually establishes a close personal relationship involving mutual rights and obligations comparable to those of a man and his wife's father or brother or two genealogically close members of the same named descent group residing in different settlements. Since *vaki-ra* usually reside in different settlements, mutual labor, which is recruited locally, is not generally an aspect of this relationship. Obligations do involve hospitality and ceremonial participation and contributions.

The ritual of *vaki-ra* can create several kinds of fictive kinship. Two men, two women, or a man and a woman may create a *vaki-ra* relationship as (rarely) parent and child, older and younger siblings, or simply as siblings. The phrasing of kinship depends to an extent on the age of the partners and the reason for the creation of the relationship. A man who lacks sons, for example, may acquire one or more through adoption, to be discussed below, or through the *vaki-ra* ritual. A person without siblings of the same sex of his or her *vaki-ra* may initiate the relationship to acquire a brother or sister.

In contrast to marriage, which customarily allies descent groups, and stipulation of common ancestry, which also signals a special relationship between groups, the ritual of *vaki-ra* establishes a more individual relationship. One does not inherit one's parents' fictive kin. One customarily offers a steer to be slaughtered at the funeral of his or her fictive relative. The children of the deceased will then be expected to reciprocate by offering a steer at the funeral of their parent's fictive relative. Prior to Merina rule, however, such individual relationships did have political implications for groups. One of the kings of Isandra was *vaki-ra* of the kings both of Arindrano-Tsienimparihy and of the southern Sakalava. He called on them for military assistance against his eastern rivals, and they brought their followers along.

Fictive kinship continues to serve several functions among the Betsileo. If one assumes that, for various reasons, people attempt to create and/or maintain a comfortable number of close personal relationships with others, as the Betsileo seem to do, one can understand why ritual kinship is more common among Betsileo whose kindreds are narrowest at the outset. Consider the frequency of ritual kinship relationships in the three villages I studied intensively. In a sample of fifty, only five contemporary Ivatans, all of them males, have ritual kin. Only two of them have more than one. One has two, the other six. Significantly, both are part-time residents of Ivato. One teaches in a Catholic school north of Fianarantsoa. The other (not in the sample on table 17) sojourns in pastoral areas west of Fianarantsoa to buy cattle to sell in Ambalavao and Fianarantsoa. Both illustrate a common context for the creation of fictive kinship. Malagasy often acquire their *vaki-ra* away from home. In so doing, they acquire rights to hospitality and entrance to social worlds in areas where they have no kin or affines.

For people who spend most of their lives in Ivato, there is no compelling need for ritual kin. Ivato, after all, has been traditionally a social and political center; the Tranovondro represent a large, dispersed, and prestigeful descent group throughout Vohibato and southern Lalangina. Several nearby villages and hamlets are inhabited by junior branches of the Tranovondro and by descendants of slaves of Ivatan ancestors. Intermarriages with other prominent descent groups and villages have established alliances over several generations. Any Tranovondro of Ivato is automatically plugged into a ready-made and extensive social network. Ritual kinship is only slightly more important in Ambalabe. In a sample of eighteen asked about their ritual kin, nine had none at all, seven had only one, and only two had two each. In Tanambao, however, ritual kinship is considerably more important. In a sample of seventeen queried about their ritual kin, only five had none at all, six had one, three had two, two had three, and one had four, for a total of twenty-two ritual kin relationships, twice Ambalabe's eleven.

In the reasons they gave for having entered into ritual kin relationships, my informants indicated or suggested many of the functions that ritual kinship has served historically for southern highlanders. Many relationships had been formed while informants were residing away from their village, usually for economic reasons—plantation work on the east coast or cattle dealing in the west or south. In a few cases my informants had been invited to participate in the ritual by non-Betsileo who "wanted to have relatives in the highlands," suggesting the historically important role of ritual kinship in trade and travel. Betsileo recall that their ancestors who pursued commerce in Bara and Tanala country needed *vaki-ra* there for protection. They assert that having ritual kin among different Bara groups was the surest passport in times when Bara raids into Betsileo country were common.[23] In other cases, friendships

established with other Betsileo during military service or other sojourns outside of Betsileo country led to ritual kinship.

Two cases in Ivato illustrate that ritual kinship also may be used to re-
solve conflict. After discovering an Ivatan's adultery with the wife of a man
from a nearby village, their elders managed to calm the dispute by forcing
the two men to go through the *vaki-ra* ritual. The adulterer declared himself
younger brother of the husband, an admission of his guilt. The elders forced
another Ivatan and a man from a neighboring village to become blood brothers to bring an end to their longstanding enmity.

Ritual kinship is part and parcel of a series of social organizational principles that structure Betsileo society historically and today. The people of
Tanambao rely more on ritual kinship than more senior Betsileo because other
kinds of social links to their neighbors and to their region are weak. Ivatans,
on the other hand, if they remain at home, do not need to increase already
populous social networks through ritual kinship. In fact, Ivatans are actually
discouraged from acquiring fictive kin. It is, I was told, taboo for a non-
Tranovondro to drink Tranovondro blood. Because of this, in those few cases
in which Ivatans have entered *vaki-ra* relationships, the ritual substituted
rum, symbolically attenuating the relationship. I was told that in the one case
in which an Ivatan's blood had been drunk by his *vaki-ra*, the latter got sick.
It is tempting to speculate that the taboo was created to discourage others
from trying to affiliate with Ivato through ritual kinship. It seems probable
that without the "easy out" provided by the taboo, attempts to establish special relationships with residents of a prestigeful and relatively wealthy village
and an important regional center would have been frequent.

Regardless of the inception of the Ivatan taboo, when data from the three
villages are compared, one sees that there is a definite inverse relationship
between seniority of village and initiation of fictive kin relationships. Respondents were asked, for each relationship, to indicate who had initiated the
relationship, the respondent or his or her fictive relative (table 17). The only

TABLE 17
Seniority and Initiation of Ritual Kinship in Three Betsileo Villages

Village	Respondent Initiated Relationship	Alter Initiated Relationship	Elders Initiated Relationship	Other or No Data	Total
Ivato	0	2	2	1	5
Ambalabe	4	7	0	0	11
Tanambao	10	9	1	1	21
Total	14	18	3	2	37

Note: $\theta = -.25$ (computed for first two columns only); rank is inversely associated with initiation of relationship.

Ivatan who had initiated a *vaki-ra* relationship was the irregularly resident cattle merchant, all of whose ritual kin resided in the extreme west of Betsileo country, where he bought his cattle. Four members of the Ambalabe sample had initiated ritual kinship, whereas seven had been drawn into the relationship. In contrast, ten people in Tanambao had initiated relationships, while nine other relationships had been initiated by their *vaki-ra*. As is true in the case of descent, affiliation, and kinship calculation, there is again a definite and explicable relationship between differential access to resources and the manner in which Betsileo use the social organizational principles their culture provides.

ADOPTION

Land transfers, which are a group concern, do not result from ritual kinship, which is an individual matter; they can, however, follow formal adoption, making adoptions both unusual and potentially disruptive, because they contradict basic social structural rules. As in industrial states, Betsileo adoption is an official relationship whereby an adult, usually childless, may acquire legally recognized children and heirs. Appropriate adoption involves close kin, particularly other members of the childless person's local descent group. However, adoption of inappropriate kin and of nonrelatives also occurs, creating several problems. Chapter 4 related a case illustrating a common relationship between ranking and adoption during the nineteenth century. Ivato's most influential leaders in Merina and French colonial times, Karl Fridaysfather, Goodmaker, and Vernon, were all adopted as adults by childless people from other villages. Their adopters desired, at the cost of bringing new heirs to their ancestral estates, to create alliances with Ivato, to gain the support and assistance of some of the most important Betsileo in the region. In so doing, adopters could absorb some of the prestige of their adoptive sons and could enjoy access to the labor of their slaves and other dependents, profiting in life by choosing to alienate their shares of their descent group estates to their adoptive sons and their descendants.

Adoption of an outsider, however, is viewed by Betsileo as a profoundly selfish act. Violating several Betsileo norms, adopters flout a collectivist ethos by asserting their independence of their own community, agnates, and other relatives. Simultaneously, they make an *individual* matter out of kinship and land, which traditionally and appropriately are *group* concerns. Not surprisingly, lands transferred through adoption have led to litigation between Tranovondro and members of the adopter's descent group. One such dispute, involving a rice field passed to the Tranovondro through the adoption of Karl

Fridaysfather, was resolved in favor of Ivato and Karl's great-great-grandson Antoine in 1967.

Today, as in the past, official adoption creates benefits for some and problems for others. Consider the case of Henri, a sixty-seven-year-old Ivatan. Just as Tuesdaysfather represents Karl Fridaysfather's descendants, the descendants of Karl's younger brother, Blacksfather, are represented by his grandson, Henri. Blacksfather, who died in 1919, had but one child, Henri's mother. Henri, who himself is childless, and two of his sisters' sons—one of whom, Pierre, is now village chief—represent the only heirs now residing in Ivato to Blacksfather's estate of 4.1 hectares in rice fields. The status of none of Blacksfather's descendants is particularly comfortable in Ivato, although Henri, as elder, bears the brunt of the informal ostracism leveled against nonagnates. To an extent, Henri has created his own local reputation as a witch by removing himself from village social life in a variety of ways. Violating convention, he sold one of his rice fields to a non-Tranovondro, using the cash in his cattle merchant business. More than twenty years of his life have been spent in western Betsileo and Bara country, where, again in violation of Ivatan practice, he acquired six fictive relatives. These are among the strangers whom he often attracts as his guests to Ivato.

Wishing to be remembered as an important ancestor, Henri has further incurred the displeasure of fellow Ivatans by legally adopting eleven people, ten males and one female. Five of the eleven are considered appropriate adoptees; they claim affiliation with Ivato through their mothers—Henri's sisters. The other six are socially inappropriate: two are patrilateral kin, two are relatives of his dead wife, and the final two are nonrelatives—men who worked for Henri during one of his sojourns outside of Betsileo country.

Only two of Henri's adopted children (sons of a sister) now reside in or near Ivato. One of them is the village chief, Pierre; the other lives in Little Ivato, a nearby satellite. Pierre cultivates not only his own rice fields—part of his maternal heritage—but also does most of the work in Henri's rice fields. Pierre's brother, who cultivates his own field in Little Ivato, also works for Henri.

Most of Henri's adoptive children, like Pierre, stand to profit as much or more from their status as heirs as Henri does from his prerogatives as adoptive father. Because of his frequent absences from Ivato, Henri could not maintain his rice fields without their labor. However, Henri, like those men and women who adopted illustrious Ivatans in the past, has also attempted to enhance his own reputation by adopting an important man. One of his adoptive children, a patrilateral kinsman, is a government official whom Henri visits from time to time in Tananarive. Henri frequently mentions their relationship in conversation. In addition to those whom he has officially adopted,

Henri has raised other children in his home; he may eventually make some of them official adoptees.

HOUSEHOLD COMPOSITION AND FOSTERAGE

Although legal adoption remains fairly unusual, fosterage is a highly significant part of Betsileo kinship, descent, marriage, and household organization. Along with strategically arranged marriages, the custom of raising relatives' children forms part of the exchange system that links Betsileo villages into a common social network.[24] Like other principles of social organization, however, Betsileo fosterage practices vary regionally and in the context of socioeconomic stratification.

Betsileo custom prescribes that the first child of any union be born in the mother's village. Although in 1967 most Betsileo children were born in maternity wards in canton seats, the mother and child still convalesced in the mother's native village. This custom cements the marriage, the status of husband and wife as parents (thereafter, both parents are called teknonymously), and the alliance between their families. Furthermore, the child's rights as a member of the mother's group are established; a man with no sons would stipulate that his daughter's first son would reside as an adult in his village rather than follow the norm of patrifiliation (cf. Bloch 1971, pp. 193–94, for similar Merina customs.) Subsequent children were often born in the mother's village, but no rigid rule operated.

Betsileo enculturation does not proceed principally within the confines of the nuclear family, but within a network of bilateral kin representing descent groups and villages of husband and wife and their parents. Table 18 describes some of the variation in household composition at a given time (1966–67) for Ivato and the two villages in Mahazony. Although both in Ivato and Tanambao the nuclear family provides the modal category of household composition, in none of the three villages does nuclear family organi-

TABLE 18

Distribution of Household Types in Ivato, Ambalabe, and Tanambao, 1966–67

Household Type	Ivato		Ambalabe		Tanambao		Total	
	No.	*%*	*No.*	*%*	*No.*	*%*	*No.*	*%*
Nuclear	14	*45.2*[a]	15	36.6	9	*45.0*	38	41.3
Expanded	13	41.9	20	*48.8*	3	15.0	36	39.1
Single person or couple	4	13.0	6	14.6	8	*40.0*	18	19.6
Total	31	100.1	41	100.0	20	100.0	92	100.0

a. Modal category italicized for each village.

zation characterize as many as half the households. In the total, combining the three villages, the expanded household, the modal category in Ambalabe (which includes affinal, collateral, and/or lineal relatives of the household head other than members of his family of procreation) is encountered almost as often as the nuclear family household. Furthermore, because expanded households typically include more people than nuclear family households, more Betsileo live in expanded households than in the other two types (nuclear; inhabited by single person or couple) combined (244 to 230 in the combined population of 474 of Ivato, Ambalabe, and Tanambao).

Assuming stable village populations, the opportunity of exporting population increase into the national economy, and no major modifications in the local ecosystems of the three villages, the relative proportion of each household type might remain constant in each village. However, individual Betsileo households, like those in other societies, do change in composition. Goodmaker's house, now inhabited by the younger son of his youngest son, illustrates variation in household composition over time. The house remains the most imposing wattle and daub structure in Ivato. Goodmaker commissioned the house and moved into it with his wife, their two youngest sons Joseph and François (their oldest son, Vernon, taught school then in Fianarantsoa), one of their two daughters, and four male slave descendants who worked for Goodmaker. Joseph, their second son, eventually married and built a house of his own. The daughter married and left Ivato. Two of the workers entered military service. Several other workers, male and female, resided in the house for various lengths of time thereafter.

When Goodmaker died, his wife, Pelagie, became household head; all the workers left, but other people joined the household. Her granddaughter (DD) and grandson (DS) moved in to be raised by Pelagie. The widow and two sons of her youngest son, François—who had died in a Spanish influenza epidemic in 1919—also resided with Pelagie. One worker, a slave descendant, was also a member of this expanded household.

Pelagie survived her husband by thirteen years. François's two sons, the older now married, remained in the house for two or three years after their grandmother's death; Pelagie's other descendants scattered. Since the two grandsons could not afford to maintain the house, their father's oldest surviving brother, Joseph, who himself had been raised in the house by his parents, moved in, along with his wife, his older son Rakoto, and Rakoto's wife. François's sons stayed on as members of their uncle's expanded household; their father's brother had, in Betsileo parlance, "replaced" Goodmaker. Eventually Rakoto built a house of his own. When Joseph died, his widow returned to their original house, now headed by her youngest surviving son. François's two sons, both now married, remained in Goodmaker's house until the older built a house of his own. In accordance with the role of ultimogeniture, François's younger son stayed in the house, where he lives today with his wife and children.

Goodmaker's house has therefore seen a succession of household types reflecting the age, sex, and socioeconomic status of each of its heads. Originally established as an expanded household capable of lodging and supporting workers and other dependents, when Goodmaker's widow replaced her husband as household head its ability to support dependents diminished considerably. The third head, a young grandson, was unable to maintain the house, even though he was supporting only his wife, children, and unmarried younger brother. The fourth head, Joseph—then leader of the eastern village—could head a larger expanded household, but since his death the house lodges a nuclear family household appropriate to the Betsileo rule of ultimogeniture in house transmission.

The case of Goodmaker's house illustrates that variation in Betsileo household organization over time is associated with the head's age, sex, and socioeconomic status, which determine ability to support dependents. Although most of Goodmaker's dependents were slave descendants who provided labor as agricultural workers or guardians of his cattle, much of the departure of Betsileo households from nuclear family organization reflects the traditional system of fosterage. More so in the past than at present, the fosterage system was ritually regulated. Like most Malagasy, Betsileo imported or brought with them from the southeast coast (one of the centers of Islamic influence in Madagascar) techniques of divination based on astrological calculation. Like most other Malagasy, too, Betsileo use terms obviously derived from Arabic to name the days of the week. Their diviners, usually non-Betsileo from Tanala country or the southeast coast, taught Betsileo that some days of the week were more propitious than others. The destiny of every child was set at birth, not only by the day, which was often incorporated as part of the child's name, but also by the combination of the day, time of day, month of birth, and conjunction of zodiac signs. In many cases and for various reasons, parents enlisted astrological experts to calculate whether the destiny (*vintana*) of a given child was compatible with their own, or whether it posed a danger to the child's close relatives. Often parents consulted diviners following a child's long illness. In other cases, parents whose previous children had died in infancy consulted astrologers as a matter of course when a new birth took place. If astrological comparison showed that the newborn's destiny was incompatible with that of either parent, it was necessary for the diviner to examine destinies of grandparents, aunts, uncles, and other relatives until someone could be found whose destiny was compatible and who would agree to raise the child.[25] Often those who were willing as well as astrologically acceptable were childless, older, or wealthier relatives who could afford to take over the child's support. (For related practices among Bara and Sakalava see Huntington 1974, pp. 153–55 and Gardenier 1976, pp. 40–46).

Astrological calculation, discouraged by Christian missions and by the French, continues today, but in attenuated fashion. Fosterage, however, remains common, which suggests that the astrological computation was never indispensable to the system. Other, more informal, considerations can dictate where Betsileo children grow up. Couples with too many dependents often farm several of them out to their relatives, usually to wealthier households and to childless relatives or kin whose children have grown up and live elsewhere. That the number of real children of contemporary foster parents of Ivato children averages only 1.1 (ranging from 0 to 3) and, more significantly, that most (96 percent) foster parents have no children of their own living in their households, supports informants' contention that foster parents are typically people with few or no children.

Betsileo also recognize that fosterage, although less certainly than formal adoption, is one way of obtaining or reinforcing rights in estates. Consider another case from Ivato. Antoine, forty-six years old in 1967, is one of two children and the only son of Tuesdaysfather. Antoine and his forty-three-year-old wife Ravao have twelve children. Like most adult men with a living father, Antoine cannot lay claim to his father's sizeable estate, but cultivates a .8 hectare rice field located almost five kilometers away, derived not as part of his descent group estate, but through adoption of Karl Fridaysfather, his FFFF. Only four of Antoine's children—three girls, aged one, two, and seven, and a boy ten years old—live with Antoine and Ravao. One twenty-year-old daughter married in 1967, but had been raised by Antoine's parents. Antoine's oldest son, twenty-five years old in 1967, has also been raised by, and still lives with, his father's parents in Ivato. An eight-year-old daughter is being raised by a patrilateral kinswoman in Ivato, and a twelve-year-old son resides in one of the two client households in the village. The head of the client household, who has no sons of his own, cultivates rice land that is registered in Tuesdaysfather's name. Not only is the client content to have his social link with his patron strengthened by caring for the patron's grandson, but the minimal descent group headed by Tuesdaysfather is ensuring also that the land will revert to a member of that group—the grandson—following the client's death.

Three of Antoine's children—a twenty-two-year-old girl, an eighteen-year-old girl, and a sixteen-year-old boy—reside in or near Ambalavao with two of Antoine's paternal uncles, both government employees. All three avail themselves of better educational opportunities in Ambalavao. Antoine and his father contribute to their support by sending white rice. Finally, a four-teen-year-old boy resides with his mother's brother in Wednesday, a nearby canton seat, while attending primary school.

Antoine and Ravao represent merely an extreme case of the common Betsileo pattern of sending children to be raised or cared for by other relatives.

Because of Ivato's senior commoner status, its reputation, and wealth relative to other Betsileo villages, one might expect Ivatans to accept foster children more often than to export them. However, almost exactly balancing, rather than exceeding, the thirty-seven Ivatan children who presently reside away from their parents' home as students or as foster children are thirty-six children from outside who now live in Ivatan households. Some of them have come to study at the Catholic primary school; others are simply being raised with relatives. These thirty-six children represent 21 percent of the present population of Ivato. In 1967, thirty-seven children born to parents residing in Ivato were living outside their parents' households. Twenty-two of them were being fostered; seven of them had been fostered in more than one nonparental household. Fifteen others were studying outside, usually residing simultaneously with kin in canton and subprefecture seats. These were being lodged and cared for temporarily, so were not truly fostered.

Since the ability to maintain dependents reflects wealth, and since wealth (control of productive rice fields and associated differential access to strategic resources) generally increases with age, several consequences involved in explaining fosterage and household composition follow. Household size and number of nonnuculear family household members should both increase with age and wealth. Expanded family households are defined by their inclusion of residents other than the head's family of procreation. Expanded household organization should therefore be correlated with wealth. Table 19 demonstrates the predicted relationship between household organization, wealth (rice area controlled by household), and age.

TABLE 19
Relationship between Land Control, Age, and Household Type in Ivato

Household Type	No.	%	Rice Field Area in Mean Hectares	Total Area	% All Area	Average Age of Household Head
Nuclear	14	45.2	.95	13.3	38.9	37.5
Expanded	13	41.9	1.4	18.1	52.9	53.5
Couple or one person	2	6.5	1.4	2.8	8.2	51.5
Matrifocal	2	6.5	0	0	0	59.5
Total	31	100.1	1.1	34.2	100.0	46.5

· *Note*: $\eta^2 = .19$ for association of household type and rice field area.

Forty-seven adult Ivatans (23 men and 24 women) have raised a total of 73 foster children, an average of 1.6 each. However, only 28 of these 47 people have actually served as foster parents, with an average of about 3 foster children each. Nineteen Ivatans have raised no children at all other than their own. Some of these are younger men and women with living fathers or fathers-in-law who still cultivate the fields that will eventually pass to their sons. Others are slave descendants and other less fortunate Ivatans who have sufficient difficulty maintaining their own offspring so as not to consider accepting other children. Ivatans do not appear to favor one sex over the other in accepting foster children, for 38 boys and 35 girls have been raised by villagers, but other Betsileo favor boys (see below).

I obtained information on the relationship between foster parent and child for most of these cases in Ivato. Nonrelatives, usually slave descendents, provided only two cases. The relatives fostered most frequently by far were agnates—brothers' daughters and sons of male household heads or of their wives. In none of these cases were outsiders using their fosterage by Ivatans to gain access to its estate. Native agnates already had rights to the local estate, whereas wives' nephews had no legitimate claim to such rights. Although in the past daughters' sons were occasionally raised in Ivato, no living Ivatan has fostered his or her daughter's son. Since most contemporary Ivatans have real sons (only one of the twenty-three mothers in Ivato has no sons [see table 46]), their fostering histories suggest that Ivatans have tried to anticipate potential conflict between agnates and nonagnates by excluding daughters' sons from their fosterage. Of all the foster children raised in Ivato, only six—all sisters' sons—represent nonagnates who might conceivably try, as adults, to claim estate rights in their uterine descent group.

On the basis of the figures in table 48, an Ivatan's decision to take in a foster child is most obviously related to the number of real children now residing in the fosterer's household. On the average just one natural child now resides in the households of Ivatan foster parents. Foster parents tend to be, therefore, in Ivato as elsewhere among the Betsileo, older people, who often expressed to me the advantages of having small children around to run errands and to make their lives less lonely.

Ivatan children currently residing outside their parental households and Ivatans' fostering of other children have been examined above. Yet to be considered are adult Ivatans who have been raised by people other than their parents. For this analysis I obtained two nonoverlapping samples. Significant differences between the two samples reflect their memberships. The first sample (almost total) involves fifty-two contemporary adult *residents* of Ivato, peasant men who are native sons and their nonnative wives. The second sample (less complete and nonrandom) is limited to thirty-two men and women who were born in Ivato but now reside elsewhere. Most of the women are residing in their husband's village, but their fosterage histories, contrasted with those of Ivato's wives, illustrate differences between the experiences of Ivato's native women and those from other Betsileo villages. Furthermore, whereas the men in the first sample are all peasants, most of those in the second sample are not; many of them—including several descendants of Goodmaker—are government employees, or otherwise successful native sons, in villagers' estimation.

Again, variable fosterage histories reflect manipulation by Ivato's senior commoners of social organizational mechanisms potentially available to all Betsileo. And again the effect is to preserve Ivatans' favored access to wealth, prestige, and power. The first sample (table 20) includes twenty-seven native males residents and twenty-five nonnative wives. Note that whereas only three of the women had been fostered, more than twice as many (nineteen) men had been raised outside their parental home as by their parents; five of them had been fostered more than once. On the basis of this sample it would appear—deceptively, as we shall soon see—that fosterage is a typical experience of boyhood, of negligible significance for girls, and one might be tempted to compare a woman's break with her parents to reside virilocally after marriage with the much earlier, long-term break between a male and his parents. (The average period of fosterage begins at age six and lasts about a decade.) In both cases Betsileo are certainly using residential changes to create and/or strengthen their special relationships with other villages.

The second sample (table 21), however, which includes twenty-four men and eight women, all native Ivatans, shows greater female participation in the fosterage system. Proportionately, slightly more of the native women (five out of eight, as compared to fourteen out of twenty-four men) had been

TABLE 20
Fosterage of Adults Now Residing in Ivato

	Men		Women		Total	
	No.	*%*	*No.*	*%*	*No.*	*%*
Never fostered	8	29.6	22	88.0	30	57.7
Fostered at least once	19	70.4	3	12.0	22	42.3
Total	27	100.0	25	100.0	52	100.0

	N	Mean	Mode	Median	Range
No. times fostered	52	0.5	0	0	0–2
Age fosterage began	20	5.7 years	1	4.5	0–15
Age fosterage ended	20	16.1 years	25	16.5	3–25
No. children of the foster parent	21	1.7	0	1.0	0–7

TABLE 21
Fosterage of Native, Nonresident Adult Ivatans

	Men		Women		Total	
	No.	*%*	*No.*	*%*	*No.*	*%*
Never fostered	10	41.7	3	37.5	13	40.6
Fostered at least once	14	58.3	5	62.5	19	59.4
Total	24	100.0	8	100.0	32	100.0

raised by people other than their parents. Fosterage, therefore, is experienced by girls and boys, though more commonly by the latter.

When fosterers are grouped by kin type and these two samples are combined, the bilateral nature of Betsileo kinship is shown: nineteen people had been fostered by patrilaterial and eighteen by matrilateral relatives. However, underneath the bilaterality that is revealed statistically is a significant difference in the kin types of fosterers for the two samples. In the first sample, thirteen of the foster parents were patrilateral relatives and only seven matrilateral. In the second sample, however, the ratio was reversed: only six paternal versus eleven matrilateral foster parents.

This difference shows that not only the ability to foster children but also being fostered oneself is related to status and wealth. Divergent fosterage histories of Ivato's native women and its wives show that senior commoners have often used daughters as well as sons to strengthen kin relationships through fosterage. Furthermore, the seniormost commoners, such as Goodmaker's descendants, who dominate the second sample, are more likely to reinforce matrilateral ties than junior commoners. The most senior commoners, of course, have used their favorable positions to propel their contemporary descendants to relatively successful positions in the extravillage economy. Today these nonpeasants do not actually cultivate the maternal estates to which their fosterage histories especially entitle them. But they have not relinquished these rights. They allow their maternal relatives to cultivate their potentially available fields, and they expect hospitality when they vacation in their mother's village and gifts of milled rice when these relatives visit them in the city. Dormant now, their prerogatives could be activated, given a change in fortune or a special need by their children.[26]

Over the generations, senior commoners have insured that their descendants' uterine rights will be preserved not only by making sure that Betsileo custom is followed scrupulously in having their child or grandchild born in the maternal village, but by carrying the custom one step further and allowing the child to be raised by its mother's people.[27] Eight of the fourteen men in the second sample who had histories as foster children had actually been raised in their mother's village. And Ivatan Tranovondro are continuing today with an entrepreneurial pattern established in the past—ten Ivatan children are currently being raised in their mother's village.

More artfully than junior commoners, Ivatans exploit the opportunities that Betsileo social organization provides them. Although they are perfectly willing to have their sons raised in maternal villages, we have seen that Ivatans discourage nonagnates from seeking foster homes in Ivato. Yet no one can fault Ivatans for poor participation in the fosterage system. After all, they import as many children as they export, and the average foster parent in Ivato can be expected to raise three foster children. Ivatans' advantageous use of the fosterage system rests on skillful choices about which kin links are to be reinforced through fosterage. As noted, not one of the seventy-three foster children raised by any adult Ivatan has been a daughter's son, and only six have been sisters' sons who might conceivably argue one day for primary membership as an Ivatan Tranovondro. And even these cases are exceptional instances in which the foster parent has few or no real children. As in their disdain for fictive kin relationships, Tranovondro of Ivato in their fosterage practices manage to protect themselves from outsiders' socially appropriate claims.

Yet, in the consciousness of Betsileo who follow them, these patterns are not simply strategies in a game plan for entrepreneurs. They form parts of a blueprint of Betsileo culture, sanctioned by the ancestors, which proper Betsileo are obliged to follow scrupulously. The discussion of marriage that follows shows another arena in which senior commoners, just as they respect the rule of childbirth in the maternal village and the maternal group's right in the child, are more likely to adhere to rules of Betsileo culture than junior commoners. The affinal relationships between *groups* is stronger among senior commoners than among their juniors.

MARRIAGE

Like fictive kinship, adoption, fosterage, and household composition, Betsileo marriage patterns vary according to socioeconomic status and have political implications. Traditionally nobles were expected to marry other nobles, senior commoners other senior commoners, junior commoners other junior commoners, and slaves other slaves. Such intrastratum marriages insured that spouses had approximately the same ritual status (recall the discussion of *hasina*, the graduated sacred force, chapter 3). Marriages of nobles also created or cemented alliances between independent Malagasy polities. Like their Merina counterparts, Betsileo kings, chiefs, and other important men (Karl Fridaysfather, for example) were polygynous. King Andrianampoinimerina of Imerina chose twelve official wives (all *andriana*—"nobles" or aristocrats), who resided in different parts of his kingdom. The king could therefore employ each wife in overseeing a different area of the royal domain. Betsileo kings selected members of groups strategic to insuring their sovereignty against both external and internal threats—noblewomen from neighboring polities and women representing the most important senior commoner descent groups within their circumscriptions. Tranovondro and other senior commoners married senior commoners, preferably members of their own descent group or, more rarely, junior commoners or nobles. Among the rules governing Betsileo marriage, none conveyed the severity of the proscription against intermarriage of free people and slaves. Even today, violations of this interdiction are very rare.

For reasons related to preservation of wealth, honor, rank, and power, nobles tended to marry closer relatives than commoners. Among senior commoners there appears to have been both a cultural and an actual preference for descent group endogamy. However, as previously noted, descent group endogamy usually involved marriages between different local branches of the same named descent group. While endogamy was allowed in the supralocal group as a whole, it occurred far less frequently within localized branches. The explanation that Betsileo themselves offer for their ancestors' behavior concerns purity and appropriateness of marriage among people with the same status. Members of the Tranovondro descent group chose other members as their spouses because the kin of each spouse were familiar with the marital history and ancestry of the other. In this way, the Betsileo say, their ancestors could be sure that their spouses had no ancestors who were slaves or members of another socially stigmatized group. When the descent groups were territorially dispersed, descent group endogamy also reinforced political alliances based on genealogy.

Betsileo maintain local descent group exogamy by asserting that descendants of the same ancestor, up to and including great-great-grandchildren, should not marry. However, violations of this prohibition occur, and Betsileo culture accommodates, although discouraging them, by allowing the related prospective spouses to sacrifice a steer as they ask the ancestors' permission to marry.[28] At least three cases of marriage of close relatives appear in the genealogy of the Tranovondro of Ivato. The closest was the case of a woman who married her paternal grandfather's grandson through another union. Ivatans use this case to illustrate their claim that close marriages bring impaired fertility and viability of offspring, an assertion that apparently serves as a major ideological basis for the interdiction in a society that values large families. The couple produced only one child, a daughter, who never bore children of her own. In another case, a woman married the grandson of her great-grandmother's sister and was childless. Ivatans cite a contemporary case to illustrate the relationship between genealogical closeness and imparied viability of offspring. Bethsmother is the great-granddaughter of the sister of her husband's maternal grandfather. Only four of their nine children, including just one son, are alive. Since the couple was told by a diviner that their sons could not reach a healthy maturity in Ivato, all were raised by relatives in other villages.

Betsileo culture permits (after the appropriate sacrifice) marriage of patrilateral parallel cousins, though I never discovered an actual case of it. Betsileo ideology also allows a man to marry his matrilateral cross-cousin. In a strictly patrilineal society this is not a case of descent group endogamy, since the mother's brother's daughter belongs to the mother's rather than the father's patrilineal descent group. However, Betsileo society is incompletely patrilineal. Individuals have rights in their mother's descent group; thus matrilateral cross-cousin marriage can also represent descent group endogamy. However, such marriages seem to have been just as rare as those involving the children of two brothers.

According to the Betsileo, the preference that senior commoners choose their spouse from a branch of their own descent group is a corollary of a more general rule that individuals marry people of similar rank. Therefore, if a marriage could be arranged with another senior commoner descent group whose genealogy was known to be pure according to Betsileo standards, this was fine, too. As a result, Betsileo males sometimes sought as spouses women from their mother's descent group, perhaps from the mother's actual local descent branch, perhaps from another branch. The Betsileo say of this custom, alluding to the customary transfer of a steer to the wife's group, "if cattle find the grazing good in a pasture one day, they will return to graze there on another."

As has been reported throughout Madagascar (cf. Southall 1971), sexual relations between the children of sisters are prohibited among the Betsileo. Since flesh and blood are believed to be transmitted through the mother, such cousins are seen as being of "one heart," and their incest would be severely stigmatized. (The relationship of this custom to kinship calculation and fosterage patterns has been discussed above.)

The distinction between same sex and opposite sex relationships is expressed in kinship terminology, which uses different terms for brother and sister depending on whether males or females are speaking. Brothers use *rahalahy* (male substance) to refer to each other, sisters *rahavavy* (female substance, which they are believed to share), whereas a woman's brother is her *anadahy* (male cross-substance) and a man's sister his *anabavy*. This usage parallels Huntington's (1974; pp. 81–87) findings for the Bara. Reference terms can distinguish children of brothers, children of sisters, and cross-cousins (children of a brother and a sister). However, when less specificity is required, Hawaiian reference terms can also be used; siblings and cousins will be lumped togther under one of the four terms mentioned previously, depending on the sex of the speaker and alter. The terms *zoky* and *zandry* are also used to refer to elder and younger sibling, regardless of sex. Variable Betsileo kinship terminology for ego's generation, therefore, can be used to express either relative seniority, cognatic kinship, or the possibility of cross-cousin marriage. Unlike Bara and Sakalava, however, Betsileo do not distinguish the maternal from the paternal uncle, referring to these kin types by the terms used for actual father (*ray* or *aba*). Among the Bara the reference term for mother's brother can be translated as "male mother," presumably in accordance with the more prominent differentiation between maternal and paternal lines noted by Huntington (1974; p. 94).

Present-day Ivatans demonstrate that the traditional preference for marrying senior commoners and Tranovondro continues. Included within my Ivatan genealogies is information on thirty-nine *terminated* marriages involving either ancestral Tranovondro or a few living Tranovondro whose marriages have been terminated, usually by death, but in a few cases by divorce. Of these, thirteen, or one-third of the total, exemplified descent group endogamy. Tranovondro was by far the most common affinal descent group; six other marriages involved members of another senior commoner descent group, Taray. Of twenty-four *extant* marriages of Ivatan Tranovondro, four wives are Tranovondro, seven Taray, and the remaining thirteen are members of nine different named descent groups.

When considerations of status and political alliance are not so compelling, choice of spouse may proceed within a wider network of locally available commoner descent groups. Neither in Ambalabe nor in Tanambao does any single descent group predominate among spouses as in Ivato. Of fifteen contemporary marriages in Ambalabe for which information on wife's descent group affiliation was available, twelve different named descent groups were represented, none accounting for more than two marriages. In Tanambao, a sample of eight wives represented as many different named descent groups. Also contrasting Ivato with the two Mahazony villages is the fact that although none of the marriages of Ivatans involved village endogamy, a few of the marriages in Ambalabe and Tanambao, where several named descent groups have local branches, did.

Arranged Marriages

Just as observance of descent group endogamy is more characteristic of senior than of junior commoners, other aspects of Betsileo marriage reflect socioeconomic status, ranking, and political factors. Compared to junior commoners, senior commoners' marriages are more often arranged by their elders, involve longer trial marriage periods, and are more stable. Although any Betsileo marriage entails mutual rights and obligations involving spouses and their relatives, senior commoners generally take these rights and obligations more seriously than juniors. Arranged unions, almost universal for first marriages in the past, are still common today, especially for senior commoners. Often members of branches of a named descent group localized in different villages agreed that their children would eventually marry. I have information about twenty-nine of the thirty-four extant or dissolved marriages of living adult male Ivatans. Of these twenty-nine marriages, representing twenty-four men, only five first wives were selected by their husbands; twenty marriages were arranged. All of the second and third wives, however, had been selected by their husbands. None of the senior commoners of eastern Ivato had chosen their first wives; all had been arranged.

Arranged marriages are not as characteristic of junior commoners and slave descendants as of senior commoners. Young Betsileo have ample opportunity to evaluate potential spouses for themselves. Young men and women attend markets and ceremonials more often than married women, and liaisons that eventually lead to marriage are often initiated at ceremonials,[29] markets, and other assemblies.

Consider a case of the initiation of a marriage among junior commoners. My field assistant Joseph Rabe, while living in Tanambao, observed, one evening in September, the negotiation of a marriage according to Betsileo custom. The close relatives of the prospective bride had gathered in the house of the eldest, Rabe's brother, to receive three visitors including the prospective groom, who had met his intended at a market. Although the bride's relatives had been informed beforehand of the visit, Betsileo custom demands that before negotiations may begin, the groom offer two monetary contributions to the wife's relatives, the first for the door to be opened and the second for being allowed to speak. In this case, he offered 30 francs for the opening of the door and 100 for permission to speak. One of the three visitors then explained that he was the spokesman of his family and, in this case, of the groom, and that they had come to ask the woman's hand.

Rabe likened the bargaining that followed to the sale of a steer.[30] The groom's spokesman first asked what price the woman's relatives wanted; Rabe's brother responded that they were asking 17,250 francs and a steer. The groom's spokesman countered with an offer of 6,000 francs, 2,000 to be given then, the remainder plus a steer after the woman had joined her husband in his village. The bargaining continued until they agreed on 12,500 francs—4,000 then, the remainder and a steer later. The groom spent the night in Tanambao with his bride; the others left. Rabe told me that it was understood that since the woman was the mother of two natural children, her husband could be legally recognized as their father by adopting them. She was to join her husband about ten days later. The remaining cash would be given to Rabe's brother to divide among her relatives in Tanambao. The steer would graze with his herd.

A case from Ivato also illustrates that individuals with little wealth and junior status may ignore marriage customs with impunity. Felix is the grandson of Alan, youngest brother of Karl Fridaysfather. Leadership of the eastern village never passed to Alan or to any of his descendants. Since land has been allocated by others, Felix (and Alan's other descendants) now farm rice field holdings that barely surpass those of local slave descendants. Felix contracted what more senior Ivatans regarded as a scandalous marriage, bringing home from the Ambalavao region a wife whom he had selected himself. Betsileo custom required that at least his father and uncle travel to her village to ascertain her descent group affiliation and to scrutinize her ancestry for imperfections. In addition to slave descent, certain descent groups carry curses, and Betsileo believe that others carry hereditary maladies, both physical and mental.

In contrast, so interested were senior commoners in their children-in-law that in the past a girl who was destined to become a senior wife was sometimes raised by her future husband's parents or grandparents. Tuesdaysfather's wife Louise lived in her husband's village for four years before they married, and this case is not atypical among senior Ivatans. Whether the couple was allowed to have sexual relations during such a time was apparently decided by their parents.

Trial Marriage

Betsileo custom appears generally to have recognized a union as a marriage only after a period of what the literature on Madagascar usually refers to as trial marriage. I witnessed two cases of trial marriage in Ivato. One involved Tuesdaysfather's eldest grandson, whose prospective wife lived in Ivato for two months, while the husband-to-be, his parents, and grandparents evaluated her. When the young man decided against her, she was reminded that a visit to her parents was overdue. According to Betsileo custom she could not return to Ivato until she was sought out. If, as in this case, no such party arrived, she would eventually realize that she had been rejected.

The trial period for first marriages of Ivatans varied between one month and four years. The longer periods are cases of older, senior Ivatans whose brides were very young when they came to the village. Subsequent trial marriages, following death or separation, sometimes lasted as long as one month; in other cases there was no trial period. Betsileo described the trial period as allowing the groom and his family to evaluate not only the potential wife's appropriateness as wife and daughter-in-law but also her procreative capacity. Often, apparently, marriages were officially sanctioned only after the woman had become pregnant. The custom whereby the first child is born in its mother's native village is related to trial marriage, the demonstration of fertility, and the Betsileo notion that, although it is dishonorable for a Betsileo woman to bear a child whose father is unknown, conceptions that take place during trial marriages are perfectly appropriate.

Another case from Ivato illustrates the process whereby trial marriages become permanent unions following the birth of a child. Tuesdaysfather's granddaughter Celeste was eventually married after a trial period in a satellite village inhabited by another branch of the Tranovondro. Social relations between the families of Celeste and her husband, Robert, were well established during her trial period in his village, prior to her return to Ivato to have her first baby, a daughter, Flora. Robert and his father visited Ivato at least twice a week following Flora's birth.[31] The couple had to wait for their church ceremony until their papers were processed by the government, which took about two months. A few days after the wedding, which took place in Ivato's church, Celeste and Flora were escorted to Robert's village by a group of sixteen of his relatives who came to Ivato bearing baskets of white rice and 150 francs to buy meat as a sidedish; following custom they offered the meal in the baby's name. The group included the groom, his parents, six paternal uncles, their wives and sons, and one of his paternal aunts.[32]

The events surrounding a Betsileo marriage, which is a process rather than an event, lack the regional scale characteristic of most of the ceremonials to be described in chapter 7. On the other hand, ties between affinally related local descent branches and villages are maintained by prestations at regional ceremonials. The prestations traditionally associated with marriage itself have more symbolic than monetary value. The convention of teknonymy, to be described in chapter 7, signals the fruition of trial marriage and the new status of bride and groom as parents. Two kinds of prestations offered by the groom and his parents to the bride's family also symbolize the union of spouses and their families.

The *ala-fady*, literally "the breaking of taboos,"[33] is presented by the groom to his future father-in-law, who must distribute it among close members of his and his wife's families as a means of informing them that the marriage is to take place. The amount of the *ala-fady* is small, and its distribution is symbolic of close kin relations. The bulk of it goes to members of the bride's father's minimal descent group. When Celeste married, her father and grandfather, who had raised her, distributed the *ala-fady*, a token amount of 100 francs, to the ten household heads who are descendants of Karl Fridaysfather, the bride's patrilineal great-great-great-grandfather, to a client attached to this group, to the bride's mother's father and mother's mother's brother, and to the bride's father's mother's brother. The native villages of the bride's four grandparents were therefore alerted. A total of fifteen people received 5 francs each and the surplus remained with Celeste's father.

The *vodi-ondry*, literally "rear end of a sheep,"[34] was paid following receipt of government authorization for the marriage. As among the Merina

(Bloch 1978), this prestation traditionally provides final social legitimation of the marriage. Half of it was used to pay for the festivities that followed the Christian ceremony. Of the other half, the bulk remained with Celeste's father and paternal grandfather. However, the three remaining nonslave descended household heads of eastern Ivato, descendants of Karl Fridays-father's two brothers, plus the bride's mother's uncle (FB) and two of his sons received about fifty francs each. Those who had received a part of the *ala-fady* were excluded from the distribution of the *vodi-ondry*.

The amount of the *vodi-ondry* is considerably less in the Ivato region than in Mahazony, where we have already seen an example of 12,000 francs and a steer given as brideprice. Ivatans are aware of this difference and contrast bridewealth in their region with Mahazony and other parts of the more pastoral and traditional south, saying that whereas in the latter it is fixed at about 15,000 francs, in their region it is left to the discretion of the families involved.[35] A new method of settling the amount of bridewealth in the Ivato region was used in 1967 for the marriage of a young male eastern villager. The *vodi-ondry*, 7,500 francs, was presented in an envelope to the bride's parents, and discussion was curtailed. Ivatans seemed to view the new method as preferable to Betsileo custom, according to which, they said, the groom's representatives had to discuss the *vodi-ondry* all day with the bride's family, remaining near her door, not entering her house, fearing a lack of sufficient funds to complete the negotiations. Exaggerated perhaps, this stereotype does recall the earlier account of brideprice negotiations in Tanambao (and Bloch's [1978] description of the Merina marriage ceremony).

Divorce and Separation

Several traditionally legitimate reasons for separation were mentioned by Betsileo informants. Knowledge of infidelity by either spouse gives the other the right to end the union; however, such cases do not uniformly lead to divorce. Several known adulterers and at least one known adulteress remain with their original spouses in Ivato. Neglect of duties of husband and father is considered the most common cause of divorce; for Betsileo this means simply that the husband does not provide sufficient food for his wife and family. Such neglect may reflect the husband's poverty; one female native of western Ivato who had married a Merina colonist in a nearby village eventually left him because his rice field produced only about 200 kilograms of paddy per year. Betsileo say that alcoholism is the most common reason for insufficient funds to buy food and supplies, and therefore is a common cause of neglect, and thus divorce. When the groom and his relatives come to offer the *vodi-ondry* to the wife's parents, the latter, having consented to the union, are supposed to remind their affinals that they are receiving an unblemished commodity (Ivatan Rakoto's term) and to caution them that it is their obligation to see that she remains this way. Accordingly, wife beating, if brutal or frequent, or associated with drunkenness or other signs of irrationality on the part of the husband, can also lead to separation.

I am acquainted with the case of a woman who left her husband because he had contracted several debts, impairing his ability to provide for her. Presumably a man can leave his wife if she is derelict in her roles of wife and mother. In the case of one temporary separation in Ivato a man was judged right to abandon his wife when he traveled to Sakalava country and to return with a new wife because his original spouse could not manage a kitchen garden and all her chickens died. A husband, I was told, can chase away his wife if she is too jealous or strikes him.

Divorce, too, appears to be less frequent among senior commoners than among people lower in the hierarchy. Marital stability reflects the wealth, general socioeconomic status, and political roles of the families and local descent groups of bride and groom. Almost without exception, the contemporary elders of eastern Ivato had their marriages arranged with Tranovondro or Taray women, and only one of these marriages has been terminated, and that by the wife's death.[36]

Arranged, tried, and maintained more effectively by senior commoners than by junior commoners and slave descendants, Betsileo marriages entail a regular series of mutual services and prestations by both husband, wife, and their families. Compensating to some degree for the wife's trial period and virilocality are the husband's traditional obligations to his father-in-law, helping with several kinds of work: planting manioc, weeding rice, cutting firewood, assisting in house construction, and lending his cattle and labor for trampling at transplanting time. But in relationships between the affinally linked villages and minimal descent groups, the mutual hospitality and other prestations are more evenly balanced. The importance and durability of affinal alliances emerge in the context of regional and occasional events, particularly in ceremonials. We move now from principles that structure Betsileo village and home life to those that regulate regional interaction, a domain in which the import of affinality, common descent, fictive kinship, friendship, neighborship, and regional politics is felt.

Differential access to strategic resources, reflecting the historical and contemporary contrasts that have been examined in previous chapters, is evident in many areas of Betsileo social organization. Nobles and senior commoners belong to descent groups structured by deeper genealogies than those of Betsileo of lower rank, who, especially as migrants, claim affiliation with stipulated descent groups and stress collateral kin ties. Higher-ranking Betsileo continue to enhance their prestige by demonstrating their connections to historic agents of state organization. Patrilineal succession to leadership positions in local descent groups is a Betsileo cultural ideal, but is most characteristic of senior commoners, reflecting their greater political prominence.

However, flexibility in patterns of affiliation with local descent groups can also operate homeostatically to even out strategic resources. The ambilineal side of Betsileo descent permits access by Betsileo with sparse patrimonies to other ancestral estates. However, there is a perpetual structural contradiction in the Betsileo descent system—the opposition between, on the one hand, ambilineality and ancestral interests and, on the other, agnation and the immediate economic interests of living descent group members. This contradiction is never fully resolved, introducing tension which is manifest in aberrant behavior by nonagnates, who often receive (and provoke) accusations of witchcraft. In the long run it is senior commoners who, with reference to their own estates, emphasize the cultural value of agnation, as one of a number of culturally permissible ploys to discourage the legitimate claims of nonagnates.

In its mixture of ambilineal and patrilineal principles, and its inciusion of kin and descent groups of many types, Betsileo social organization is similar to that of many other Malayo-Polynesian and Malagasy peoples. Betsileo patterns of kinship and descent are variations on common Malagasy themes. In a sense these patterns, found among a geographically and economically intermediate people, also mediate the contrast between the cognatic principles that structure traditional Merina local kin groups and the strong patrilineal stress of Bara local group affiliation and political succession. However, Betsileo are much less endogamous than either Merina or Bara and have correspondingly clearer lineal genealogies, which can be used as a framework for regional integration, along with another contrasting principle, local group exogamy.

Betsileo of different rank use the social organizational principles their culture provides them in different ways. Senior commoners, represented as the guardians of the land and traditions of the ancestors, manipulate traditional rules and cultural values to increase their differential access to resources and social honor. Senior commoners stress lineal over collateral kinship and retain more extensive genealogical knowledge than juniors. They respect the maternal rights and obligations of their agnatic descendants and use the fosterage and adoption systems to increase their descendants' well-being. Simultaneously, by skillful management of their own web of kin obligations they have preserved a core of agnatic estate rights against legitimate claims of uterine descendants. Similarly, senior commoners are discouraged from acquiring ritual kin, from adopting outsiders, and from raising uterine claimants to their estate. Junior commoners, lacking the seniors' local and regional networks based on long-residence, political role, and alliance through marriage, kinship, and phratry organization, use fictive kinship and wide-ranging collateral kinship calculation for social and material survival.

Other contrasts between Betsileo of different rank emerge in considering marital relationships between individuals and groups. Senior commoners preserve their regional influence, and ties based on past links of descent and marriage, by respecting the cultural values of rank and, derivatively, regional descent group endogamy. Their marriages are political alliances that connect groups as well as individuals. It is no surprise that they are more carefully arranged and maintained through scrupulous observation of rights and obligations between spouses and their families and that they are more stable than the marriages of junior commoners, who pay much less attention to the descent group affiliation of their spouse. Regional variation between the agricultural east (Ivato) and the more pastoral south (Mahazony) also shows up in marital prestations, which are monetary and less substantial in the former. Men in Mahazony still use cattle in bridewealth payments, like Bara and other groups to the south and west. Variation in region and rank shows up just as strongly in the system of ceremonial feasting and prestations that I now examine.

CHAPTER SEVEN

The Overdetermination of Betsileo Ceremonial Life

Ceremonials held for different reasons and of varying scale bring Betsileo from different villages together throughout the year. Some, like tomb-centered ceremonials in which dead bodies are handled, wrapped in new shrouds, and/or transferred to new tombs, are confined to the winter ceremonial season, between June and September, whereas others, including funerals, can occur at any time. Ceremonials afford opportunities for kin, in-laws, and fictive kin to express their mutual obligations, for relatives and neighbors to socialize, and for regional status and prestige of individuals and groups to be demonstrated. In addition, certain Betsileo social groups, including the common descent group—uniting descendants of people buried in the same tomb—emerge only at ceremonials. Most important, however, in the consciousness of the natives who organize and take part in them, ceremonials allow Betsileo to recall, commemorate, and/or appease their dead ancestors. The persistence of Betsileo ceremonials is guaranteed by their overdetermination—the plethora of cultural values and meanings they express and functions they serve, but their functions and effects vary in the context of different material conditions. Before relating Betsileo ceremonial life to dimensions of variation set forth in previous chapters, however, certain common beliefs, values, and principles embodied and expressed in ceremonials must first be examined.

THE SUPERNATURAL REALM

Huntington's (1974, p. 96) statement that "the conspicuous burial of the dead is the ultimate activity of Malagasy systems of religion, economics, and social prestige" is as true of the Betsileo as of the Bara or Merina. Ironically, for people whose ceremonial life pays so much attention to the dead, Betsileo, apparently like other Malagasy, have little to say, other than the stock informant's answer of "custom," about why they do what they do. Students of the Malagasy have commented on vagueness and inconsistency in their religious beliefs (e.g., Bloch 1971, pp. 124–27; Dez 1956, p. 122). On death, for example, at least two spirits leave the body. One goes to a mountaintop, or, nowadays, to heaven or hell, and has no more to do with the living. The other stays nearby, wandering the hills, occasionally invading homes and dreams, assembling with other such spirits in the tomb to receive offerings from the living. Ancestral spirits are conceived in still other ways in particular contexts, some of which are examined below. Inconsistency in these and other aspects of Betsileo religion may be partially a reflection of Christianization, which has proceeded much farther than among the Bara (cf. Huntington 1974, p. 53), but not as far as among the Merina (Bloch 1971). I suspect, however, that much of the vagueness in Betsileo cosmology predates their Christian experience and is an aspect of cultural flexibility that has enabled the Betsileo to deal with major social changes.

The Betsileo supernatural realm consists of beings, powers, and forces. Among the beings are gods, souls, several categories of ancestral spirits, ghosts of evildoers and legendary beings, spirits of nature and water. The major sacred force is *hasina* (chapter 3), which flows from the land through ancestors to living people and into the sociopolitical order, and thus incorporates nature and culture, past and present, dead and living, acephaly and the state in a single conceptual order. However, the Betsileo also must deal with the dark side of the force, the occult powers controlled by sorcerers and witches, people who mock the social order by using its most potent symbols (e.g., food and tomb, major symbols of kinship) in inappropriate contexts. As Haile (1900, p. 401) noted, Betsileo cosmology recognizes no conditions and events that lack cause, and, in a highly personalistic world structured by kinship and marriage, causes are often personalistic. Causes are revealed by diviners, who examine and interpret patterns of seeds or beans as they fall in a grid-like setting. Causes of illness, sterility, diminishing prosperity, or other misfortune include malicious use of occult powers by others, ancestral displeasure, infringement of taboos, spirit possession, loss of soul, and action by ghosts. Diagnosis made, the diviner suggests a course of action, usually involving the sacrifice of an ox, designed to effect a cure, and exacts a fee for his labor.

Betsileo curers possess a variety of skills and control various kinds of knowledge and techniques. Some are general practitioners and others specialists, for example in calculating what Gardenier (1976) (in an analysis of similar practices among the central Sakalava) calls "day and destiny." These astrologers determine, on the basis of day, date, time of birth, and zodiac signs, one's lifetime horoscope, and suggest ways of combating particularly dangerous or unfortunate destinies. Astrology and divination are also used to set dates of ceremonies and a series of details connected with ceremonial performance. Medico-religious specialists also prepare, dispense, or prescribe concoctions made from native herbs, roots, barks, and pieces of wood, sometimes obtained from colleagues in the Tanala forest or imported and sold in a market town. Charms and antidotes to poison and wizardry (which are not distinguished) are obtained through the same channels. Charmed figurines guarded nineteenth-century Betsileo villages, and missionaries reported that people paid an ox for a talisman that offered generalized protection. Betsileo therefore provided multiple causes and cures for many conditions and events whose actual causes lay beyond their control or understanding.

Prior to the spread of Christianity among the Betsileo, missionary G. A. Shaw (1878, p. 2) described their religion as more concerned with the wonder-working spirits of the dead than with a supreme being. To be sure, pre-Christian Betsileo recognized a creator-god, Andriananahary or Zanahary, as maker of earth and sky, but he had little to do with human affairs. Customarily Zanahary was invoked to initiate ceremonials, as cooked rice, pieces of beef, and vessels containing rum were laid out on banana leaves placed on shelves in the northeastern corner of the house of the patriarch-sponsor. Zanahary, whose offering was placed on the top shelf, was invited to come, partake, and leave. The ancestral spirits, whose offerings were placed on the next shelf down, were much more critical to the ceremonial's success; their significance is discussed below. Christian missionaries chose still another Malagasy deity, Andriamanitra, the sweet lord or the fragrant prince, as equivalent to the Christian god. Betsileo speak of Andriamanitra in church, but even Ivato's devout Christians still invoke Andriananahary at ancestral ceremonials.

As many students of Madagascar have noted, one of the terms for ancestor, *razana*, has multiple referents. It can denote ancestors, dead relatives, or placenta, and is the root of *karazana* and *firazana*, which mean descent group (people with common ancestors) in many parts of Madagascar. The term and its compounds (*tanindrazana*, the land of the ancestors; *fombandrazana*, the customs of the ancestors) recur among all Malagasy peoples and demonstrate the importance of the past and the dead for the present and the living.[1] The Betsileo, like other Malagasy, terminologically preserve ancestors and dead kin in the human realm. Significant is the fact that when Malagasy talk of people in the abstract, they use a term translatable as "living people," rather than simply "people." The humanity of the dead is not forgotten; it is always necessary to distinguish living people from dead people.

As will be discussed more fully below, the Betsileo have complex and inconsistent notions about the afterlife. Two souls or spirits separate from the body, but neither is identical to the ancestors who are addressed at ceremonials. The Betsileo do not attempt to reconcile the fact that their ancestors— their bodies and spirits—have multiple locations in time and space. In ceremonies, ancestors are addressed as *razana*, and by name. The term *fahasivy* ("the ninth or the ninths") is also used as a reference (not address) term for ancestors. It comes from the ninth row in seed divination, which identifies the ancestors as factors in the problem being diagnosed.

All Betsileo ceremonies (except funerals) customarily began with the previously described offering to and invocation of Andriananahary, the ancestors of the hosts, and the dead slaves that served them in the afterworld. Offerings for each were placed on successively lower shelves. A case analyzed later in this chapter illustrates that such offerings and invocations necessarily preceded the opening of the ancestral tomb for reasons other than burying someone. Other content of such ancestor worship sessions could include thanksgiving for a successful harvest, an increasing herd of cattle, growing wealth or prosperity, fertility of self or descendants, recovery from illness, or return home from a long journey. Such ceremonies might also be held because a diviner had diagnosed ancestral displeasure, perhaps because a descent group taboo had been violated (that displeasure would be acknowledged in the session designed to overcome it), or because an ancestor had appeared in a dream. Problems that lead to the diagnosis of ancestral ill will include illness, sterility, other misfortune, or someone's death. Other sessions called on the ancestors to intervene with other spiritual beings (e.g., Vazimba, the quasi-historical early inhabitants of the land. Certain sites believed to be associated with the Vazimba, including purported burial sites, are tabooed; if these taboos are broken unwittingly, an animal sacrifice is necessary.) It would seem that Betsileo could always find an appropriate occasion for holding such a ceremony, although, as is indicated below, ceremonials clustered in the postharvest season. Betsileo beliefs in ancestral ability to work good and evil seem much more similar to Bara (Huntington 1974, pp. 73–74) than to Merina, who, states Bloch (1971, pp. 125, 162), believe that their ancestors have little power over the living and offer no direct benefit to them.

In addition to gods, souls, and spirits, Betsileo recognize a category of undifferentiated ghosts, similar to the *angatra* of the Merina (Bloch 1971, p. 124). This vaguely conceived but potentially dangerous category seems to include remote and forgotten ancestors, and ghosts of nonrelatives, which can be malevolent, especially if one has affronted them in life. Also included are spirits of the bush (*lolo*), other nature spirits, and a few monstrous creatures.

Missionaries (cf. Moss 1900, pp. 476–77) described spirit possession among the Betsileo in terms that recall Huntington's (1974, p. 200 et seq.) description of *bilo* (a nature spirit) possession of Bara women, including its choreomania (dancing fever). I never observed Betsileo spirit possession, although I suspect that one of the curing sacrifices I mention below was intended to correct such a condition. Nor did I observe soul loss, also described by nineteenth-century missionaries (Cf. Haile 1899, p. 332). To expel an unwanted spirit or to restore a roving one to its owner, consultation with a specialist, fee, and animal sacrifice were ordinarily remedial.

A more abstract dimension of Betsileo supernaturalism is their beliefs and behavior about certain sacred places, rocks, raised stones, streams, paths, and other parts of the landscape. Taboos against stepping on Vazimba land have been mentioned. To obtain fertility, women anointed raised (phallic) stones or rocks, and sometimes sacrificed roosters at these sites in the countryside. Merchants also anointed rocks believed to insure fertility—of their money. If no other cause could be determined for misfortune, infringement of an (unknown) taboo connected with a sacred spot was always a possibility. *Hasina*, efficacious force, is somehow connected with these spots and taboos, but no informant could say just how.

In chapter 3 I noted that *hasina* has a dark side, called *hery*. People can manipulate occult forces to work evil. Gardenier (1976) reports that the central Sakalava fear public assemblies since witches (strangers) work from a distance; their evil eye can modify food or drink as it is being consumed, rendering it poisonous. Mouth-covering is a precaution against this. Sorcery against a relative, on the other hand, involves actually placing poison in the victim's food or drink. Huntington (1974, p. 109) reports that Bara fear witchcraft, for example, by affinals, at postharvest ceremonies, particularly postburial gatherings, since witchcraft may have been implicated in the death, and there may be scores to settle. Bloch (1971, p. 152) notes that a "surprising" number of Merina do die at ceremonies—scenes of drinking, dancing, bullbaiting, wrestling, sexual license, and generally raucous behavior. Betsileo display similar fears of malevolent intent of outsiders and strangers and similar exaggerated "party" behavior at their major ceremonies.

The central Sakalava (Gardenier 1976), whose mobile stockbreeding existence is not compatible with large corporate local groups, think that black magic can be worked by relatives (closeby) or strangers (at a distance). For the Merina (Bloch 1971, p. 58), however, the categories of relative (*havana*) and witch are mutually exclusive. One is supposed to live with, work with, share food with, trust implicitly, and even marry relatives. Betsileo are intermediate. Ivatans, for example, think that one villager, affiliated through uterine links, works witchcraft, but they are doubtful about whether he would actually harm his own relatives. Yet, on an ideal level, they say that sharing food converts strangers (like affines) into kin, and that food sharing between actual or fictive relatives is based on trust; one has faith that the "relative" who prepares and serves the food will not poison it.

Because of the cultural values that witches' behavior mocks, witchcraft stands out as the systematic inversion of ceremonial in Betsileo life (see figure 5). Witches' behavior is reminiscent of what goes on at ceremonies, but witches do these things in inappropriate contexts. Bloch (1971, p. 155) notes that in ordinary life Merina respect the separation of the dead and the living, However, in an appropriate context—the *famadihana* or ritual rewrapping and reburial of one or more corpses—living and dead come in close contact. The children and siblings of the focal corpse not only view the body of a loved one for the first time since death, but by the end of the ceremony they have adjusted to his or her death by dancing with the corpse, jostling it, and tossing it in the air. So, notes Bloch (1971, p. 168), is emotional distance from, and eventual adjustment to, the death of someone close accomplished among the Merina. The close relatives of the dead break another ordinary taboo at the *famadihana*; they stand on the tomb. They affirm their common kinship by their common sacrilege and relationship to the focal dead (Bloch 1971, pp. 167–68). In the same context, as also among the Betsileo, the mat on which the corpse is deposited is fought over by women, who sleep with it to enhance their fertility. In the context of tomb-centered ceremonials, then, the fertility (an aspect of nature) of living people is enhanced through customs that renew the membership of the (decaying, returning to nature) dead in the cultural realm as corpses are rewrapped. The *famadihana*, in other words, is a complex mediator of the nature-culture opposition among Merina and Betsileo.

Witches, however, are mediators out of context; they become, in the words of Burton and Hicks (1976), "classificatory monsters" because they so accurately mimic the most sacred behaviors. Witches invert appropriate ceremonial behavior through solitary (versus social) action in an inappropriate context. *Famadihanas* are daytime affairs; Betsileo fear the night; witches

Ceremonial	Witchcraft
day	night
social	individual
kinship	non- or distant kinship
"naked" are clothed	witch removes clothes
common sacrilege affirms kinship values	individual sacrilege denies kinship values
symbols of death used benevolently to renew human fertility	symbols of death used malevolently to destroy human life
appropriate mediation of nature-culture opposition	witches are classificatory monsters

Fig. 5 Witchcraft as a Contextual Inversion of Ceremonial

are active at night. Like close relatives at a *famadihana*, witches dance around and atop tombs, but those of nonrelatives (or, perhaps, distant kin). In the *famadihana*, corpses that the Betsileo describe as "naked" (Dez 1956, p. 120) are reclothed, whereas frenzied witches remove their clothes as they desecrate family tombs. Among the northern Sakalava (Feeley-Harnik 1978, p. 410) witches are believed to use parts of the dead or things that have been in contact with the dead to work evil against the living. Although Betsileo witches do not actually invade tombs, their desacralized use of the tomb helps create their efficacy as witches. Witches are therefore believed to seize on and to mimic the structure and content of society's most potent set of sacred symbols, decontextualizing them in order to desecrate them.

I do not know whether or not Betsileo witches really exist. When I asked a man suspected of being a witch whether he was one, he smiled, but did not deny his label. I doubt, though, that he engages in the kinds of witching activity just mentioned. Nevertheless, the belief in witches, by parodying basic values, helps to make their structure and meaning unmistakable and thus to reinforce and renew them.

Having described the supernatural beings, powers, and forces that intrude on Betsileo social life, I turn to the interarticulation of religious acts and beliefs, social life, and the individual life cycle.

THE LIVING AND THE DEAD

Consideration of the Betsileo life cycle demonstrates the constant articulation of living and dead, of descendants and ancestors, through a series of observances that help bridge the opposition of life and death. All first children and most others are born in their mother's native village (or are taken there from maternity wards while their mother recuperates). Eventually the father and his family arrive to escort mother and child to his village. Traditionally they offer a meal of rice and meat symbolizing transfer of primary rights in the child from mother's to father's group. Yet through birth in the maternal village the child's rights as member of the mother's descent group and potential cultivator of its estate have been communicated and guaranteed. For a boy, circumcision reinforces these rights. A neighborhood specialist is paid for his services in a small-scale ritual held in the father's village. Close maternal relatives, including mother's brother and maternal grandparents, traditionally attend.[2] The ritual continues close ties of boy and maternal relatives; although circumcision continues today, the mother's brother's reportedly customary swallowing of the foreskin has been abandoned.

Betsileo regard early childhood as an enigmatic and dangerous period. Because they believe that children may be attacked by envious spirits, they refer to their children and address them with a derogatory nickname, for example "little dog," or "slave." Betsileo never praise children for being attractive or healthy, since this might attract spirits who could destroy them.[3] In order to join the ancestors, a Betsileo is expected to have attained fully human personality. Excluded from the ancestral tomb if they die young, children are in effect given a trial period before they are regarded as fully human. Their real identity concealed from malevolent spirits by the convention of the child's nickname, they are scrutinized for viability. Should they pass from the critical years into adolescence, they can identify themselves with the ancestors by taking an ancestral name and be buried in the ancestral tomb. Should they, on the other hand, incur ancestral or other spiritual envy or enmity, they are relegated to separate children's tombs, or, in the old days, to burial in the rice fields.[4] Entering adolescence, through a name-changing ceremony a boy can assume an adult name.

The name-changing ceremony is witnessed rarely among contemporary Betsileo. In the past Betsileo were known by at least three different names at different stages of their lives: a child's name, an adult name assumed in a ceremonial context, and a teknonymous name incorporating the name of one's child or younger sibling. Suppressing a childhood name for reasons other than teknonymy occasioned a ceremonial involving the slaughter of a steer and the proclamation that the individual would no longer be known by the childhood name, but by whatever adult name had been chosen, always an ancestral name. Ceremonial assumption of an adult name constituted a descendant's plea to the ancestor for a special relationship in which the ancestor would act as personal intermediary between his namesake and other spiritual entities. Although ancestral names can come from either side, Ivatans appear to prefer patrilateral names, representing illustrious figures of the past.[5] The ceremony can be viewed as a ritual statement of the individual's incorporation within a descent group consisting of dead and living representatives.

Adult names do not always stick. Ivatans cited the case of Tuesdaysfather's only son Antoine, who, in a ceremony held in the cattle corral, took on two adult names at once, that of Goodmaker, his patrilineal great-grandfather, and that of Soana, a matrilateral ancestor. Neither name stuck. Teknonymy, in contrast, occasions no ceremonial. The family is merely expected to address and to refer to new parents teknonymously, as *Rai-* ("father of") and *Reni-* ("mother of") followed by the newborn's name. Others follow their example. Still another Malagasy name, with one or more foreign first names—generally French, occasionally English—appended, may be used for government and school records and generally in the external world. Such a name is often chosen for a child by its mother and father.

Later in life, most Betsileo begin a trial period, often arranged, with a prospective spouse. Once a woman demonstrates her fertility by pregnancy, she returns to her native village, where, soon after the child is born, her husband and her in-laws seek her out. Removal to the husband's village with a first-born child signals that what is expected to be a durable marriage has been established. The alliance of husband's and wife's minimal descent groups and villages is symbolized by the ritual offering and acceptance of a meal given in the baby's name.[6] Thereafter, a person's status as a parent and future ancestor is recognized by the convention of teknonymy.

Throughout the rest of his life a man expresses his obligations to his wife's father, and ultimately to her brother, who replaces her father on his death, through his labor. Obligations to her relatives and village are met at ceremonials held by her native villagers and other close relatives. The wife's group reciprocates at ceremonials held in her husband's village and in those of his close relatives. Still another status change, involving eldest or eldest surviving siblings, may be confirmed by teknonymous assumption of the name of a recently born sibling. This convention communicates that one has replaced his father as village elder or head of a minimal descent group.

Funerary tribute measures a Betsileo's socioeconomic status and lifetime achievement. Deceased people corporeally join other members of their descent group in the ancestral tomb, while spiritually they gain admittance to the vaguely conceived ancestral afterworld atop Ambondrombe, a mountain in Tanala country southeast of the Betsileo heartland (see below). When death terminated a marriage, relationships between the affinally linked groups could be, but were rarely, continued by levirate and sororate. Much more commonly a widow was (and still is) expected to remain with her sons in her husband's village, relying on their support and eventually interred in their tomb. A widow with no sons is customarily invited to remain in her husband's village; however, most such women ultimately return to their native villages, since their positions can easily become uncomfortable. Ivatans asserted that childless widows had no real claim in their husband's village and could be sent home whenever his relatives wished.

Betsileo do not think of death, which permeates their lives, as termination, but as an inevitable rite in passage along an indefinite path linking past and future. Some of Maurice Bloch's statements about Merina eschatology also apply to the Betsileo. Bloch (1971, p. 124) describes the Merina as lacking interest in the afterlife, and he reports many inconsistencies in their eschatological beliefs; both are also true of the Betsileo. Betsileo share the Merina belief in two souls: *ambiroa* and *fanahy*. The *ambiroa* gradually develops in childhood and survives death. It is vaguely associated with the tomb. Rum, tobacco, household utensils, and other offerings left in the tomb after each opening seem to be intended for the use of the *ambiroa* of the *razana* (dead or ancestors) in the tomb. The *ambiroa* are also believed to wander around the hills; they occasionally visit tombs, and houses of their living kin; they can come in dreams and make demands, as the *ambiroa* of

Karl Fridaysfather appeared in a dream of his son Goodmaker and directed him to build a new tomb and transfer his bones from the sepulcher of the western village. As among the Merina, *ambiroa* can be mischievous, avenging lifetime affronts. As memory of the less illustrious dead fades, their *ambiroa* merge into a general ghost category, also feared but never directly addressed in Betsileo rituals. For both Betsileo and Merina, the second soul, *fanahy*, moved to Ambondrombe, a mountain on the southeastern edge of Betsileo country (there is apparently another with the same name in Imerina.) The ancestral spirits on Ambondrombe presumably followed Betsileo customs, worshipping their ancestors, attending markets and ceremonials, just like the living. Missionaries equated *fanahy* with the Christian soul concept and sent good and bad ones to heaven and hell rather than Ambondrombe. My Christianized informants were uncertain about where the *fanahy* goes now; they seem to maintain vague beliefs in both heaven and Ambondrombe.

Memories of ancestors are revived, however, when descendants take their names; older brothers replace their fathers and stand as fathers to their younger siblings; parents are socially defined with reference to their descendants—teknonymy identifies them as ancestors. In enculturation, in ritual, and in conversation Betsileo remember their ancestors with admiration and fondness. Recall is constantly reinforced as remains are seen and handled in the tomb. Genealogies extend several generations into the past, and events associated with the lives of important ancestors are recounted.

Betsileo extend to their children and grandchildren considerable warmth and succor, and they know that their ancestors felt and acted similarly. Nevertheless, adult children are expected to repay their parents with hard work, respect, and unquestioning obedience, and a parent may justly reject and disinherit a child who shirks these responsibilities. The relationship between dead ancestor and living descendant is also a projection of that between parent and adult child; ancestral favor must be curried, and a specialist is needed to diagnose ancestral displeasure, since the dead cannot caution their descendants as parents caution children.

Although my informants were vague about the identities of envious spirits who threatened their young children, it was my impression that ancestral spirits could be involved, and that Betsileo feared that since older people often foster their grandchildren, there is a danger that departed ancestors will seek to foster their young descendants by spiriting them away to the afterworld, particularly if the living parents have affronted them. Such fears are reinforced by practice, as parents, concerned about spiritual action against their children, entrust them to fosterage by grandparents, who have more weight with the afterworld. Indeed, curers often diagnose ancestral displeasure as the cause of illness, misfortune, infertility, or failure of plans, and outward success is a sign of ancestral favor. Individuals sponsor certain ceremonials because they are concerned about ancestral displeasure or because they want to thank the ancestors for intervention in human affairs or otherwise to curry or maintain ancestral goodwill.

As Betsileo feel ambivalent about their ancestors, they also attribute ambivalence to their ancestors' feelings about the living. They extend their protection to all their descendants, guaranteeing them a place on the ancestral estate. They act as intermediaries with unrelated ghosts, gods, nature spirits, and other spiritual entities and contribute to the success of some of their descendants. But they insist that they be remembered and honored by ceremonial sacrifices, by attention to the tomb and the local estate, by continuing respect for elders, and they are capable of expressing their displeasure by sending sickness, misfortune, and even death.[7]

Symbols of the continuity of life and death permeate Betsileo ceremonials. Raw silk obtained from worms, which were raised throughout the Betsileo south and west until early in this century, was used to manufacture the most magnificent of all shrouds, the *lamba landy*, due a person of high status on burial, rewrapping, or tomb transfer. From bodily putrescences of high status corpses—preserved in a pot—came their reincarnations in the form of a worm or snake, which, when offered cooked rice, accepted it to demonstrate the transformation (cf. Richardson 1875, p. 73). From not-yet-human babies (as the Betsileo view them) buried in the rice fields came new life, rice, the foundation of Betsileo existence. The season for handling the dead immediately precedes transplanting, even as new rice is growing in nursery beds. The shroud offered by the living encloses the dead; the dead reciprocate, suffusing with the stuff of life both the shroud and the straw mat on which ancestral remains are allowed to repose. Women fight for bits of old straw and cloth, place them in their beds, and ask the dead to make them fertile. In reality, funerals and other tomb-centered ceremonials celebrate death while promoting new life. Missionaries complained regularly about licentiousness at such events (cf. Shaw 1878, p. 7).

The inverse of teknonymy, which establishes one as ancestor, is the name-changing ceremony, which establishes one as descendant. Significantly, no steer is sacrificed when a child is born; it is the ancestors' gift to the living. The ancestor, who has been symbolically reborn when a descendant sacrifices a steer and changes his name, offers a concrete gift—a child—to his descendant, and his descendant thereafter symbolizes his own direct contribution to the ongoing descent group by incorporating the name of this child into his own. Just as cattle and their byproducts are used agriculturally to reproduce the source of Betsileo life (rice), gifts of cattle to ancestors are essential, in the Betsileo view, to renewal of human life. Cattle serve therefore, in fact and in symbol, as necessary agents in the perpetuation of life. Note that the customary offering after a child's birth is rice and pieces of meat, not a whole sacrificial steer. Just as steers are appropriate gifts for the ancestors, children and rice are viewed as symbolically interlinked evidence of ancestral reciprocation.

In symbols and practice, therefore, ceremonials reaffirm the social basis of Betsileo life: the continuity of the descent group, of bilateral kinship, the persistence of social and socioeconomic divisions, hierarchical and otherwise, conceived as intrinsic to Betsileo life. Closer examination of Betsileo ceremonials reveals several additional dimensions. I will return to them after describing and analyzing the different ceremonials and people's reasons for attending them.

SEASONALITY AND SCALE OF BETSILEO CEREMONIALS

Seasonality governs most Betsileo ceremonials, particularly tomb-centered regional events like *famadihana*, the ceremonial inauguration of a new tomb, involving transfer of mortal remains from at least one old tomb to the new structure. A definite ceremonial season spans the Malagasy winter, from June through September. Table 22 analyzes Betsileo ceremonials according to scale and seasonality. My fourfold classification of scale perhaps masks a gradual increase in participation from familial through village through neighborhood through regional ceremonials. Circumcision attracts fewest people. Normally held in the boy's paternal village, circumcision unites maternal and paternal grandparents and siblings with the parents and their son, who is usually circumcised between his first and second year. The operation is performed on a winter morning (Betsileo believe that cold weather facilitates

TABLE 22

Classification of Southern Betsileo Ceremonials according to
Scale, Seasonality, and Frequency

| | Seasonality | |
Scale	Seasonal	Year-Round
Familial	Circumcision	
Local (village)		Marriage ceremony
		Saondrazana (vow
		fulfillment)
		Curing sacrifice
Neighborhood	Rewrapping inside tomb	*Infant's funeral*
	Naming ceremony	
	Rewrapping outside tomb	
	Lanonana[a]	
Regional	*Famadihana*[a]	Adult's funeral[a]

a. Most common ceremonials.

healing) by a paid specialist who provides the service for several villages. The boy is not allowed to sleep the preceding night. His fatigue, aided by rum, helps him fall asleep after the operation.

Other seasonal ceremonials are tomb-centered, involving handling and rewrapping of the dead bodies within them. The scale of tomb-centered ceremonials varies with the status and wealth of the sponsor, ranging from primarily village affairs, in which bodies are simply wrapped in new shrouds inside the tomb, through events attracting an entire neighborhood, or, when a new tomb is inaugurated, a whole region. Cases of the first and last kind are discussed below. I never observed the neighborhood ceremonial occasioned by removal, rewrapping, and replacement of bodies in the same tomb (but see Dez 1956, p. 115). This ceremony is much more common among the Merina (see Bloch 1971, p. 146–61) than the Betsileo.

Of events that are not seasonally confined, weddings, curing sacrifices, and vow fulfillment ceremonies (*saondrazana*, literally "thanking the ancestors") are of smallest scale. The marriage ceremony per se is a creation of state organization (government authorization must be obtained) and European contact (small-scale Christian ceremonies attracting close relatives of the bride and groom are sometimes held). The several steps traditionally involved in the gradual establishment of a proper Betsileo marriage have been discussed in chapter 6. Betsileo culture uses no major ceremonies to mark arrangement of a marriage by elders, trial marriage, negotiation of bridewealth, notification of the bride's relatives, childbirth, the paternal meal offered in the mother's village, and teknonymy.

Other ceremonies are addressed toward ancestors but do not involve opening tombs or handling remains. Of largest scale and closest to a party of any Betsileo ceremonial is the *lanonana* or thanksgiving ceremony, which ranges from a neighborhood to a regional affair but is of smaller scale than a tomb inaugural (*famadihana*) or adult's funeral. *Lanonana* are held for a variety of reasons but have as a common theme thanksgiving to ancestral spirits for some successful outcome. Typically they are held following the instructions of a ritual specialist, though they may also be homecoming ceremonials. *Lanonana* occur throughout the year, but the larger ones are concentrated in the winter ceremonial season. Consider one example: I attended a *lanonana* held in a hamlet genealogically affiliated with western Ivato on a Wednesday in September 1967. It commemorated the recovery, following treatment by a traditional Betsileo curer, of the granddaughter of François, the organizer. François's daughter, who lives in Bara country with her husband, a policeman, took her child to a physician when she first became ill. When he was unable to effect a cure, she brought the child home to consult a curer. Following apparently successful treatment, the curer was paid cash, but he also attended the *lanonana* and received a large share of the raw beef of the slaughtered steer, which was purchased in a nearby village, where one of the organizer's daughters is married. Each of his three sons-in-law contributed 1,000 francs to the steer's cost of 14,000 francs ($56.00 U.S., 1967). Most local household heads attended this *lanonana*, but very few women from eastern Ivato were present, betokening the differential participation in ceremonial life of men and women, which is examined further below. Representatives of about thirty-five villages attended, most from neighboring communities. The sixteen Ivatan household heads present gave between 20 and 50 francs each, the typical contribution for a neighbor or distant relative at this kind of ceremony. Estimating average village parties of five persons each for the neighboring villages, there were between 200 and 300 people present. If each guest gave at least 20 francs, the organizer came near recouping the cost of the steer.

Similar to *lanonana*, but of only village scale, are curing sacrifices and vow-fulfillment ceremonies. Both involve sacrifices of one steer, in the first case at the direction of a curer who has diagnosed ancestral displeasure, transgression of a taboo, or, rarely, spirit possession or loss of soul as a cause of illness and has prescribed cattle sacrifice as a cure. The second type of ceremony, vow fulfillment, is a personal ritual in which an individual sacrifices a steer to fulfill a vow made to ancestors, presumably (but Betsileo were vague about this) to repay general ancestral blessing or some instrumental action or intervention on the individual's behalf. Ivatans assert that such local rituals were more common in the past; the strength of the local Roman Catholic church has contributed to their demise. However, sixty-one-year-old Ivatan Etienne, locally regarded as Ivato's least devout Christian and most traditional Betsileo, did not let Catholicism deter him from holding an ancestral ceremony in his home. Etienne had vowed, somewhat indefinitely, to make a sacrifice when his herd reached sufficient size, which turned out to be ten. On a table in the northeastern corner of his house, Etienne arranged bits of rice and beef from the slaughtered steer in separate piles on a banana leaf.[8] He then addressed his father, who had resided uxorilocally in Ivato, his mother, his maternal grandfather (by a second and subsidiary union) Karl Fridaysfather, as well as collateral ancestors of the eastern descent branch.

Of nonseasonal ceremonials an adult's funeral is the only event of regional scale. Funerals, as cases discussed below illustrate, vary in scale depending on age, social attributes, and political prominence of the deceased and his or her kin. Other things being equal, number of participants and the geographic range of their villages increase with the age of the deceased. The funerals of prominent senior commoners may attract more than 1,000 people representing more than 100 villages, whereas an infant's funeral attracts mostly close kin, neighbors, and residents of the child's village. The typical crowd might number between 300 and 400.

FACTORS IN CEREMONIAL ATTENDANCE

Tables 23 and 24 provide more detailed information on the seasonal occurrence of Betsileo ceremonials. In table 23 responses to an interview schedule on ceremonial attendance from informants in Ivato and the two Mahazony villages are arranged according to the different types of ceremonial they attended in specified months of 1966 and 1967. It shows how many respondents attended ceremonials (ceremonial mentions) rather than how many ceremonials actually took place. Table 24, in contrast, involves Ivato alone; its figures document the monthly occurrence of particular ceremonies between June 1966 and November 1967 rather than ceremonial mentions. The correspondence between the two tables probably largely reflects the fact that my interview schedules were filled out at the end of winter, 1967, so that people remembered the funerals and other events they had attended from June through September 1967 more often than earlier events.[9]

Despite the skewing introduced by the timing of my interviews, some significant patterns are demonstrated in tables 23 and 24. As expected, funerals are most widely distributed throughout the year. Although, like tomb-centered ceremonials, *lanonana* cluster in the winter, they are more widely distributed than other winter ceremonials, occurring as early as March and as late as November (table 23). Only one *famadihana* occurred outside of the winter, in April; all the others were held between July and October. Table 23 demonstrates that informants in all three villages attended ceremonials, whether funeral, *lanonana*, or *famadihana*, during every month of the year, but with a marked clustering between July and September. August was the modal month in all three villages. Statistics thus confirm that the ceremonial season that exists in Betsileo consciousness[10] is borne out in their actual ceremonial attendance.

Interview schedule results also demonstrate the regional nature of Betsileo ceremonials and the kinds of social relationships that motivate Betsileo to attend them. Only 13 percent of the ceremonials attended by Ivatans had

TABLE 23

Remembered Ceremonial Attendance, Combining Ivato, Ambalabe, and Tanambao

| Type of Ceremonial | Number of Individuals Attending (by month) | | | | | | | | | | | | Totals | |
	1	2	3	4	5	6	7	8	9	10	11	12	No.	%
Funeral	1	2	1	0	3	5	7	43	18	2	1	2	85	46.7
Lanonana	0	0	2	0	1	6	14	14	8	1	6	0	52	28.6
Famadihana	0	0	0	1	0	1	6	19	6	4	0	0	37	20.3
Marriage	0	0	0	0	0	1	0	0	0	0	3	0	4	2.2
Circumcision	0	0	0	0	0	1	0	2	0	1	0	0	4	2.2
Total by month	1	2	3	1	4	14	27	78	32	8	10	2	182	100.0

TABLE 24

Specific Ceremonials Attended and Mentioned by Ivatans,
June, 1966–November, 1967

| Type of Ceremonial | Number of Ceremonials Attended (by month) | | | | | | | | | | | | | | | | | | Totals | |
| | 1966 | | | | | | | 1967 | | | | | | | | | | | | |
	6	7	8	9	10	11	12	1	2	3	4	5	6	7	8	9	10	11	N	%
Funeral	2	1	0	0	0	0	1	1	1	0	0	1	1	3	6	3	2	0	22	66.7
Lanonana	1	0	1	0	0	1	0	0	0	0	0	0	0	1	2	1	0	0	7	21.2
Famadihana	0	0	0	1	0	0	0	0	0	0	0	0	0	0	1	0	0	0	2	6.1
Marriage	0	0	0	0	0	0	0	0	0	0	0	0	0	0	0	0	0	1	1	3.0
Circumcision	0	0	0	0	0	0	0	0	0	0	0	0	0	0	0	0	1	0	1	3.0
Total by month	3	1	1	1	0	1	1	1	1	0	0	1	2	6	7	3	3	1	33	100.0

been held in that village; the figure was similar (15 percent) in the two Mahazony villages. However, ceremonials did draw most of their personnel from the canton where they were held. About three-fourths of the ceremonials mentioned by the villagers in Mahazony were in that canton, and 92 percent of the ceremonials mentioned by respondents in Ivato, which is located on the borders of two cantons, involved one of them.

Betsileo attend an average of about five ceremonials a year, and some participate in three times as many. Thus, in their lives Betsileo attend perhaps hundreds of these events. Any Betsileo can be expected to make a major contribution to a *famadihana* involving transferal of the remains of any grandparent or great-grandparent. Any Betsileo can be expected to attend a *lanonana* sponsored by a parent, sibling, child, and probably an uncle or an aunt. Any Betsileo can be expected to be a major participant in a funeral involving the village of any grandparent, and possibly great-grandparent, or of close affinals, either through one's own marriage or the marriages of children, siblings, or parent's siblings.

Whenever a respondent mentioned a ceremonial, he or she was asked to indicate his or her relationship to the focal individual (sponsor or deceased). Table 25, considering only Ivatans' responses, groups such links into three categories. In a quarter of the cases, Ivatans attended ceremonials involving unrelated individuals. Usually they identified these individuals as their neighbors, but some said that they were attending as friends, or pointed to a relationship based on patronage-clientship or former master-slave status, or said that no relationship was involved. About a third of the ceremonials were attended because of affinal links, and about 40 percent of all links were purely consanguineal. Betsileo bilaterality in kinship rights and obligations re-emerges here; Ivatans are equally likely to attend ceremonials involving the mother's as the father's side, the wife's as the husband's.

TABLE 25

Consanguineal, Affinal, and Other Links to Ceremonials Attended by Ivatans

	No.	Totals by Category	
	No.	No.	%
Consanguineals			
Matrilateral	24		
Patrilateral	25		
Siblings and their descendants	5		
Descendants	3		
Same local descent group	8		
Same named, but not local, descent group	6		
Subtotal	71	71	39.9
Affinals			
Wife's relatives	12		
Husband's relatives	12		
Other affinals	36		
Subtotal	60	60	33.7
Unrelated, identified as			
Neighbor	33		
Unrelated	8		
Client	4		
Friend	2		
Subtotal	47	47	26.4
Total		178	100.0

Although similar ties based on kinship, descent, affinity, and neighborhood provide entries to ceremonials in the two regions, there is an important contrast between Ivato and the Mahazony villages in *types* of ceremonials attended. Half of the ceremonials attended by Ivatans were funerals; about a third were *lanonana*, and only 12 percent were *famadihana*. In contrast (table 26) *lanonana* was the most common ceremonial mentioned in the Mahazony villages (44 percent of the responses), followed by *famadihana* (33 percent)

TABLE 26

Types of Ceremonials Attended: Ivato Compared with the Two Mahazony Villages

Type of Ceremony Mentioned	Ivato (n = 209)[a]	Mahazony (n = 90)
Funeral	51%	17%
Lanonana	30	44
Famadihana	12	33
Other	7	6
Total	100	100

a. Ceremonial mentions.

and then funerals (17 percent). The smaller number of funerals attended by Mahazony villagers may reflect both lower population density in the south and the more restricted social networks of junior commoners, or it may be sample error or chance.[11] However, one major difference does stand out. People in Mahazony attend a greater variety of traditional ceremonials than people in the agricultural east. Not only are *lanonana* more common in the south, the ceremony of largest scale, the *famadihana*, is commonplace in the south, but very rare in the east. Respondents in Ambalabe and Tanambao together mentioned eighteen different *famadihana*, sixteen held in 1966 or 1967, compared to only seven, two of which took place in these years, cited by Ivatans. The greater frequency of tomb inaugurals in Mahazony is the most obvious expression of *greater ceremonial activity* in the more sparsely populated south. Some of the reasons for this difference, and for the very different functioning of exactly the same ceremonial forms in the context of demographic and socioeconomic variation, are examined later in this chapter, after considering some actual Betsileo ceremonies.

CASE ANALYSIS OF BETSILEO CEREMONIALS

Rewrapping Ceremonies (Famadihana)

As noted, Betsileo *famadihana* are ceremonies that center on transfer of mortal remains from old to new tombs. When removed from a tomb or a temporary burial site, corpses or fragments are always wrapped in new shrouds (old, decaying shrouds are never removed). Most generally, the term *famadihana* applies to rewrapping of the dead (from roots that mean "to turn over the dead"). Among the Betsileo I studied the term is used almost exclusively for the inaugural ceremony held in the postharvest season following a new tomb's completion. Remains are transferred to the new sepulcher from one or more old burial sites.

Bloch (1971, p. 145 et seq.) surveys the term's varied and different meanings among the Merina. Despite a high emigration rate, most Merina colonists preserve their links with the "land of the ancestors" by contributing to the upkeep of a tomb in their ancestors' village (where their own land is farmed by distant relatives or by sharecroppers, who are often slave descendants). They expect to be buried in this tomb. Merina who die outside the community where their tomb is located are usually buried temporarily. About two years later, during the postharvest ceremonial season, the corpse is "returned" to the ancestral tomb. This "return *famadihana*" constitutes the term's primary meaning to the Merina. When Merina talk about rewrapping ceremonies, they have in mind the obligation to inter, eventually, any dead person with his other relatives. Bloch (1971, p. 162) speaks of the "terror" that Merina have of being buried alone. Although they are vague about its nature,

Merina believe that the dead do enjoy some kind of an afterlife, and life is incomplete unless one is surrounded by kin.

However, Merina also use *famadihana* for three other ceremonies. First is the opening of a new tomb, along with rewrapping and transfer of remains from temporary burials and old tombs to the new building. This, as noted, is the principal meaning for the Betsileo. Among the Merina *famadihana* also refers to removing corpses and remains from a tomb, rewrapping and returning them to the original sepulcher. Dez (1956, p. 115) describes this practice for the Betsileo, and I was told that it happened, but never observed a case. A variant, which I did observe, consists of rewrapping within the tomb; a case is described below. The final meaning of *famadihana* for the Merina is transfer of a corpse from one old, established tomb to another. Bloch (1971, p. 146) reports that this ceremony is very rare, since it signals a change in social identification (burial group affiliation) of the corpse.[12]

Bloch reports that the (return) *famadihana* has become increasingly important in Merina society, probably in proportion to increasing emigration. Long distances between death site and tomb site and the Merina custom of a burial delay of no more than three days often necessitate temporary burial and eventual return *famadihana*. Although Betsileo also have a high emigration rate, colonists who settle permanently outside their own homeland build new tombs there rather than having their remains sent back home. (However, Betsileo who die while working, attending school, in military service, or temporarily absent for other reasons are returned home and buried in the family tomb.) Since the current importance of *famadihana* for Merina is based on retention of homeland ties in the face of emigration, the situation in the past was probably much more similar to contemporary Betsileo practices. When people actually lived in the communities where their tombs were located, they could be buried immediately, and no return *famadihana* was necessary. John Haile (1892, p. 407), a late-nineteenth-century observer of the Merina, called the practice an innovation less than a century old and still limited to Imerina. Reasons for the spread of rewrapping ceremonies to Betsileo country are considered below. But to summarize, for the Merina the primary meaning of *famadihana* is return *famadihana*, whereas for the Betsileo, the term applies principally to tomb inaugurals, a case of which I now analyze.

From Wednesday, July 26 through Friday, July 28, 1967 we[13] attended a *famadihana* near Little Ambalavao, a village in the canton of Mahazony. We had hoped to encounter a *famadihana* in one of the villages around Ivato, but none was held during our field stay, as there are fewer such ceremonies held in the agricultural east, a regional contrast previously mentioned. Our entry to this *famadihana* was provided by Cecille, a sixty-five-year-old woman who resided in Tanambao. The remains of her maternal grandmother, a member of the Maromaitso descent group, were to be transferred to a newly constructed tomb in a valley near the villages of Little Ambalavao and Maso. Samuel, a resident of Little Ambalavao, had organized the *famadihana*, involving the transfer of the bones of his grandfather and other deceased Maromaitso from two old tombs (donor tombs), the less ancient of which was located near the new tomb. The other, an ancient, traditional Betsileo structure, was located in the hills above the new site. The new tomb, whose construction had begun in 1960, was completed in 1966. Samuel, with the accord of the other local Maromaitso, decided to petition the canton chief to hold the transferal ceremony during the next ceremonial season, the winter of 1967.

Conflict between Maromaitso descent branches localized in Little Ambalavao and nearby Maso, both with ancestors involved in the transfer, was generated over the official center for the ceremony. Living participants are ritually greeted at a "green hut," a shack roofed with foliage by the organizers of the event. As the person who had petitioned the government for permission to hold the ceremony, Samuel wanted to construct the reception hut in his own village, Little Ambalavao. However, Lawrence, elder of Maso, argued that the hut should be constructed in the valley, not only nearer the new tomb, but also closer to one of the donor tombs, which Lawrence's grandfather and namesake had constructed. The remains of the earlier Lawrence and his descendants both in Little Ambalavao and Maso were to be transferred. Unable, even after consultation with fellow descent group members in the two villages, to reconcile their opinions, Samuel petitioned the canton chief to judge their claims. The administrator's decision was that there be two reception huts, one in Little Ambalavao hosted by Samuel and the other, near the tombs, built by the people of Maso, with Lawrence as host. Lawrence's hut, nearer the ceremonial center, was to prove more successful, slightly outdrawing Little Ambalavao in guests and their contributions.

Since we spent only three days among the Maromaitso of Little Ambalavao and Maso, it is difficult to evaluate the significance of the conflict. Although monetary receipts totalled only 18,000 francs ($72.00 U.S., 1967), this sum was equivalent to more than 1,000 kilograms of paddy, about half the average annual production of a hectare of rice land in Mahazony. Receipt of such a sum, when nonmonetary contributions are also considered, would enable a *famadihana* organizer to profit from, rather than merely recouping his personal investment in, the ceremonial. The prestige signalled by receiving and distributing gifts may have been an even more potent factor. At any rate, the tension was reduced, if not permanently dissipated, when Samuel, the younger of the two men, apologized to Lawrence, and offered him a steer, which Lawrence accepted, as atonement for his rivalry. The principle of age won out, as it usually does in Betsileo conflicts.

As the event got underway visitors made their presence and contributions known at one or both of the reception huts. Following Betsileo custom, young men were designated as official welcomers at each hut. Their job was to utter a ritual greeting to the guests who entered. In the welcoming speech, which we heard several times, the young man began by thanking (the Christian) God for the safe arrival of each party. He recalled to them the reason for constructing the new tomb, that the old tomb was too crowded. He told of the manner in which fifteen families (*fianakaviana*), representing descendants of ancestors in the tomb, had divided equally the cost, 135,000 CFA ($540.00 U.S., 1967), of the mason's fee and additional expenditures on cement and other building materials. He related that work on the tomb had begun in 1960 and had been completed in 1966. The young greeter also told the guests of the petition to the government and receipt of authorization for the *famadihana*.[14] He ended his speech by reiterating his welcome.

A representative of each guest party then responded to the greeting, thanking God and the ancestors for successful completion of the tomb and authorization for the *famadihana*. Following a practice witnessed at all major Betsileo and Merina (Bloch 1971, p. 154) ceremonies, the guest then enumerated the gifts his party had brought, stating the number of baskets of white or cooked rice; pots and pans; shrouds for the dead, either Betsileo-manufactured traditional silk shrouds or factory-made textiles. The guest's speech was followed by a ritual acceptance speech delivered by the host. The offerings were carefully recorded in a notebook by members of the greeting party. They would eventually be reciprocated.

Some of the parties (representing forty-one villages) visited only one reception hut, while others (thirty-seven villages) divided their contributions between the two. The average village party consisted of about seventeen people. In all, representatives of at least seventy-eight villages—about 1,300 people—attended.[15] In the main they came from Mahazony and adjacent cantons. However, people who had ancestors in the tombs came from as far as 115 kilometers away.

The ceremony culminated on Friday, with the opening of the two old tombs and the transfer of their remains to the new sepulcher.[16] Remains were first gathered from the older tomb, located in the hills about a kilometer away. Before a *famadihana* may be held, a diviner[17] must determine a propitious day for the transferal to take place. For this *famadihana*, Friday had been selected. At a specific hour, determined by the same diviner, young adult men, "strong men," journeyed to the tomb, carrying spades and accompanied by musicians and a group of elders. Arriving at the tomb, the oldest elder approached the tomb's entrance and ritually addressed the ancestors as follows: "Oh! Yesterday we came to advise you that you would be changing

homes. We now ask your permission to open your door." The speaker
was reportedly calling the souls (*ambiroa*) of the dead home from their
wanderings.

The elders then spilled a bit of rum over the tomb before ordering the
young men to start digging. The musicians, hired as well as local, played
drums, flutes, trumpets, rattles, and accordians as the young men got to
work. In a half hour they uncovered the entrance and dislodged the outer
slab. A second slab, inside the tomb, was easier to open. The assembly then
waited a few minutes for the tomb's air to clear. To light the interior of the
tomb, a traditional Betsileo candle, a cloth wick floating in beef fat in an iron
receptacle, was, as demanded by custom, used, rather than a factory-pro-
duced kerosene lantern or candle. After the air had cleared, one of the young
men entered the tomb and a few minutes later announced his discovery of a
mound representing the mortal remains, reduced to dust by more than a century in the tomb. Contemporary local Maromaitso do not even attempt to
trace actual genealogical descent from these fragments.

Next, two women carried a straw mat and a white "calico" cloth into the
tomb, where they joined with the men in collecting the remains. More intact
remains are simply wrapped in a straw mat, and the decaying shrouds already
around them are not removed. Here the addition of the calico cloth was necessary to keep the ancestors' dust from spilling. They spread the calico over
the mat and placed the ancestral dust on it. The remains were then rolled up
in these coverings and the bundle fastened with straps. As they emerged from
the tomb, the musicians began playing a series of lively tunes and several
people quickly surrounded the bundle. Amid shouting and dancing, women
argued about who was to receive the straps, which are believed to convey
good fortune and fertility; they were especially sought after by childless
women. Still at the ancient tomb site, the bundle was untied and laid down;
the calico bundle was removed from the mat and wrapped in an additional
layer of calico cloth. Women, again to promote fertility, took pieces of the
mat, to be placed in their beds or under their mattresses (cf. Dez 1956, p.
119). Amid music and shouting the ancestral bundle was then carried around
the ancient tomb. The ancestors having been allowed to say good-bye to their
old home, their bearers suddenly rushed away, running, followed by the others who attended the exhumation, down the slope leading to the new tomb.

Reaching the valley, the ancestral bundle was laid down in front of the
entrance to the new tomb, where it was wrapped with more expensive raw
silk shrouds donated by guests. As it was being wrapped, ten people, eight
women and two men, danced around. On the dancers' heads were furnishings
for the new domicile: pottery, wooden soup ladles, spoons, small baskets to
place dishes in, and straw mats. The dancers included several young couples
who sought ancestral blessing of their union and numerous progeny.

Next, the remains of the people who had been buried in the old tomb in the valley, only a few meters distant from the new structure and located under the same rocky overhang, were exhumed. Most of them still recognizable, they were divided into three bundles, men, women, and children respectively and, after having been wrapped in shrouds, were interred in the new tomb. Older people accompanied the bundles into the tomb, where others were already actively preparing the new household, placing pots and other cooking and eating utensils, tobacco, and rum in the back room of the tomb.

On the tomb's roof, exemplifying a widespread Malagasy practice, were displayed the heads of the nine steers that had been slaughtered and consumed. Once all ancestral remains had been placed in the tomb, it was closed, and Lawrence began the closing oration, thanking people present and absent for all they had done to make the ceremony a success. He also thanked the administration and local authorities for having "facilitated" the efforts made by the elders in preparation for the ceremony. Once his speech was concluded, the *famadihana* officially ended; the assembly began to disperse at about 4:00 P.M.

Affect Toward the Dead

There appear to be differences in affect of living to dead and in the emotional reactions of participants between the Merina rewrapping ceremonies described by Bloch (1971, p. 153–55) and those I observed among the Betsileo. These differences reflect the contrast in the primary meaning of the *famadihana* for Merina and Betsileo. For the Betsileo the ceremony inaugurates a new tomb, rewraps and transfers several corpses. For the Merina, on the other hand, the ceremony is most commonly for a recently dead relative who is being transferred from temporary burial to the ancestral tomb. The attitude of the participants in the Betsileo *famadihana* just described was generally jubilant and happy. There was some trepidation when the older of the two donor tombs was opened (for the first time in many years), since people were unsure about what they would find in it. But soon thereafter the mood became as joyous as that described for the Betsileo *famadihana* studied by Dez (1956).

Although Merina take advantage of any *famadihana* to tidy up (rewrap) all the remains in the ancestral tomb, the focal individual is a recent corpse who is being rewrapped for the first time. Bloch (1971, pp. 155, 153) describes the corpse's close relatives, who are seeing and touching it for the first time, as initially "frightened" and "profoundly moved." He reports that a general anxiety—which I did *not* note among the Betsileo—prevails on such occasions, reflecting a feeling that death might be catching. By the end of the Merina ceremony, however, fear yields to "joyous excitement" and "Bacchanalian high spirits" (Bloch, 1971, p. 154) as close relatives of the dead, rewrapping complete, finally accept the loss of their loved one. As they dance with the corpse, toss it in the air, and hear its bones crack from the rough treatment, they finally accept, psychologically, that a former loved one is now a corpse, and living participants define their common social identity by commiting sacrilege together (Bloch 1971, pp. 167–68).

My best opportunity to observe Betsileo affect in similar circumstances—first rewrapping of a recently dead corpse—came in an Ivatan ceremonial. The ceremony was held by our sponsor, to rewrap his dead wife and ancestors, on the occasion of his receipt of a cabinet post in the Malagasy government. From his (and his eldest daughter's) point of view, his wife was the focus of the ceremony. For villagers, however, the tomb-opening meant a chance to present important ancestors like Goodmaker and Karl Fridays-father with new shrouds. Like close Merina kin described by Bloch, the sponsor's daughter, who had the job of rewrapping her mother, was clearly uneasy about seeing and touching the corpse for the first time. However, her spirits lightened noticeably once she entered the tomb; she commented on the good state of preservation of her mother's body. However, she did seem relieved when the rewrapping was complete.

Rewrappers of older corpses seemed not to be bothered in the least. The men who rewrapped Goodmaker's remains were almost gleeful in pointing out to me some areas of still intact skin. Outside the tomb and throughout the festivities, villagers who were less directly involved in the in-tomb proceedings were as joyful and exhuberant as participants in the Mahazony tomb inaugural just described, or as any group of party-goers.

The Common Descent Group

As noted in chapter 6, certain Betsileo social groups exist only in a ceremonial context. We may recognize, for example, major participants in a tomb-centered ceremonial as members of the same common descent group, consisting of descendants of a given ancestor (or group of related ancestors interred together), be the ancestor male or female, the descendants male or female, or the genealogical links connecting them male or female. As noted in chapter 6, the common descent group differs from the smaller, localized descent branch, which is more patrilineal and which includes descendants who actually make their living off the ancestral estate. By bringing all descendants together, tomb-centered ceremonials remind people who cultivate the ancestral estate of the residual rights of the others. By contributing to the high cost of constructing a new tomb, and by participating in the organization of the ceremonial, common descent group members reinforce their potential rights in the ancestral estate. Alliances based on past marriages between descent groups of different villages are also recalled and may be reinforced through common ceremonial participation.

Like any Betsileo *famadihana*, the Mahazony tomb inaugural described above was a regional affair. Major contributions were offered by people from several different villages who claimed to be members of the Maromaitso descent group. In many cases when I asked about descent group affiliation, people told me that, although members of different descent groups in the villages where they resided, they were attending the ceremonial as Maromaitso. Other large offerings were made by affinals of the hosts. Nine steers and cash contributions totaling at least 18,000 CFA ($72.00 U.S., 1967), were received in the two reception huts. A total of thirty-six shrouds were presented, including twelve traditional silk Malagasy textiles and twenty-four factory-made wrappings. About 350 baskets of white rice were presented. Six of the steers came from affinals,[18] the other three from people who had ancestors in the tombs. A gift's value depended on closeness of genealogical or affinal connection.

Certainly the 135,000 francs expended on the construction of the new tomb were not recouped from the 18,000 francs that the two hosts received as contributions. However, the personal financial burden of the *famadihana* does not appear to have been onerous for either of the two organizers, since the rice brought by village parties was sufficient to feed the guests, and the cash contributions were more than sufficient to provide rum. The mason's fee was equivalent to about $550 U.S., and the contribution of each of the fifteen "families" who equally divided the cost of the tomb (over several years) was the equivalent of the selling price of about 600 kilograms of paddy, representing about half the average annual production of the average rice field in this area. In addition to the mason's fee, each family was expected to purchase four or five bags of cement, increasing the contribution considerably. Including the cost of cement, each family expended the equivalent of about $50 U.S. dollars for the tomb. The cash value of the tomb was certainly greater than that of any house in either Little Ambalavao or Maso, and further expenses were incurred in contributions to the two reception huts.

Although their contributions gave members of all fifteen families the right to be buried in the new tomb, certainly not all expected to activate this right. In accordance with the policy, described in chapter 6, of maximizing rights to different ancestral local descent group estates and burial rights in different ancestral tombs, a Betsileo may contribute to the cost of several new tombs throughout his or her lifetime. These burdens can be onerous, and can lead to debt, as shown below.[19]

Other Reburials

The case just discussed was a major *famadihana*, which, of Betsileo ceremonials, attracts most people. Though they are regional affairs, *famadihana* are among the most infrequent ceremonials in the Ivato region, although much more common in Mahazony. They are everywhere confined to the winter ceremonial season, clustering in August and September, just prior to transplanting in Mahazony. Individuals from Ambalabe and Tanambao attended seven *famadihana* in 1967. In contrast, only one resident of Ivato attended a *famadihana* that year.

I did observe another type of secondary funerary ceremonial in Ivato in October, 1967, soon after our sponsor had been elevated to an important post in the government of then President Tsiranana. Spurred on by his eldest daughter, he sponsored a rewrapping ceremony in which the tomb of the eastern village, where his patrilineal ancestors and his wife, among others, are buried, was opened and the bodies inside wrapped in new shrouds. A ceremonial demonstrating his new status and attracting people from Ivato's satellite villages in the same rice plain, it was still a smaller-scale event than a *famadihana*. While guests were entertained in Ivatan homes, only one steer was slaughtered.

On Friday, October 6, preparatory to the opening of the tomb the following morning, a ritual session including an address and offering to the ancestors took place in the house built by Goodmaker, constructor of the tomb and our sponsor's grandfather. The offering was made, as tradition demands, in the northeastern corner of the second floor of the imposing wattle and daub house that is now inhabited by Goodmaker's youngest grandson. Glasses of Malagasy rum were placed on shelves of a cupboard.[20] As is traditional, the highest was offered to Andriananahary. Below it was a glass for the ancestors of the eastern village, the real focus of the ritual. A glass for Ivato's former slaves was placed on a stool much closer to the ground.

Village spokesman Rakoto began his address to the ancestors by excusing himself for speaking, since, he said, he was not the seniormost member of his generation, but pointing out that he, rather than one of the older men in attendance, had been designated spokesman of the village by Goodmaker. Rakoto told the ancestors that the purpose of his speech and of the offering was to inform them that the tomb was to be opened the following day, not to inter someone, but to cover their bodies with new cloth. When a tomb is to be opened for any reason other than burial, it is necessary to let the ancestors know in advance through this kind of session.

The ancestors addressed by name (figure 6) were the forefathers of eastern Ivato, including Vernon (father of Tuesdaysfather and our sponsor), Vernon's brother Joseph (Rakoto's father), Goodmaker (father of Joseph and Vernon), Karl Fridaysfather (father of the last), Marie-Claire (Karl's daughter by a secondary union and mother of Etienne, an old man in attendance), Norasmother (Goodmaker's sister), Peter (father of Karl Fridaysfather) and Hundredmaster (apical ancestor of the eastern village). Subsequently, two other tomb residents, Karl's two brothers, Blacksfather and Alan, were addressed

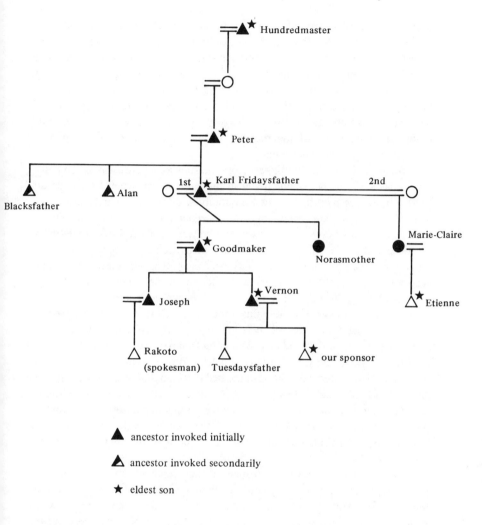

Fig. 6 Ancestors Addressed at Ivatan Rewrapping Ceremony, October, 1967

in the names of their descendants in Ivato, who were present. A contingent of descendants of Goodmaker's most intimate friend, representing senior commoners from a nearby village, several of whose women have married men from Ivato, also attended the session.

Rakoto asked that the ancestors also bless the Roman Catholic mass to be held in association with the tomb ceremonial the following day, and in this context he mentioned again the name of Karl Fridaysfather, who introduced

Catholicism to Ivato around the turn of the century. The prayer finished, those present drank the sacrificial rum, as a substitute for the beef that this ritual would consecrate in a more traditional session. Since no slave descendant attended, the rum that had been offered to Ivato's former slaves was given to Tuesdaysfather's twenty-five-year-old grandson, the youngest participant. Someone explained to me that the young man was viewed as a type of slave because of his generation and age. Most people left the session around midnight, although some of the men stayed and drank more rum, and many villagers did not sleep that night.

A sacrificial steer, the biggest from the sponsor's herd, was killed before 5:00 A.M. and was being butchered in the cattle corral when I arose around 5:30. The young men had opened the tomb by 8:00 A.M., when most people arrived at the tomb site. Rewrappings proceeded throughout the morning.

Distinctions between the sexes and between core and marginal Ivatans are observed in the placement of bodies in the tomb. Its nine beds are arranged in three tiers of three masonry beds each. The separation of beds and sections in the tomb of eastern Ivato reiterates several social distinctions of life. Generally, the beds observe sex differences; four are reserved for females, four for males. One remains unoccupied. Only Karl Fridaysfather, as patriarch of the tomb, lies in the same bed as his wife, its matriarch, and some of their male descendants. The core Tranovondro of eastern Ivato and principal wives occupy the ritually superior northern wall of beds, with the wives and female agnates placed in the bed between that of Goodmaker above and that of Karl which is lowermost.[21] A separate bed is reserved for childless women—adopters and agnates—who have provided inheritances for contemporary Ivatans. Of the additional beds reserved for males one houses the remains of distant relatives of members of the patriline, while the other is used for Karl's brothers.

When I asked them why so many distant relatives (more than a dozen people representing neither agnates nor their spouses) had been placed in the tomb, Tuesdaysfather and Rakoto pointed out that the tomb is not crowded, which is true, since only eight of the beds are occupied by the forty-one corpses. Karl and Goodmaker, I was told, collected around them many impoverished and unhappy people. The large number of beds and bodies in this relatively recently built tomb reflect the regional importance of these men and their descendants and the refuge they provided to their childless, husbandless, and parentless kin (as well as to their more fortunate adoptive parents). Junior commoners, like the Maromaitso of Mahazony whose *famadihana* has been described, have no need for a tomb with nine beds, and so suffice with six.

Note, too, in the tomb, that a kind of alternating generation affective relationship is expressed. Goodmaker is buried with his grandchildren and with his youngest son, who, Betsileo say, is like a grandson, just as an oldest son is similar to and replaces the father. With Karl are his two grandsons, Vernon and Joseph, who, like their grandfather, served as leaders of the eastern village. Betsileo view a man's relationships with his youngest son and his grandsons as particularly warm, and they express this in tomb placement.

As the rewrapping ceremonial proceeded some corpses, particularly Goodmaker and our sponsor's wife, received more careful attention than others. The visiting senior commoner elder covered the corpse of Goodmaker, his ancestor's intimate friend. Men rewrapped male remains, while women shrouded deceased females. As they worked, all drank liberally of local rum. Inside the tomb the rewrappers used wine, rather than the traditional rum, to wash their hands. Emerging from the tomb, they washed their hands again, using water but no soap. Once all the corpses had been wrapped, the tomb was closed. The doors are supported by stone hinges. The spaces around the outer door were filled with rocks, pebbles, and mud. Rum and bits of tobacco were left in the tomb for the ancestors to enjoy.

Although this was the only such rewrapping ceremony I attended or heard about that year apparently it is customary among the Betsileo (see Dez 1956). The rewrapping ceremony, however, appears to be held only when the organizer or organizing party can afford to slaughter a steer and entertain large numbers of guests. Like certain other Betsileo ceremonials, particularly the name-changing ceremony described above, the rewrapping is among other things a desirable but nonobligatory statement of an important change in status, in this case, a national political appointment. The small ceremony that we attended in Ivato conveyed information to our sponsor's peasant kin and neighbors about his new position in the national hierarchy. To his colleagues in government and regional and national politics who attended, it conveyed information about the strength of his rural base.[22]

Funerals

In contrast to *famadihana*, which are limited to the months of June through October, and in contrast to other secondary funerary ceremonials, which also cluster in these months, are funerals, which can take place at any time of year. Note, however, that so great was the role that seasonality played in the Betsileo past in determining when ceremonies would be held that when kings, princes, chiefs, and even senior commoner governors died, their bodies were often preserved as long as eight months for interment in the winter, after the harvest. Traditionally, a special corps of funerary attendants treated bodies of dead kings in the following manner. The corpse was suspended from a rafter in the wooden palace and squeezed dry by plank-wielding attendants, its humors draining into a pot through holes cut in the feet. The pot was placed in a lake for several days, then removed. Betsileo told me that should a snake or large worm emerge from the pot it was offered cooked rice. Should it accept and eat the rice, it was taken to be the reincarnation of the deceased king (see also Richardson 1875, pp. 73–74; Shaw 1878, p. 6; Moss 1900, p. 476).

Bloch (1971, pp. 138–40) reports that Merina funerals, which, as noted previously, are more often temporary burials than those of the Betsileo, take place between one and three days (today's Betsileo maximum) after death. A more lavish ceremony than the funeral—the return *famadihana* (cf. p. 228)— will be necessary when the corpse is eventually taken back to the land of the ancestors to be buried in the ancestral tomb. Since most Betsileo still reside in their ancestral homeland or, as emigrants, have constructed new tombs in the area of colonization, there is usually no need for the Merina pattern of temporary burial and eventual *famadihana*. The funeral itself can be a full-fledged ceremony, and the meaning of *famadihana* can contract to designate mainly the ceremony that inaugurates a new tomb. With immediate burial in the ancestral tomb, Betsileo rewrapping ceremonies also become nonobligatory statements of status changes rather than necessary rituals incorporating dispersed descendants into the tomb of the ancestors and the society of the past.

But there is another difference involving burial practices between contemporary Betsileo and Merina. Even for those Merina who die in the land of the ancestors, interment in the ancestral tomb may have to be postponed, since Merina prohibit tombs from being opened more than twice a year. Furthermore, Merina children who die must await an adult's death to accompany them into the ancestral tomb. These customs permit Merina to hold more elaborate tributes to the dead in the postharvest period of greater wealth. Bara similarly may save up for an elaborate regional ceremony called a *havoria* in the postharvest season following someone's death (Huntington 1974, pp. 107–12). Context and effects of these different ways of celebrating death are examined below.

In regional scale, the Betsileo funeral immediately follows the *famadihana*. The number of participants at a funeral and the geographical range of their villages vary with age, socioeconomic and ritual status, and other attributes of the deceased and his or her close kin. This can be illustrated by a series of contrasting cases.

The Funeral of a Senior Commoner

In mid-August, 1967, while living in Ivato, we received news of the death of a prominent native Ivatan, Goodmaker's sole surviving child, Therese. A woman in her nineties and the aunt of our sponsor, his brother Tuesdays-father, and village spokesman Rakoto, Therese was the last surviving member of their fathers' sibling group of five. On Wednesday, August 16 we arrived in the hamlet where the funeral would take place. Therese's body had been placed in the ancestral corner. The hamlet's name, "there at the palace," recalls that it once belonged to Betsileo nobles. Therese and her husband acquired the hamlet and its estate by purchase between 1900 and 1910. Three houses are located in the hamlet proper. One was the domicile of Therese, her husband, and their eldest son—like his retired father, a schoolteacher— and the son's wife. The second house, the hamlet's most opulent, is inhabited by the younger of Therese's two resident sons and his wife; they are peasants. Therese's daughter and her husband live in the third.

Informants had varying opinions about the descent group affiliation of Therese's hamlet, some considering it a Taray hamlet, representing her widower's descent group, others calling it a Tranovondro village, because Goodmaker, Therese's father, had acquired title to it. Because Alfred, Therese's husband, was poor, Goodmaker bought them their estate, considering him a good match for his daughter. Not only did he belong to the prestigious Taray descent group, albeit one of its poorer branches, he was one of the first peasants in the area to be trained as a schoolteacher, in Fianarantsoa, before the French conquered Madagascar.

Always an independent person, Therese originally opposed the match her father and Alfred's elders had arranged. Her objection to marrying a man who lacked rice fields was met when her father bought them the estate. Ivatans say that Goodmaker was sure that schoolteachers would prosper from French administration of Madagascar, a relatively accurate judgement. Therese took time to settle down with her husband. She once bragged to her niece that, soon after their marriage, she had run away to Tulear on the southwest coast, whence her father had forceably brought her back; her husband received her because of his dependence on her inheritance. Her wild rice plants sown, Therese settled down, raised several children with the assistance of slave descendants and her husband, and turned to the female sphere of political activity among the Betsileo—arranging strategic marriages for her children, nieces, nephews, and grandchildren.

Attendance at Therese's funeral thus reflects several attributes of the deceased and her family. Her funeral was a tribute to an independent and active person, and the oldest surviving member of her sibling group. Her husband had been a well-known local schoolteacher; her oldest son taught primary school in their canton seat; one of her grandsons was a bureaucrat in Tananarive and another, an instructor at the Catholic secondary school in Fianarantsoa, had earned a university degree. Furthermore, the deceased was the child of Goodmaker, in his time one of the region's most illustrious figures; sibling of Vernon, another notable in regional politics; and aunt of our sponsor, a current national political figure. Moreover, along with her spouse's descent group, her own was one of the major senior commoner descent groups in northern Vohibato.

For these reasons, among the several hundred people who came to her funeral were a number of government employees and elected officials. The guests were received in sixteen houses in her own and nearby settlements, including that of the mayor of her canton seat, also a national assemblyman. The funeral also reflected the strong ties of Therese's family to Catholicism. When we arrived, Therese's attendants were singing Christian chants, rather than traditional Malagasy funeral songs, and the interment took place on Thursday, before dusk, both taboo for burials according to Betsileo cultural dicta.

The sixteen households that had agreed to act as hosts supplied the rice, and five cattle were killed. Beef from some of the slaughtered steers was cooked and consumed at the ceremonial; in this case, it was sent for cooking to each of the sixteen host households. As a funeral terminates, raw beef of at least one steer is given to village representatives, to be taken home and redistributed. Condolences and contributions, generally monetary, were presented to at least three different reception groups, and notebooks listing gifts were kept by all three. One notebook was maintained at the house of Alfred, the widower. Another, listing offerings of seventy-one villages, was maintained by members of Therese's younger son's household. A third notebook was kept in Ivato, listing the contributions of its satellites and other neighboring villages, some of which, rather than attending the funeral, had simply presented their contributions and condolences to Therese's nephews in Ivato on hearing of her death.

I consulted two of the three notebooks listing contributions, that compiled in Ivato and that kept by Therese's younger son. He listed representatives of 71 villages; 16 others had offered condolences and contributions in Ivato. Probably well over 100 villages paid their respects to Therese and her kin. Her younger son and his wife seemed proud to proclaim to me that they had received a total of 25,000 francs (about $100 U.S.) in cash contributions. This allowed them, they said, to recoup their expenditure on the one sacrificial steer they had contributed; they even made a profit. One of the five slaughtered steers came from the herd of Therese and her husband. Her two sons gave one each, and her siblings' children in Ivato paid 10,000 francs ($40.00 U.S., 1967) for the steer they slaughtered, purchased in a village near Ivato. Its cost was divided into four equal shares, representing the children of her three brothers and one sister. A fifth steer was given by her closest relatives from her mother's village of origin.

Steers were offered by others, generally affinals, but were declined on the grounds that there was sufficient meat already. Money, generally 6,000 francs ($24.00 U.S., 1967), was accepted instead. The parents-in-law of one of Therese's sons were obliged to pay substantially more—10,000 francs— for the following reasons. Therese's son, who resides in Tulear on the south-west coast, rarely visits Therese's hamlet, preferring to stay with his wife's parents when he visits his homeland. Resenting this neglect, his brothers and father haughtily declined the offer of a steer by their co-parents-in-law, who were told "since your son-in-law never visits us and thus has never brought us a steer, we would be unable to reciprocate by offering you a steer should there be a death in your family." We were told that the co-parents-in-law were distraught, pleading that their steer be accepted. They were allowed to pay more instead. Therese's oldest son told me that the sum they agreed on was not calculated on the basis of the wealth of the affinals, but was a symbol of atonement for their social distance from his family.

Governing contributions to Betsileo funerals is what Elman Service (1966) and Marshall Sahlins (1968) have called the principle of balanced reciprocity, the expectation that what is given, closely calculated, eventually will be received in kind. The exchange between the people of Therese's hamlet and their socially distant affinals illustrates this principle, as did Ivatans when they told me that Therese's family had sacrificed a steer when her brother Joseph, Rakoto's father, had died in Ivato. Many of the villages in Ivato's rice plain gave, even though they were not Tranovondro or Taray and in some cases were slave descendants, as they know that Therese's family in Ivato can be depended on to reciprocate their condolences and to offer equivalent gifts in the future.

As at a *famadihana*, the value of a contribution reflects closeness of genealogical and affinal ties, as well as geographical proximity where neigh-borliness is the only social tie. Other settlements in the valley shared more in the cost of Therese's funeral, not only by lodging guests, but also in their larger monetary contributions, than more distant villages.[23] Most villages attending the funeral gave the customary 50 francs, whereas more closely related village representatives gave much more. The fact that notebooks listing village, name of representative, and amount of contribution are scrupulously kept at all Betsileo ceremonials betokens close calculation of social debts and obligation.

The Funeral of a Junior Commoner

Expectably, the scale of a junior commoner's funeral is smaller. My assistant, Joseph Rabe, was a participant-observer at the funeral of Joesfather, a seventy-five-year-old man who was regarded as the head of the Maromaitso descent branch localized in the village of Tanambao and its hamlet Amboangy, where Joesfather lived and died. The funeral began the morning of Saturday, August 12, 1967 and ended with his interment on Monday, August 14, at dusk, as Betsileo tradition prescribes. Joesfather had been a semi-invalid for some twenty-five years, following a fall, and suffering from acute asthma. When it became obvious on Friday that his physical condition was deteriorating dramatically, his relatives in Amboangy summoned other kin. Soon after his death, the men bathed, dressed, and placed his corpse in a traditional straw mat coffin. The customary alcove of the deceased was prepared in the northeastern section of the house, the ancestral corner, and Joesfather's coffin was placed therein. Young men carried news of his death to relatives in different villages and to the administrative authorities in the canton seat.

In Amboangy and Tanambao, Joesfather's relatives prepared to receive their guests. The reception, following tradition, took place in a separate room, called the "males' hut," of his home, where condolences and offerings were officially presented and received.[24] The reception committee included the deceased's six closest local male relatives. With a Maromaitso mother born in Tanambao, my field assistant was among them. The committee was obliged to remain in the reception room from Saturday until Monday. Betsileo term these men "judges," because they decide whether steers offered for slaughter at the funeral will be received. The decision to accept or reject is made according to the individual case, but generally it is refused if made by a fairly distant relative of the deceased or if the familial or pecuniary situation of the would-be donor is known to be precarious. Offers by close relatives of the deceased, or of his wife, according to Rabe, were more often accepted. Furthermore, if the donor insists with sufficient fervor, the judges may ignore other considerations and accept the gift.

Beginning on Saturday, arriving day and night, the guests paraded through the reception hut to present their (highly ritualized) condolences and offerings in the name of their families (*fianakaviana*), their local descent groups and villages (*fokonolona*), and individually. This scene came to an end only a few hours before the corpse was borne to the tomb, a kilometer away. Ten houses in Tanambao and four in Amboangy lodged and fed the guests; household heads received a share of the beef each time a steer was killed, but from their own granaries supplied cooked rice for the guests. Like Therese, Joesfather was a Christian, a Protestant rather than a Roman Catholic. Although to a lesser extent than Therese's, Joesfather's funeral bore witness to the sincerity of his conversion. Protestant and Catholic chants were sung around the deceased's alcove, and, in contrast to the *famadihana* and to Betsileo custom, no hired musicians attended and no musical instruments were played.

The young men left Monday morning to dig out the entrance to the tomb, and around 2:00 P.M., after the midday meal, Joesfather's corpse was removed from his house, carried around it a few times as farewell, and borne, in an hour's time, to the tomb. On arrival around 3:00 P.M. the corpse was placed on top of the tomb to await the funerary orations and chanting until the sun had set. Protestants stood on one side and Catholics on the other; small groups who did not wish to be associated with either were scattered about. A few meters away from the assembly stood a steer, which would be slaughtered at the close of the funeral, its raw meat distributed to the guests, in the customary way, by village rather than by individual. A pastor from Mahazony spoke for the Protestants and Joseph Rabe for the Catholics. The tomb was opened at six, and at six-thirty, when it was fully dark, the corpse was taken into the tomb, which was almost immediately closed. The guests began to disperse as the funeral ended around 7:00 P.M.

The funeral of this man, oldest male member and head of the junior commoner branch of the Maromaitso localized in Tanambao and Amboangy illustrates, though I cannot be certain it typifies, funerals of men of similar age, status, and affiliation in the canton of Mahazony. The organization of the funeral and reception of the guests devolved on Joesfather's cousins, in the absence of siblings and sons. Joesfather's only son had predeceased him by several years.

As a member of the reception committee, Rabe had access to the notebook that listed the villages attending and the amounts of their contributions. Apparently not all of the parties from the seventy-nine villages attending (fifty-two of the villages were in Mahazony, though five other cantons were included) presented offerings, since a total of only forty-nine contributions—representing just twenty-seven villages—were recorded. Contributions included money and shrouds (two of Betsileo silk, fifteen factory-made coverings). Fourteen steers were offered, of which seven were accepted and seven declined. The would-be donors then gave money instead. Their average gift was only about 1,700 francs ($6.80 U.S., 1967), considerably less than the 6,000 francs accepted in lieu of a steer at Therese's funeral. Once again, the value of the gift reflected closeness of genealogical or affinal connection. However, fictive kinship (the *fatidra* relationship), which in chapter 6 was cited as being more important in Mahazony than in Ivato and more significant for junior than for senior commoners in general, was also a basis for a few valuable gifts of shrouds or cash. Cash—about 100 francs each—was offered by seventeen elders representing ten neighboring villages, who stated their relationship to the deceased as one of *firaisana*, neighborhood. As noted, seven steers, given by contributors from six villages, were killed. One of them came from the herd of the deceased. Three were provided by close kin (cousins and nephews) representing other local descent groups: his mother's native village, and two villages where his sisters had married. The remaining three were given by affinals: his wife's father, daughter's husband, and a representative of his stepfather's village. Significant lessons from this case, when compared with the senior commoner's funeral, include its smaller scale, the role of the "judges" in accepting or rejecting offers of cattle, and the larger number of cattle actually slaughtered. These contrasts are discussed below in the analysis of variation in the functioning of Betsileo ceremonials in different socioeconomic and demographic contexts.

DETERMINANTS OF CEREMONIAL ATTENDANCE

Although all Betsileo take some part in ceremonial life, in the same region and even in the same village some people regularly attend more ceremonials than others, and some of this variation reflects sex, age, and social and economic status. In about a year, one Ivatan, Rakoto, a fifty-five-year-old man, went to 15 ceremonies, whereas one female Ivatan said that she had attended only 2. The most significant distinction determining ceremonial participation appears to be sex. Ivatan men annually attended between 3 and 15 ceremonials, women between 2 and 7. Men went to ceremonials about twice as often as women, a mean of 9.4 compared to 4.4.[25]

There is also a statistical association between wealth and ceremonial attendance. The eight Ivatan men who attended ten or more ceremonials had an average rice holding of 1.6 hectares, producing an average of 3.4 metric tons of paddy per year. The ten men who attended nine or fewer ceremonies had an average holding of only .9 hectare, producing an average of only 2.1 metric tons annually. Those men who gather the largest annual harvests[26] tend to participate in more ceremonials than less fortunate peasants. Generally they are older men, who are expected to maintain regional political ties. Because of their wealth and age, they also can afford to leave home more often; they have dependents and/or hired hands to take care of village work.

There is, however, a curvilinear relationship between age and ceremonial attendance. Among those who attended ceremonials most frequently are young, unmarried males, generally excluded from my sample, who use these occasions to meet and woo young females. On the other hand, older, wealthier men, as figures of regional significance, are invariably asked to represent Ivato at ceremonials in its neighborhood and region. Depending on their health and energy, and their evaluation of the prestige of the ceremonial sponsor or deceased and of the importance of maintaining ties between Ivato and the ceremonial site, senior Ivatans may choose either to attend themselves or to designate a younger man as representative. Through their own or their representatives' participation, senior Ivatans preserve regional social and political alliances. Thus, for different reasons elders and young men attend ceremonials more frequently than other Betsileo.

The Ivatan who attended the largest number of ceremonials was Rakoto, who went to fifteen. Rakoto is fifty-five years old and still energetic enough to walk long distances to a variety of regional events. On the other hand,

Pierre, the twenty-eight-year-old village chief, who ranked sixteenth on a list of twenty-five Ivatans according to annual rice production, but who ranked second in ceremonial attendance (fourteen), seemed to avail himself of virtually every opportunity to attend ceremonials, whether as a designate of an elder or because of some distant kinship or affinal connection. For Pierre, ceremonials offered recreational, economic, nutritive, and sexual benefits. Especially during the lean season, from December through February, before the harvest, Pierre was a veritable funeral hopper. At ceremonials he consumed nutritious meals of rice and beef, made sexual liaisons, and obtained raw meat to bring back to his wife and young children. Any younger, poorer Betsileo can, if he wishes, use the ceremonial system to gain access to these benefits.

BETSILEO CEREMONIALS: FUNCTION AND CONTEXT

The rest of this chapter indicates why it would be foolhardy to attempt to explain Betsileo ceremonials with reference to a single function or effect that they accomplish. The functions and effects of Betsileo ceremonial are numerous. Ceremonials help distribute food; they link local groups into regional systems; they provide opportunities to establish and reinforce alliances based on marriage; they give concrete form to common descent groups; and, at different times and places, they reduce, maintain, or increase differential access to strategic resources. Most significantly, the implications of Betsileo ceremonial life have varied historically and still vary from region to region and in the context of socioeconomic stratification.

Regional Distribution and Adaptation

In addition to their manifest purposes—to bury the dead, transfer bones, fulfill kinship obligations, and honor the ancestors—Betsileo ceremonials are also feasts; cooked rice, meat, and rum are always available.[27] Frequent attendance at ceremonials by poorer Betsileo permits them to conserve the rice in their own granaries and to avoid spending cash that might otherwise go to (generally Merina) butchers in local markets. However, most Betsileo attend not because they are hungry but to honor the dead, the ancestors, and living sponsors, and simply to enjoy themselves. Many people did, nevertheless, recognize the nutritional benefits of ceremonials. One informant told me that although the government officially discouraged ceremonial slaughter of cattle, it did not push the matter, since it recognized an important source of nutrition for peasants.

It is intriguing to note that one of the periods that Betsileo assert to be a common time of death—the December-February rainy season—coincides with the lean period just prior to harvest, when granary supplies are lowest.[28]

I lack sufficient data to test the possibility of an actual rainy season clustering of deaths. However, such a clustering—should future data confirm it—would ensure that the funerary distribution of rice, meat, and rum would automatically and homeostatically increase at precisely that time of year when Betsileo nutrition is poorest, when rice supplies, especially of poorer households, have been exhausted. It is between December and February that poorer Betsileo normally contract debts, borrowing paddy that they must repay twofold at harvest. It is also during these months that poorer Betsileo reluctantly turn from the rice they prefer to the protein-poor manioc that they tolerate as their daily staple.

Oral traditions discussed in chapter 3 suggest that funerary slaughter of cattle was customary in the southern highlands, as is generally true throughout Madagascar, prior to Merina conquest.[29] Ceremonial slaughter continued among an increasingly agricultural, decreasingly pastoral Betsileo population, whose settlement pattern emphasized small, dispersed hamlets located near rice fields. In the absence of markets, and given such a settlement pattern, ceremonial slaughter necessitated regional distribution, since beef could be neither consumed nor stored in a single hamlet. Hamlets were linked by ties of common descent, membership in the same named descent group, affinal ties, fictive kinship, and other bases of association, so that representatives of several hamlets could be expected to attend any ceremonial.

Ceremonials still provide dramatic expression of social integration on a regional scale, while simultaneously distributing beef over wide areas, although over time, with denser population and agglomeration into villages, the geographic range of ceremonials has contracted. However, the possibility of activating multiple affiliative links remains. The point here is not so much what motivates individual Betsileo to attend ceremonials but the fact that so many ways of gaining access to ceremonials exist. These potential linkups may be activated or not depending on the individual circumstances. Thus, ceremonial attendance may be seen not just as a mechanism of regional sociopolitical integration but also as part of individual adaptive strategies.

A biologically useful strategy might also be seen in another, less frequent, Betsileo ceremonial, the curing sacrifice. In this fairly rare ritual, a curer prescribes that the afflicted person sacrifice an ox and drink its blood. Illness, although diagnosed as brought on by ancestral displeasure, witchcraft, spirit possession, or soul loss,[30] may actually be malnutrition, or may express increased susceptibility to disease because of malnutrition. As Roy Rappaport (1968) has argued for the Tsembaga Maring of New Guinea, if one individual in a household or village suffers from illness related to malnutrition, then it is likely that other members of the household or village are also suffering nutritionally. Ceremonial slaughter of an ox not only appeases the ancestors, but also eases hunger and provides high quality protein for other villagers. Since the curing sacrifice, unlike most other ceremonies, may occur at any time of year, nutritional crises may be met. The only such curing sacrifice I heard about during my fieldwork among the Betsileo involved a resident of a landpoor village of slave descendants near Ivato. I suspect that differential access shows up medically and that such sacrifices are correspondingly more frequent among slave descendants and junior commoners than among richer Betsileo.

Markets now offer an alternative to the nutritive function of ceremonials, given cash from such crops as tobacco, coffee, and surplus rice. Peasants with cash can, if they wish, go to market and buy beef every week. (Missionary John Haile [1899, p. 328] reported in 1899, before the market had fully penetrated their homeland, that Betsileo never ate meat except as guests at other people's tables and at funerals.) Although ceremonials have served many functions in addition to regional food distribution, the contrast in frequency of tomb-centered ceremonials between the south (e.g., Mahazony) and east (e.g., Ivato), reflecting differential market penetration, must be significant. Within a radius of ten kilometers from Ivato, where winter ceremonials are fewer and smaller in scale, are three canton seats that hold weekly markets on different days. With more cash and easier access, Ivatans attend markets much more frequently than people from either of the two Mahazony villages, whose markets are less accessible.

The market also provides an alternative to ceremonials as a place for young people to meet members of the other sex, whom they sometimes marry. Again, this consideration may be more important for junior commoners, fewer of whose marriages are arranged, than for seniors, among whom arranged marriages continue to be the practice.

Ceremonial and Stratification

In several studies (e.g., Harris 1974; Rappaport 1968; Suttles 1974), anthropologists have examined the adaptive value of intercommunity feasting, which is often ceremonially organized. Several economic and ecosystemic functions have been attributed to ceremonials; for example, stimulating surplus production, redistributing human and animal populations with respect to strategic resources, and leveling out temporary resource imbalances between communities located in different microenvironments. By and large these studies have involved *tribal* populations and have focused on negative feedback effects of ceremonial in apparently stable human ecosystems. As the preceding section has shown, similar functional arguments can be made about certain aspects of Betsileo ceremonial. Thus, by providing opportunities for impoverished and/or malnourished people to eat, and, in areas like Mahazony, by allowing the relatively poor to make smaller contributions than the relatively wealthy, Betsileo ceremonials can help to even out access to food and other strategic resources.

However, an interpretation of Betsileo ceremonials demands much more. The functions and effects of Betsileo ceremonials vary regionally today, and they have varied historically. Rights and obligations connected to ceremonials have been among the positive feedback mechanisms that have contributed to the rise of socioeconomic stratification and state organization among the Betsileo. Furthermore, Betsileo history shows that ceremonial participation can assume new and very different functions in a stratified and state-organized society. Accordingly, Betsileo ceremonial life will now be approached from the viewpoint of variation and change. Specifically, in those parts of the Betsileo homeland where stratification and state organization are most developed, the contributions of ceremonial toward increasing, rather than evening out, differential access to strategic resources stand out and will be emphasized.

To see how this works, recall the cases discussed above. We have seen that the size and regional scale of a Betsileo ceremonial directly reflect the focal individual's reputation, which varies depending on his or her access to strategic resources, including power, wealth, and prestige. However, although the total value of guests' contributions also increases with the focal person's reputation and stratum, ceremonial expenditures by his or her immediate family may not. Thus, although several people attended and were fed at the funeral of senior commoner Therese, more steers were actually killed at the funeral in Tanambao of Joesfather, a junior commoner. The *monetary* contributions to the senior commoner's funeral were larger, however, and her son and daughter-in-law boasted that their guests had provided more than enough money for them to recoup the cost of the steer they had sacrificed. No profit appears to have accrued to Joesfather's relatives. The junior commoner's relatives therefore collected less and personally gave up more than the senior commoners.

In the south and west, several customs keep wealth differentials from being widened through ceremonial contributions. Reception committees at funerals, for example, are expected to decide whether to accept or decline a steer by evaluating the donor's economic status. Furthermore, all steers must be slaughtered and their meat immediately consumed or given away. Since they are neither hoarded nor converted into their actual cash value, they cannot be used to increase the wealth of the dead person's close relatives. The burden of providing cooked rice and other food aside from beef is customarily distributed among several households.

Close calculation of the value of prestations and the obligation to return equivalent value would also seem to soften exacerbation of wealth differentials through ceremonial observances. However, if two groups participating in the same ceremonial system are of unequal socioeconomic status, as is commonly the case in the Ivato region, merely equivalent exchange cannot function to level, but at best maintains the status quo, and can even force those with marginal resources into debt.

I suggest that exactly the same cultural forms, in this case ceremonials, can function differently in different regions and in relation to socioeconomic attributes of organizers and participants. Here again, the longstanding contrast between the agricultural east and the more pastoral south and west is implicated. Thus, in less stratified, more pastoral Mahazony, the obligation to contribute to ceremonials increases with relative wealth. Richer people are expected to give more. This means that in the long run resources are balanced out, there is regional redistribution of rice, meat, and cash, and there is no progressive buildup of the wealth of certain minimal descent groups over others. Around Ivato, on the other hand, in a more densely populated region where nobles, senior commoners, junior commoners, and slave descendants live in neighboring settlements and participate in the same ceremonials, ceremonial prestations, guided by a more rigid standard of balanced reciprocity, contribute to socioeconomic differentiation.

In a subsistence-focused economy where cash is in short supply, an offering of 500 francs from a person whose granaries are loaded with rice and whose purse is filled with cash is obviously less of a burden than a poor person's gift of the same amount. The obligation of the relatively poor to return *equivalent value* to the relatively wealthy can lead to financial hardship and debt when there is no ready access to means of reciprocation. In areas where stratification is developed, therefore, the leveling, redistributive function of ceremonials is of reduced significance. Senior commoners not only boast about their receipts but also excuse their own smaller expenditures and the smaller shares of beef that they offer at ceremonials by claiming that their Christianity and enlightened progressiveness force them to underplay customary ceremonial observances. Therese's relatives offered precisely these excuses for only killing five steers at her funeral. In Mahazony the funeral of a person of her status would have demanded the slaughter of several more cattle.

Ceremonial and the State

With the growth of the state, and particularly after Merina conquest, Betsileo began to participate in new kinds of ceremonials. And, as has been indicated, the functions and implications of Betsileo ceremonies changed—from leveling to siphoning wealth—in the context of stratification and state organization. In several instances ceremonial obligations and observances began to hurt rather than help most of their Betsileo participants, particularly with the addition of Merina demands.

Chapter 4 described how the Merina administration used the funeral of a king of Isandra to exact massive revenues. During more than four months of funerary ceremonies, the Merina queen collected a piaster, equivalent then to a steer, from every male over the age of ten in Isandra; she also requisitioned the equivalent of 500 additional steers from the Isandran population. Revenues were collected as government officials had the royal corpse paraded through three regional capitals, and at its final resting place. State seizure of and control over customs and institutions that had evolved in a different context and that were formerly regulated by kinship and other nongovernmental means can be seen in other aspects of the Betsileo (and Merina peasant) condition when Merina nobles ruled them. Adoption and rejection of children, formerly affairs administered by kinship and descent groups, were eventually identified as legal actions requiring government registry and fees (cf. Haile, 1899, p. 331). Similarly, as in Imerina, Betsileo circumcision was a small-scale seasonal affair performed on a boy during his second year of life, involving his closest maternal and paternal kin. The Merina transformed circumcision into a revenue-collecting and censusing device, by requiring that all boys be circumcized at seven year intervals, and that they be sponsored by a couple who paid a fee to the national treasury. Under Merina rule, lower-level Betsileo officials held annual circumcisions of boys over five months old (Shaw 1878, p. 10), again with a fee to the state.

In several other ways, state administrations, whether Betsileo or Merina, have transformed ceremonials from redistributive and leveling devices, as they still are among the Taimoro of the southeast coast, into occasions for collecting state revenues, siphoning peasants' wealth, and thus further exacerbating differential access to strategic resources. Recall from chapter 3's discussion of the evolution of Betsileo statelets that in early Lalangina the "privilege" of sacrificing steers at funerals and other ceremonials was reserved for nobles and senior commoners. I would suggest that such sacrifice, rather than being a privilege dear to the hearts of Betsileo elites, was actually a leveling device in which large numbers of subjects would avail themselves of meals hosted by wealthier people, free from the obligation of reciprocating. The "privilege" of slaughtering steers was gradually extended to junior commoners and now is a universal Betsileo custom. As the privilege of hosting such feasts, and the canon of balanced reciprocity, became culturally obligatory for junior commoners and, nowadays slave descendants, the material effects of the ceremonial system gradually changed. Whereas formerly ceremonial participation had equalized access to strategic resources, it now accelerated socioeconomic differentation by *siphoning* scarce resources from poor to rich.

Ceremonial also provided a formal context for collecting state revenues. In the ceremonial distribution of sacrificial beef among Betsileo and Merina alike, the rump became the noble's due. It was traditionally presented to kings, princes, or their noble or senior commoner representatives; when several steers were sacrificed, "rump" might actually be presented as one or more whole animals for the noble's herd.[31]

Not only did the Merina modify Betsileo ceremonials, they introduced and fostered the diffusion of their own ceremonials and tomb architecture throughout the southern highlands. Continuing a fashion adopted by high status Betsileo in Merina days, most Betsileo tombs constructed in this century have used the traditional Merina sepulcher as a model. Prior to Merina incorporation, only the tombs of Betsileo elites had been imposing structures, and in Isandra and other areas of the south and west, nobles traditionally had been interred in caves (as among contemporary Bara; see Huntington 1974, pp. 96–97). Traditional commoner tombs were excavated in the ground and roofed by a stone slab; their entrances were filled in with earth and rocks, and corpses reposed on mats placed on the dirt floor (cf. Shaw 1878, pp. 7–8).

Construction of tombs after Merina models entailed much greater expense for the Betsileo than their traditional burial places. The gradual dissemination of the Merina tomb complex began as high status Betsileo, like ancestral Ivatans Karl Fridaysfather, Owen, and Goodmaker, commissioned Merina structures. The western Ivato tomb was constructed in Merina days by Merina masons, at a cost of forty cattle and two slave women. In 1914, Goodmaker brought three of the masons who had constructed the tomb of a Merina prime minister to Ivato to construct the eastern tomb. Ivatans estimated that, if constructed today, this sepulcher, which cost around 1,000 francs between 1914 and 1917, would cost about 500,000 francs, or $2,000 U.S. in 1967. Note that the value of this senior commoner tomb is between three and four times the cost of the junior commoner tomb in Mahazony whose *famadihana* was described above.

Betsileo construct tombs for various reasons. The decision to construct the Mahazony tomb whose inauguration has been described appears to have been triggered by the utilitarian consideration that the old tomb was too full. On the other hand, Ivatans told me that the western village tomb was not at all full when Goodmaker commissioned the eastern village sepulcher. The Ivato case illustrates, therefore, that new tombs may also be commissioned by economically ascendant individuals and groups as status symbols. Since successful individuals generally initiate construction, one might wonder whether tomb construction functions to divert wealth from entrepreneurial use into a nonproductive status symbol, thus leveling major socioeconomic contrasts. Apparently not totally, since when a new structure is initiated by economically ascendant individuals, members of the common descent group who are unlikely themselves to be buried in the new tomb are also expected to contribute. When people are poor, neither they nor their local descent segment is likely to commission a new tomb. Indeed, their obligations to contribute to the cost of several tombs limits the amount they can spend on the tombs where they are most likely to be buried. However, if they are to fulfill culturally specified notions of a wide bilateral network of rights and obligations and to honor several ancestors, they cannot shirk such responsibilities, on pain of social ostracism and at the risk of ancestral displeasure.

Obligations based on common descent and on bilateral kinship and marriage therefore mitigate the potential leveling effect of the expense of tomb construction, and thus help to maintain wealth differentials in Betsileo society. Siphoning of wealth from poor to rich can also be seen when Betsileo ceremonials are viewed in the context of social, economic, and political relationships to outsiders. In several ways, tomb construction and associated *famadihana*, and other Merina-derived tomb ceremonials, have channeled strategic resources from Betsileo into Merina hands. Furthermore, comparison of Merina and Betsileo ceremonial expenses suggests that not only Betsileo but Merina have suffered as a result of their ceremonial obligations. John H. Haile (1892, p. 408 et seq.), a British missionary, described obligations associated with tomb and ceremonial in the Merina countryside late in the nineteenth century. Haile noted that many Merina peasants who would have been reluctant to spend $40 (or piasters) on their houses lavished $200 on their tombs. Specialized masons were hired to dress and fit stones, and Haile estimated the cost of splitting stone slabs for a tomb as between $6 and $16. Once the stone slabs had been split, they were carried to the tomb site by 200 to 300 villagers, and at the conclusion of each day's work, oxen and pigs were killed which, according to Haile, represented a major expenditure.

Once the tomb was finished, a date was set for its inaugural *famadihana*. Haile noted that silk funerary shrouds were bought in the market at prices ranging between $7 and $16.[32] The status of the deceased determined the number of shrouds used to envelop his or her corpse; Haile had observed cases in which as many as seven or eight, at a cost of $100, had been used.

As among contemporary Betsileo, winter is the season for *famadihana* in Imerina. Haile interpreted a winter ceremonial season as consonant with the torpor of death and in its context as the agricultural off-season. One might also point to the greater cash revenues available to peasants just after the harvest.[33] Haile noted that for a month before the *famadihana*, the close relatives of the deceased were expected to follow a special diet designed to impart plumpness of face and form. As among the Betsileo, the date of the ceremony was fixed by a diviner, usually for August or September. As the ceremony, which lasted a week, began, music was played at the old burial site to call the ghosts together and, eventually, to announce to them their impending move. Organizers hired a band of musicians to play throughout the *famadihana*, paying them between three and sixteen dollars. Haile (1892, p. 415) reported that, in earlier times, the head and body of wealthy corpses were encircled with silver chains; money was also deposited in piles around the corpse, and wealth items were placed in the tomb. There was, according to Haile, a tacit understanding that in cases of penury, the descendants might fall back on this store, but only in the event of a funeral or *famadihana*. While token sums of money were still interred when Haile lived in Imerina, he attributed Merina abandonment of using tombs as storage vaults to increasing fear of grave robbers, which he attributed to a declining respect for the ancestors.

Though there is reason to doubt the total objectivity of a missionary's account of traditional Malagasy ceremonial, there must be some accuracy in his characterization of tomb construction and *famadihana* as occasions on which the living were impoverished to aggrandize the dead, and, I add, the rich. Haile states that because of ceremonial expenses, many Merina were plunged into poverty or involved in debt from which they were never able to extricate themselves. He attributes the continuation of ceremonial outlays to pressure by kin to satisfy ancestral expectations. Bloch (1971, p. 148 et seq.) makes similar comments about the causes and effects of rewrapping ceremonies among contemporary Merina, noting, for example, that for every *famadihana* he attended, the people directly involved (usually children and siblings of the focal corpse) had to sell cattle or land. Current Merina *famadihana* expenses are exceeded only by the cost of constructing a new tomb. Despite major expense and debt, Bloch (1971, p. 162) notes that Merina continue to participate in these customs. People must, after all, be surrounded by their kin in the vaguely conceived Merina afterlife; the return *famadihana* is a sacred obligation. A major factor is terror, in a world cognized through a kinship model, of being buried alone and spending eternity away from relatives.

Haile also reported that the custom of secondary burials in winter was maintained by the nineteenth-century Merina convention, which the Betsileo at least have avoided, that no tomb could be opened for one year after its ceremonial inaugural; those who died during this year would be buried temporarily and transferred to the tomb, occasioning another major ceremonial the following year (Haile 1892, p. 414).[34]

Nineteenth-century Betsileo lived in a stratified society governed by Merina and their agents, and in which Merina controlled commerce and such skilled trades as masonry. Even today, Merina are the major Malagasy commercial figures in the southern highlands, and Merina masons still build Betsileo tombs. Within the context of tomb construction and *famadihana*, Merina have reaped profits from the sale of rum,[35] silk shrouds, and other ceremonial items; bands of Merina musicians have availed themselves of Betsileo demand for their services; and masons have acquired cash by talking Betsileo into elaborate tombs.[36] As Haile reported for Imerina, the expectation of cash and labor contributions toward the construction of tombs from people with little cash has created debts, which Betsileo have been expected to repay with substantial interest to Merina creditors and their agents, local senior commoners. Ivatans relate that three generations of ancestors, Karl Fridaysfather, Goodmaker, and Vernon, increased their estates in slaves and/or land and cattle not only through adoption and other social manipulations, but through usury. The massive burden of peasants' forced contributions to the funerary ceremonies of a post-Merina Isandran king has been described. Thereby, too, peasants contracted debts as a result of their participation in state-regulated ceremonials. Individuals were forced to sell rice, cattle, slaves, and even their rice fields, to meet demands conceived by their overlords. In Betsileo days, as under Merina rule, peasants could be reduced to slavery for inability to pay their debts.

It is apparent, therefore, that no single functional explanation of Betsileo ceremonials can be defended. Functions of ceremonials have varied according to region, stratum, other socioeconomic considerations, and the intervention of the state in the regulation of ceremonial and regional distribution. In some cases, e.g. Mahazony, as may have been true generally prior to the evolution of stratification and state organization among the Betsileo, ceremonials can still function as adaptive mechanisms of regional redistribution, making food generally available on a fairly constant basis and leveling out differential access to strategic resources between communities. However, as stratification developed and became more pronounced, rigid maintenance of the norm of balanced reciprocity—which was undoubtedly inherited from a similar, but more flexible, ideology of reciprocation in the more egalitarian past—meant that ceremonials could no longer function merely to redistribute wealth when they brought together members of different communities and different strata. Rather, since ceremonial attendance and prestations measured prestige, wealth differentials were actually magnified. The wealthier, the more prestigious the host, the greater the number of people in attendance and the greater the web of ceremonial debt relationships governed by balanced reciprocity. Moss (1900, p. 475) reported an even more startling change in Betsileo ceremonial in the context of stratification, noting that although the number of oxen sacrificed increased with the wealth of the host family (cf. Haile 1899, p. 332), the largest shares of the funerary meat were being given to the wealthiest and most influential people, while poorer Betsileo some-times got no meat at all. Ceremonial's transformation from leveler to siphoner therefore seems to have been well-advanced by the turn of this century.

Furthermore, to the roster of ancestral Betsileo funerary practices, the Merina added, and promoted the spread of, a new type of tomb that was more expensive and more reliant on Merina skills than the traditional Betsileo structure. Transmitted with Merina tombs was the *famadihana* complex.[37] Both tomb and *famadihana* stimulated Betsileo, like Merina peasants, to in-vest wealth in nonconvertible, nonproductive symbols of prestige, while pro-viding a new market for Merina skills and products, and abundant profitable opportunities for Merina artisans and business people.

As Bloch (1971) reports, the ideal Merina (homeland) peasant commu-nity (excluding slaves and their descendants) is modeled on kinship, coopera-tion, and a degree of egalitarianism. Although peasants hide their differential wealth in their ordinary lifestyle, they may appropriately spend as much as (or more than) they can afford on ceremonies and the ancestral tomb. Today's Merina emigrants can invest their differential wealth in the land of the ances-tors, in a social fund built around ancestral tomb and house, both of which are visited rarely, for holidays and ceremonies. Bloch describes social pres-sure to continue to make such investments. He reports, for example, a shop-keeper's complaint that neighbors were pressuring him to sponsor a rewrap-ping ceremony in order to block his accumulation of money. Another informant told Bloch (1971, p. 162), "The neighbours will think us wicked to have money while the dead do not have new (shrouds)." In these cases, as in the cargo-fiesta system of highland Latin America (cf. Harris 1964), the distribution of wealth is being rearranged in two ways: (1) intracommunity and intrastratum wealth differences are being leveled out, as those with a temporary advantage are forced to make larger contributions of time, food, and money to ceremonials; and (2) peasants, reliant on outsiders' skills and permissions for key aspects of ceremonials, are forced to participate in an extravillage market economy. Major contributors, mystified by their obliga-tions to dead kin, pass their wealth on to outsiders and incur debts to wealthier people, rather than reinvesting it in their own community of living kin and neighbors.

In the context of stratification, ceremonial obligations have had many similar effects among the Betsileo. Finally, to various degrees, state officials have usurped all Betsileo ceremonials and used them as occasions for col-lecting revenues (cf. Dez 1956, p. 119). In some instances, state demands were extremely onerous and led not only to exacerbation of wealth differ-ences among Betsileo but also to debt slavery and the transfer to the Merina and their agents of Betsileo ancestral lands.

Betsileo ceremonials, which cluster in the postharvest period between June and September, demonstrate the continuing importance of the physical and/ or (believed in) spiritual remains of dead ancestors in ongoing Betsileo life. Differences in the context and effects of Betsileo ceremonials in time and space are another aspect of sociocultural variation related to such material factors as economy, population density, market access, and socioeconomic stratification. Their emic justification aside, the persistence of Betsileo ceremonials is guaranteed by their overdetermination (the plethora of functions they serve), but functions and effects vary in the context of different material conditions.

Chapter 7 once again has focused not on how cultural forms (in this case, ceremonials) *originate* to fill particular functions, but on how the functions, effects, and impact on other institutions of certain cultural forms *change* as material conditions vary. Among the effects of ceremonial life on social organization are the following: common descent groups form, uniting members of different local groups; regional alliances based on descent and marriage are given behavioral expression; people keep up bilateral networks and have opportunities to meet and evaluate marriage partners.

Ceremonials also play a role in regulating access to strategic resources. In the more pastoral, more sparsely populated Betsileo south and west, as probably was generally the case early in the process of socioeconomic differentiation and state formation, ceremonials help even out regional and intercommunity differences in access to strategic resources, as (perhaps temporarily) poorer people were allowed to give less and receive more than (perhaps temporarily) more fortunate people. On the basis of oral traditions, eighteenth-century Betsileo ceremonials in the agricultural east were still levelers rather than siphoners. Only elites—nobles and senior commoners—could sponsor ceremonies; they had to foot the bill for the rest of the population, and thus could not invest their greater wealth in their own or their family's material advancement. Over time, however, the right to sponsor ceremonials was extended to the poor along with the rich, and people began rigidly to stress balanced reciprocity (rather than gifts based on ability to pay). Concomitantly, the rich could use their prestige and web of ceremonial invitations to tie the less fortunate into a network of reciprocating. As has been true for the Merina as well, the web of ceremonial obligations—sponsorship and repayment—has forced the less fortunate to sell cattle and land.

Equally important, ceremonial obligations have forced Betsileo into market and state relations. Ceremonial expenses (rum, dancers' fees, musicians' fees, wrestlers' fees, government permits) necessitate cash and therefore sale of crops, animals, labor, or, in the most extreme case, ancestral land. As chiefdom turned to state, and conqueror replaced conqueror, government progressively intervened in ceremonial life, using circumcision to census and tax, and most life cycle or seasonal rituals to collect taxes or fees.

Differences in function and context of Betsileo cultural forms (in this case ceremonial) were again illustrated with the contrast of Ivato and the two Mahazony villages, sampling regional diversity and socioeconomic stratification. The people of Mahazony lead a much richer ceremonial life for several reasons: (1) ceremonial remains more leveler than siphoner; (2) market access (an alternative to several historic functions of ceremonial) is more difficult; (3) there are fewer Christians in the south than around Ivato. In the Ivato region, on the other hand, senior commoners use their Christianity as an excuse for their own (relatively) small contributions to others' ceremonies and to the reduced scale of their own. They get away with this because Christianity, modernity, senior commoner status, education, and political prominence—all of which Ivatans now have—enhance prestige, inspire trust, and keep ordinary people somewhat baffled about the actual workings and consequences of the ceremonial system.

Still, in the face of growing market access and awareness of some of the siphoning, debt-producing results of ceremonial participation, Betsileo of the agricultural east are participating in ever fewer ceremonies.

A final change related to context: the *famadihana*, a Merina innovation, spread rapidly in Mahazony, where the equalizing aspect of ceremonial stood out; it provided one more link in regional social integration and one more occasion for ceremonial partying and feasting. More tombs are also needed here because of descent group fragmentation, emigration, and the multiple descent group affiliations of villages. In the Ivato region, on the other hand, the funeral is the major ceremonial event, and even funerals of major figures (like senior commoner Therese) are less lavish (in cattle slaughter and rum consumption) than those in the south and west.

CHAPTER EIGHT

The Past in the Present and the Future

Any study of variation within a culture or among related cultures almost inevitably exposes unity as well, and this has been true of the present work. Historical and contemporary variation among the Malagasy generally, and the Betsileo in particular, has been viewed against a background of contrasts in material conditions simultaneously acting on and processed through a shared sociocultural heritage. As noted in chapter 1, material conditions are those that govern a group's access to strategic and valued resources. They include aspects of the physical environment and biome as they are processed by cultural systems. Along with customary means and relations of production, material conditions also include trade, warfare, and participation in other regional relationships. Most important for the present study, however, are the contrasting material conditions arising from and within the context of socioeconomic stratification and the state.

The exploration of unity and diversity in Malagasy life has proceeded through a gradually narrowing analytic focus, from natural and cultural contrasts encountered on the island of Madagascar to variation between three Betsileo villages. Chapter 2 examined the divergence of the Proto-Malagasy and tried to identify aspects of physical environment, local economy, and participation in regional systems that have figured in that differentiation. Chapters 3 and 4 explored the sociopolitical implications of environmental and economic contrasts between two parts of the Betsileo heartland, reconstructed the growth of socioeconomic stratification, and examined the effects on local life of state formation and of Merina and French conquest. Contrasts between Ivato, Ambalabe, and Tanambao then served to illustrate specific aspects of sociocultural variation associated with region, economy, demography, and different positions in the hierarchy of rank, wealth, and power.

The contrasts uncovered in chapters 5 through 7 included social relations of production reflecting the different descent group structures of the three villages; other contrasts include cultivation practices, diet, and housing. Among the aspects of kinship, descent, and marriage that vary with differential access are the relative importance of ancestral versus collateral kinship calculation, genealogical depth, strictness of agnation in local descent group affiliation, fictive kinship, fosterage, household composition, descent group and village endogamy, the initiation of marriage, bridewealth, and marital stability. Differences in ceremonial life in the two regions reflected ceremonial's continuing redistributive, leveling role in the south and west, compared to its siphoning and impoverishing effects in the agricultural east.

Some of the variations that have been considered involve different functions, effects, meanings, or contexts of shared cultural forms; others have been differences in scale. However, contrasts generally have not been seen as absolute or qualitative differences but as variations or transformations on themes that recur throughout Madagascar. Several factors have contributed to cultural unity among Malagasy peoples. A major input is the sociocultural heritage of the Proto-Malagasy, common to the island's divergent daughter populations. Other reasons for cultural unity include contacts through trade, migration, and warfare, diffusion, and inclusion within common political boundaries.

The relationship of the current work to other materialist and evolutionary studies should be made clear. Many previous studies—Julian Steward's (1955) best known works, for example—have shown the role of *common* material conditions in generating sociocultural similarities, both diachronic and synchronic, among *unrelated* populations. This is also a major aim of Marvin Harris's cultural materialist determinism as revealed in the following quote:

> By a deterministic relationship among cultural phenomena, I mean merely that similar variables under similar conditions tend to give rise to similar consequences (Harris 1977, p. xiii).

These goals are perfectly appropriate, and such studies have increased our understanding of how similar forces generate similar sociocultural results. However, the aim of the present work has been different. I have attempted to show how and why encounters between *identical* (or at least similar) cultural raw material and *dissimilar* material conditions tend to result in *dissimilar* consequences. This is simply an application to cultural data of the Darwinian model of branching evolution—descent with modification—through natural selection.[1] The cultural features examined here have not been seen as *generated* quasi-mechancially by material conditions or natural selective forces. Of interest instead has been the *modification* of cultural material, which was there at the outset, as a result of determinate encounters. Since cultural heritage can be held constant, even more obviously when comparing Betsileo than when dealing with Madagascar as a whole, the role of specific material conditions in effecting sociocultural change is particularly clear.

Criticizing (incorrectly, I think) the materialist determinism of Steward and others, Sahlins (1976, p. viii) insists that culture conforms to material constraints "according to a definite symbolic scheme which is never the only one possible." However, the uniqueness of a particular cultural adaptation depends on whether one is talking about specific details of cultural content or about relatively similar forms and functions. Thus, although the specifics of a recipe or fairy tale might never be independently reinvented, many formal and functional analogies *have* developed independently in different cultures. There are certain generalized, functionally interlinked features of state organization, for example, or of chiefdoms, "big man" systems, or segmentary lineage organization. Of course, all cultural details cannot be explained in such studies, but many significant features can. It is unrealistic to expect any approach to explain everything. A combination of approaches enhances understanding of how culture is constituted and how it works and changes.

Sahlins's criticism is not as applicable to the current study, since a common "symbolic scheme" has oriented Betsileo culture's *variant* conformity to material constraints. I have not treated culture as mechanically generated from nature, but as gradually modified through its interaction with material forces. Culture was there at the beginning.

Nevertheless, this work probably qualifies as a variant of the "practical reason" approach that Sahlins (1976) sees linking Morgan, Malinowski, Steward, and Marx. Sahlins accuses the practical reason school of "impoverishing" the study of culture, which

> degenerates into one or another of two common-place naturalisms: the economism of the rationalizing individual (human nature); or the ecologism of selective advantage (external nature). (Sahlins 1976, p. 83).

Although I *have* attributed cultural variation in Madagascar to material conditions (natural selective forces), I hope that I have managed to avoid the "impoverishment" of culture that Sahlins decries. I do not share his belief that there is an unbridgeable gap between a materialist approach and a "cultural account." As understood by Sahlins (1976, p. 55), at issue is

> whether the cultural order is to be conceived as the codification of man's actual purposeful and pragmatic action; or whether, conversely, human action in the world is to be understood as mediated by the cultural design, which gives order at once to practical experience, customary practice, and the relationship between the two.

Sahlins (1976, p. 55) contends that these views are irreconcilable: the truth does not lie "somewhere in between, or even on both sides (i.e., dialectically)."

Is it not possible, however, that the truth *does* lie on both sides, not dialectically, but simply and simultaneously? That is, is culture not both adaptive ("useful") and meaningful? Humans do have biological needs (which vary, within limits, from population to population and individual to individual) and socially generated needs (which vary much more widely), and they use culture to satisfy them. And, since no human exists without culture, human action is always mediated by a cultural design.

Some of the terms and distinctions of Sahlins's argument seem themselves to derive from a western world view that opposes culture and nature and that believes that "individuals" exist. Betsileo, and no doubt many other people that anthropologists have studied, see things very differently. First, the very notion that culture and practical reason are, should be, or can be *opposed* is one that a Betsileo would not easily understand. Sahlins (1976, p. 85) criticizes Malinowski (perhaps justly) for seeing culture in terms of

> the struggle of the individual subject to achieve his own ends in the face of *constraining* cultural conventions. Meaningful analysis thus gives way to manipulative rationality, to the formal analysis of means-ends relations based on an eternal teleology of human satisfactions (italics added).

Although Malinowski may have been led by his own western bias to find "economic man" in the Trobriands, an anthropological statement that some people act selfishly (i.e., so as to deprive others) or that they manipulate cultural rules for advantage is not necessarily to understand a culture as "the organized effect of individual businesslike economizing" (Sahlins 1976, p. 95). The very terms of Sahlins's argument carry a western bias into the evaluation of ethnography: although Betsileo seek certain (culturally perceived) satisfactions, they have difficulty conceiving of "the individual."[2] We have seen that the senior commoners of Ivato realize certain social (predominantly kin-based) ends that deprive others of socially appropriate means of satisfying their own (culturally perceived) needs.[3] Yet Ivatans, far from struggling against "constraining cultural conventions" (Sahlins 1976, p. 85; note here the imposition of another, curious, western opposition—culture *against* man), are, of the Betsileo I studied, the foremost advocates of maintaining the ancestral traditions. Senior commoners are the "culture-keepers." More than junior commoners and slave descendants, they uphold, follow, and benefit from cultural rules.

We are not, after all, dealing with a "primitive" society; ethnographic data should not be forced into such dichotomies as West versus rest, western versus tribal, or kinship-based versus capitalist (Sahlins 1976, pp. 54, 212). The Betsileo live in a state-organized society, as different from the !Kung or Mbuti as the contemporary United States is from Madagascar. Betsileo senior commoners constantly emphasize transgenerationally sanctioned dicta that help mystify differential access under the veil of ancestors, kinship, and sacred force. To say that senior commoners manipulate and benefit from cultural rules is not, therefore, to impose on the Betsileo our (western) consciousness of ourselves (cf. Sahlins 1976, p. 86). Nonethnocentrically—and accurately—stated, Ivatans follow certain cultural rules more frequently and more carefully than other Betsileo. Doing this helps them reproduce, and even increase, their differential access to strategic and culturally valued resources. Although some Ivatans recognize this effect, they, like most Betsileo, simultaneously see their behavior as culturally necessary. In other words, *Betsileo* ideology neither separates nor opposes culture and practical reason.

Although Betsileo have no conception of "the individual," people do act for themselves and for groups in ways that would be considered selfishly nepotistic in our own society. However, those who act, in a collectivist society, as maximization theory expects "individuals" to act—for example, by alienating ancestral lands through sale or inappropriate adoption—alienate themselves as well. They become witches, scorning society, inverting culture; they are the only "individuals" among the Betsileo.

WHAT HAS CHANGED AND WHAT HAS REMAINED THE SAME?

This work recognizes that culture is not generated out of nothing; it is there from the start, interacting with material conditions in its descent with modification. How does this compare with biological evolution? A major feature of biological evolution is its fortuitous character; from an array of available phenotypes natural forces select those fittest to survive and reproduce in a given environment. Given environmental perturbations or gradual shifts, adaptable varieties are not simply created but must be chosen from what the range of phenotypical differences has to offer. In the biological realm, then, natural selection can only depend on and operate on the variety at hand. Contemporary human populations also evolve, that is, adapt to changed circumstances, by phenotypical modification.[4] However, behavior patterns can vary much more quickly and flexibly because they are less genetically restricted than among other animals. Culture, based on learning, can be set to work in adapting to change. Materialists see flexibility and adaptability as basic characteristics of the genus *Homo*, viewing such "uncommitted potentiality for change" (Bateson 1972, p. 497) as itself a product of evolutionary selection. Variation is the stuff of which both biological and sociocultural evolution are made.

Nevertheless, the cultural evolution of specific human populations also has a conservative component: it proceeds in the face of prior structures (a given sociocultural heritage) and is affected by the organizational material (sociocultural patterns) at hand when the change begins. Several anthropologists agree, and a few (e.g., Oliver 1962) have systematically demonstrated that human populations and their cultural ways cannot be regarded as blank checks on which environment can freely and mechanically write. Recognizing this, Roy Rappaport (1971a, pp. 23–24) has defined adaptation as

> the processes by which organisms or groups of organisms maintain *homeostasis* in and among themselves in the face of both short-term environmental fluctuations and long-term changes in the composition and structure of their environments (italics added).

The feedback between materialist, ecological, and evolutionary approaches in anthropology has considerably expanded our understanding of cultural evolutionary processes. Furthermore, I also believe that because of the growth of structuralism, materialists and other anthropologists are paying, and will continue to pay, more attention to relationships between prior structure and the material context of change. Although Lévi-Strauss's (cf. 1967, pp. 57–58) most characteristic and familiar use of the term "structure" is for universal attributes of the human mind or brain that are supposedly responsible for the cross-cultural recurrence of similar cultural forms or manifestations, he also occasionally uses "structure" to refer to the sociocultural manifestations and representations themselves. In this case his structuralism can more easily be used within a materialist analysis. For example, when Lévi-Strauss tells us that the structure of the Dobuans is very different from the structure of the Trobrianders (1967, p. 42), he is not talking about universal mental structures. Nor is he when he writes that ". . . the great lesson of totemism is that the form of the structure can sometimes survive when the structure itself succumbs to events" (1966, p. 232).

The interaction between prior structure (sociocultural heritage) and material conditions forms a framework for understanding a variety of types of evolutionary processes (figure 7).

We have seen that Steward (1955) explicated sociocultural regularities or analogies involving form and function among widespread unrelated populations. He was demonstrating convergent evolution; he offered middle range generalizations intended to explain similarities attributable to common material conditions. Both flexibility (human populations are not so bound by their sociocultural heritage or prior structure that they may not change as material conditions change) and a certain inevitability (material conditions limit the variety of potential responses) are basic to Steward's formulations.

Materialist studies have also tried to explain similarities and differences among related populations, groups like the Malagasy that now are separate but that share a common sociocultural heritage. It is in such cases, as well as in studies of specific evolution (Sahlins and Service 1960), that materialists

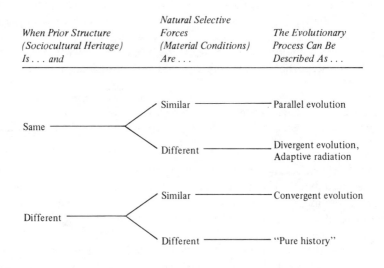

When Prior Structure (Sociocultural Heritage) Is . . . and	Natural Selective Forces (Material Conditions) Are . . .	The Evolutionary Process Can Be Described As . . .
Same	Similar	Parallel evolution
	Different	Divergent evolution, Adaptive radiation
Different	Similar	Convergent evolution
	Different	"Pure history"

Fig. 7   Interrelationship of Prior Structure and Material
Conditions in Types of Sociocultural Evolutionary
Processes

must examine what Lévi-Strauss describes as "the structure which underlies the many manifestations and remains permanent throughout a succession of events" (Lévi-Strauss 1967, p. 22). When related groups separate and encounter similar material conditions, not only are they likely to retain much of their common prior structure and cultural content, they can also be expected, to some extent, to change in parallel ways. Such parallel evolution is the basis of chapter 2's cultural adaptive typology of Malagasy populations (i.e., those within a given type). Material conditions encountered in different places can, of course, never be identical; they must be evaluated as relatively similar or dissimilar by examining a combination of specified variables. Thus, although sociocultural manifestations encountered in Polynesia can be viewed as variations on a common proto-cultural theme, some Polynesians are more alike culturally and structurally than others, and many of these parallels can be linked to similar material conditions (Sahlins 1958).

Like convergence, parallel evolution concerns the production or retention of similarities. If neither material conditions nor prior structure are common to the populations under consideration, there is little basis for materialist comparison of them. One is in the realm of "pure history." However, by holding prior structure constant, and viewing sociocultural variation among related populations against a background of variation in material conditions, a processual, materialistic explication of variation and transformations becomes possible. This has been my object in the current work.

Although anthropological investigations of *divergent evolution*, which often culminates in an *adaptive radiation* of related populations, are not new, they are less common than studies of convergent evolution. Models essentially of adaptive radiation have been previously applied by Sahlins (1958) to Polynesia, by Gulliver (1955) to the Jie and Turkana of Uganda, and by Steward (1956) and his students to Puerto Rico. Such a model makes it possible to see sociocultural differences among related populations as so many variations on a common theme, and to link this variation—considered synchronically or diachronically—to differences in material conditions. Applied to the twenty or so ethnic units of Madagascar, or to three contrasting southern Betsileo villages, the model has enabled me to explore and elucidate certain relationships between form, content, structure, behavior, and change, on the one hand, and material factors on the other.

Maurice Bloch (1975) has also used the related populations of Madagascar to examine the structure or structures that underlie variant manifestations and remain permanent throughout a succession of events, and to explicate relationships between material variation and transformations of structural relations and cultural representations. His comparison of Zafimaniry (a swiddening Tanala offshoot) and Merina illustrates a particular problem that confronts any anthropological analysis of Malagasy populations: sociocultural forms are often so similar that perceiving variation demands that attention be diverted from the shared *forms* themselves toward (1) variable *behavior* motivated by interpretation of similar forms; (2) variable *meanings* of the same forms (in Victor Turner's [1975] words, different signata of the same signans); (3) variable *contexts* into which these forms and associated behavior enter; (4) variable *functions* of the same forms and associated behavior; and (5) variable *modes of articulation* of forms, behavior, and their contexts with other such forms, behavior and contexts.

For example, Bloch (1975, p. 216) finds only minor differences between Merina and Zafimaniry kinship terms as forms. Merina, but not Zafimaniry, use terms recognizing age distinctions among father's siblings. This probably reflects differential inheritance of permanent rice fields in the former but not in the latter. Bloch found, however, that a much more important difference between Merina and Zafimaniry involved variant use of the same terms. For example, Zafimaniry widely extended affinal terms (beyond such primary affinals as parents-in-law) and limited the term *havana* to kin. The endogamous Merina, however, used *havana* for both kin and affinal relations. Bloch relates these differences in "tactical meaning" to contrasts in rural social organization, themselves linked to varying material conditions. Furthermore, he considers how the Zafimaniry horticultural economy, now faced with limits to further expansion in the forest, is being transformed. Research in a village where a change from swiddening to irrigation was well underway led Bloch to suggest that a

> radical transformation is possible quasi-mechanically from the (traditional) Zafimaniry system, without any categories or ethical principles being changed or even challenged but simply by the introduction of permanently held land invested by the labour of previous generations (1975, p. 219).

The radical transformation in social structure involved marriage patterns: a shift from a moiety pattern to the local endogamy of rural agricultural Imerina. This ramified throughout social organization, so that the Zafimaniry were developing demes similar to those of Imerina, "where affinity is played down and where unbridgeable barriers are established between outsiders and insiders" (Bloch 1975, p. 219).

Betsileo state formation, as discussed in chapter 3, provides yet another example of an approach that looks beyond formal similarities. The growth of stratification and state organization in the agricultural east during the eighteenth century was simply without parallel in the west. But again, the similarity of cultural *forms* among Malagasy populations, especially among those as closely related as western and eastern Betsileo, has led certain scholars (e.g., Dubois 1938) and many Betsileo to view Isandra as every bit as much of a state as Lalangina. The two polities shared a common heritage, were exposed to the same regional changes, and had access to an ethnomodel of state organization that was developing and diffusing all over Madagascar during the eighteenth century. A common term, *mpanjaka*, was applied to their heads of government; indeed the term is widely used throughout Madagascar to refer to the head of a territorial group. Furthermore, a similar structural relationship of *mpanjaka* and heads of senior commoner descent groups as territorial and administrative agents was common to the ethnomodels of political organization both in Lalangina and Isandra. But, as in the case of Bloch's analysis of the shared form, but variant meanings, of kinship terms among Merina and Zafimaniry, analysis of meanings, behavior, functions, contexts, and levels of articulation *beneath* the formal similarities of the two Betsileo states is necessary to demonstrate the relationship between material conditions and sociocultural variation.

Consider also chapter 7's discussion and analysis of form and scale, content and functions of Betsileo ceremonials. Several ceremonials are common to Betsileo, Merina, and other Malagasy. Some of them, and the ideology that orients participation, perhaps reflect proto-Malagasy cultural heritage; others have been spread by political conquest, emulation, and diffusion, such as the *famadihana* and the associated Merina-type tomb that have grown in popularity in many areas of the southern highlands since the nineteenth century. However, although ceremonial forms and orienting ideology are shared, considerable explicable variation is revealed when one considers who organizes and sponsors them, who attends, who gives what, when and where they occur, and their overall material context and effects. The same ancestor-oriented ceremonial forms have acquired new and different functions depending on context.

In early Lalangina ceremonial slaughter of cattle was the perquisite of a few, and a redistributive, leveling effect seems likely. Associated in the minds of ordinary Betsileo with their seniors, and therefore carrying prestige, the privilege of sponsoring ceremonials once it was extended to junior common-ers spread quickly down the hierarchy, and the same forms assumed new functions corresponding to a directional change (growth of state organiza-tion). Offerings to the ceremonial sponsor continued to be governed by the principle of reciprocity inherited from prestate organization, but in the con-text of socioeconomic stratification, the expectation of equivalent offerings coupled with the direct relationship between prestige and number of partici-pants actually—in a gradual, positive-feedback relationship—exacerbated socioeconomic contrasts. Variant functioning of the same form can also be demonstrated in synchronic as well as historical variation; for example, by comparing ceremonials in Mahazony and the Ivato region.

Furthermore, the introduction and spread of new forms provide a changed context to which old forms and functions must adapt. Markets, in-troduced by the Merina, spread first to densely populated areas of the Bet-sileo heartland. The diffusion of markets, now universal in Betsileo canton seats, demanded peace and regulatory officials, and markets came to assume several regional and political functions once associated with ceremonials. Markets functioned like ceremonials in regional distribution and gradually provided an alternative form for several other functions; they replaced cere-monials as sites of governmental proclamations. Market days became occa-sions for census taking and extracting levies. Market participation, rather than ceremonial, provided opportunities for peasants to bring grievances to superordinates and granted the latter opportunities to assess conditions and sentiments of their subjects. In a sense, one can interpret events surrounding the death of an Isandran king, which were described in chapter 4, as a meet-ing of functional alternatives: his funerary ceremonial occasioned market ac-tivity. The two alternatives were then one, but gradually ritual regulation of regional distribution has been supplanted by commerce. Chapter 7's com-parison of Mahazony and the Ivato region demonstrates that the shift of these functions from ceremonial to market is still incomplete. The spread of markets reflects population density, and in regions of low density ceremonials are still more important.

We have seen several examples of a directional process whereby the state manipulates and even usurps ancestral forms, using them to identify and control subjects, to maintain and even to enhance resources at its disposal. The Merina used traditional Betsileo funerals and fostered the diffusion of their own tomb type and *famadihana* and thereby promoted poverty, debt, and transfer of Betsileo ancestral estates to Merina ownership. Circumcision became an occasion for censusing and for collecting fees. Betsileo have certainly responded to these changes, as best they could, by reducing the scale of their rituals, by relying more on the market, and by diminishing the frequency of ceremonial events. Such deemphasis of ceremonial has, as one might expect, been most marked in areas of dense population and developed socioeconomic contrasts, where the siphoning effects outweigh regional distribution and leveling.

Continuity as well as change in the face of modified circumstances—the gradual nature of the evolutionary process, and its incorporation of prior structural units and cultural content—is also exemplified in my reconstruction of the origin and growth of Betsileo statelets and nobilities. The prevailing explanation for complex political developments in Madagascar has been that state organization, or at least "the idea of the state," was introduced by foreigners and imposed on Malagasy populations as a radical transformation of their life-styles. However, an evolutionary interpretation seems more plausible. During the seventeenth and eighteenth centuries, southern highlanders organized against raids stimulated by coastal populations. They restructured their sociopolitical organization—on the basis, however, of the demographics of the prior structure—as the most populous descent groups provided defensive coordinators, leaders, and officers. Warfare thereafter became a way of life sustained by Europeans' demand for slaves and the readiness of Malagasy to supply them; successful defenders ultimately became offenders, and success reflected the support, in human bodies, that military leaders could muster. The largest descent groups enjoyed a military advantage and eventually extended their range and became elite members of nascent statelets. A prestate sociopolitical organization that may have been based on autonomous descent groups interlinked by genealogy, marriage, trade, and fictive kinship gradually evolved into one in which minor descent groups and branches were subordinated to major groups. Far from disappearing from the emerging states, descent groups and descent structure have remained vigorous elements of Betsileo sociopolitical structure through the present. Often their internal authority structure has been grafted onto state organization; senior descent branches supplied governors in Lalangina and northern Vohibato, and probably elsewhere.

Throughout the process of state formation, the doctrine of *hasina* linked past and future in the transforming structure, as rulers' authority originated in commoner descent group heads, who in turn could draw on it—as owners or caretakers of the land—through their ancestors from nature itself. Unapparent to actors at any given moment, the *hasina* concept, maintained as form, was undergoing the same progressive differentiation as polity, economy, and the kinship-descent structure. Furthermore, new kinds of political relations were made more acceptable by being rendered in the kin terms of the past. Subject was to sovereign as ancestors to nature, elders to ancestors, parents to grandparents, younger to older brothers, sons to fathers. These continue as the main differential relationships in Betsileo society. In each case junior gives labor, respect, and obedience (or, for the dead, respect and ceremonial attention) and receives blessing, means of livelihood, and fertility. Drawing on this historic and enduring pattern, political superiors were as fathers to their citizens as they appropriated their labor and its products.

The roles of descent group organization and the *hasina* concept in Betsileo sociopolitical transformation offer excellent illustration of Emmanuel Terray's (1972, p. 87) observation that

> An institution is in itself merely a foundation: while apparently unchanged, it may acquire new attributes, sustain new relations, and play very different roles. Today it may be at the service of democratic power and tomorrow provide a basis for the aristocracy.

Local descent groups (estate-centered groups) flourished during the growth of the state in Lalangina. If degree of corporateness of descent groups reflects control of an estate, there is every reason to believe that, as population became less mobile, as estates became more permanent, and as access to estates was increasingly safeguarded by state organization, Betsileo descent groups actually became *more corporate* as the state matured. Changes in inheritance laws in Lalangina actually favored and strengthened corporate, local descent groups. A previous exclusively patrilineal right to inheritance was changed to bilateral inheritance, which kept estates under local descent group control by transferring lands of people without heirs to collateral members.

Although the Merina disturbed the relationship between Betsileo descent groups and their ancestral lands by their policy of establishing colonies of loyal Betsileo in recalcitrant areas, they also used preexisting Betsileo sociopolitical organization—like the rulers of Lalangina before them and the

French after them—by using Betsileo nobles and senior commoners as administrators. By widening perquisites both of noble and senior commoner status, the Merina both reaffirmed and widened gaps in the previous status quo.

These examples help clarify my earlier assertion that consideration of the relationship—the interaction—between prior structure and material conditions is *as essential* to materialist models as is demonstration of analogous sociocultural developments attributable to similar material conditions among unrelated populations. A widespread and enduring misconception about materialist analysis is that it must be limited to evolutionary stages and functional ecological explanations. However, a materialist approach is fully capable of realizing the following program enunciated by Maurice Godelier:

> To go further than a structural morphology means, therefore, trying to account for the forms, functions, modes of articulation and conditions of transformation of the social structure *within the concrete societies*[5] studied by the historian and the anthropologist (Godelier 1972, xli) (italics added).

Julian Steward (1955) warned against separating the analysis of form and function, and of giving priority to either. The examples discussed in this book suggest that it is often necessary to look above, below, and around sociocultural forms if we are to understand relationships between form and function, levels of articulation, sociocultural processing of and responses to material variation, and contexts of variation.

Lévi-Strauss's lesson for materialist anthropology is not direct and obvious. Materialists, who are concerned not just with the universal but with the specific, the limited, and the general, cannot take as their starting point Lévi-Strauss's usual equation of structure with universal features of the human mind. However, his subsidiary uses of the term are perfectly compatible with the materialist view that prior structure constitutes a significant input into the analysis of change. For example, Marvin Harris's (1974) materialist analysis of Melanesian cargo cults constantly refers to a structure that underlies the many manifestations and remains permanent throughout a succession of events (although he does not use these terms.) The events—material modifications affecting cult participants—have included missionization, economic exploitation, and political domination. Underlying the several manifestations is an enduring representation of relations of production and distribution that belongs to societies that recognize and respond appropriately to the achieved status known as "big man." Harris appropriately considers interrelationships of prior structure and material conditions in a concrete setting. The implication of his analysis is clearly that given equivalent material changes, the particular sociocultural response (cargo cults) would not occur if prior structure, including hierarchical ordering of the social structure in question, accommodated status differences greater or lesser than the contrast between the big man and his supporters.

In addition to those dimensions of Betsileo life summarized above, several others can likewise be seen as permutations on a common theme, explicable in terms of similar interactions between prior structure and historical material conditions. A final illustration of the continuing effects of historical patterns helps us understand how present-day Betsileo are dealing with forces of change.

LABOR MOBILIZATION IN A CHANGING ECONOMY

Although labor for certain cooperative tasks in rice cultivation was once recruited from a neighborhood or even a region, villages are today more or less self-contained units of labor conscription. Nevertheless, labor mobilization is more of a problem for some Betsileo than others. Again consider contrasts between Ivato, Ambalabe, and Tanambao. Ivatans offer their labor to covillagers in transplanting and trampling, harvesting and threshing. Western villagers work for easterners only slightly less regularly than for other westerners, and vice versa. Slave descendants give their labor to commoner covillagers, and the latter partially reciprocate. Richer than peasants in Mahazony, Ivatans invest in plows and harrows (only 54 percent of Ivatan rice field owners own neither plow nor harrow, compared to 80 percent in Ambalabe and 91 percent in Tanambao). Accordingly, and because they have more cash to hire rice field laborers, Ivatans invest considerably less of their own labor in rice cultivation than peasants in Mahazony. For the selected tasks in rice cultivation discussed in chapter 5 (cf. table 11), Ivatans invested only 540 person-hours for the average field and 844 person-hours per hectare, as compared to respective figures of 1,021 and 2,042 in Ambalabe and 966 and 2,610 in Tanambao. By the end of the rice cycle, once paddy has been stored in the granary, 86 people will have worked on the average rice field in Ivato, compared to 101 and 74 in Ambalabe and Tanambao respectively (cf. table 27). To understand the relationship between historically determined social relations of production and contemporary patterns of labor conscription, note that in absolute rather than per hectare figures, the average rice field in Ambalabe involves the most work by the most people. Why?

Degree of cooperation in Betsileo village life, including willingness to work for other villagers, reflects prior bases of association. Members of the three senior commoner descent branches localized in Ambalabe have in their historic membership in the same phratry a preexisting basis for cooperation. Members of the two junior commoner, land-poor descent groups of northern Ambalabe also exchange labor. Labor exchange between the junior commoners of northern Ambalabe and the senior commoners of the southern village

TABLE 27

Personnel Working on Specified Tasks in Rice Cultivation, for Average Field in
Ivato, Ambalabe, and Tanambao

Task	No. of Workers (by village)			Correlation (η^2)
	Ivato	Ambalabe	Tanambao	
Plow	1.8	.6	2.5	.02
Hand till	.4	3.2	7.6	.36
Trample	10	11	4.6	.06
Uproot seedlings	3.5	4.6	2.8	.08
Carry seedlings to field	1.8	1.2	1.2	.06
Transplant	9	14.7	11.8	.13
1st weeding	2.6	4.8	4.6	.08
2nd weeding	2	3.5	2.4	.04
Reap	11	9.2	6.9	.10
Carry to threshing floor	15.6	11.4	8.2	.08
Arrange stalks	5.6	3.8	2.6	.18
Stomp pile of stalks	4.9	4.3	2.5	.13
Thresh	12.3	10.8	7	.08
Beat	.9	3.7	2.7	.23
Carry paddy to granary	4.6	14	6.8	.31
Total personnel (sum of averages)	86	101	74.2	
Total personnel per hectare	134	202	201	

is less regular, but still common. The core status of the Tranovondro in Ivato and allegiance of local clients and slave descendants provide a ready-made structure for labor recruitment. However, greater reliance on modern agricultural technology has reduced the need for cooperative labor, and fewer people work on the average rice field than in Ambalabe, and when they work they do not work as long or as hard.

In Tanambao, in contrast to both Ivato and Ambalabe, older peasants with smaller plots work harder and longer for marginally higher yields (per land unit). Table 27's figure for total personnel per hectare in Tanambao (201), however, which is virtually identical to the figure for Ambalabe (202), is very deceptive. The people of Tanambao have considerable difficulty recruiting the 74 people who work in the average rice field. Only one man in Tanambao has a one hectare field, and he certainly does not find 200 people to help him farm it. Tanambao's labor recruitment problem, which is revealed statistically, is very much recognized by the people of the village. Repeated failures of residents of nearby villages and even covillagers to appear after having been "invited" to participate in transplanting and trampling in 1967 led the people of Tanambao to adopt a local labor allocation plan devised by my field assistant, Joseph Rabe. People formed a cooperative association, with male and female managers in charge of making sure that all members appeared for any other member for customary tasks associated with age and sex. A fine was to be extracted by the village elders for failure to report. It remains to be seen how well the plan has worked. However, given little prior basis for solidary association among the people of Tanambao, I would predict its failure.

Access to labor is merely one of several strategic resources that are differentially allocated among the Betsileo. Differential access to labor is seen when we compare villages representing different segments of a socioeconomic continuum; it is also obvious within settlements (which, as Sahlins [1972, p. 74–78] notes is generally characteristic of a "domestic mode of production.") Unequal access to labor is, however, particularly obvious in villages like Ivato where rank, seniority of descent, agnation, and age are determinants of access both to land and to labor. Tuesdaysfather and Rakoto, the wealthiest and seniormost Ivatans, head expanded households that include clients and slave descendants as well as adult children and grandchildren. Even for rice-cultivating tasks that normally devolve on the field owner, these men can also rely on other household heads, including adult sons and grandsons, younger brothers, and clients. Table 28 demonstrates relationships between ages of Ivatan rice field owners and labor in their rice fields. Both mean absolute number of person-hours invested in rice cultivation and person-hours per hectare increase with age of owner. (Tables 49 and 50 reverse dependent and independent variables and demonstrate that owner's age increases as labor expenditure, absolute and per hectare, increases.)

Since throughout the Betsileo heartland transplanting is compressed into two or three months, and since several rice fields and owners draw on the same labor pool, a reliable labor supply is essential. Ivatans recount that their ancestors employed resident astrologers from Tanala country and the south-

TABLE 28

Relationship between Age of Ivatan Rice Field Owners and Labor
in Their Rice Fields

Owner's Age (yrs.)	No.	Mean Total Person-Hours Expended for Owner	Person-Hours per Hectare
30 or younger	7	378	750
31–40	5	440	568
41–50	3	821	1,089
51–60	5	1,086	985
61 or older	6	1,266	1,142
Total	26	782[a]	890[b]

a. $\eta^2 = .56$ (age associated with total person hours)

b. $\eta^2 = .23$ (age associated with person-hours per hectare)

east coast to determine (and probably ritually guarantee) the schedule for transplanting in a given year. Although the contemporary Betsileo I studied had dispensed with this use of astrology, the distinction between irrigated and rainfall-dependent fields does allow staggering in the transplanting schedule, with the irrigated fields transplanted before November rains. In his field notes Joseph Rabe includes a case that illustrates some of the problems encountered by peasants whose access to labor is tenuous. I translate:

> Trampling and transplanting of the rice field of Manga of Ambalabe (a junior commoner) were to have taken place October 18, 1967. Like every year, he had invited relatives and friends to join in the work. He left a few people to start the work while he awaited at least fifty people who had been asked. Seven *vata* (about 200 kilograms) of paddy had been milled for the midday meal; several chickens had been killed; several liters of rum had been purchased, and meat as well. How disappointed he was when the people he had invited didn't show up; what useless expense (especially since the price of chickens had risen during the transplanting season). He had to spread the work over two days with the few people and cattle at his disposal.

Such a situation rarely if ever confronts a senior commoner in Ambalabe or, especially, in Ivato.

Since older, wealthier men control the largest rice holdings and have surest access to labor, the hypothesis is suggested that cooperative labor parties and communal meals occasioned by cultivation of their fields might function to redistribute and level some of their differential wealth. And, as in the case of ceremonials in some parts of the southern highlands, some leveling effect can be perceived. Table 29 plots age of owners against costs of a year's rice cultivation (including outlays on communal meals and wage labor). The linear relationship between age and cost of the average rice field is particularly clear (Pearson's r of .72 is significant at the .01 level of confidence for

TABLE 29

Relationship between Age of Ivatan Rice Field Owners and Cost[a] of Rice Cultivation

Age Group (yrs.)	No.	Mean Total Cost	Mean Cost per Hectare
30 or younger	5	4,000	7,800
31–40	5	8,000	8,600
41–50	2	11,000	19,500
51–60	3	14,300	10,400
61 or older	4	18,750	17,600
Totals and grand means	19	10,500	11,700

a. CFA, includes expenditures for food at communal meals as well as cash payments.

a two-tailed test). Although older Betsileo do have privileged access to land and labor, and have to pay more for it, the contrast in field cost is considerably less significant when age is plotted against field cost *per unit of land* (Pearson's *r* of .43 is barely significant at the .05 level of confidence for a one-tailed test). In part, then, older men spend more on their fields simply because their fields are larger. I conclude therefore that, since their increased product almost makes up for their increased outlays, cooperative labor on their behalf reflects their seniority, age, prestige, and control over a spectrum of strategic resources and serves a very minor leveling function indeed. As in the case of ceremonials in the agricultural east, today's cooperative labor parties, whatever leveling function they may have served in the past, are best interpreted within the context of stratification and differential access to strategic resources.

Although contemporary labor recruitment and cultivation costs are more obviously related to stratification than to redistribution, the organization of labor, like ceremonial organization, has evolved through a variety of contexts; transformations have involved forms, scale, functions, effects, and interrelationships. Commenting on the difference between the contemporary transplanting scene and transplanting-trampling in ancestral times, Ivatans recall work parties in the fields of Karl Fradaysfather and Goodmaker. As they remember it, transplanting in the fields of these important men was a regional affair fully comparable in number of participants (Ivatans drew the analogy) to major contemporary tomb-oriented ceremonials. Descent branch heads came from several villages. Before the adoption of harrowing, old men brought their cattle for trampling, along with younger people to take part in trampling and transplanting. Steers were always slaughtered and served with rice and vegetables. Anyone could offer labor and share in the communal feast. The rice fields of Karl and Goodmaker have been fragmented through inheritance, and although the largest shares, held today by Rakoto and Tuesdaysfather, still attract the largest labor parties, the scale of the cooperative aspects of rice cultivation has diminished considerably, and labor even in these fields has become mostly a village affair.

I believe, however, that, as was the case with ceremonials, the correlation between access to cooperative labor and wealth once functioned as a leveling mechanism, and that the redistributive function has declined gradually but directly with the growth of stratification and the state. For example, I believe that if one did a detailed study of labor allocation within Ambalabe—a village located in a region where a leveling effect is still attached to ceremonial—one would find that personnel, person-hours, and cultivation costs per hectare were greatest for older, wealthier, senior commoner villagers. Unfortunately, my data from Ambalabe are not detailed enough to demonstrate this.[6] However, other kinds of evidence do tend to confirm the interpretation of cooperative labor as functioning as part of an adaptive system that also includes ceremonial.

Consider table 30, which calendrically arranges frequency of ceremonial attendance, actual ceremonial events, number of rice fields being worked, and harvests of the major sources of vegetal protein other than rice: beans, peanuts, and cape peas. Note that people attend ceremonials most frequently from June through September, a postharvest period in which granaries are full. Note, too, that with beef and rice widely available at ceremonials, the vegetal protein crops are no longer being harvested. The transplanting season then begins as the ceremonial season ends, and continues the tradition of communal feasting, though in a different context. Through January and February, Ivatans are weeding their rice fields; granary stores are, for poorer peasants, almost exhausted; communal feasting has ended until the harvest, and people are contracting debts. In these months peasants harvest most of their beans and, until the harvest season is over, other sources of vegetal protein. Remember, too, that Betsileo assert that more people, especially the old, die during the rainy months of January and February than at other times of the year. Their funerals—regional events—then provide renewed opportunities for communal feasting that can help to tide poorer peasants through the harvest.

Like the organization of ceremonials, the customary assignment of cooperative tasks on the basis of age and sex and the obligation to work for elders are sanctified with reference to ancestral ways. Concern about maintaining tradition and propitiating ancestors dominates the cognized model that supports recurrent aspects of Betsileo behavior and their calendrical spacing. It would be incorrect and foolish to assert that Betsileo attend ceremonials and lend their labor to others just to keep their stomachs full. An apter inter-

TABLE 30

Ceremonials, Major Rice Cultivation Tasks, and Harvests of Vegetal Protein Crops, by Month, 1967

| | *Month* | | | | | | | | | | | |
	1	*2*	*3*	*4*	*5*	*6*	*7*	*8*	*9*	*10*	*11*	*12*
Three village sample, ceremonial attendance	1	2	3	1	4	14	27	78	32	8	10	2
Actual ceremonials, Ivato	1	1	0	0	1	2	6	7	3	3	1	1
Number of rice fields being worked, Ivato	17	9	24	55	32	6	7	14	40	35	53	45
No. bean harvests, Ivato	4	9	5	2	0	0	0	0	0	0	0	0
No. peanut harvests, Ivato	0	3	3	4	1	0	0	0	0	0	0	0
No. cape pea harvests, Ivato	0	1	4	4	4	0	0	0	0	0	0	0

pretation would see cooperative labor and ceremonial as long-established aspects of Betsileo life that can and have functioned through a variety of contexts, and that provide a cultural framework that people can work through for several ends, including, but not limited to, nutrition, debt avoidance, kinship obligations, and desire for prestige. Although people can, indeed must, use institutions provided by their culture, and thus act in a variety of ways, the institutions, their functions and effects, and their relationships to other institutions evolve in reacting or adapting to a larger context. As in previous centuries, events beyond the central highlands of Madagascar, and beyond Madagascar itself, are still altering the context of Betsileo adaptation; they are being met by changes in Betsileo life.

Consider the increasing incorporation of Betsileo peasants within a monetary and market economy. Some of the ways in which money and markets have encroached on ceremonial's traditional role in regional distribution and have modified forms, frequency, scale, and functions of ceremonials have been examined. Consider now certain effects of cash and markets on the organization of labor. We have seen that fewer people assemble for cooperative labor in rice cultivation than in the past. Plows are replacing hand tillers; harrows are rendering tramplers and their cattle herds obsolete. In the past, owners of large fields could rely on a variety of social organizational principles, including descent, political role, marriage, fictive kinship, and regional reputation, not to mention slavery, to draw the labor they needed for their fields.

Increasing use of plows, harrows, and chemical fertilizers, along with modern nursery care, row transplanting, and more thorough weeding, have reduced labor requirements and increased yields per unit of land and labor. Augmented productivity means greater income, which means that Ivatans and others like them can better afford to hire labor for their fields. Concomitantly, people in and around Ivato are coming to expect payment when they offer their labor to covillagers and neighbors. The Ivatan women who transplant in rows demand cash payment for their work, but a traditional transplanting job in the same village is still rewarded with a communal meal. However, as cash payment becomes more and more common, people are not as willing as formerly to take on jobs with only food as a reward, and this creates ever greater difficulty in recruiting free labor. Correspondingly, more and more tasks that formerly involved at least a modicum of cooperation are now devolving on the owner and members of his household. In view of these trends, and with estate fragmentation and village population growth, rice agriculture loses its regional significance, and except for a few wealthy and prestigious men, is no longer even a neighborhood affair.

Contrasts between Ivato, Ambalabe, and Tanambao in labor organization, technology, and costs of rice cultivation are explicable in terms of the same kinds of historically-determined socioeconomic variables that explain other differences between the three villages. The varying historic fortunes of the three villages also enable us to predict, for other villages of these types, manner of contemporary involvement and articulation with the national economy and government, along with receptiveness to aspects of modern life and readiness to change. No law of evolutionary potential (Service 1960), no privilege of historic backwardness appears to operate for the contemporary Betsileo. Ivatans, favored in the past, remain favored in the present. Many Ivatans can, if they wish, pay cash for a variety of goods and services because they control more land, and their land is—or they can afford to make it—more productive. One source of cash is sale of crops including rice, and here a contrast between the three villages is instructive. Compared to only 31 percent of the rice field owners of Ambalabe, 46 percent in Ivato sold rice. In Tanambao, but for different reasons, even more people (52 percent) sold rice. Much of the rice sold in Ivato was surplus beyond household subsistence needs, whereas Tanambao's impoverished peasants were being forced to sell rice badly needed for their own consumption in order to pay a head tax, which has since been abolished.

Ivato's senior commoners will continue to prosper for other reasons. Although more rice fields in Ivato than in the Mahazony villages have uncertain, rainfall-dependent water supplies, senior commoners have more certain access to *labor*, the compensatory effect of which can be determined only after a long-term study. Furthermore, just as Ivatans try to limit their obligations by closely calculating their networks of personal relations, they also invest in labor-saving technology and are willing to reduce size of cooperative labor parties because they recognize the potential or actual leveling, draining effect, added inefficiency, and problems in recruiting and managing large groups of laborers.

HISTORICAL PATTERNS AND THE WORLD OUTSIDE

The historically-granted advantages attached to Ivatans' senior commoner status emerge not simply in their participation in the national economy, but in all aspects of contemporary life. Because they live in a densely populated area and because of prior regional links, they have greater access to agents of the outside world, including an agricultural advisor, a school, a priest, nearer markets and government officials, better access to transportation, hospitals, and maternity wards.

Ivatans not only have more chance to confront, but are also more willing to confront, national life. Perhaps, in retrospect, the warmth and openness of our initial reception by Ivatans are not solely attributable to our sponsor; several encounters I observed when with Ivatans convinced me that they are more willing than most other rural Betsileo to deal with outsiders. After all, Ivatans have a history of benefiting from their associations with outsiders. A school is locally available, and Ivatans send their children there at age six. Almost all Ivatan males, and at least half of the women, are literate, and some have partial high school educations. A few speak good French. With better educations and greater exposure to alien viewpoints, Ivatans now cognize many effects of Betsileo customs that other rural Betsileo still ignore. A few Ivatans informed me about the nutritional importance of ceremonials, admitted that contribution to construction costs of several tombs might be a bad investment, and complained about having to feed too many agricultural workers.

To illustrate how Ivatans and many other senior commoners have continued historic Betsileo trends in adapting to twentieth-century life, the case of our sponsor can be examined. Oldest son of three generations of oldest sons, our sponsor grew up in the presence of his grandfather's and father's regional prominence (both were officials of the French administration), and was regularly indoctrinated with tales of the successes of his great-grandfather Karl Fridaysfather. He and his slightly younger brother, Tuesdaysfather, were both enrolled in the village school, but their parents soon saw that Tuesdaysfather had no real interest in schoolwork, and groomed him as eventual manager of the local estate. Our sponsor's grandfather (Goodmaker), father (Vernon), and eventually paternal uncle (Joseph) concentrated their resources on his education, supporting medical training in France. In middle age he became a physician in a Betsileo subprefecture seat and entered national politics. A legislative career in Tananarive culminated in a cabinet appointment.

Once established as a physician, our sponsor began to do for other members of his minimal descent group what earlier members had done for him. He helped pay for the education of his youngest brother, who, in the Betsileo view, stands as a son to him. Most of his own children proved interested and talented in school and now include a trained midwife, a "doctor" with partial medical training, a government schoolteacher, and a well-placed bureaucrat. Our sponsor provides an exaggerated case of the benefits that accrue to peasants as a result of a relative's national success. Most senior commoner villages lack patrons who pay their taxes, arrange appointments of agricultural advisors, bring piped water into the village, and buy modern agricultural equipment for village use. Typically, however, the external relative does provide food and lodging on a temporary basis, more permanent lodging for a child in school, loans and gifts, help finding a job, and advice and assistance on matters linking peasants to the outside world.

Our sponsor, then, is a recent illustration of Ivatans' ability to capitalize on changes in government and modifications in relationships between Betsileo villagers and outsiders. He, during the French and Malagasy administrations, and his father and grandfather under colonial rule, did what his great-grandfather had done in Merina days and they and their village (need I add) now provide the main characters in a book about the Betsileo.

During the seventeenth century, a sparser southern highlands population with a more homogeneous sociopolitical organization tried to maintain itself as its relationships with other Malagasy began to change. Events beyond the control of these pastorally oriented horticulturalists initiated a rapid change from tribal to stratified society, from acephaly to state organization. A set of common externally imposed circumstances reached and transformed populations coping with a variety of contrasting environments. Parallel changes reflected the common regional variables; diversification followed contrasts in local ecosystems. In Lalangina, abundant rainfall supported an agricultural economy and allowed the major Betsileo state to develop; to centralize progressively, to differentiate sociopolitical systems and subsystems, and to stratify. A comparable development, including an agricultural economy, through irrigation, came to the south and west only a century later with Merina conquest and pacification and ensuing French colonial rule. Socioeconomic differences accompanying stratification meant that life-styles and behavior patterns of Betsileo came to vary, and common institutions came to benefit and to be used differently by Betsileo of different rank. Such contrasts pervade Betsileo life today.

In the face of change, through pre-Merina conquest and reconquest, through Merina annexation and rule, through French colonialism, Betsileo have modified, borrowed, created, varied, and evolved. In the context of the Malagasy Republic, forms and variations of the past continue to affect, indeed to orient, contemporary behavior. On a small scale, events in the southern highlands of Madagascar mirror events that have played out on the whole island. In their historical and contemporary variation, in their modification of prior forms in meeting changed circumstances, and in their tenacity in preserving the essentials of an ancestral cultural plan, their *fombandrazana*, in the face of change, the Betsileo illuminate problems, solutions, and obstacles common to a large segment of humanity—tribal populations pushed rapidly from a world governed by kinship and reciprocity toward one of political regulation, inequality, and exploitation. Yet, curiously, the rapidity of their conversion may be their salvation. Unlike populations who have directly undergone the long, gradual, historical growth of capitalism and industrialism, the Betsileo, like many other populations of Madagascar, continental Africa, and Oceania, face the late twentieth century with communal, tribal forms, which, though altered, are too close to forget and too vital to eradicate.

APPENDIX

TABLE 31
Socioeconomic Contrasts in Ivato, Selected Variables

Identification Number[a]	Rice Area Cultivated (has.)	Age	Total White Rice (kg.) Produced 1967 harvest	Total White Rice Consumed in Household Annually (kg.)	Surplus or Deficit (kg.)	Production/ Consumption Ratio	Name (Fictitious)	Social Identity[b]
235	2.58	61	5,881	1,686	4,195	348.8	Etienne	E
194	3.16	55	5,209	2,433	2,776	214.1	Rakoto	E
218	2.5	63	4,075	730	3,345	558.2	Tuesdaysfather	E
201	1.2	53	2,357	1,217	1,140	193.7	Zafy	W
272	1.05	38	2,306	1,095	1,211	210.6	Jean-Paul	W
232	1.53	30	2,173	973	1,200	223.3	Jules	E
311	1.12	75	2,153	2,433	−280	88.5	Rangahy	X
240	1.11	65	2,114	852	1,262	248.1	Marcel	E
215	1.15	49	1,864	1,460	404	127.7	Rasabotsilahy	E
209	0.95	51	1,711	852	859	200.8	Goodsfather	E
291	1.99	51	1,634	730	904	223.8	Monsieur Charles	W
243	1.47	40	1,326	1,400	−74	94.7	Rady	E
255	0.99	50	961	973	−12	98.8	Jean Rainibia	E
257	0.65	67	923	973	−50	94.9	Rainizana	C
275	0.73	28	538	1,217	−679	44.2	François	W
189	0.5	43	538	2,433	−1,895	22.1	The Sergeant	S
250	.33	61	480	1,460	−980	32.9	Ramaria	XE
228	.84	40	461	608	−147	75.8	Antoine	E
294	.28	51	423	973	−550	43.5	Tsimba	W
282	.85	51	384	730	−346	52.6	Donné Rainiboto	XW
185	.5	31	346	852	−506	40.6	Jean de la Croix	S
187	.19	30	231	608	−377	40.0	Zandry	S

a. See also genealogy in figure 4 and maps 4 and 5.
b. E = Eastern Ivato, Tranovondro
   W = Western Ivato, Tranovondro
   S = Slave Descendant
   C = Client
   X = Hamlet

TABLE 32

Cultivated Land Use in Ivato (1967) Compared to Subprefectures of Fianarantsoa
and Ambalvao

Ivato	
Population of Ivato	175
No. rice field owners	31
Mean rice holding per owner	1.1 ha.
Total area of rice fields cultivated	34.2 ha.
Per capita rice holding	0.2 ha.
Total secondary food crop area	45.1 ha.
Per capita secondary food crop holding	0.26 ha.
Total cultivated food crop area per capita	0.46 ha.
Percent of total in rice fields	43.5%
Fianarantsoa	
Per capita rice holding	0.22 ha.
Per capita secondary crop holding	0.2 ha.
Total cultivated area per capita	0.43 ha.
Percent cultivated land in rice	53.0%
Ratio of cattle to people	0.5
Ambalavao	
Per capita rice holding	0.23 ha.
Per capita secondary crop holding	0.1 ha.
Total cultivated area per capita	0.34 ha.
Percent cultivated land in rice	67.0%
Ratio of cattle to people	1.6

Sources: Fianarantsoa and Ambalavao, government records for 1966; Ivato, author's field notes.

TABLE 33

Labor Expenditure in an Ivato Rice Field, 1966–67

Task	Performed By	Month or Date	Person-Hours	Man-Hours	Woman-Hours
Production					
Manahalaka	young men	May-June	24	24	0
Mitatatra; hydraulic system maintenance	young men	May-June	36	36	0
Manamaina, manevina; drainage	young men	May-June	12	12	0
Miasa; till or first plow	men	September 9–17	70	70	0
Manala songo; till with spade areas of rice field that cannot be reached with plow	young men	September 9–17	24	24	0
Pregerminate paddy seed	men	September	1	1	0
Prepare nursery	men	September 22	12.5	12.5	0
Seed nursery	men	September 22	6	6	0
Guard from birds	owner (man)	September 23–24	4	4	0
Transport and apply dung, chemical fertilizer	young men	October 26–28	48	48	0
Manatsaka; remove weeds from bunds	young men	November 5–7	36	36	0
Manampoka; second plowing	men	November 5–7	32	32	0
Mamona evina; cover over drainage furrows in rice fields and work corners if plowed	young men	November 5–7	16	16	0
Manao laheritra; harrow and spade	men	November 12–13, 16–17	30.5	30.5	0
Trample flooded field	young men	November 18	100	100	0
Mananjary tany; break up remaining clumps with spade	older men	November 18–19	52	52	0
Transplant; pull out seedlings from nursery	women	November 18–19	48	0	48
Transplant; carry seedlings to rice fields	young men	November 18–19	10	10	0
Transplant; place seedlings in soil	adult women	November 18–19	108	0	108
Transplant; hold string for row planting	men	November 18–19	18	18	0
First weeding	men and women	December 9–13	121	60.5	60.5
Second weeding	men and women	December 28–30	132	66	66
Harvest; reaping	young men	March 30	104	104	0
Harvest; carry rice on straw to threshing floor	young women	March 30–31	105	0	105
Harvest; arrange straw and place in pile	adult women	March 30–31	83	0	0

TABLE 33—*continued*

Task	Performed By	Month or Date	Person-Hours	Man-Hours	Woman-Hours
Stomp on stack	old men and women	March 30–31	133	56.5	56.5
Prepare threshing floor	men	March 30–31	5	5	0
Thresh	young men	April 3	36	36	0
Beat to remove remaining grains	older men	April 3	36	36	0
Dry paddy	men	April 4–16	28	28	0
Winnow	men and women	April 4–16	120	60	60
Dry winnowed paddy	men	April 4–16	10	10	0
Transport to and arrange in granary	men and women	April 4–16	32	16	16
Subtotal			1,613	1,010	603
			(950/ha)	(62.2%)	(37.4%)
Preparation for Consumption					
Remove and dry paddy prior to pounding (husking) as needed	women		182	0	182
Pound	woman and children		550	0	550
Total			2,345	1,010	1,335
				(43.1%)	(56.9%)

Note: The rice field examined is the principal field of Rakoto, a prominent, fifty-five-year-old member of Ivato's eastern Tranovondro branch. The field is located only 300 meters from Rakoto's home; the soil type is *fotaka*, and Rakoto chose *vary lahy* as his rice variety when he seeded his nursery in 1966. A great deal of the field repair, including hydraulic maintenance and field preparation, was done by Rakoto's twenty-five-year-old son, twenty-five-year-old stepson, and two hired hands. The field's area is 1.7 hectares. The figures given are actual person-hours expended; they have not been adjusted to a per hectare basis.

TABLE 34

Labor Expended in an Ivato Rice Field, by Owner, Other Males, and Females

Task	Total Person-Hours	Owner Hours	Other than Owner	
			Man Hours	Woman Hours
Production				
Repair bunds	0	0	0	0
Maintain hydraulic system	22	22	0	0
Drain	11	11	0	0
Till or first plowing	137	111	26	0
Till with spade areas of rice field that cannot be reached with plow	33	33	0	0
Prepare nursery	3	3	0	0
Pregerminate paddy seed	0	0	0	0
Seed nursery	.5	.5	0	0
Guard from birds	0	0	0	0
Fertilize	0	0	0	0
Remove weeds from bunds	19	19	0	0
Second plowing	57	19	38	0
Cover over drainage furrows in rice field and work corners if plowed	0	0	0	0
Harrow and spade	57	19	38	0
Trample flooded field	54	4.5	49.5	0
Break up remaining clumps with spade	14	0	14	0
Transplant; pull out seedlings from nursery	26	6.5	0	19.5
Transplant; carry seedlings to rice field	8.5	0	0	8.5
Transplant; place seedlings in soil	68	0	0	68
Hold string for row planting	0	0	0	0
First weeding	129.5	38	60	31.5
Second weeding	88	0	44	44
Additional weeding	0	0	0	0
Harvest; reap	52	6.5	45.5	0
Harvest; carry rice on straw to threshing floor	75	0	0	75
Harvest; arrange straw and place in pile	30	0	0	30
Harvest; stomp on stack	30	0	7.5	22.5
Prepare threshing floor	2	2	0	0
Thresh	55	5.5	49.5	0
Beat to remove remaining grains	11	0	11	0
Dry paddy	16	10	0	6
Winnow	68	34	0	34
Dry winnowed paddy	8	5	0	3
Transport to and arrange in granary	30	7.5	15	7.5
Subtotal	1,104.5	357 + 398 = 755		349.5
		68.4% male labor		31.6%

TABLE 34—*continued*

Task	Total Person-Hours	Owner Hours	Other than Owner	
			Man Hours	Woman Hours
Preparation for Consumption				
Remove and dry paddy prior to pounding (husking) as needed	182	0	0	182
Pound	300	0	0	300
Total	1,586.5	357 + 398 = 755		831.5
		47.6% male labor		52.4%

Note: The rice field considered belongs to Jules, a thirty-year-old eastern villager. It is the more productive of his two fields. Although located 4 ½ kilometers from his home, it is the field which Jules worked more intensively. Its yield exceeded that of his nearer field absolutely and rivaled the closer field on a per hectare basis. The soil type is *fotaka*, and Jules planted *vary lava* in 1966. At harvest time in 1967, Jules's paddy production from this field was approximately 2,250 kilograms. Since the field's actual area is one hectare, these are both absolute and per hectare figures. Note that because of the field's distance, Jules neglected in 1966–67 some of the tasks carried out in Rakoto's field examined in table 33. Unlike Rakoto, Jules, whose oldest son was only four in 1967, invested a considerable amount of his own time and labor in rice cultivation.

TABLE 35

Population of Ivato, Ambalabe, and Tanambao by Sex, Dependence, and Age

	Population by Village		
	Ivato	Ambalabe	Tanambao
Sex			
No. males	88	114	39
% males	50.3	52.5	47.6
No. females	87	103	43
% females	49.7	47.5	52.4
Dependence			
No. adults	84	131	44
% adults	48.0	60.4[a]	53.7
No. children	91	86	38
% children	52.0	39.6[a]	46.3
Age (yrs.)			
Mean age	22.0	n.d.	24.6
Age range	0–83	n.d.	1–97
Median age	13	n.d.	16
Sample size for age data	167	n.d.	74
Summary			
Men	40	67	21
Women	44	64	23
Boys	48	47	18
Girls	43	39	20
Total population	175	217	82

a. Age data were not obtained for most of the population of Ambalabe. The classification of population into adult and children was crude and is not comparable to the classification in Ivato and Tanambao, where all those fifteen years old and above were reckoned as adults.

TABLE 36

Comparison of Rice Fields with *Fotaka* (Mud-Clay) versus *Fasika/Baibo* (Sandy) Soil for Selected Variables

	No. Fields in Sample	Mean Size (ha.)	Mean Paddy Yield, 1967 (kg./ha.)	Mean Cost of Cultivation (CFA)	Mean Person-Hours/Ha.[a]	Mean No. Personnel Involved
Fields with *fotaka* **soils**						
Ivato	17	.65	2,432	12,833	822	94
Ambalabe	15	.47	1,962	14,357	2,207	86
Tanambao	16	.31	2,339	17,643	2,845	70
Fields with *fasika/baibo* **soils**						
Ivato	17	.64	2,054	8,636	668	86
Ambalabe	5	.35	2,154	12,750	1,194	82
Tanambao	2	.38	—[b]	—[b]	—[b]	52

a. Selected tasks as in table 11.
b. Sample too small for meaningful data.

TABLE 37

Association of Soil Type and Rice Variety Harvested 1967, Combined Sample Data from Three Villages

| | Rice Variety (by field) | | | | | | | | | | | |
| Soil Type | Angika | | Lava | | Lahy | | Ambalalava | | Others and Combinations | | Soil Type Total | |
	No.	%	No.	%	No.	%	No.	%	No.	%	No.	%
Fasika/baibo	8	72.7	5	21.7	5	12.8	1	14.3	4	22.2	23	23.5
Fotaka	0		11	47.8	27	69.2	3	42.9	8	44.4	49	50.0
Others and combinations	3	27.3	7	30.4	7	17.9	3	42.9	6	33.3	26	26.5
Rice variety total	11	100.0	23	99.9	39	99.9	7	100.1	18	99.9	98	100.0
Percentage of total rice crop	11.2		23.5		39.8		7.1		18.4		100.0	

Note: Vary is the Betsileo term for rice. Vary lahy is the ancestral variety, and predominates in Ambalabe, Tanambao, and in the combined three village sample. It is usually planted on the preferred fotaka soil. More recently introduced, long-grained vary lava, has become Ivato's most common rice type, but is ignored totally in Ambalabe and planted in only four of Tanambao's twenty-five sampled fields. A versatile rice, lava spans all soil types. Angika, the lowest yielding, least labor-intensive variety, is usually planted in sandy, baibo, soils, never in esteemed fotaka fields.

TABLE 38

Association of Soil Type and Rice Variety Harvested 1967, by Village

	Rice Variety (by field)					
Soil Type	Angika	Lava	Lahy	Ambalalava	Others and Combinations	Total
Ivato						
Fasika/baibo	7	5	3	0	2	17
Fotaka	0	9	8	0	1	18
Others and combinations	3	5	0	0	0	8
Total	10	19	11	0	3	43
Ambalabe						
Fasika/baibo	1	0	1	1	1	4
Fotaka	0	0	10	3	2	15
Others and combinations	0	0	6	3	2	11
Total	1	0	17	7	5	30
Tanambao						
Fasika/baibo	0	0	1	0	1	2
Fotaka	0	2	9	0	5	16
Others and combinations	0	2	1	0	4	7
Total	0	4	11	0	10	25

TABLE 39

Comparison of Rice Varieties Harvested in 1967 for Selected Variables, by Village

Rice Variety	No. Fields in Sample	Mean Size (ha.)	Mean Paddy Yield, 1967 (kg./ha.)	Mean Cost of Cultivation (CFA)	Mean Person-Hours/Ha.[a]	Mean No. Personnel Involved
Lahy						
Ivato	12 (41 total)	.54	2,520	14,000	940	100
Ambalabe	19 (29)	.53	2,580	16,700	2,470	120
Tanambao	11 (20)	.35	2,040	12,100	2,780	60
Lava						
Ivato	19	.66	2,220	13,700	730	90
Ambalabe	0	0	0	0	0	0
Tanambao	4	.35	2,950	25,200	3,140	90
Angika						
Ivato	10	.71	1,620	7,600	520	90
Ambalabe	1	.25	1,610	7,000	620	30
Tanambao	0	0	0	0	0	0

a. For selected tasks in table 11.

TABLE 40

Annual Person-Hours Expended per Hectare in Selected Tasks for Average (Mean) Rice Field

| | *Village* | | | | | |
| | *Ivato* | | *Ambalabe* | | *Tanambao* | |
Task	*No.*	*%*	*No.*	*%*	*No.*	*%*
Seeding	2	0.2	6	0.3	8	0.3
Tillage						
Hand till	12	1.4	298	14.6	354	13.6
Plow	39	4.6	24	1.2	38	1.5
Subtotal	51	6.0	322	15.8	392	15.1
Transplanting						
Trample	61	7.2	104	5.1	78	3.0
Uproot seedlings	22	2.6	60	2.9	51	2.0
Transport seedlings to field	14	1.7	16	0.8	19	0.7
Transplant	100	11.8	184	9.0	219	8.4
Subtotal	197	23.3	364	17.8	367	14.1
Weeding						
No. 1	147	17.4	604	29.6	859	32.9
No. 2	91	10.8	292	14.3	481	18.4
Subtotal	238	28.2	896	43.9	1,340	51.3
Harvest						
Reap	53	6.3	112	5.5	127	4.9
Carry to threshing floor	145	17.2	144	7.0	157	6.0
Arrange stalks in pile	45	5.3	46	2.2	54	2.1
Stomp pile of stalks	41	4.9	54	2.6	49	1.9
Subtotal	284	33.7	356	17.3	387	14.9
Threshing						
Thresh	41	4.9	72	3.5	81	3.1
Beat	31	3.7	26	1.3	35	1.3
Subtotal	72	8.6	98	4.8	116	4.4
Total	840	99.8	2,040	99.6	2,610	99.8

TABLE 41
Personnel Involved in Selected Tasks for Average (Mean) Rice Field

	Village		
Task	Ivato	Ambalabe	Tanambao
Transplanting			
Tramplers			
Mean no.	11	12	8
Minimum no.	1	2	2
Maximum no.	40	54	18
Uprooters			
Mean no.	4	5	3
Minimum no.	1	1	1
Maximum no.	14	12	5
Transporters			
Mean no.	2	1	1
Minimum no.	1	1	1
Maxmimum no.	10	2	3
Transplanters			
Mean no.	9	15	11
Minimum no.	2	2	2
Maximum no.	25	35	25
Weeding			
No. 1			
Mean no.	3	5	5
Minimum no.	1	1	1
Maximum no.	10	20	18
No. 2			
Mean no.	3	6	4
Minimum no.	1	1	2
Maximum no.	7	16	10
Harvest			
Reapers			
Mean no.	11	10	7
Minimum no.	1	1	1
Maximum no.	25	25	15
Carriers			
Mean no.	16	12	9
Minimum no.	1	1	1
Maximum no.	60	30	30
Arrangers			
Mean no.	6	4	3
Minimum no.	2	1	1
Maximum no.	15	8	6
Stompers			
Mean no.	5	5	3
Minimum no.	1	1	1
Maximum no.	12	12	6

TABLE 41—*continued*

Task	Village		
	Ivato	*Ambalabe*	*Tanambao*
Threshing			
Threshers			
Mean no.	12	11	7
Minimum no.	1	1	1
Maximum no.	40	35	12
Beaters			
Mean no.	10	4	3
Minimum no.	2	1	1
Maximum no.	30	12	7
Total mean no. of personnel[a]	94	100	75

a. Includes nursery preparation, seeding, tillage, and all aspects of transplanting, weeding, harvesting, and threshing.

TABLE 42

Annual Person-Hours Expended in Selected Tasks for Average (Mean) Rice Field

Task	Village		
	Ivato	*Ambalabe*	*Tanambao*
Seeding	1	3	3
Tillage			
Hand till	8	149	131
Plow	25	12	14
Subtotal	33	161	145
Transplanting			
Trample	39	52	29
Uproot seedlings	14	30	19
Transport seedlings to field	9	8	7
Transplant	64	92	81
Subtotal	126	182	136
Weeding			
No. 1	94	302	318
No. 2	58	146	178
Subtotal	152	448	496
Harvest			
Reap	34	56	47
Carry to threshing floor	93	72	58
Arrange stalks in pile	29	23	20
Stomp pile of stalks	26	27	18
Subtotal	182	178	143
Threshing:			
Thresh	26	36	30
Beat	20	13	13
Subtotal	46	49	43
Total	540	1,021	966
Mean field size (ha.)	0.64	0.5	0.37

TABLE 43

Comparison of Rice Fields with Perpetual versus Interrupted Water Supplies in Ivato and Ambalabe for Selected Variables

	No. Fields in Sample	Mean Size (ha.)	Mean Paddy Yield, 1967 (kg./ha.)	Mean Cost of Cultivation (CFA)	Mean Person-Hours per Ha.[a]	Mean No. Personnel Involved
Perpetual water source						
Ivato	26	0.62	2,183	12,895	728	88
Ambalabe	20	0.48	2,053	17,000	2,101	108
Interrupted water source						
Ivato	17	0.66	2,208	11,167	867	105
Ambalabe	13	0.54	2,057	11,700	1,799	85

a. Selected tasks as in table 11.

TABLE 44

Type of Kin Relationship Mentioned, according to Sex, in Combined Three Village Sample

	Male		Female		Total	
	No.	%	No.	%	No.	%
Parent or other lineal from there	107	35.3	72	37.7	179	36.2
Collateral	102	33.7	61	31.9	163	33.0
Ego's kinswoman married there	61	20.1	54	28.3	115	23.3
Relative of spouse or spouse of relative	21	6.9	2	1.0	23	4.7
Fictive	9	3.0	0	0	9	1.8
Adoptive	1	0.3	2	1.0	3	0.6
Other	2	0.6	0	0	2	0.4
Total	303	99.9	191	99.9	494	100.0
Percentage of total sample		61.3		38.7		100.0

Note: Lambda, C = 0.005, R = 0.000, RC = 0.002.

TABLE 45

Type of Kin Relationship Mentioned, according to Village

	Ivato		Ambalabe		Tanambao		Total	
	No.	%	No.	%	No.	%	No.	%
Parent or other lineal from there	176	41.7	1	2.6	2	5.9	179	36.2
Collateral	120	28.4	21	55.3	22	64.7	163	33.0
Ego's kinswoman married there	94	22.3	12	31.6	9	26.5	115	23.3
Relative of spouse or spouse or relative	19	4.5	4	10.5	0	0	23	4.7
Fictive	8	1.9	0	0	1	2.9	9	1.8
Adoptive	3	0.7	0	0	0	0	3	0.6
Other	2	0.4	0	0	0	0	2	0.4
Total	422	99.9	38	100.0	34	100.0	494	100.0
Percentage of total sample		85.4		6.9		7.7		100

Note: Lambda, C = 0.000, R = 0.127, RC = 0.103.

TABLE 46

Fertility of Adult Women in Ivato

Childbearing Histories	Sample Size	Mean	Mode	Median	Range	Total
Living children	26	4.3	3	3.5	0–12	110
Living males	26	2.2	1	2	0–7	56
Living females	26	2.1	2	2	0–7	54
Dead children	25	1.5	0	1	0–6	37
Dead males	24	0.7	0	0	0–3	16
Dead females	24	0.9	0	1	0–5	21
Childless women	26	—	—	—	—	3
Boyless women	26	—	—	—	—	4
Girless women	26	—	—	—	—	6

Note: There are forty-four women aged eighteen or older in Ivato; twenty-six of them are or have been married, and thus enter the sample. I gathered information from all twenty-six married women in Ivato, with ages ranging from twenty-two to eighty-three, on their childbearing histories.

TABLE 47

Secondary Crop Cultivation in Ivato

(1966–67 data, samples from interview schedules)

Secondary Crop	*No. of Planters Cultivating Secondary Crop (by month)*												*Total No. Sampled Planters*
	6	7	8	9	10	11	12	1	2	3	4	5	
Manioc planted	0	1	4	5	1	0	0	0	1	1	0	0	13
Sweet potatoes planted	1	1	1	0	0	0	*3*	3	2	1	1	0	13
Beans planted	0	0	5	1	0	*7*	2	0	0	1	0	0	16
Harvested	0	1	0	0	0	1	1	0	1	2	1	2	
Cape peas planted	0	0	0	0	0	*4*	1	0	0	1	0	0	6
Harvested	0	0	0	1	0	0	0	0	0	0	2	1	
Peanuts planted	0	0	0	0	0	*6*	1	0	0	0	0	0	7
Harvested	0	0	0	0	0	0	0	0	1	1	2	0	
Corn planted	0	1	2	0	0	*10*	2	0	0	0	0	0	15
Harvested	0	0	0	0	0	0	1	0	4	3	2	0	
Taro planted	2	1	1	0	0	0	0	1	0	0	0	0	5
Tobacco planted	0	0	0	0	1	1	2	4	*5*	2	0	0	15
Harvested	1	1	0	0	1	0	0	0	1	1	0	*5*	

Note: Modal months in italics.

TABLE 48

Fostering by Ivatans

	Mean	*Mode*	*Median*	*Range*
No. males fostered[a]	0.8	0	0	0–10
No. females fostered	0.7	0	0	0–4
Total no. fostered	1.6	0	1	0–11
No. informant's living children	4.2	3	3	0–12
No. informant's children residing in informant's household	0.9	0	0	0–4

a. From a sample of 47 adult Ivatans.

TABLE 49

Relationship[a] between Total Person-Hours Expended on behalf of Ivatan Rice Field Owners and Age of Owner

Total Person Hours[b]	No.	Mean Age
100–399	8	33
400–699	5	42
700–999	6	48
1000–1299	3	51
1300+	4	60.5
Total	26	44.5

a. $\eta^2 = 0.47$
b. Includes all sampled fields for each owner.

TABLE 50

Relationship[a] between Person-Hours Expended per Hectare in Ivatan Rice Fields and Age of Owners

Person Hrs./Ha.	No.	Mean Age
400–499	4	39.5
500–599	5	39
600–699	3	49
700–799	3	41
800–899	2	58
900–999	4	42
1000+	5	50
Total	26	44.5

a. $\eta^2 = 0.18$

TABLE 51

Relationship[a] between Village and Cash (CFA) Value Expended on Average
Rice Field

	Ivato	Ambalabe	Tanambao	Mean Combined Sample	η^{2a}
Tillage, wages	184	77	328	187	0.04
Tillage, food	173	429	600	362	0.07
Chemical fertilizer	1,280	0	0	552	0.37
Transplanting; wages and food	1,464	1,644	1,026	1,416	0.04
Weeding, wages	822	1,027	636	843	0.02
Harvest, food and women's shares	2,437	2,285	2,280	2,346	0.002
Threshing, food	941	688	536	746	0.08
Transport to granary, food	224	461	204	298	0.05
Total cash value expended per field	7,742	7,214	6,000	7,100	0.03

a. Village as control variable versus each item of expenditure as dependent variable.

TABLE 52

Costs of Rice Cultivation (Per Hectare) in Ivato, Ambalabe, and Tanambao

	Amount Expended by Village (CFA)[a]		
Item of Expenditure	*Ivato*	*Ambalabe*	*Tanambao*
Tillage, wages paid	288	154	887
Tillage, cost of feeding workers	270	858	1,620
Chemical fertilizer cost	2,000	0	0
Transplanting, wages and/or food	2,288	3,288	2,770
Weeding, wages	1,284	2,054	1,717
Harvest, food and cash value of shares given to female workers	3,808	4,570	6,156
Threshing, food	1,470	1,376	1,447
Transport to granary (food)	350	922	551
Total	11,758	13,222	15,148

a. $\eta^2 = 0.08$ for association between village as control variable and total cash value expended per hectare as dependent variable.

Notes

1. In a study of the Bara, southern neighbors of the Betsileo, Huntington (1974, pp. 12, 26) also notes that the discreteness of ethnic labels in Madagascar has increased with political consolidation, and that Bara ethnicity also originated in the nineteenth century. See also Eggert (1979) for relevant comments on Mahafaly ethnicity.

2. Fortunately, English-language ethnographic works on Madagascar are now more abundant. In addition to articles on several groups, book-length studies are available for, among others, the Merina (Bloch 1971), Bara (Huntington 1974), Sakalava (Gardenier 1976), and an Islamized group of Malagasy speakers in the Comoro Islands (Lambek 1978).

3. This is no longer the case. In fact, what young Malagasy perceived as too much French control of their education was a major reason for political events that led to a change of government in 1972.

4. Tanambao, Ivato, Ambalabe, and most other village names used herein are fictional.

5. It turned out that one of the principal reasons it had taken me a month to find that descent groups were named was the declining importance of territorially dispersed groups based on stipulated descent since the Betsileo have been living under state organization.

6. Bloch (1971, pp. 31–32), Huntington (1974, pp. 109–12), and Gardenier (1976, pp. 8–9, 139–42) discuss similar fear of strangers, who, as among the Betsileo, are regarded as potential witches, sorcerors, poisoners, vampires, or heart- and liver-snatchers by rural Merina, Bara, and Sakalava. These suspicions of strangers belong to social worlds, all these anthropologists note, where only kin can be totally trusted.

7. Bloch (1974) and Keenan (1973a, 1974b) have analyzed formal Merina speech making on such ritual occasions as marital negotiations and funerals. As among the Merina, Betsileo orators use formalized speech on ritual occasions (see chapter 7), drawing on proverbs and oral lore. Still, Betsileo recognize that not all orators are equally effective. Rakoto is regarded as an especially good one.

8. Throughout this work I generally translate Betsileo personal names into their closest English equivalents, since readers of a first draft complained that the Malagasy

names were almost impossible to follow for someone not familiar with the island. First of all, almost all names begin with *R* and are very long. The Betsileo version of Tuesdaysfather, for example, is Rainitalata, of his great-grandfather—Fridaysfather—Rainijomalahy. After several characters have been introduced it becomes difficult for the nonspecialist to tell them apart. Furthermore, as is discussed more fully in chapter 7, Betsileo commonly use at least three Malagasy names at different times in their lives and often have European first names as well. Thus I feel comfortable occasionally using French and English first names in discussing cases below. However, all names have been changed or disguised in order to protect informants' identities.

9. One recent example is Pasternak (1972). Bloch's (1971) study of the Merina, which involved fieldwork in two villages—one in old Imerina, the other in a recently colonized area—also comments on variation in a complex society.

CHAPTER 2

1. For a contrary view see Southall (1971).

2. Bloch's (1975, 218–21) work among the Zafimaniry (see also Coulaud 1973), a Tanala-like swiddening group east of the northern Betsileo, indicates that this is no longer the case. Zafimaniry retain their ethnicity even when using sedentary agriculture.

3. Population figures are those reported in the government census of 1964.

4. Lombard (1973) has written of Sakalava growth and expansion.

5. For more information about Merina history and ethnography, see Bloch (1971), which focuses primarily on the colonial and contemporary period. Bloch (1977) offers a reconstruction of Merina state formation at variance both with my own understanding of sociopolitical process in Madagascar and with recent archeological findings in Imerina (Wright and Kus 1976, n.d.). Delivré evaluates Merina history through the late nineteenth century, ferreting out probability and anachronism in Callet's *Tantaran'ny Andriana* (Chapus and Ratsimba, vol. 1–4, 1953, 1956, 1958) and other oral traditional accounts. Condominas (1960) offers a quick, readable review of Merina history, and Julien (1908) is a thorough study of Merina social and political institutions and their impact on Madagascar generally. Callet's collection mentioned above remains the major source on Merina history, compiling oral traditions of earliest times through King Andrianampoinimerina, for whose reign it is strongest. Despite Delivré's reservations, I also find Malzac (1930) an interesting work on Merina history. For King Radama's accomplishments, see Valette (1962). Other sources on the Merina include Isnard (1953) and Molet (1956).

CHAPTER 3

1. Extending north of the Ankona-Matsiatra almost up to the Mania River was the territory known as Manandriana, which, following Merina annexation, was placed in the southernmost province of Imerina proper. South of the Ankona-Matsiatra lay the Betsileo province, with a capital established in 1830 at Fianarantsoa. Although it was subsequently brought under the administration of Fianarantsoa and considered a Betsileo area, Manandriana's early exclusion was historically logical, for, on the basis

of oral traditions, before the nineteenth century, Manandriana was a sparsely populated area, which experienced no internal evolution of socioeconomic stratification and state organization (cf. Dubois 1938, pp. 14, 16, 139–40). Manandriana's nobility seems to have originated with Merina assistance and support and was immediately incorporated as part of Imerina. I thus exclude Manandriana, which spanned the eastern part of the subprefecture of Ambatofinandrahana, the northwestern part of Ambohimahasoa, and the western half of Ambositra, from my examination of the traditional political organization of the southern highlands. Furthermore, like Manandriana, most of the rest of the north of contemporary Betsileo country, that is, the area between the Mania and the Ankona-Matsiatra Rivers, experienced no evolution of stratification and political organization independent of Imerina. None of the seats of the three northern Betsileo subprefectures (Fandriana, Ambositra, Ambatofinandrahana) lay within a traditional Betsileo petty state. Most of Ambatofinandrahana is west of Manandriana, Ambositra east of it, and Fandriana northeast of it. Origin traditions of the northern Betsileo, which I collected through a macroregional questionnaire, confirm that the Betsileo north was organized politically and became densely populated as part of the growth of the Merina state, beginning in the early nineteenth century.

2. Portuguese trade interest in Madagascar lasted only until about 1650. During the sixteenth and early seventeenth centuries Dutch, English, and French used the Malagasy shores for provision of their voyages to the East Indies. In exchange for cattle, fowls, fruits, and rice, they offered utensils, trinkets, beads, and other ornaments (cf. Deschamps 1965; Kent 1970).

3. In an insightful essay contrasting shifting and sedentary cultivators, Ralph Linton (1939) asserted that the Betsileo were once cultivators of dry rice. While his analysis stands as a good typological contrast of Tanala and Betsileo, I could find no evidence that the ancestors of the Betsileo were ever shifting horticulturalists. I know of no oral tradition that argues as Linton does, and when I asked Betsileo if their ancestors had ever practiced the *tavy* cultivation of the Tanala, all emphatically denied it. According to oral traditions, the pre-wet-rice economy was one of stockbreeding, supplemented with hunting, fishing, collecting and cultivation of roots and tubers including *colocasia*, still grown by Betsileo. Furthermore, archaeological survey (Wright and Kus 1976, mss.) has uncovered no evidence for dry rice cultivation by the earliest inhabitants of Imerina. Early wet rice or tuber cultivation in small swampy valleys is much more likely to have characterized the early Merina economy.

4. On the basis of their 1975 archaeological survey of central Imerina, Wright and Kus (1976) find evidence for an increase in warfare (more heavily fortified sites on more easily defensible hilltops) and population growth in south central Imerina during the Ankatso phase, second oldest in the ceramic sequence for central Imerina.

5. Much of the information provided and analyzed below comes from my own ethnographic and ethnohistorical fieldwork among the Betsileo in 1966 and 1967. My reconstruction of the histories of Lalangina and Isandra is, however, based in large part on oral historical accounts gathered by Father Dubois (1938).

6. In analyzing Merina oral traditions, Delivré (1974, p. 58, 69–70) distinguishes between more or less fixed (at least after 1850) royal ethnohistory (type A sources) and more variable histories of families (type B sources).

7. The seven subprefectures include three northern subprefectures—Fandriana,

Ambositra, and Ambatofinandrahana—and one southern subprefecture—Ihosy—
which are outside the pre-Merina heartland and which assumed Betsileo ethnic affiliation, either as immigrants or for administrative reasons, after Merina conquest. Ambohimahasoa, Fianarantsoa, and Ambalavao are the three contemporary subprefectures in the traditional Betsileo heartland.

8. A similar early rivalrous uncentralized period, termed *manjaka hova* or *fan-
jakan'i Baroa*—the latter term also used by the Betsileo—is recalled in Merina oral
traditions (Delivré 1974, p. 159).

9. Delivré (1974, pp. 198–99) uncovers similar ascending anachronisms in Merina oral traditions.

10. My reconstruction of the histories of Lalangina and Isandra is based largely
on oral traditions collected by Father Dubois and included in his monumental *Monographie des Betsileo* (1938). While my own oral historical research was conducted
largely in northern and southern Vohibato, and forms the basis for most of chapter 4's
analysis, I was able, while in the field, to check many of Dubois's Lalanginan and
Isandran accounts for accuracy. In addition, a macroregional questionnaire distributed
throughout Vohibato, Lalangina, Isandra, and, indeed, the entire region of contemporary Betsileo ethnicity, provides a substantial corpus of new, quantitative information missing from Dubois's account. Because Lalangina and Isandra were the major
pre-Merina Betsileo political units, I include them even though most of my own research was done in northern and southern Vohibato. Northern Vohibato is similar to
Lalangina in its local ecosystems, while southern Vohibato approximates Isandra. In
chapters 5 through 8 my analysis of local ecosystems in these regions can, to an
extent, be generalized to the historical contrast between Lalangina and Isandra.

One of my major interests before, during, and after my field research in Madagascar, reflecting my general interest in sociopolitical transformations, has been to
reconstruct Betsileo history in a way that makes sense in terms of what we know about
processes of state formation in other parts of the world. In pursuing these aims, not
only did I collect the ethnohistorical data in the field and through a questionnaire, but
I also investigated, when in the field and through subsequent library research, Dubois's vexing presentation of oral traditions about origins of Betsileo nobilities and the
contrast between Isandra and Lalangina. My brief analysis of oral traditions of Lalangina and Isandra collected or published by Dubois is based on a 112-page section
of his 1,500-page book. The analysis is mine; Dubois amassed the traditions, but
without providing a context. My analysis of traditions collected by Dubois, in combination with my own diachronic research in Madagascar, totally reverses the relative
importance of Lalangina and Isandra, whereas Dubois accepted as fact informants'
statements about the historical priority of Isandra, which in reality became prominent
only after Merina annexation (cf. Shaw 1875, p. 64).

11. In one version the first king dies while attacking the Tanala and his son
succeeds, while in the other, the people oust the first king and establish his younger
half brother as their ruler. In this account the kings' father had two wives, an official
and senior wife who was a noblewoman, while the second wife was a slave. The first
king, the older son, was the child of the slave, the favorite wife. When the king
became a leper his people expelled him, and he fled south to Arindrano where, following a miraculous cure, he was elected king of Tsienimparihy, whose former king

Andriamanely had just been chased out by his own subjects. Andriamanely went on to Bara country where he became the ancestor of a Bara noble descent group called Zafimanely.

These contradictory accounts of the first two kings of Lalangina are more significant as sociological than as historical documents. They indicate, for example, that an individual derives his social position from both parents, rather than simply from the father. Contemporary Betsileo continue to favor stratum endogamy. The child of a mixed union is tainted by the subordinate status of one of his parents. The belief that the mother of the first Lalangina king was a slave justifies his deposition and replacement by a prince with two noble parents. Her slave status aside, the fact that she was a junior wife can also be used to justify her son's expulsion. Yet principles that conflict with these also play a part in establishing seniority. Age confers seniority; the Betsileo say that the oldest son replaces his father. One sees, too, in this oral traditional account, as in the later history of Lalangina, an example of the rights of Betsileo rulers to designate their heirs, and of subjects to overthrew their rulers. Finally, the tradition of expulsion of a leprous king is also an argument on Lalangina's part for its superiority to Tsienimparihy. Not only did the king of the southern statelet come from Lalangina, but he also was the leprous son of a slave and junior wife who was unwanted and had been banished by his own subjects.

12. For a remarkably similar development in Inca history see Godelier (1977, p. 191).

13. Bloch (1977, pp. 308–12) similarly attributes the transition between two sociopolitical types which, following Isnard (1953), he labels "pre-takeoff state" (whose reality I doubt for agricultural areas of the central highlands, as described by Bloch) and "takeoff state" to marsh irrigation—administrative intervention to transform marshes, through drainage and earthworks, into rice producing land.

14. Shaw comments on a high incidence of litigation over inherited land among nineteenth-century Betsileo, apparently stimulated in large part by bribes and delays occasioned by unsalaried Merina and Betsileo officials.

15. Survey evidence reported by Wright and Kus (1976, n.d.) also confirms that fortifications preceded the advent of state organization in central Imerina.

CHAPTER 4

1. As Bloch (1971, pp. 68–71) observes about Merina society, few nobles actually ruled in Betsileo polities. The status of *andriana* was merely a necessary, not a sufficient, condition of *mpanjaka* status. As chapter 3 has shown, senior commoners were as prominent in Betsileo as in nineteenth-century Merina government, wielding much more power than most *andriana*.

2. Most probably, these negotiations date to the time of Radama. Their attribution to Andrianampoinimerina's reign exemplifies an ascending anachronism (Delivré 1974, 198–99).

3. Bloch (1971, pp. 68–70) reports similar demotions of whole groups of *andriana* to *hova* status among the Merina.

4. If a senior commoner male marries a noble female, he is expected to reside uxorilocally, with his wife's people. Betsileo males are reluctant to leave their kin and

ancestral estate. For commoner women, who may follow customary virilocality, the problem does not exist.

5. For a discussion of a similar problem in interpreting Merina oral traditions see Delivré (1974, pp. 32–33).

6. Condominas (1960, p. 57) mentions the same policy used by Andrianampoinimerina in pacifying central Imerina.

7. The other brothers settled nearby hamlets, and the two sisters married out.

8. See Dubois's (1938, pp. 888–89) discussion of the place of *anakandriana*, whom he calls clan heads, in the Betsileo stratification system.

9. Gardenier (1976, p. 110) reports that purchased slaves were their owner's fictive kin among the Sakalava.

10. It is difficult to estimate the percentage of *andevo* in the rural Betsileo population. Individuals rarely acknowledge slave origin, and it is considered improper to ask people if their ancestors were slaves. When non-*andevo* informants identify someone as a slave descendant, and even when they have to use the word *andevo*, they whisper. Phenotype provides no clue.

11. We must recognize that this bit of Merina history may be a rationalization for conquest.

CHAPTER 5

1. The administrative structure described here existed in 1966–67. Certain modifications have followed subsequent changes of government.

2. CFA: francs of the French African Community, worth about 250 per American dollar and 50 per French (new) franc, in 1966–67; also called FMG or *franc malgache*.

3. See also table 47 for a calendar of secondary crop cultivation in Ivato.

4. Rice's relative contribution to the total food crop again reflects historical economic contrasts discussed in previous chapters. With higher rainfall, the Ivato area supports a greater variety of crops than the south (e.g., the canton of Mahazony and the subprefecture of Ambalavao), where irrigated rice makes a proportionately larger contribution to the diet.

5. An hour's pounding yields about 3.5 kilograms of husked (white) rice.

6. Mahazony was more recently settled than Ivato. Whereas Ivato's founding ancestor arrived in the seventh generation above the contemporary grandparental generation represented by Tuesdaysfather, the apical ancestors of the three southern Ambalabe descent groups claim to have arrived in Mahazony in the sixth, fifth, and fourth generations respectively above the current age peers of Tuesdaysfather.

7. Based on average of paddy production, 1966 and 1967 harvests.

8. These tables analyze, for two rice fields in Ivato, calendar dates and labor expenditures for all aspects of rice field maintenance, preparation, and rice cultivation. Table 33 provides calendar information and analyzes labor expenditures in terms of man-hours, woman-hours, and aggregated person-hours. Table 34 includes data on owner's labor contribution and that of other males and of females.

9. Table 11 provides a calendar for the major aspects of rice cultivation in Ivato, indicating how many field owners carried out each task by month. Several tasks usu-

ally, but not universally, associated with rice cultivation, including hydraulic system and bund maintenance, and second plowing, as well as winnowing, paddy drying, and women's daily pounding and preparation are illustrated in tables 33 and 34. These tables give a better approximation, for a much smaller number of cases, of the total labor requirements in person-hours associated with rice among the Betsileo. The tasks listed in table 11 encompass only between 65 and 75 percent of the person-hours involved in rice cultivation in Ivato.

10. Only 11 percent of the fifty-five fields studied in Ambalabe and Tanambao had this soil type. This is one of the major reasons for lower average labor requirements in Ivato (840 person-hours per ha. in Ivato, compared to 2,040 in Ambalabe and 2,610 in Tanambao (cf. table 10) for the tasks included in table 11.

11. Average ages were 30.4 (SD = 12.5), 30 (SD = 12.7), and 29.4 (SD = 13.9) for Ivato, Ambalabe, and Tanambao respectively. Average distances were 0.96 km. (SD = 1.2), 0.96 (SD = 1.2), and 0.92 (SD = 1.2), in the same order.

12. Harder work, however, is no sure path to higher yields; the people of Ambalabe worked harder than those of Ivato and got smaller per hectare yields.

13. "To eat," in Betsileo as in Merina parlance, is "to eat rice," *mihinam-bary*. Manioc, sweet and Irish potatoes, as well as beans, greens, beef, pork, and fowl, are to be eaten as *laoka*, accompaniments to rice; they should not stand alone. A husband's primary duty, Betsileo say, is to provide adequate rice for his wife and children.

CHAPTER 6

1. Southall (1971) offers a lengthy argument for the generally cognatic nature of Malagasy systems of kinship and descent. Huntington (1974, p. 65 et seq.) takes issue with Southall and argues that the Bara are "split-lineal" because of their prominent differentiation of male and female principles and paternal and maternal lines. Wilson (1971) and Lavondès (1967) describe Tsimihety and Masikoro-Sakalava respectively as essentially patrilineal. "Cognatic" elements certainly characterize Merina kingroups (Bloch 1971, p. 62). To an extent, this variant terminology reflects preferences and analytic frameworks of the different ethnographers. On the other hand, some of it is attributable to actual variance in Malagasy kinship and descent systems. No doubt some groups are more patrilineal, and others more cognatic, than others. I have suggested some of the material conditions that might underlie this variation elsewhere (Kottak 1971), but some of my statements there must be revised in the face of new ethnography. However, this is beyond the task of the current work.

2. Such genealogical depth appears unusual in Madagascar, characterizing neither the Bara as described by Huntington (1974), the Sakalava studied by Gardenier (1976), nor—except for the ruling line—the Merina as reported by Bloch (1971). A taboo on mentioning names of the dead militates against descent demonstration among the Sakalava (Gardenier 1976, p. 87). Bloch (1971, pp. 170–71, 222) reports that the Merina tend to forget the names of the dead after their corpses have been ritually rewrapped in the *famadihana* ceremony (see chapter 7).

3. The continuing link between emigrants and their ancestral homeland, which is the focus of Bloch's (1971) study of contemporary Merina social organization, does not characterize the Betsileo. Perhaps reflecting their more mobile heritage, Betsileo

have built new tombs on the estates they have settled as migrants rather than retaining burial rites and actually being interred in a tomb in the "land of the ancestors" (cf. Bloch 1971, p. 213).

4. The named kin groups or demes (*karazana*) of traditional Merina society were, in contrast, once local and corporate with respect to an agricultural estate (Bloch 1971, pp. 43–46, 59). Today, like Betsileo named descent groups, Merina deme members are geographically dispersed and never mass for common action.

5. Both traditionally and today, the village has been the unit of recruitment for cooperative labor among the Merina (Bloch 1971, pp. 60, 94–100).

6. Bloch (1971, pp. 60–65) uses the Merina term *fianakaviana* to designate an endogamous, local subdivision of a deme, into which it may develop as its population grows and it acquires a name. Betsileo *fianakaviana* contrast with their Merina namesakes in being more exogamous, ancestor-oriented, and agnatically biased in composition. Nevertheless, like the Merina, Betsileo also use *fianakaviana* more generally, much as Americans use the terms "kin," "relatives," and "family" in discussing their own (personal) kindred.

7. However, the apical ancestor of this minor descent group was a younger brother. The group descended from his oldest brother, which now supplies the political leadership of Ivato, has always been headed by agnates.

8. On the basis of Huntington's research (1974, pp. 138–39), although Bara have the option of affiliating with a maternal *tariky*, and do so occasionally, agnation is a much stronger moral value governing local descent group affiliation than among the Betsileo. Furthermore, multiple *tariky* affiliation is rare among the Bara, whereas joint or alternating local descent group affiliation is more common among the Betsileo. Merina affiliation practices are also more definitive than those of the Betsileo.

In theory, because of deme endogamy, Merina children inherit the same deme and *fianakaviana* membership through father and mother. In fact, because endogamy is incomplete, many Merina have to choose between paternal and maternal kin groups. The significant kin group consists of people who plan to be buried in the same tomb. Because tomb upkeep is expensive, Merina choose, soon after marriage, to activate membership in just one tomb and tomb association. Tomb group affiliation among the Merina is therefore in Murdock's (1968) terms optative-exclusive (Bloch 1971, pp. 116 et seq.).

9. The northern Betsileo studied by Southall (1971, p. 147) are similar in enjoying multiple descent group memberships depending on where they are and in claiming more exclusive and important membership in one of them.

10. Bloch (1971, pp. 193–94) reports that part of the agreement that leads to a Merina marriage may specify that one or two of the couple's children will be raised by the wife's parents.

11. Huntington (1974) reports that women are customarily buried with their relatives rather than affinals among the Bara.

12. Huntington (1974) reports that among the Bara agnatic ancestors are believed to enforce the norm of patrifiliation with local descent groups and tombs by inflicting illness on descendants who reside in their mother's village. Although I found no evidence for a similar belief among the Betsileo, I have formed the impression that Ivato's nonagnates experienced greater psychological stress than agnates, but I lack

the data to confirm this opinion. This stress was manifest in frequent visits to other villages, complaints about sickness, and more antisocial behavior, such as abetting suspicions about practicing witchcraft. On the basis of Bloch's reports, these stresses seem to be absent in Merina social organization, which is much more cognatic than the kinship systems of either Betsileo or Bara.

13. Linton Freeman's (1965, p. 108 et seq.) coefficient of differentiation, *theta*, Θ, a descriptive statistic designed to measure association between a nominal and an ordinal variable, was calculated to assess the relative reduction in prediction error achieved by considering rank order of village as an independent variable (senior, senior/junior, and junior, represented by Ivato, Ambalabe, and Tanambao respectively, were ranked on a descending scale: 3, 2, and 1).

14. This focus on tomb, mortal remains, and associated ceremonials recalls the socially powerful link to ancestral homeland and tomb described by Bloch (1971) for geographically dispersed Merina deme members. However, Betsileo focus on particular ancestors in the tomb whose descendants they are, whereas Merina use tomb, remains, and ceremonies to symbolize their connection through kinship (expressed collaterally rather than lineally—ancestral names are forgotten) to territorial demes in old Imerina.

15. Lavondès (1967, pp. 40–41) makes a similar observation about potential membership in eight "clans" among the Masikoro (Sakalava). In fact, because of endogamy and neglect of nonstrategic kin ties, Betsileo rarely if ever actually participate in the affairs of eight ancestral groups.

16. Wilson (1971, p. 206) reports for the Tsimihety that only agnates (and, derivatively, affines and fictive kin) may appropriately participate in tomb-centered ceremonials. Since possibilities of uterine inheritance of land are limited, there is no Tsimihety equivalent to the Betsileo common descent group.

17. Bloch (1971, p. 84) reports that today's Merina, because of migration and reaggregation, also see the contemporary *fokonolona* as a group of neighbors rather than of kin.

18. *Hava* designates kin or "large family" among the Bara (Huntington 1974, pp. 188–91).

19. Southall (1971, p. 150) states that the same is true of the northern Betsileo, and Bloch (1971, p. 116) reports that Merina informants found the mother's side somehow weaker than the father's.

20. Southall's (1971) information on the northern Betsileo parallels Huntington's (1974, pp. 81 et seq.) findings about the Bara conception of the kinship roles of mother and father. Mothers confer flesh and blood; fathers are associated with strength, order, and bones. My own Betsileo informants, although linking mother and blood, never expressed the Bara idea that the role of the father's semen in conception is to give order (and perhaps skeleton) to the blood in the mother's womb. Although calling the father's side more important, my informants also never precisely echoed the Bara belief that a person's mystical link to the ancestors (in the *tariky* tomb) is traced exclusively through the father. In fact Betsileo call on male and female ancestors in their rites.

21. Furthermore, informants named their mother's village (forty-two times) slightly more often than their father's (thirty-five times). One might be tempted to

interpret these figures as biased by the fact that more males reside in paternal than in maternal villages; so residing, males might be expected sometimes to forget their own village when asked to identify all villages where they had relatives. However, this interpretation is incorrect; females in the sample, who were usually residing in their husband's rather than in their father's village, mentioned matrilateral kin even more frequently than males.

22. Bloch (1971, pp. 58–60, p. 98–102) focuses on the tremendous moral value that Merina, like Betsileo, attach to kinship, expressed by the term *havana*. Because of endogamy, in the traditional localized demes of old Imerina, kin, affines, and neighbors were one and the same. Merina emigrants, however, often live in recently established villages and hamlets among nonkin. In such a situation, people gain access to cooperative labor, share resources, and offer solace during life crises through the fiction of kinship, converting unrelated neighbors into *havana mpifankatia*, "kin because they are loved." While using fictive kinship to organize their everyday lives, however, Merina emigrants admit that these *havana* are not "real," and keep up their relationships with "real" *havana* through marriage and participation in tomb-centered rituals in the "land of the ancestors."

23. Merina migrants use a form of fictive kinship called *havana mpifankatia*, rather than blood siblingship, in the recently settled area studied by Bloch (1971, p. 98 et seq., pp. 206–7). The obligations associated with the *fatidra* relationship are considered too strong for neighbors, and Merina have used them mainly to facilitate trade and travel in hostile territory. Huntington (1974) and Gardenier (1976) report blood siblingship among Bara and Sakalava, and indeed it is widespread in Madagascar.

24. Cf. Carroll, ed. (1970) for similar effects and several cases of fosterage and adoption practices in Oceanian societies.

25. This horoscope system appears to have operated more flexibly among the Betsileo than among Bara and Sakalava, and, as suggested in chapter 3, this is related to a more positive Betsileo attitude toward population growth, when compared to their less populous, more pastoral neighbors to the south and west. Gardenier reports for the Sakalava that some destinies were too potent (dangerous to the child's kin) to be corrected even by ritual experts, and infanticide was practiced in these cases. My Betsileo informants stressed *incompatibility* of destinies between child and parents and danger to the child; this contrasts both with Bara (Huntington 1974, pp. 153–55) and Sakalava (Gardenier 1976, pp. 43–46). The Betsileo system, favoring fosterage, supported population growth and redistribution; in other parts of Madagascar infanticide limited population growth.

26. When Merina women reside virilocally, they leave their estate rights in trust with their brothers. There are similarities between the Betsileo nonpeasant's treatment of maternal land rights and the Merina situation described by Bloch (1971, pp. 54–55).

27. Bloch (1971, p. 96) mentions, but provides little data on the "extensive" Merina fosterage system. He does report that children are commonly fostered by their matrilateral kin (1971, p. 193).

28. Similar customs are reported for other Malagasy groups. Huntington (1974, p. 191) reports that three-fourths of all Bara marriages link first or second cousins.

Close kin endogamy is therefore much more characteristic of Bara than Betsileo. Bloch (1971, p. 52) also reports that the favored marriage among free Merina was between second cousins, the grandchildren of a brother and sister. Huntington suggests that incest between cousins is common among the Bara. Like Betsileo and Merina in the past (Bloch 1971, p. 58), Bara atone for incest by sacrificing a steer for the ancestors. Such a sacrifice, states Huntington (1974, p. 191) serves to mark the limits of kinship. If the boy's family refuses to make the sacrifice, the families no longer deem themselves related.

29. Traditional funerals and other Betsileo and Merina tomb-centered ceremonials were condemned by European missionaries as occasions of rampant drunkenness and licentiousness.

30. These negotiations recall, but are less elaborate and ritualized than, the initiation of a marriage among the Merina. Many parts of Bloch's (1971, pp. 178, 187; 1978) analysis of the ceremonial inferiority of the groom and his relatives during marital negotiations and the marriage ceremony apply to the Betsileo and other Malagasy groups.

31. This pattern of visiting bears some resemblance to Huntington's (1974, pp. 88–90) description of the father's role after childbirth among the Bara. Huntington notes that the child's identification with its father and patriline is gradual, strengthening after the child leaves the maternal village. During the period of the new mother's recuperation Bara men, like Betsileo, are expected to be available to fetch and carry for their father-in-law. Gardenier (1976, p. 81) reports bride service—the son-in-law's customary completion of a specified task for his wife's father—among the Sakalava, but this follows marriage rather than childbirth. Similarly, Merina husbands work five or six days each year for their father-in-law, after having been ritually denigrated during the marriage ceremony itself (Bloch 1978).

32. Some prominent features of Merina marriage are missing among the Betsileo. They include the avoidance between groom and wife's father prior to marriage, informal avoidance between husband and parents-in-law after marriage, and avoidance by groom's father of participation in the marriage ceremony (Bloch 1971, pp. 180, 195; 1978). Furthermore, Merina apparently lack trial marriage.

33. A reminder perhaps of a more endogamous Betsileo past, the *ala-fady* once may have figured in the initiation of (incestuous) marriage among the Merina (Bloch 1971, p. 58). Among the Bara incest is *mila-fady* and the atonement ceremony is called *mangala tongo*. *Ala-fady* reshuffles parts of these terms. Since most Bara marriages are between cousins, such sacrifices are common. Although Betsileo marry more distant relatives and more nonrelatives than Bara or Merina, they preserve, in the custom of distributing the *ala-fady* to notify the girl's four grandparental villages, the demonstration of kinship through the incest atonement offering, as interpreted by Huntington (1974, p. 191).

34. Presentation of the hindquarters of any animal signals the ritual superiority of the recipient. Although many Malagasy groups still use animals in marital prestations, Betsileo in the Ivato region, like the Merina, have substituted cash.

35. Bloch (1971, pp. 179, 195) attributes a decline in the monetary value of the *vodi-ondry* among the Merina, less even than in Ivato, to church propaganda. The Merina groom's presentation of the *vodi-ondry* is an act of obeisance symbolizing his

acceptance of kinship ties with and the fatherlike authority of his wife's father. Its presentation establishes a Merina marriage, which, lacking trial marriage and demonstration of fertility (perhaps also attributable to Christianity), is more of an event and less a protracted process than among the Betsileo.

36. The marital bond is weaker among the Bara. Huntington (1974, pp. 75, 138) reports frequent divorce, the average person having been married at least twice. Marital instability is associated with the Bara woman's burial in a parental tomb, rather than her husband's, as among the Betsileo, and with the Bara woman's mobility— particularly her frequent visits to her natal village and to see her kinswomen—as opposed to far less circulation by males. Betsileo of both sexes frequently visit others, but the male-female contrast here is less developed than among the Bara. Gardenier (1976, pp. 83, 108) also reports frequent divorce among the Sakalava of Ambongo. Bloch's (1971) ethnography suggests that divorce is less common among the Merina.

CHAPTER 7

1. Except for the Sakalava, whom Gardenier (1976, p. 109) characterizes as child-oriented rather than ancestor-oriented, and whose ties to cemeteries are not particularly strong.

2. Huntington (1974, p. 90) reports that attendance of the boy's mother and maternal uncle is also customary at the Bara circumcision ritual. The operation, which takes place near the time of weaning and is done by the ritual head of the boy's agnatic local group, marks an important part in the boy's gradual separation from mother's group, establishment of male identity and paternal authority, and inclusion in the agnatic order.

3. Similarly, among the northern Sakalava (Feeley-Harnik 1978, p. 407) babies are thought to be dangerously close to the spirit world.

4. Similarly, Bara interred very young infants on wet land (*tany le*) (Huntington 1974, p. 89).

5. Among the Sakalava of Ambongo (Gardenier 1976) a man can symbolically offer his dead father rebirth by bestowing the latter's name on his own son. In such a case the normally authoritarian Sakalava father-son relationship is partially equalized, since their actual relationship has been symbolically inverted. Bara also often confer a dead man's name on his grandchild; the former takes a death name (Huntington 1974, p. 111).

6. Betsileo fear accepting food from strangers, since poisoning (or sorcery) is a common diagnosis of severe illness and death. Sharing food converts strangers into allies.

7. Among the Bara (Huntington 1974, pp. 72–74), local ancestors insist that their patrilineal male descendants reside virilocally; men residing elsewhere encounter illness and misfortune as evidence of ancestral wrath. In general, neither good nor evil comes from maternal ancestors. In sharp contrast to Huntington's findings among the Betsileo's southern neighbors, Bloch (1971, p. 125) denies that the Merina worship their ancestors to obtain benefits or avoid displeasure. At no time did his informants suggest that they feared ancestral punishment for leaving the land or tomb of the ancestors. Only minor offerings (e.g. honey) to the *ambiroa* in Merina tombs, rare and insignificant, suggest that the dead can directly affect the affairs of the living.

Bloch (1971, p. 162 et seq.) stresses that Merina rewrapping ceremonials are under-taken neither to obtain ancestral blessing nor to avoid harmful effects of ancestral displeasure, but in order to remove guilt (*tsiny*) that builds up (especially among Me-rina colonists who live apart from kin) when kin obligations, particularly toward those who are buried alone, are avoided. The dead, Bloch reports, are believed to enjoy some kind of life, and no life can be properly lived without kin. Thus the continuance of Merina ceremonies that place the dead in the tombs of the ancestors.

8. The postharvest thanksgiving or "harvest home" ceremonies described among later nineteenth-century Betsileo by Shaw (1878, p. 4) and Haile (1900, p. 8) have probably merged with the *lanonana*, vow-fulfillment, and other non-tomb-centered, ancestor-oriented ceremonies of today. The ceremonies described by the missionaries, which always involved cattle sacrifice, dancing, singing, wrestling, and other festive activity, were held to acknowledge and demonstrate appreciation for spiritual bless-ings manifest in prosperity in herds and harvest.

Describing a Betsileo ancestor-worship session Haile (1899, p. 334) notes that a hornful of rum, along with morsels of rice and meat were presented, spread out on a banana leaf, on separate shelves reserved for creator god (Andriananahary or Zana-hary), ancestors of supplicants, and slave ancestors respectively. Once the spiritual entities invoked in the ritual had their fill, women scrambled for the morsels, which were believed to grant fertility. I only noted a seeming connection between the sym-bolism of this ceremony and that of rewrapping ceremonies after leaving Madagascar. In rewrapping ceremonies in which corpses are removed from tombs, they are laid down on a mat in a hut covered with banana leaves. Once they are wrapped in new silk shrouds, women fight for bits of the mat. Banana leaves are linked to the ancestral blessing of fertility therefore in two Betsileo ceremonies, one involving spiritual con-sumption of food offered by the living, the other involving physical contact of living with the embodied dead.

9. These interview schedules were filled out during the latter part of Malagasy winter, 1967, from July to September. I intended to compose lists of all ceremonials attended by these respondents during one year. However, informants in all three vil-lages tended to concentrate on the ceremonials they had attended most recently, often forgetting earlier ones. To combat this tendency, I habitually asked Ivatans I inter-viewed, after they had completed their initial listing, whether they might have forgot-ten other ceremonials attended during the past year, particularly funerals, which are not confined to the ceremonial season. Since, however, I was not present when he was conducting all of his interviews, I have no way of knowing, but have reason to doubt, that Rabe was as persistent. Differences in researchers' persistence may ac-count, therefore, for certain differences in the number of ceremonials mentioned by respondents in the three villages.

10. Bloch (1971, p. 147) reports that the law limits Merina *famadihana* to the months of July through September inclusive.

11. Only twenty-three informants responded to this interview schedule in the two Mahazony villages, compared to twenty-seven adults in Ivato.

12. For rewrapping ceremonies that seem as akin to Bloch's Merina as to the southern Betsileo I studied, see Dez's (1956) account of Betsileo rewrapping customs. Dez reports that families would save up for a lavish entrance into the family tomb, burying a corpse temporarily near what would be, in three or four years, its final

resting place. I never discovered a case of such a practice among the Betsileo I studied.

13. Betty Kottak, Joseph Rabe, and I.

14. Dez (1956, p. 119) points out that, at least since the time of Merina Queen Ranavalona I (1825–61), fees, which were sometimes exorbitant, have been paid to government officials to obtain authorization for ceremonials. For related points see Shaw (1877, p. 84) and Bloch (1971, p. 148).

15. This ceremony was, therefore, more than twice as large as the largest (500 people) of the eight *famadihana* attended by Bloch (1971, p. 148). Bloch suggests, however, that Merina *famadihana* can be much larger than those he observed.

16. The following description is based on my own observations and on notes taken by Joseph Rabe, my field assistant.

17. Among the Merina, too, (Bloch 1971, p. 151) an astrologer determines all the arrangements for the *famadihana*, including date, day, and time, and the path the corpse or remains must follow from old place of burial to tomb.

18. Of the six steers donated by affinals, one came from Lawrence's wife's brother, one from the father-in-law of a female native of Maso, one from the village where Lawrence's daughter had married, two from relatives of husbands of Little Ambalavao native women, and one from Samuel's wife's father. Note the lack of a clearcut preponderance of either "wife-givers" or "wife-receivers" among the affinals, also true of my data on affinal prestations at other ceremonials.

19. In contrast to the Betsileo, Merina at least avoid expenses connected with the upkeep of multiple ancestral tombs. Bloch (1971, p. 116) reports that a decision about a future burial place is made soon after marriage, since no one wants to pay for the upkeep of more than one tomb. Betsileo continue to reinforce multiple estate rights because, with ancestral land actually being cultivated by a greater proportion of the Betsileo population, there is a greater chance that they might eventually activate rights in landed estates associated with various tombs. Since land is abundant among the Merina colonists described by Bloch (1971), tomb affiliation is not a route to land use. For such people, as Bloch shows so well, the tomb is the linking symbol to the glory of a past society rather than a repository of demonstrated ancestral remains and potential or actual land-use rights.

20. In the traditional ancestor worship session, meat rather than rum is offered; most Ivatans no longer observe this custom. When meat is offered it is placed on banana leaves.

21. Bloch (1971, p. 144) states that newly interred corpses are placed in the tomb's most honored position, the upper northern bed. However, ancestral priority determines placement in Betsileo tombs, an aspect of the deeper genealogical connections that Betsileo maintain with their ancestors. The Merina tend to forget the names of their relatives once a *famadihana* has been held for them (Bloch 1971, pp. 170–71). In the tomb of eastern Ivato, Goodmaker, who commissioned the tomb, lies in the ritually honored position.

22. A much louder statement of status change is made when an individual commissions, on his own, the construction of a new tomb, and thus establishes himself as an apical ancestor of a new descent line.

23. Despite the smaller scale of the contemporary Merina funeral, Bloch (1971, pp. 138, 142) also notes the active role of neighbors, who provide money and rice, and offer the deceased person's kin protection against witches on the night following death. The Merina emigrant community appears to be most clearly activated as a social unit by the funeral. To an extent this is also true of Betsileo villages, particularly when they include members of several descent groups or different strata.

24. Rather than simply a separate room, the Bara (Huntington 1974, pp. 98–101) use two huts for a funeral. One, as among the Betsileo, is called the "males' hut." Here, visitors express condolences and make offerings and are greeted in a highly formalized manner. The corpse reposes in "the house of many tears," where women ritually weep, in an order that begins (and ends) with the deceased's closest female relative.

25. Computing the correlation ratio, η^2, 42 percent of the variation in frequency of ceremonial attendance was associated with sex.

26. Forty percent of the variation in ceremonial attendance (η^2) is associated with total annual crop.

27. Huntington (1974, p. 40) also notes that wide distribution of beef at rituals is an important addition to the Bara diet.

28. Future research, including examination of medical and canton records of dates of death will be necessary before I can judge the intriguing Betsileo assertion that more people, especially the old, die during the winter months and during the rainy season (December through February) than at other times of year. What can be asserted, however, on the basis of my data, is that in 1967 more Ivatans did attend funerals during the winter, especially in August and September, than during other months. It is surprising (and I find it hard to believe that it is not due either to dimming of respondents' recollection or to chance) that no Ivatan attended funerals between August and November, 1966, nor in March or April, 1967.

29. The *famadihana* and other rewrapping ceremonials were, however, introduced by the Merina; see note 37.

30. I suspect that such curing sacrifices may still be prescribed for spirit possession and soul desertion, two Betsileo maladies reported by nineteenth-century missionaries (Haile 1899, p. 332; Moss 1900: p. 476–7); I observed neither. Spirit possession is common among the Bara (Huntington 1974, p. 199 et seq.), Sakalava (Gardenier 1976, pp. 142–56), and the Malagasy-descended people of Mayotte Island in the Comoros (Lambek 1978). The possessions that Huntington describes are the work of nature spirits; they cluster in the springtime months just prior to the rainy season and occasion long-lasting (two weeks) regional gatherings. The eventual cure follows protracted dancing and special license by the possessed. As is generally true in Madagascar, Bara victims are usually women. I never observed an acknowledged case of Betsileo spirit possession; nor did I witness soul loss, described by nineteenth-century missionaries. People who have temporarily lost their *ambiroa* are lethargic and lose weight. Eventually a curer ritually conducts the *ambiroa* back into the afflicted person's body. Cattle sacrifice (including the Bara victim's drinking of blood as it gushes from the animal) is part of the treatment for all such maladies.

31. Shaw (1877, p. 84) reported that the senior commoner head of each village

was entitled to half of the "sirloin" of every sacrificial animal, with the other half going to the native king. Merina overlords and their Betsileo representatives retained this ceremonial tribute.

32. Funerary shrouds are known as *lamba mena*, or red mantles, although, as Bloch (1971, p. 146) notes they need not actually be red; the term distinguishes these special coverings from those (white) *lambas* that Merina wear in everyday life. High costs are still incurred to provide the dead with new shrouds; each costs about $12.00 U.S. (1967), and each child and sibling of the focal corpse in a particular *famadihana* is expected to provide one. The other skeletons must also be "tidied up," which means still more shrouds and more expense (cf. Bloch 1971, pp. 148, 157–58).

33. Merina *famadihanas* are delayed for at least two years after a death, which, as Bloch (1971, p. 147) notes, allows the family to save up for the ceremony. Huntington (1974, p. 108 et seq.) cites similar motives for the Bara *havoria*, a gathering held in the postharvest season following someone's death, the (nonobligatory) second stage in a funerary process that begins with temporary interment and ends with final placement of a fleshless (dry) corpse in a communal casket in the ancestral burial cave. Huntington (1974, p. 108) calls the *havoria* a "conspicuous display of wealth," and the most elaborate event in Bara social life. All expenditures are announced to the public, including fees for dance specialists, wrestlers, and cattle riders, the number of slaughtered cattle, and the amount of rum. Huntington seems to suggest that most of these expenses are borne by the host and his close relatives; thus the significance and effects of balanced reciprocity as practiced by Merina (Bloch 1971, p. 154) and Betsileo cannot be assessed.

34. On the basis of a study in a different part of the Betsileo homeland, Dez (1956, pp. 115–17) describes *famadihana* customs more similar to those of the Merina than of the southern Betsileo I studied. Dez reports that Betsileo tombs are opened only at intervals and that temporary burials are followed by *famadihana* held three to four years later, allowing the family to save up to purchase shrouds, rum, rice, and cattle, and to meet other expenses. I observed no such customs among the Betsileo I studied. However, the previously noted delay of burial, particularly of high status corpses, was clearly an attempt to fit an unexpected event (death) into a postharvest ceremonial schedule.

35. Describing changing Betsileo funerary customs, Shaw (1877, p. 81) comments on rum's intrusion into Betsileo funerals, and blames much of the change on the Merina. He notes that the amount of sugarcane grown—chiefly by the Merina, who also made most of the rum—had increased tenfold in a few years. He describes Betsileo exchanging funerary bullocks with Merina for pitchers of rum. Moss (1900, pp. 475–76) notes that heavy debts were incurred at Betsileo funerals, especially over the rum.

36. For a discussion of similar hardships for some and benefits for others associated with participation in another ceremonial system, the cargo-fiesta complex in highland Latin America, see Harris (1964).

37. Haile (1892, pp. 406–7) characterizes rewrapping of the dead among the Merina as a relatively recent cultural innovation, only about 100 years old. Haile's account also asserts that the *famadihana* complex had not yet spread beyond Imerina.

Bloch (1971, p. 147) also suggests that rewrapping was less important in the past. Bloch (1971, p. 161) reports, after all, that the Merina conceive of all *famadihana* as return *famadihana*, necessary to unite the dead with relatives in the ancestral tomb. The incidence of return *famadihana* must have increased directly with Merina emigration, and the return *famadihana* is now the most important ceremony for Merina residing outside their ancestral homeland. When the Merina still resided in their ancestral communities, burial in the ancestral tomb could be direct, as among contemporary Betsileo. In the absence of temporary burial and return *famadihana*, the primary meaning of the term among contemporary Betsileo, as perhaps among ancestral Merina, is the opening of a new tomb and transfer of ancestral remains to it.

CHAPTER 8

1. Correspondingly, encounters between identical cultural raw material and similar material conditions tend to give rise to similar consequences in form, function, *and* cultural content (parallel evolution), just as (in Steward's studies) encounters between dissimilar cultural raw material and similar material conditions result in some degree of formal and functional convergence.

2. Although I described Betsileo fictive kinship as an "individual" relationship, this was my label, not Betsileos'. This Betsileo institution actually phrases what is analytically perceptible as an individual relationship in kinship terms, i.e., as a conceptual analog of a group relationship, but without the obligations and social implications that accompany any actual group relationship.

3. And might not this also be true of the contemporary United States? How much of our own behavior really involves "individual businesslike economizing," or even struggling to achieve individual (rather than, say, family or factional) needs? How much of Americans' behavior is actually based on economic rationality? It seems that our own primary motives should be more closely scrutinized by anthropologists.

4. Human populations continue to adapt to environmental change through genetic, physiological, and sociocultural adaptation. The last, however, is our most distinctive adaptive apparatus.

5. And no such account can be content with polarization of concrete historic societies into such categories as West versus rest (Sahlins 1976, p. 54) or Western versus tribal (Sahlins 1976, p. 212). This work has shown, I think, that the material determination of nonindustrial stratified societies differs from the more prominent immediate local and regional ecological determination that has hitherto been argued for tribal societies and hunter-gatherers. Oppositions like West/rest or capitalist/kinship mask tremendous contrasts between stratified and unstratified nonindustrial societies, and also obscure the continuum of sociopolitical structures observable cross-culturally.

6. Data that argue further against the interpretation of contemporary cooperative labor as a leveling mechanism are included in tables 51 and 52, which comparatively summarize field costs in Ivato, Ambalabe, and Tanambao. Note (table 51) that although the cost of cultivating the average field does not vary appreciably ($\eta^2 = 0.03$) between the three villages, per hectare costs (table 52) increase more noticeably

($\eta^2 = 0.08$) from Ivato to Ambalabe to Tanambao. Relying still on traditional technology and the ancestral custom of communal meals at work parties, the peasants of Mahazony spend more per unit of land worked and per unit of rice produced than their neighbors to the north.

Bibliography

Bastian, G.
  1967 *Madagascar: étude géographique et économique*. Tananarive: Nathan.
Batchelor, R. T.
  1877 Notes on the Antankarana and their country. *Antananarivo Annual* 3:27–31.
Bateson, G.
  1972 *Steps to an ecology of mind*. New York: Ballantine.
Battistini, R. and Vérin, P.
  1966 Irodo et la tradition Vohemerienne. *Revue de Madagascar*, pt. 9.
Besson, "Dr."
  1897 Étude ethnologique sur les Betsileo. *Notes, reconnaissances et explorations*, pp. 538–52.
Bloch, M.
  1968 Astrology and writing in Madagascar. In *Literacy in traditional society*, edited by Jack Goody, pp. 278–97. London: Cambridge University Press.
  1971 *Placing the dead*. London: Seminar Press.
  1975 Property and the end of affinity. In *Marxist analyses and social anthropology*, edited by M. Bloch, pp. 203–28. London: Malaby.
  1977 The Disconnection between power and rank as a process: an outline of the development of kingdoms in central Madagascar. In *The evolution of social systems*, edited by J. Friedman and M. Rowlands, pp. 303–40. London: Duckworth.
  1978 Marriage amongst equals: an analysis of the marriage ceremony of the Merina of Madagascar. *Man* 13:21–33.
Burton, J. W., and Hicks, D.
  1976 Chaos triumphant: archetypes and symbols in *The Exorcist*. In *The American dimension: cultural myths and social realities*, edited by W. Arens and S. P. Montague, pp. 117–23. Port Washington, N.Y.: Alfred.
Callet, F.
  1908 *Tantaran' ny Andriana*, 2 vols. Tananarive: Imprimerie Officielle. Translated into French by G. S. Chapus and E. Ratsimba.
Carneiro, R. L.
  1970 A theory of the origin of the state. *Science* 169:733–38.
Carroll, V., ed.
  1970 *Adoption in eastern Oceania*. Honolulu: University of Hawaii Press.

Chapus, G. S., and Ratsimba, E.

1953   *Histoire des rois*, vol. 1. Tananarive: Académie Malgache. French translation of *Tantaran' ny Andriana* by F. Callet.

1956   *Histoire des rois*, vol. 2. Tananarive: Académie Malgache.

1958   *Histoire des rois*, vols. 3 and 4. Tananarive: Académie Malgache.

Collins, C.

1897   The *fandroana* or annual festival of the Taimoro; together with some other
customs of that tribe. *Antananarivo Annual* 21:149–51.

Condominas, G.

1960   *Fokon'olona et collectivités rurales en Imerina*. Paris: Berger-Levrault.

Coulaud, D.

1973   *Les Zafimaniry: un groupe ethnique de Madagascar à la poursuite de la
forêt*. Tananarive: Fanontam-Boky Malagasy.

Dahl, O. C.

1951   *Malgache et Maanjan: une comparison linguistique*. Oslo: Egede Institutett.

Davenport, W.

1959   Nonunilineal descent and descent groups. *American Anthropologist* 61:
557–72.

Decary, R.

1930   *L'Androy (extreme sud de Madagascar), I. Géographie physique et hu-
maine*. Paris: Société d'Éditions Géographiques, Maritimes et Coloniales.

Delivré, A.

1974   *L'histoire des rois d'Imerina: interprétation d'une tradition orale*. Paris:
Klincksieck.

Deschamps, H.

1959   *Les migrations intérieures à Madagascar*. Paris: Berger-Levrault.

1965   *Histoire de Madagascar*, 3d ed. Paris: Berger-Levrault.

Deschamps, H., and Vianès, S.

1959   *Les Malgaches du sud-est*. Paris: Presses Universitaires de France.

Dez, J.

1956   Le retournement des morts chez les Betsileo. *Société d'Ethnographie de
Paris*, pp. 115–22.

Dubois, H-M.

1938   *Monographie des Betsileo*. Paris: Institut d'Ethnologie.

Dyen, I.

1965   A lexicostatistical classification of the Austronesian languages. *International Journal of American Linguistics* 31, no. 1.

Eggert, K.

1979   *Mahafaly* as a misnomer. In *Human adjustment in time and space in Madagascar*. New York: Wenner-Gren Foundation for Anthropological Research.

Faublée, J.

1954   *La cohesion des sociétés Bara*. Paris: Presses Universitaires de France.

Feeley-Harnik, G.

1978   Divine kingship and the meaning of history among the Sakalava of Madagascar. *Man* 13:402–17.

Ferrand, G.
1891 *Les Musulmans à Madagascar et aux Îles Comores. v.I: Les Antaimorona: aperçu succinct de la situation, étude de documents Arabico-Malgaches.* Paris: Leroux.

Firth, R.
1968 First published in 1957. A note on descent groups in Polynesia. In *Kinship and social organization*, edited by P. Bohannan and J. Middleton, pp. 213–23. Garden City, N.Y.: Natural History Press.

Flacourt, Etienne de
1661 *Histoire de la grande île de Madagascar.* In *Collections des ouvrages anciens concernant Madagascar*, edited by Alfred Grandidier et al., 9: 1–426. Paris: Union Coloniale.

Flannery, K. V.
1972 The cultural evolution of civilizations. *Annual Review of Ecology and Systematics* 3: 399–426.

Freeman, L.
1965 *Elementary applied statistics: for students in behavioral science.* New York: Wiley.

Fried, M. H.
1960 On the evolution of social stratification and the state. In *Culture and history*, edited by S. Diamond, pp. 713–31. New York: Columbia University Press.

Friedman, J.
1974 Marxism, structuralism and vulgar materialism. *Man* 9: 444–69.

Gardenier, W.
1976 *Witchcraft and sorcery in a pastoral society: The central Sakalava of west Madagascar.* Ann Arbor: University Microfilms International.

Godelier, M.
1972 *Rationality and irrationality in economics.* Translated from the French by Brian Pearce. London: NLB.
1977 *Perspectives in Marxist anthropology.* Translated from the French by Robert Brain. Cambridge: Cambridge University Press.

Goodenough, W.
1968 A problem in Malayo-Polynesian social organization. First published in 1955. In *Kinship and social organization*, edited by P. Bohannan and J. Middleton, pp. 195–211. Garden City, N.Y.: Natural History Press.

Gulliver, P. H.
1955 *The family herds: a study of two pastoral peoples in east Africa, the Jie and Turkana.* New York: Humanities Press.
1965 The Jie of Uganda. In *Peoples of Africa*, edited by J. L. Gibbs, Jr., pp. 157–96. New York: Holt, Rinehart, and Winston.

Haile, J. H.
1892 *"Famadihana,"* a Malagasy burial custom. *Antananarivo Annual* 16: 406–16.
1899 Betsileo home-life. *Antananarivo Annual* 23:326–37.
1900 Some Betsileo ideas. *Antananarivo Annual* 24:1–16, 401–7.

Hance, W. A.
   1957   The economic geography of Madagascar. *Tijdschrift voor Economische en Sociale Geografie* 48: 161–72.
Harris, M.
   1964   *Patterns of race in the Americas.* New York: Walker.
   1968   *The rise of anthropological theory.* New York: Crowell.
   1974   *Cows, pigs, wars, and witches.* New York: Random House.
   1977   *Cannibals and kings: the origins of cultures.* New York: Random House.
Hudson, A. B.
   1967   *The Barito isolects of Borneo.* Ithaca, New York: Cornell University, Department of Asian Studies, Data paper no. 68.
Huntington, W. R.
   1973   Community spirit in a Malagasy village. *South African Outlook* 103.
   1974   *Religion and social organization of the Bara people of Madagascar.* Ann Arbor: University Microfilms International
   1978   Bara endogamy and incest prohibition. *Bijdragen Tot de Taal-, Land-, en Volkenkunde* 134:30–62.
Isnard, H.
   1953   Les bases géographiques de la monarchie hova. In *Éventail de l'histoire vivante: hommage à Lucien Febvre*, pp. 195–206. Paris: A. Colin.
Julien, G.
   1909   *Institutions politiques et sociales de Madagascar*, 2 vols. Paris: Guilmoto.
Keenan, E. O.
   1973   A sliding sense of obligatoriness: the polystructure of Malagasy oratory. *Language in Society* 2:225–43.
   1974   Norm-makers, norm-breakers: uses of speech by men and women in a Malagasy community. In *Explorations in the ethnography of speaking*, edited by R. Bauman and J. Sherzer, pp. 125–43. New York: Cambridge University Press.
Kent, R.
   1970   *Early kingdoms in Madagascar (1500–1700).* New York: Holt, Rinehart, and Winston.
Kottak, C. P.
   1971   Cultural adaptation, kinship, and descent in Madagascar. *Southwestern Journal of Anthropology* 27:129–47.
   1972a   A cultural adaptive approach to Malagasy political organization. In *Social exchange and interaction*, edited by E. Wilmsen, pp. 107–28. Ann Arbor: Anthropological Papers of the Museum of Anthropology, University of Michigan, no. 46.
   1972b   Ecological variables in the origin and evolution of African states: the Buganda example. *Comparative Studies in Society and History* 14:351–80.
   1977   The process of state formation in Madagascar. *American Ethnologist* 4:136–55.
   1978   *Anthropology: the exploration of human diversity.* 2d ed. New York: Random House.

Lambek, M.
  1978 *Human spirits: possession and trance among the Malagasy speakers of Mayotte (Comoro Islands)*. Ann Arbor: University Microfilms International.
Lavondès, H.
  1967 *Bekoropoka: quelques aspects de la vie familiale et sociale d'un village Malgache*. Paris: Mouton.
Lee, R.
  1968 What hunters do for a living, or, how to make out on scarce resources. In *Man the hunter*, edited by R. Lee and I. DeVore, pp. 30–48. Chicago: Aldine.
Lévi-Strauss, C.
  1966 *The savage mind*. Chicago: University of Chicago Press.
  1967 *Structural anthropology*. Translated from the French by C. Jacobson and B. G. Schoepf. Garden City, N.Y.: Doubleday.
Linton, R.
  1933 *The Tanala: a hill tribe of Madagascar*. Chicago: Field Museum of Natural History, Anthropological Series, v. 23.
  1939 The Tanala of Madagascar. In *The individual and his society*, edited by A. Kardiner, pp. 282–90. New York: Columbia University Press.
Lombard, J.
  1973 *La royauté Sakalava: formation, developpement, et effondrement du XVII au XXe siècle; essai d'analyse d'un systeme politique*. Tananarive: Office de la Recherche Scientifique et Technique Outre-Mer.
Malzac, V.
  1930 *Histoire du royaume hova*. Tananarive: Imprimerie Catholique.
Meggers, B. J.
  1975 The transpacific origin of Mesoamerican civilization: a preliminary review of the evidence and its theoretical implications. *American Anthropologist* 77:1–27.
Molet, L.
  1956 *Le bain royal à Madagascar*. Tananarive: Imprimerie Luthérienne.
Moss, "Mrs."
  1900 Betsileo funeral customs. Translated from a native account. *Antananarivo Annual* 24:475–77.
Murdock, G. P.
  1949 *Social Structure*. New York: Macmillan.
  1968 Cognatic forms of social organization. First published in 1960. In *Kinship and social organization*, edited P. Bohannan and J. Middleton, pp. 235–53.
Nielsen-Lund, J.
  1888 Travels and perils among the wild tribes in the south of Madagascar. *Antananarivo Annual* 3:440–56.
Oliver, S. C.
  1962 *Ecology and cultural continuity as contributing factors in the social organization of the Plains Indians*. University of California Publications in American Archaeology and Ethnology, 48 (1).

Pasternak, B.
   1972   *Kinship and community in two Chinese villages.* Stanford: Stanford University Press.
Peake, P. G.
   1878   The Bezanozano, or Bush People. *Antananarivo Annual* 4:31–43.
Rakotoarisoa, J. A.
   1979   Principaux aspects des formes d'adaptation de la société traditionnelle malgache. In *Human adjustment in time and space in Madagascar.* New York: Wenner-Gren Foundation for Anthropological Research.
Rappaport, R. A.
   1968   *Pigs for the ancestors: ritual in the ecology of a New Guinea people.* New Haven: Yale University Press.
   1971a The sacred in human evolution. *Annual Review of Ecology and Systematics* 2:23–44.
   1971b Nature, culture, and ecological anthropology. In *Man, culture and society,* rev. ed., edited by H. Shapiro. pp. 237–68. New York: Oxford University Press.
Richardson, J.
   1875   Remarkable burial customs among the Betsileo. *Antananarivo Annual* 1:70–75.
Sahlins, M. D.
   1958   *Social stratification in Polynesia.* Seattle: University of Washington Press.
   1968   *Tribesmen.* Englewood Cliffs, N.J.: Prentice-Hall.
   1972   *Stone age economics.* London: Tavistock.
   1976   *Culture and practical reason.* Chicago: University of Chicago Press.
Sahlins, M. D., and Service, E. R.
   1960   *Evolution and culture.* Ann Arbor: University of Michigan Press.
Sanders, W. T. and Price, B. J.
   1968   *Mesoamerica: the evolution of a civilization,* New York: Random House.
Service, E. R.
   1960   The law of evolutionary potential. In *Evolution and culture,* edited by M. Sahlins and E. R. Service, pp. 93–122. Ann Arbor: University of Michigan Press.
   1966   *The hunters.* Englewood Cliffs, N.J.: Prentice-Hall.
   1971   *Primitive social organization: An evolutionary perspective.* 2d ed. New York: Random House.
   1975   *Origins of the state and civilization: the process of cultural evolution.* New York: W. W. Norton.
Shaw, G. A.
   1875   Notes on Ikongo and its peoples. *Antananarivo Annual* 1:64–69.
   1876   Rough sketches of a journey to the Ibara. *Antananarivo Annual* 2:102–10.
   1877   The Betsileo: country and people. *Antananarivo Annual* 3:73–85.
   1878   The Betsileo: religious and social customs. *Antananarivo Annual* 4:2–11.
   1893   The Arab element in south-east Madagascar: as seen in the customs and traditions of the Taimoro tribe. Pt. I. *Antananarivo Annual* 17:99–109.

1894   The Arab element in south-east Madagascar: as seen in the customs and traditions of the Taimoro tribe. Pt. II. *Antananarivo Annual* 18:205–10.

Sibree, J.

1877   The Sihanaka and their country, translated and adapted. *Antananarivo Annual* 3:51–69.

1878   The Sakalava: their origin, conquests, and subjection. *Antananarivo Annual* 4:53–65.

1897   The manners and customs, superstitions and dialect of the Betsimisaraka. Pt. I. Translated from a Malagasy ms. *Antananarivo Annual* 21:67–75.

1898a Some Betsimisaraka folk-tales and superstitions. *Antananarivo Annual* 22:214–17.

1898b Remarkable ceremonial at the decease and burial of a Betsileo prince, translated from an account written by an unnamed Betsileo informant. *Antananarivo Annual* 22:195–208.

Singer, R., Budtz-Olsen, O. E., Brain, P., and Saugrain, J.

1957   Physical features, sickling and serology of the Malagasy of Madagascar. *American Journal of Physical Anthropology* 15:91–124.

Southall, A.

1971   Ideology and group composition in Madagascar. *American Anthropologist* 73:144–64.

1979   Faliarivo and the model of Malagasy kinship. In *Human adjustment in time and space in Madagascar.* New York: Wenner-Gren Foundation for Anthropological Research.

Steward, J. H.

1955   *Theory of culture change.* Urbana: University of Illinois Press.

1956   *People of Puerto Rico.* Urbana: University of Illinois Press.

Suttles, W.

1974   Variation in habitat and culture on the Northwest Coast. First published in 1960. In *Man in adaptation: the cultural present*, 2d ed., edited by Y. A. Cohen, pp. 128–41. Chicago: Aldine.

Terray, E.

1972   *Marxism and "primitive" societies.* New York: Monthly Review Press.

Thompson, V. and Adloff, R.

1965   *The Malagasy Republic: Madagascar today.* Stanford, California: Stanford University Press.

Turner, V.

1975   Symbolic studies. *Annual Review of Anthropology* 4:145–61.

Valette, J.

1962   *Études sur le règne de Radama Iᵉʳ.* Tananarive: Imprimerie Nationale.

Vérin, P.

1975   *Les echelles anciennes du commerce sur les côtes nord de Madagascar.* Lille: Service de Reproduction des These, 2 vol.

1979   L'installation des Malgaches à Madagascar: premières données sur leur adaptation; discussion des données culturelles. In *Human adjustment in time and space in Madagascar.* New York: Wenner-Gren Foundation for Anthropological Reserach.

Vérin, P., Kottak, C. P. and Gorlin, P.
  1970   The glottochronology of Malagasy speech communities. *Oceanic Linguistics*, 8:26–83.
Wilson, P.
  1967   Tsimihety kinship and descent. *Africa* 37:133–53.
  1971   Sentimental structure: Tsimihety migration and descent. *American Anthropologist* 73:193–208.
  1977   The problem with simple folk. *Natural History* LXXXVI, 10:26–32.
Wittfogel, K.
  1957   *Oriental despotism: a comparative study of total power.* New Haven: Yale University Press.
Wright, H. T.
  n.d.   Early communities on the island of Mayotte and the coasts of Madagascar. Mss., University of Michigan, Museum of Anthropology.
Wright, H. T., and Kus, S.
  1976   Reconnaissances archéologiques dans le centre de l'Imerina. *Taloha* 7:19–45.
  n.d.   An archaeological reconnaissance of ancient Imerina. Unpublished paper, University of Michigan, Museum of Anthropology.

Index

329